T0212933

Communications
in Computer and Information Science 1625

More information about this series at https://link.springer.com/bookseries/7899

Vladimir Golenkov · Viktor Krasnoproshin ·
Vladimir Golovko · Daniil Shunkevich (Eds.)

Open Semantic Technologies for Intelligent Systems

11th International Conference, OSTIS 2021
Minsk, Belarus, September 16–18, 2021
Revised Selected Papers

Springer

Editors
Vladimir Golenkov ⓘ
Belarusian State University of Informatics
and Radioelectronics
Minsk, Belarus

Viktor Krasnoproshin ⓘ
Belarusian State University
Minsk, Belarus

Vladimir Golovko ⓘ
Brest State Technical University
Brest, Belarus

Daniil Shunkevich ⓘ
Belarusian State University of Informatics
and Radioelectronics
Minsk, Belarus

ISSN 1865-0929   ISSN 1865-0937 (electronic)
Communications in Computer and Information Science
ISBN 978-3-031-15881-0   ISBN 978-3-031-15882-7 (eBook)
https://doi.org/10.1007/978-3-031-15882-7

This Springer imprint is published by the registered company Springer Nature Switzerland AG
The registered company address is: Gewerbestrasse 11, 6330 Cham, Switzerland

Preface

This collection contains articles that were presented at the 11th International Scientific and Technical Conference on Open Semantic Technologies for Intelligent Systems (OSTIS 2021) which was held at the Belarusian State University of Informatics and Radioelectronics, the leading Belarusian university in the IT field, during September 16–18, 2021.

The OSTIS conference has been held annually since 2010 in Minsk, Belarus, in mid-February and is dedicated to the development of flexible and compatible technologies that provide fast and high-quality construction of intelligent systems for various purposes.

The OSTIS conference is now well known and recognized, and also has a wide geography of participants, including Belarus, Russia, Ukraine, the USA, Latvia, Kazakhstan, and Tajikistan.

OSTIS conferences are carried out in collaboration with other commercial and scientific organizations, including the Russian Association of Artificial Intelligence and the Belarusian Public Association of Artificial Intelligence Specialists.

The main topic of the reports at the OSTIS 2021 conference was the standardization of intelligent systems. In total, 46 papers were submitted to OSTIS 2021 from authors in five countries. All submitted papers were reviewed by Program Committee members together with referees. As a result, 28 papers were selected for presentation, in the form of reports, at the conference.

Throughout all three days of OTIS 2021 well-known scientists in the field of artificial intelligence made their reports, as well as young scientists, who had the opportunity to present and discuss their scientific results. Also, the first version of the open semantic technology standard for component design of intelligent systems of the new generation was presented and discussed, and with the participation of partner companies a presentation of applied projects built on the basis of this technology was held.

This year, a collection of selected papers from the conference is published in Springer's Communications in Computer and Information Science (CCIS) series for the second time. The collection includes the 20 best papers from OTIS 2021 selected by the OSTIS Program Committee. These papers have been extended by their authors and the papers have been reviewed again by an international group of experts.

The collection is intended for researchers working in the field of artificial intelligence, as well as for enterprise specialists in the field of intelligent systems design.

June 2022

Vladimir Golenkov
Viktor Krasnoproshin
Vladimir Golovko
Daniil Shunkevich

Organization

General Chair

Vladimir Golenkov — Belarusian State University of Informatics and Radioelectronics, Belarus

Program Committee Chairs

Vladimir Golovko	Brest State Technical University, Belarus
Viktor Krasnoproshin	Belarusian State University, Belarus
Daniil Shunkevich	Belarusian State University of Informatics and Radioelectronics, Belarus

Program Committee

Sergey Ablameyko	Belarusian State University, Belarus
Alexey Averkin	Plekhanov Russian University of Economics, Russia
Elias Azarov	Belarusian State University of Informatics and Radioelectronics, Belarus
Tatiana Gavrilova	St. Petersburg University, Russia
Larysa Globa	National Technical University of Ukraine "Igor Sikorsky Kyiv Polytechnic Institute", Ukraine
Vladimir Golenkov	Belarusian State University of Informatics and Radioelectronics, Belarus
Vladimir Golovko	Brest State Technical University, Belarus
Valeriya Gribova	Far Eastern Federal University, Russia
Natalia Guliakina	Belarusian State University of Informatics and Radioelectronics, Belarus
Aliaksandr Hardzei	Minsk State Linguistic University, Belarus
Stanislaw Jankowski	Warsaw University of Technology, Poland
Nadezhda Jarushkina	Ulyanovsk State Technical University, Russia
Vladimir Khoroshevsky	Dorodnicyn Computing Centre of RAS, Russia
Boris Kobrinskii	Federal Research Center "Computer Science and Control" of RAS and Pirogov Russian National Research Medical University, Russia
Viktor Krasnoproshin	Belarusian State University, Belarus
Oleg Kuznetsov	V. A. Trapeznikov Institute of Control Sciences of RAS, Russia

Ilya Levin	Tel Aviv University, Israel
Boris Lobanov	United Institute of Informatics Problems of the National Academy of Sciences of Belarus, Belarus
Natalia Loukachevitch	Lomonosov Moscow State University, Russia
Kurosh Madani	Université Paris-Est Créteil Val de Marne, France
Liudmila Massel	Irkutsk National Research Technical University, Russia
Gennady Osipov	Federal Research Center "Computer Science and Control" of RAS, Russia
Pavel Osipov	Riga Technical University, Latvia
Grabusts Pēteris	Rezekne Academy of Technologies, Latvia
Alexey Petrovsky	Federal Research Center "Computer Sciences and Control" of RAS, Russia
Anatoliy Sachenko	Ternopil National Economic University, Ukraine
Altynbek Sharipbay	L.N. Gumilyov Eurasian National University, Kazakhstan
Daniil Shunkevich	Belarusian State University of Informatics and Radioelectronics, Belarus
Sergey Smirnov	Institute for the Control of Complex Systems of RAS, Russia
Igor Sovpel	IHS Markit, Belarus
Dzhavdet Suleymanov	TAS Institute of Applied Semiotics, Russia
Valery Taranchuk	Belarusian State University, Belarus
Valery Tarassov	Bauman Moscow State Technical University, Russia
Yuriy Telnov	Plekhanov Russian University of Economics, Russia
Volodymyr Turchenko	University of Toronto, Canada
Alexander Tuzikov	United Institute of Informatics Problems of the National Academy of Sciences of Belarus, Belarus
Anna Yankovskaya	National Research Tomsk State University, Russia
Alla Zaboleeva-Zotova	Volgograd State Technical University, Russia

Additional Reviewers

Ilya Azarov, Belarus
Vladimir Golenkov, Belarus
Vladimir Golovko, Belarus
Natalia Guliakina, Belarus
Larysa Globa, Ukraine
Boris Kobrinsky, Russia

Vladimir Krasnoposhin, Belarus
Dmitry Lande, Ukraine
Altynbek Sharipbay, Kazakhstan
Igor Sovpel, Belarus
Dzhavdet Suleymanov, Russia

Partnering Organizations

Belarusian Public Association of Artificial Intelligence Specialists
JSC "Savushkin product"
Intelligent Semantic Systems LLC

Contents

On the Current State and Challenges of Artificial Intelligence

Vladimir Golenkov[1]([✉]) [iD], Natalia Guliakina[1] [iD], Vladimir Golovko[2] [iD],
and Viktor Krasnoproshin[3] [iD]

[1] Belarusian State University of Informatics and Radioelectronics, Minsk, Belarus
{golen,guliakina}@bsuir.by
[2] Brest State Technical University, Brest, Belarus
[3] Belarusian State University, Minsk, Belarus
krasnoproshin@bsu.by

Abstract. In the article, the strategic goals of Artificial intelligence and the main problems of scientific and technological activities in this field are described. The problems relevant for the development of the main directions and forms of its activity are defined. Approaches to their solution, based on a new technological wave, are suggested. Issues important for the development of this scientific and technological discipline are discussed.

Keywords: intelligent system · ontological approach · artificial intelligence · General theory of intelligent systems

1 Introduction

This article is an extension of the studies described in [7,8]. The problem of the transition of **Artificial intelligence** (AI) as a *scientific and technological discipline* to a fundamentally new level – the level capable of ensuring the development of the **new generation ICS** market based on *semantically compatible AI technologies* – is considered.

The analysis of works in the field of *AI* shows that this area of *human activity* is in a serious methodological crisis. Therefore, the purposes of this article are:

– identification of the causes of this crisis;
– clarification of measures to resolve it.

It is currently relevant to research not only the phenomenon of *intelligence* and the *model of intelligent activity* but also methodological problems of *AI* in general as well as ways to solve them.

The crisis condition of *AI* is a natural stage in the evolution of any complex systems and technologies:

– at the first stage, there is an accumulation of particular solutions;

V. Golenkov et al. (Eds.): OSTIS 2021, CCIS 1625, pp. 1–18, 2022.
https://doi.org/10.1007/978-3-031-15882-7_1

– the second stage is characterized by the analysis of the resulting variety and its transformation into a coherent system of a qualitatively higher level.

The solution of crisis problems requires:

– a fundamental systemic rethinking of gained experience (rethinking of the principles of the ICS design, operation, and reengineering);
– awareness that:
  - *Cybernetics, Computer Science, and AI* are an integrated fundamental science that requires a single mathematical apparatus;
  - it is necessary not to increase the diversity of points of view but to learn to coordinate them, to ensure their *semantic compatibility*, improving the appropriate methods.

At the current stage of the *AI* development, it is necessary to proceed from the automation of certain *types of human activity* to its integrated automation.

It is essential to focus on the creation of an effective *technology* aimed at the permanent evolution of such a *system*. This requires improving not only the quality of the systems themselves but also the quality of their interaction. I.e., the **new generation ICS** should have a high level of **socialization** and such skills as:

– *mutual understanding* with partners;
– *coordination* of their actions in the process of collective activity in the event of "emergency" (unforeseen) situations;
– *sharing responsibility* with partners for timely and qualitative achievement of a common goal.

All the listed features of the *new generation ICS* assume a high level of their **semantic compatibility**. This requires shifting the emphasis from *data* processing (data science) to *knowledge* processing (knowledge science), i.e., taking into account the **semantics** of the processed information [13, 19, 20].

Without these attributes of *ICS*, it is impossible to implement such projects as Smart City [14], Smart Enterprise [6, 16], Smart University [2, 3], Smart Hospital [18], Smart Society.

The complexity of the ICS and *AI technologies* currently being developed has reached a level at which their development requires not just large *creative teams* but also a significant skill enhancement and quality improvement of these teams.

2 Activity Structure in the Field of AI

To consider the development problem of the *AI activity* as a *scientific and technological discipline* and, in particular, the problem of complex automation of this *activity*, it is required to clarify its structure.

Artificial intelligence is an interdisciplinary field of *scientific and technological activities*, the main objectives of which are:

- the building up of the formal theory of *ICS*;
- the creation of the *technology* for the *design, implementation, maintenance, reengineering, and operation of ICS*;
- the transition to a comprehensive level of automation of all *types of human activity*, based on the mass usage of ICS, which assumes:
  - the presence of *ICS* capable of understanding and coordinating their activity;
  - the building up of the *General theory of human activity*, carried out in the conditions of a new level of its automation (the theory of Smart Society activity).

Artificial intelligence as an *area of the human activity* includes the following *types of activity*:

- *scientific and research activities*;
- *the development of the technology for the design of ICS*;
- *the development of the technology for the restoration of the designed ICS*;
- *engineering, educational, and business activities*.

The considered decomposition of *activity* is not a customary feature of the decomposition of *scientific and technological disciplines*. Usually, the decomposition of *scientific and technological disciplines* is performed in contensive directions that correspond to the decomposition of *technological systems* investigated and developed within these *disciplines*, that is, correspond to the allocation of various types of components in these *technological systems*. For *AI*, such directions are research and development of:

- formal models and languages for the representation of knowledge and knowledge bases;
- logical models of knowledge processing;
- artificial neural networks;
- computer vision subsystems;
- subsystems for natural language text processing (syntactic analysis, understanding, synthesis);
- and many other aspects.

The importance of the *AI* decomposition is determined by the fact that:

- the allocation of various *types of activity* allows setting the problem for the development of their automation tools clearly;
- it can be easily generalized for all *scientific and technological disciplines*. That makes it possible to consider the automation of activity within all *scientific and technological disciplines* on a common basis since the automation of *activity* within various *scientific and technological disciplines* may look similar and sometimes can be implemented using the same *ICS*.

3 Modern Problems of AI

Let us consider possible tendencies of evolution (quality improvement) of activities in the field of *AI* as well as the evolution of products of this activity.

3.1 Problems of Scientific and Research Activities

Currently, scientific research in the field of *AI* is developing in a wide variety of directions (*knowledge representation models*, various types of *logic*, *artificial neural networks*, machine learning, decision-making, goal-setting, behavior planning, situational behavior, multi-agent systems, computer vision, recognition, data mining, soft computing, and much more).

However:

- there is no coherence of the system of *concepts* and, as a result, no *semantic compatibility* and *convergence* of these directions;
- there is no awareness of the need for *convergence* between different directions of *AI*;
- there is no real movement in the direction of building up the *General theory of intelligent systems*.

3.2 Development Problems of the Technology for the ICS Design

The modern *AI technology* is a family of particular technologies focused on the development of various types of *ICS* components. As a rule, they implement various models of information representation and processing, focused on the development of various *ICS* classes.

Therefore:

- the high complexity of the *ICS* development requires highly qualified developers;
- the developed *ICS* are not capable of independently coordinating their activities with each other;
- there is no compatibility of technologies for the *design of various ICS classes* and *AI* and, as a result, their *semantic compatibility* and interaction are not ensured;
- there is no compatibility between *particular technologies for the design of ICS components* (knowledge bases, problem solvers, intelligent interfaces);
- there is no *complex technology for the ICS design*.

3.3 Development Problems of the Technology for the Implementation of the Designed ICS, Their Operation, Maintenance, and Reengineering

Attempts to develop the *new generation computers* focused on the usage in *ICS* were unsuccessful. They were not oriented to the whole variety of *problem-solving models* in ICS, that is, they were not *universal*.

ICS can use various combinations of *models for solving intelligent problems.* However, traditional (von Neumann) *computers* are not able to productively interpret the entire variety of *models.*

At the same time, the development of specialized *computers* focused on the interpretation of a single *problem-solving model* does not solve the problem.

Currently, there is no integrated approach to the technological support of all stages of the ICS life cycle. The semantic unfriendliness of the *user interface,* the lack of built-in intelligent help systems lead to low efficiency of operation of all ICS capabilities.

3.4   Engineering Problems

The solid experience of developing *ICS* for various purposes has been gained. However:

– there is no clear systematization of the variety of *ICS,* that corresponds to the systematization of automated *types of human activity;*
– there is no *convergence of ICS* that provide automation of one type of *human activity;*
– there is no *semantic compatibility* (semantic unification, mutual understanding) between ICS. It leads to the lack of a coherent system of used *concepts;*
– the analysis of the complex automation problems asserts that further *automation of human activity* requires not only an increase in the level of *intelligence* of the corresponding *ICS* but also the realization of their ability:

   • to establish *semantic compatibility* (mutual understanding) both with other *computer systems* and with their users;
   • to maintain this *semantic compatibility* during their evolution as well as the evolution of users and other *computer systems;*
   • to coordinate their activities with users and other *computer systems* in the collective solution of various problems;
   • to participate in the distribution of work (subproblems) in the collective solution of various problems.

The implementation of the listed capabilities can create an opportunity for full automation of *system integration of ICS* into interacting complexes and automation of reengineering of such complexes. This, in turn, will make it possible:

– for the ICS to adapt independently to solve new problems;
– to improve the operation efficiency for such complexes;
– to reduce the number of errors compared to the "manual" (non-automated) performance of *system integration.*

Thus, the next stage of automation of *human activity* requires the creation of *ICS* which could combine themselves to solve complex problems together.

3.5   Problems of Educational Activities

Many universities are training specialists in the field of *AI*. At the same time, it is necessary to note the features and problems of the current state of this activity:

- *activity* in the field of *AI* combines a high degree of research intensity and complexity of engineering work. Therefore, the training of competent specialists requires the simultaneous formation of both research and engineering-practical skills and knowledge as well as the system and technological culture and thinking style. From the point of view of teaching technique and psychology, the combination of fundamental scientific and engineering-practical training of specialists is an intricate pedagogical problem;
- there is no *semantic compatibility* between different academic subjects, which leads to a "tesselation" of information perception;
- there is no systematic approach to training young professionals in the field of *AI*;
- there is no personification of training and an attitude to the identification and development of individual abilities;
- there is no purposeful formation of motivation for creativity, working skills for real development teams;
- there is no adaptation to real practical activity.

Any modern technology should have a high rate of its development. But this requires:

- highly qualified personnel;
- high rates of increase in the level of the experience.

Thus, *educational activities in the field* of *AI* and the corresponding technology should be deeply integrated into all other *types* of *AI activity*.

3.6   Problems of Business Activities

The need for automation of *human activity*, as well as the development of *AI technologies*, have led to a significant expansion of work on the creation of *applied ICS* and the creation of a large number of proprietary organizations focused on the development of such applications.

However:

- it is difficult to ensure a balance of tactical and strategic directions of developing all types of *AI* activities as well as a balance between them;
- currently, there is no deep *convergence* of various types of *AI* activities, which significantly complicates the development of each of them;
- the high level of research intensity of work imposes special requirements on the qualifications of employees and their ability to work as part of *creative teams*;
- to enhance the skills of employees and ensure a high level of development, it is necessary to actively cooperate with scientific schools and departments that train young professionals, widely participate in relevant conferences, seminars, and exhibitions.

3.7   Methodological Problems of AI Development

The core problems of *AI* development include:

– the building up of the **General (formal) theory of ICS**, in which the logical-semantic compatibility of all directions of *AI*, knowledge representation and problem-solving models, and all components of ICS would be ensured;
– the creation of **infrastructure** that provides intensive permanent development of the *General theory of ICS* in a variety of directions, which guarantees the maintenance of the logical-semantic consistency of this *theory* and the compatibility of all directions of its development.

The listed *AI* development problems require solving many subproblems. Let us consider the most important of them.

The building up of the *General (formal) theory of ICS* assumes:

– the clarification of the requirements imposed on the *new generation ICS* – the clarification of the features of *ICS*, that determine the high level of their *intelligence*;
– the **convergence** and *integration* of all kinds of *knowledge* and different *problem-solving models* within each *intelligent computer system*.

The main requirement for the *new generation intelligent computer systems* is a high level of their *socialization*, i.e., a high level of display of such skills as:

– *mutual understanding* with partners (with other *computer systems* or users);
– *negotiability* (ability to coordinate plans and intentions with partners);
– an *ability to coordinate* their actions with the actions of partners in unforeseen circumstances;
– an *ability to share responsibility* with partners for timely achievement of a common purpose.

Mutual understanding is:

– an ability to *understand* partners:
  • an ability to understand messages received from partners;
  • an ability to understand the motivation of partners' actions;
– an ability to be understandable to partners:
  • an ability to clearly formulate messages addressed to partners;
  • an ability to work and comment on their actions so that they and their causes are clear to partners.

The *ability to share responsibility* with partners, which is a necessary criterion for decentralized control of collective activities, implies:

– an ability to monitor and analyze collectively performed activities;

– an ability to be fast in reporting unfavorable situations, events, trends to partners as well as to initiate appropriate collective actions.

The level of *socialization* of intelligent computer systems is the level of their communicative (social) compatibility, which allows them to independently form groups of *intelligent computer systems* and their users as well as independently correlate and coordinate their activities within these groups when solving complex problems in partially predictable conditions.

Of special note are the following features of the *new generation intelligent computer systems*:

– the **degree of convergence** of *intelligent computer systems* and their components and the corresponding **degree of integration** (depth of integration) of *intelligent computer systems* and their components;
– **semantic compatibility** between *intelligent computer systems* in general and **semantic compatibility** between the components of each *intelligent computer system* (in particular, compatibility between various *types of knowledge* and various *knowledge processing models*), which are the key indicators of the degree of **convergence** (junction) between *intelligent computer systems* and their components;
– **unification** and **standardization** of *intelligent computer systems* and their components [1].

The peculiarity of the listed features of *intelligent computer systems* and their components is that they play an important role in solving all the key problems of the current stage of *Artificial intelligence* development and are closely related to each other.

The epicenter of the modern development problems of *activity* in the field of *Artificial intelligence* is the **convergence** and *deep integration* of all types, directions, and results of this *activity*. The level of interrelation, interaction, and **convergence** between various types and directions of activity in the field of *Artificial intelligence* is currently insufficient. This leads to the fact that each of them develops separately, independently of the others. The question is about the **convergence** between such directions of *Artificial intelligence* as the knowledge representation, the solution of intelligent problems, intelligent behavior, understanding, etc. as well as between such *types of human activity in the field of Artificial intelligence* as scientific research, technology development, application development, education, business. Why, when contrasted with the long-term intensive development of scientific research in the field of *Artificial intelligence*, the market of *intelligent computer systems* and the complex technology of *Artificial intelligence*, which provides the development of a wide range of *intelligent computer systems* for various purposes and is available to a wide range of engineers, have not yet been created? Because the combination of a high level of research intensity and pragmatism of this problem requires for its solution a fundamentally new approach to the organization of interaction between scientists who work in the field of *Artificial intelligence*, developers of tools for design automation of *intelligent computer systems*, developers of tools for implementing *intelligent computer systems*, including hardware support tools for *intelligent computer systems*, developers of applied *intelligent computer systems*. Such purposeful interaction should be carried out both within each of these forms of activity in the field of *Artificial intelligence* and between them. Thus, the basic tendency of further development of theoretical and practical works in the field of *Artificial intelligence* is the **convergence** of the most diverse types (forms and directions) of *human activity* in the field of *Artificial intelligence* and a variety of products (results) of this activity. It is necessary to eliminate barriers between different types and products of activity in the field of *Artificial intelligence* to ensure their compatibility and integrability. The problem of creating a rapidly developing market of semantically compatible *intelligent computer systems* is a challenge addressed to specialists in the field of *Artificial intelligence*, which requires overcoming "the Babel" in all its occurrences, the formation of a high culture of negotiability and a unified, coordinated form of representation of collectively accumulated, improved, and used knowledge. Scientists, who work in the field of *Artificial intelligence*, should ensure the **convergence** of the results of different directions of *Artificial intelligence* and build up the *General formal theory of intelligent computer systems*. Engineers, who develop *intelligent computer systems*, should cooperate with scientists and participate in the development of the *technology for the design of semantically compatible intelligent computer systems*.

The separateness of various research directions in the field of *Artificial intelligence* is the main obstacle to the creation of the *technology for the design of semantically compatible intelligent computer systems*.

Convergence (semantic compatibility) of all developed *intelligent computer systems* (including applied ones) transforms a set of individual (independent) *intelligent computer systems* for various purposes into a group of actively interacting *intelligent computer systems* for joint (collective) solutions of complex (comprehensive) problems and for permanent support of semantic compatibility during the individual evolution of each intelligent computer system.

Convergence of particular artificial entities (for example, technological systems) is the propensity for their unification (in particular, for standardization), i.e., the quest for minimizing the variety of forms of solving similar practical problems – the aiming at ensuring that everything that can be done in the same way is done thataway but without deviating the required quality. The latter is essential since improper standardization can lead to a significant impedance of progress. The limitation of the variety of forms should not lead to a limitation of the content and possibilities. Figuratively speaking, "words should be cramped, and thoughts should be free".

Methodologically, **convergence** of artificially created entities (artifacts) comes down to (1) identifying fundamental similarities of these entities and (2) implementing the detected similarities in the same way.

Metaphorically speaking, it is required to switch from "semantic" to "syntactic" equivalence.

Among the general methodological problems of the *AI* development the following can be attributed:

- the lack of mass awareness that the creation of a market of the *new generation* ICS that have *semantic compatibility* and a high level of *socialization*, as well as the creation of complexes (ecosystems) that consist of such ICS and provide automation of various *types of human activity*, is impossible if the development teams of such systems and complexes do not significantly increase the level of *socialization* of all their employees. The quality level of the development team, i.e., the grade of qualification of employees and the consistency level of their activity, should exceed the quality level of the systems developed by this team. The considered problem of the activity consistency of specialists in the field of *AI* is of particular importance for the building up of the *General theory of the new generation ICS* as well as the *technology for their development and operation*;
- not all scientists who work in the field of *AI* accept the pragmatism, the practical focus of this *scientific and technological discipline*;
- not everyone accepts the need:
    - for **convergence** and integration of various directions of *AI* to build up the *General theory of ICS*;
    - for **convergence** of various types of activity in the field of *AI*;
- a relevant obstacle to the **convergence** of the results of scientific and technological activities is the emphasis on identifying not similarities but differences represented in the same form;
- there is no comprehensive approach to the technological support of all stages of the ICS life cycle;
- at the core of modern organization and automation of *human activity* is "the Babel" of an ever-expanding variety of *languages*. Within the *General theory of ICS*, one *universal formal language* – an ancestor language – should be allocated, in relation to which all other used *formal languages* are *sublanguages*. *Denotational semantics* of the specified *universal formal language* should be set by the corresponding *formal ontology* of the highest possible level.

4   Building Up of ICS with a High Level of Socialization

The **new generation** systems are based on the following propositions:

- **semantic information representation**, which assumes the absence of *homonymous signs* and *synonymy*. The semantic representation of the information construct in general has a non-linear (graph) character and is called *semantic network*;
- the **universal language of semantic information representation**, which is characterized by the simplest possible *syntax* that provides the *knowledge* representation with unlimited possibilities of transition from *knowledge* to *meta-knowledge*;

- the *ontological model of knowledge bases*, which consists in the ontological structuring of information. This implies a precise *stratification of the knowledge base* in the form of a hierarchical system of *subject domains* and their corresponding *ontologies*. Each ontology provides a semantic *specification of the concepts* that are key ones within the corresponding *subject domain*;
- *associative access to stored information*, which is carried out according to the specified size and configuration;
- a *dynamic graph model of information processing*, which consists not only in changing the states of memory elements but also in the ability to change the configuration of connections between them;
- an *agent-based information processing model*, which considers the *information processing operation* as the *activity* performed by some group of independent *information agents* [22];
- *decentralized situational control of the information processing operation*, which is performed by a group of independent *agents*. The *initiation condition for agents* is the appearance in the current state of the *knowledge base* of the *situation* and/or the *event* that corresponds to the agent;
- an *ontological model of knowledge base processing*, which assumes localization of the *application scope* of the *method* and *information agent* in accordance with the *ontological model* of the processed *knowledge base*;
- the *ontological interface model* of the *system*, which includes:
  - an ontological description of the *syntax* of all *languages* used for *communication* with external *subjects*;
  - an ontological description of *denotational semantics of languages* used for *communication* with external *subjects*;
  - a family of *information agents* that provide *syntactic* and *semantic analysis* (translation into an internal sense bearing language) as well as *understanding* (immersion into the *knowledge base*) of any entered *message* that belongs to the *external language*;
  - a family of *information agents* that provide *synthesis of messages*, which (1) are addressed to external subjects, (2) *semantically equivalent* to the specified *fragments of its knowledge base* that define the *meaning* of the transmitted *messages*, (3) belong to one of the *external languages*, the full ontological description of which is in the ICS *knowledge base*;
- *multimodality* of *ICS* (its hybrid character considered in details in [11,17]), which assumes a variety of:
  - *types of knowledge* that are part of the *knowledge base*;
  - *problem-solving models* used by the *problem solver*;
  - *sensory channels* that provide *monitoring* of the *environment state*;
  - *effectors* that carry out *impact* on the *environment*;
  - *languages of communication* with other subjects;
- *internal semantic compatibility* between the ICS components, which is characterized by the introduction of general, matching for various fragments *concepts* in the *knowledge base*. It consists in *convergence* [12,15,23]

and *deep integration* inside the *system* for various types of *knowledge* and *problem-solving models*. As a result, effective implementation of *multimodality* is ensured;

– **external semantic compatibility**, which consists in the generality of the used *concepts* and the core *knowledge*;
– high level of **socialization**;
– orientation to the usage of ICS as *cognitive agents* as part of **hierarchical multi-agent systems**;
– **platform independence** that assumes:

  • a clear *stratification* of each *ICS* (1) on a *logical-semantic model*, which contains not only *declarative knowledge* but also the knowledge that has *operational semantics*, and (2) on a *platform* that provides *interpretation* of the specified *logical-semantic model*;
  • universality of the *platform* for interpretation of the *logical-semantic model*. This ensures the interpretation of any *logical-semantic model* if it is represented in the same *universal language of semantic information representation*;
  • the variety of *platform* implementation options for *interpretation of logical-semantic models*. It assumes the possibility of their implementation on *modern* and *new generation universal computers*;
  • the possibility of transferring a logical-semantic model (*knowledge base*) to another *platform for interpretation of logical-semantic models*.

The proposed **technology for the design, implementation, maintenance, reengineering, and operation** of the **new generation** *ICS* is based on the following propositions:

– implementation of the development and maintenance *technology* in the form of the **intelligent computer metasystem**, which fully complies with *standards* of the *new generation* ICS. Such a *metasystem* includes a formal ontological description of:

  • the current version of the *standard*;
  • the current version of *methods and tools for design, implementation, maintenance, reengineering, and operation*.
  Thereby, the *technology for the ICS design and reengineering* and the technology for the design and reengineering of the technology itself are identical;
– **unification** and **standardization** of *systems and methods of their design, implementation, maintenance, reengineering, and operation*;
– permanent evolution of the **standard of systems** and *methods* of their *design, implementation, maintenance, reengineering, and operation*;
– **ontological system design** [4,5,10] that involves:

  • the coordination and time-efficient formalized fixation (in the form of *formal ontologies*) of all *concepts of the current state* of the hierarchical system that underlie the *standard* being permanently evolved;
  • full and prompt documenting of the *current state* of the *project*;

- • the usage of the *"top-down" design technique*;
- **component design** focused on the assembly of *systems* based on constantly expanding libraries of *reusable components*;
- **comprehensive design**:
  - • support for the *ICS design* as independent *objects*, taking into account the specifics of those classes to which the designed systems belong;
  - • support for their implementation, maintenance, and reengineering;
- **complex convergence**: "vertical" – between different *types of activity* in the field of *AI* – and "horizontal" – within each of these *types of activity*;
- organization of development and permanent evolution of the *technology* in the form of an **open international project**, that provides:
  - • free access to the usage of the current version of the *technology*;
  - • an opportunity to join the team of *technology* developers;
- the formation of an open international **creative team**, whose members have a high level of **socialization** and share the goals of the project;
- **phasing** of the formation process for the market of *semantically compatible systems*, which *actively interact* with each other, the initial stages of which are:
  - • development of *logical-semantic models* (knowledge bases) of *applied ICS*;
  - • software implementation of the *platform for the interpretation of logical-semantic models* on modern computers;
  - • installation of the developed *logical-semantic model of the applied system* on the software platform for interpreting such models, followed by *testing* and *reengineering* of each model;
  - • development and permanent improvement of the logical-semantic model (knowledge base) of the *metasystem*, which contains (1) a description of the *standard of the new generation ICS*, (2) a *library* of reusable knowledge and *problem-solving methods*, (3) *methods* and *tools for design support* of *various types of ICS components*;
  - • development of an *associative semantic computer* as a hardware implementation of the *platform for the interpretation of logical-semantic models*;
  - • transferring the developed *logical-semantic models of new generation systems* to new, more efficient implementation options for the platform of interpretation of these models;
  - • the development of the *new generation system market* in the form of an ecosystem – the ecosystem that consists of actively interacting systems and is focused on the complex automation of all *types of human activity*;
  - • the creation of the **knowledge market** based on the *new generation ICS*;
  - • *reengineering* automation of *systems* being operated in accordance with new versions of the *standard of ICS*.

5 Advantages of the Approach to Building Up a New Generation ICS

Semantic information representation ensures the elimination of duplicating information. This mitigates complexity and improves the quality of:

- the development of various *knowledge processing models*;
- *semantic analysis* and *understanding* of information received (transmitted) from external entities (from users, developers, other ICS);
- *convergence* and *integration* of different types of knowledge within each ICS [9, 21];
- *semantic compatibility* and *mutual understanding* between different *systems* as well as between *systems* and humans.

The concept of the *semantic network* is considered as a formal clarification of the concept of *semantic information representation*, as the principle of information representation that underlies the new generation of *computer languages* and *computer systems* themselves – *graph languages* and *graph computers*.

Semantic network is a nonlinear (graph) *sign construct* that has the following features:

- all elements of this *graph structure* (nodes and bindings) are *signs* of the entities described and, in particular, *signs of relations* between these entities;
- all *characters* included in this *graph structure* do not have *synonyms* within this structure;
- the "internal" structure (organization) of the *signs* included in the *semantic network* does not need to be taken into account while its *semantic analysis* (understanding);
- the meaning of the *semantic network* is determined by the *denotational semantics* of the *signs* included in it and the configuration of their *incidence relations*;
- one of the two *incident signs* included in the *semantic network* is a relation sign.

The *agent-oriented information processing model* (in combination with the *decentralized situational control of the process*) and *semantic information representation* mitigate the complexity of processing the general *knowledge base*. Such a model also improves the quality of integration of various *problem-solving models*.

The deletion or addition of a syntactically elementary fragment of stored information, as well as the deletion or addition of each *incidence relation* between such elements, has a clear semantic interpretation. It provides a high level of *semantic flexibility of information*.

Ontologically oriented structuring of the *knowledge base* ensures a high level of *information stratification*.

High-capacity metalinguistic capabilities of the language of internal information representation provide a high level of *reflexivity of ICS*.

The level of *individual learnability* of systems, their ability to rapidly expand
their *knowledge* and *skills* are provided by:

- the *semantic flexibility* of stored *information*;
- the *stratification* of this information;
- the *reflexivity of ICS*.

The level of *joint learnability* of systems is ensured by the level of their
socialization, the ability to effectively participate in the activities of various
groups, and, principally, the high level of *mutual understanding*.

The level of *socialization* of the new generation ICS fundamentally changes
the nature of the interaction of *computer systems* with humans whose activity
they automate. There is a transition from controlling these automation tools to
the equitable partnering meaningful relationships.

Each *new generation ICS* is able to:

- independently or by invitation join a group that consists of ICS and/or
  humans. Such groups are created (on a temporary or permanent basis) for
  the collective solution of complex *problems*;
- participate in the distribution of *problems* – both "one-off" and long-term
  ones (responsibilities);
- monitor the status of the entire process of collective activity, coordinate activity with other group members in case of possible unpredictable changes in the
  conditions (state) of the corresponding environment.

The high level of intelligence of *systems* and, respectively, the high level of
their independence and purposefulness allows them to be full members of a wide
variety of communities. Within these communities, *new generation systems* gain
the rights to independently initiate a wide range of actions (problems) performed
by other members of the community and to participate in the correlation and
coordination of the activities of the community members.

The ability of the *system* to coordinate its activity with other similar systems,
adjust the activity of the entire *group*, adapting to changes in the environment,
allows significantly automating the activity of the *system integrator* both at the
stage of creating a *new generation ICS group* and at the stage of its updating
(reengineering).

The advantages of the *new generation ICS* are ensured by:

- the language of internal *semantic encoding of information* stored in the memory of these systems;
- the organization of dynamic graph associative semantic memory of the *new
  generation intelligent computer systems*;
- the *semantic representation of knowledge bases* of the new generation intelligent computer systems and by *ontological structuring of knowledge bases* of
  these systems;

– *agent-oriented problem-solving models* used in the *new generation intelligent computer systems* in combination with decentralized control of the information processing operation.

6   Conclusion

In the complex automation of types and *areas of human activity*, the following main directions can be distinguished:

– the creation of an open community (of the *new generation ICS* and professionals in the field of *AI*), which provides comprehensive automation and development of all types and areas of activity in the field of *AI* as an integral *scientific and technological discipline*;
– enlargement of the human-machine community to the level of providing comprehensive automation and development of all *scientific and technological disciplines*.

ICS focused on supporting individual and/or collective *human activity* in various *scientific and technological disciplines* can be divided into the following *classes*:

– *intelligent portals of scientific knowledge*;
– *intelligent portals of technological knowledge*;
– *intelligent systems for the design automation* of artificial systems;
– *intelligent systems for automating the preparation for production process* of artificial systems;
– *intelligent automated systems for production control* of designed artificial systems;
– *intelligent systems for maintenance automation* of artificial systems;
– *intelligent systems for reengineering automation* of artificial systems;
– *intelligent computer systems for supporting the efficient operation* of artificial systems;
– *intelligent training systems* that provide automation of individual training of professionals in various disciplines;
– *intelligent computer systems for the organization of comprehensive training of professionals* in various specialties using all available forms and methods of training and motivation.

References

1. IT/APKIT Professional Standards. http://www.apkit.webtm.ru/committees/education/meetings/standarts.php. Accessed 7 May 2012
2. Alrehaili, N., Almutairi, Y., Alasmari, M., Assiry, A., Meccawy, D.M.: A unified E-Government service - an essential component of a Smart City. IARJSET 4(7), 1–4 (2017). https://doi.org/10.17148/iarjset.2017.4701

3. Alrehaili, N.A., Aslam, M.A., Alahmadi, D.H., Alrehaili, D.A., Asif, M., Malik, M.S.A.: Ontology-based smart system to automate higher education activities. Complexity **2021**, 1–20 (2021). https://doi.org/10.1155/2021/5588381
4. Benavides, C., García, I., Alaiz, H., Quesada, L.: An ontology-based approach to knowledge representation for computer-aided control system design. Data Knowl. Eng. **118**, 107–125 (2018). https://doi.org/10.1016/j.datak.2018.10.002
5. Dietrich, J., Elgar, C.: An ontology based representation of software design patterns. In: Software Applications, pp. 528–545. IGI Global (2009). https://doi.org/10.4018/978-1-60566-060-8.ch036
6. Dietz, J.L.G.: Enterprise Ontology. Springer, Heidelberg (2006). https://doi.org/10.1007/3-540-33149-2
7. Golenkov, V., Guliakina, N., Davydenko, I., Eremeev, A.: Methods and tools for ensuring compatibility of computer systems. In: Golenkov, V. (ed.) Open Semantic Technologies for Intelligent Systems (OSTIS), vol. 3, pp. 25–52. Belarusian State University of Informatics and Radioelectronics Publishing, Minsk (2019)
8. Golenkov, V., et al.: From training intelligent systems to training their development tools. In: Golenkov, V. (ed.) Open Semantic Technologies for Intelligent Systems (OSTIS), vol. 2, pp. 81–98. Belarusian State University of Informatics and Radio-electronics Publishing, Minsk (2018)
9. Haarslev, V., Hidde, K., Möller, R., Wessel, M.: The RacerPro knowledge representation and reasoning system. Semant. Web **3**(3), 267–277 (2012). https://doi.org/10.3233/SW-2011-0032
10. Haav, H.M.: A comparative study of approaches of ontology driven software development. Informatica **29**, 439–466 (2018). https://doi.org/10.15388/Informatica.2018.175
11. Kolesnikov, A.V.: Hybrid Intelligent Systems: Theory and Technology of Development. SPbSTU, Saint-Petersburg (2001)
12. Kovalchuk, M.V.: Convergence of science and technology - a breakthrough into the future. Russian Nanotechnol. **6**(1–2), 13–23 (2011)
13. Manin, Y., Marcolli, M.: Semantic Spaces (2016)
14. Nicola, A.D., Villani, M.L.: Smart City ontologies and their applications: a systematic literature review. Sustainability **13**(10), 5578 (2021). https://doi.org/10.3390/su13105578
15. Palagin, A.V.: Problems of transdisciplinarity and the role of informatics. Cybern. Syst. Anal. **5**, 3–13 (2013)
16. Rajabi, Z., Minaei, B., Seyyedi, M.A.: Enterprise architecture development based on enterprise ontology. J. Theor. Appl. Electron. Commer. Res. **8**(2), 13–14 (2013). https://doi.org/10.4067/s0718-18762013000200007
17. Rybina, G.V.: Dynamic integrated expert systems: technology for automated acquisition, presentation and processing of temporal knowledge. Inf. Meas. Control Syst. **16**(7), 20–31 (2018)
18. Shahzad, S.K., Ahmed, D., Naqvi, M.R., Mushtaq, M.T., Iqbal, M.W., Munir, F.: Ontology-driven smart health service integration. Comput. Methods Programs Biomed. **207**, 106146 (2021). https://doi.org/10.1016/j.cmpb.2021.106146
19. Spivak, D.I., Kent, R.E.: Ologs: a categorical framework for knowledge representation. PLoS ONE **7**(1), e24274 (2012). https://doi.org/10.1371/journal.pone.0024274
20. Taranchuk, V.: Tools and examples of intelligent processing, visualization and interpretation of GEODATA. J. Phys. Conf. Ser. **1425**(1) (2019). https://doi.org/10.1088/1742-6596/1425/1/012160

21. Tuzovsky, A.F., Yampolsky, V.Z.: Integration of information using Semantic Web technologies. Probl. Inform. **2**, 51–58 (2011)
22. Wooldridge, M.: An Introduction to Multiagent Systems. Wiley, Chichester (2009)
23. Yankovskaya, A.E., Shelupanov, A.A., Kornetov, A.N., Ilinskaya, N.N., Obukhovskaya, V.B.: Hybrid intelligent system of express diagnostics of organizational stress, depression, deviant behavior and anxiety of violators based on convergence of several sciences and scientific directions. In: Works of Congress on Intelligent Scientific Publication in 3 Volumes, pp. 323–329. Stupin A. S. Publishing House, Taganrog (2017)

Intelligent Services Development Technology Using the IACPaaS Cloud Platform

Valeria Gribova⬤, Philip Moskalenko⬤, Vadim Timchenko$^{(\boxtimes)}$⬤, and Elena Shalfeyeva⬤

Institute of Automation and Control Processes, Far Eastern Branch of Russian Academy of Sciences, Radio St., 5, Vladivostok 690041, Russia
{gribova,philipmm,vadim,shalf}@iacp.dvo.ru

Abstract. The paper presents a technology for the development of intelligent multi-agent services. This technology is put to reduce the labor-intensiveness of their creation and maintenance. Its key aspect is an independent development of knowledge and databases, a user interface and a problem solver (as a set of agents), and their assembly into an intelligent service. The principal specifics of the technology are: two-level ontological approach to the formation of knowledge and databases with a clear separation between the ontology and information formed on its basis; the ontology-based specification of not only the domain terminology and structure, but also of the rules for knowledge and data formation, control of their integrity and completeness; division of all software components into procedural and declarative parts; unified semantic representation of the latter (including declarative parts of software components), etc. The proposed approaches are implemented on the IACPaaS cloud platform where expert-oriented formation of each service component with an appropriate tool is provided. An example of service development which demonstrates the technology usage is given.

Keywords: Intelligent system · Multi-agent system · Intelligent software development technology · Hierarchical semantic network · Cloud platform · Cloud service

1 Introduction

Development and maintenance of an intelligent system (IS) with knowledge are hard and labor-intensive processes. This is primarily due to the fact that a knowledge base (KB) is a part of such a system's architecture which brings in some specificies. That's why special tools are used. The typical representatives are: Level5 Object, G2, Clips, Loops, VITAL, KEATS, OSTIS, AT-technology,

This work was partially supported by the Russian Foundation for Basic Research (projects 19-07-00244 and 20-01-00449).

RT Works, COMDALE/C, COGSYS, ILOG Rules, Protégé and others [1–5]. The considerable differences between them are determined by the formalisms used to represent knowledge, methods and tools for their acquisition, forming and debugging, the used inference mechanisms, and also technologies for IS with a KB (hereinafter KBS – knowledge based system) development and maintenance.

However, the problem of creating tools for development and maintenance of KBS is far from being solved. Scientific publications mention the following main problems that need to be dealt with. First of all, there is still an open issue of including domain experts into the process of creating and maintaining knowledge bases, ensuring their real impact on the quality of software systems being developed. Experience in developing complex software systems shows that the intermediation of programmers between designed software systems and experts significantly distorts the contribution of the latter ones. When making a new generation of tools, it is not programmers who should dominate, but experts who are able to accurately represent their knowledge [6, 7]. The developed models and methods of knowledge acquisition solve the problem of their initial formation, however, as noted in [8], it is the maintenance phase that is the most complex and significant. The KB is a component of KBS which is changed much more often than other components, so providing of expert-oriented knowledge creation and maintenance tools is an important and relevant task. KB maintenance implies its refinement or improvement, which at the same time does not break the performance of the IS (i.e., a change in the knowledge base should not lead to the need of changing the solver and its user interface). Among the problems of existing tools for creating KBS, the following is also worth mentioning: the use of various approaches and mechanisms for creating knowledge bases, solvers and interfaces, complex linking of these components, or vice versa, the lack of a clear separation between KBS components, which makes it difficult to reuse solutions when creating other KBS. Our long-term experience in creating practically useful KBS for solving problems in various domains has shown an urgent need to construct problem-oriented shells with accompanying instrumental support.

The key requirement for any complex software system, including KBS, is its viability, which is implemented in software engineering through: architectural solutions (separation into loosely coupled components with logically clear functions), declarative representation of software components of a system, automation of code fragments generation, reuse of components, separation of competencies between developers of different types. One of the well-known solutions for implementing the requirement to involve domain experts in the KBS development process is the ontology-based (metainformation-based) KB formation, using a semantic knowledge representation model (the knowledge base is separated from the ontology) [9].

In software engineering, an agent-based approach is actively applied to create viable software systems [10], which in comparison with object-oriented programming has potentially greater flexibility, gives the possibility of agent reuse, and simplifies parallelization (which is important for IS as many tasks have great computational complexity [11]). However, the issue of creating a comprehensive technology that supports the development of all KBS components with ontological knowledge bases remains open.

To address these challenges in the development and maintenance of viable KBS we have proposed a concept of the development toolkit [12], which supports the following technological principles:

- knowledge base, problem solver and user interface (UI) are developed separately;
- a single language is used to describe the ontology of knowledge (metainformation for the knowledge base) and models of all declarative components (their metainformation);
- a unified declarative semantic (conceptual) representation of all information resources (ontologies, knowledge bases, databases) and software components of KBS is used – a labeled rooted hierarchical binary digraph with possible loops and cycles (thus universality of their software processing and user editing can be achieved);
- formation and maintenance of knowledge bases is carried out by domain experts and is based on knowledge ontologies;
- UI of the knowledge base editor is generated for experts on the basis of ontology (metainformation);
- method of problem solving is divided into subproblems, each one is solved by a correspondent software agent, either a reflective or a reactive one [13] – a component of a problem solver;
- software agents are provided with an API for access to information resources;
- KBS is available as a cloud service.

The paper presents the technology [14] for the development of a KBS as a cloud multi-agent service, using such toolkit. It is implemented on the IACPaaS cloud platform, which brief overview is provided. Also, a short example of service development which demonstrates the technology usage on the platform is given.

2   Technology Overview

Technological foundations supported by the proposed toolkit concept are consistent with the general trend when KBS development is based on the use of methods and tools for ontological modeling of design and specification processes of developed systems, i.e. ontological engineering tools (Ontology-Based (-Driven) Software Engineering [15]); reusability of ready-to-use solutions (components); involving stakeholders in the development process through knowledge portals.

Methods of formalizing knowledge based on the domain ontology and ontologies of known intelligent problems allow us to create structured and at the same time understandable to domain experts knowledge, as well as systematization of terms.

Further, knowledge, formalized on the basis of an ontology, are either integrated with ready-to-use problem-oriented software solvers, or require the creation of new software components. Thereby the proposed technology for the development of intelligent services consists of the following processes: *assembly of an intelligent service from components* and possibly *development of those*

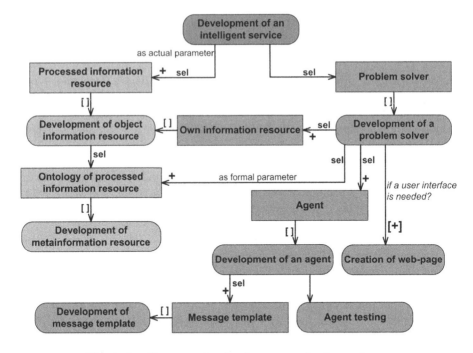

Fig. 1. Intelligent service development technology scheme.

components (Fig. 1). Components are represented by rectangles, and activities – by rounded rectangles. The components are information ones (metainformation and information) and software ones (a problem solver, its agents, message templates for their interaction, UI). Symbols on arcs have the following meaning. **sel** – searching for and selecting the appropriate component (to which an arc is pointing). [ ] – optionality, i.e. the pointed activity is performed if the required component is absent or if the condition (italic text on the arc) is true. + ("plus") – multiplicity, meaning that the selection or creation (development) of the corresponding component can be performed more than once.

3   Development of an Intelligent Service

An intelligent *service* consists of a *problem solver* (which has been integrated with *formal parameters* and with a *UI*) and actual parameters (*input actual parameters* – information resources accessible only for reading and *output actual parameters* – information resources accessible for CRUD modification). Distinction of service components into information and software ones pursues the following objectives:

– independent development by different groups of specialists;
– reuse – the same problem solver can be bound with various information resources and vice-versa.

In both cases the compatibility (between those two types of components) is provided at the level of *formal parameters* of the *solver*.

A *formal parameter* of the *problem solver* is an information resource which represents metainformation (ontology), an actual parameter is one of the information resources which represent information and which are formed in terms of this metainformation.

The declarative specification of a *service* is formed in two stages:

1. creation of a new information resource of "service" type with setting of its name and *Service structure* information resource (representing a language for declarative specification of platform services) as metainformation;
2. creation of content of this new information resource (service assembly) with the use of *Editor for digraphs of information* [16], where the process of editing is controlled by metainformation *Service structure* and consists of the following:
   - a link to the *problem solver* (to the root vertex of digraph which represents it) is created,
   - for each *formal parameter* of the *solver* (in order of its appearance in the description of solver) a link to the corresponding actual parameter (to the root vertex of digraph which represents it) is created.

4   Development of Knowledge Bases and Databases

4.1   General Description

Network (graph) structures are now widely used as a visual and universal mean for representing various types of data and knowledge in different domains. In principle, with the help of such structures that are best suited for explicitly representing associations between different concepts, it is possible to describe any complex situation, fact or problem domain. At the same time, as noted, for example, in [17] various kinds of information (data and knowledge), regardless of the concrete syntax of the language for their representation, in the abstract syntax, in the general case, can be represented as (multi-) graphs, possibly typed.

All information resources (processed by a service) have the unified declarative representation – a labeled rooted hierarchical binary digraph with possible loops and cycles. Thus, universality of their processing is achieved.

In accordance with a 2-level approach for formation of information resources [18,19], two types of them are distinguished by the abstraction level of represented information. They are information resources which represent ontology (i.e. metainformation – abstract level) and information resources which represent knowledge and data bases (i.e. information – object level).

4.2   Development of Object Information Resources

Development of an *information resource* which is processed by an intelligent service and represents information requires another information resource which represents its metainformation to be present in the storage. Otherwise it must be developed as described in the Sect. 4.3. The development of an *information resource* consists of two stages:

1. creation of a new information resource with setting of its name and metainformation;
2. formation of its content by means of the *Editor for digraphs of information* where the process of editing is controlled by set metainformation.

During the work of the *Editor for digraphs of information* it forms and maintains a correspondence between the arcs of digraphs of information and metainformation. Formation is carried out in "top-down" way: from vertices which are composite concepts to vertices which are atomic concepts. This process starts from the root vertex. In this case the user doesn't have to sharply envision and keep in mind the whole structure (connections between vertices) of the formed digraph as in the case of "bottom-up" way.

The UI of the *Editor for digraphs of information* is generated by the metainformation. This implies that as the latter one describes an ontology for knowledge or data in some domain so its experts can create and maintain knowledge bases or databases in terms of their customary systems of concepts (without mediators, i.e. knowledge engineers).

4.3   Development of Metainformation Resources

The development of a *metainformation* resource consists of two stages:

1. creation of a new information resource with setting of its name and metainformation (in such case it is an information resource which contains the description of the *language for metainformation digraph representation*);
2. formation of its content in a "top-down" way (starting from the root vertex of the digraph) with the use of the *Editor for digraphs of metainformation* (this step also makes up the maintenance process which may automatically modify correspondent object information in order to keep it in consistency with modified metainformation).

A digraph of metainformation describes the abstract syntax of a structural language in terms of which digraphs of information are further formed. The language for metainformation digraph representation is declarative, simple, and at the same time powerful enough to describe arbitrary models, which are adapted to the domain terminology and to the form adopted by the developers of KBS components as well as tools for their creation. A detailed description of the language is given in [20].

Users of the *Editor for digraphs of metainformation* are metainformation carriers who are usually knowledge engineers and systems analysts from various fields of professional activities. The editing process model which is set into the basis of the *Editor for digraphs of metainformation* has much in common with the one which is the basis of the *Editor for digraphs of information*.

The differences are caused only by formalism of representation of the correspondent digraphs and by the fact that metainformation digraph can have an arbitrary form (limitations are set only by expressive means of the *language for metainformation digraph representation*), whereas information digraph has a structure limited by its metainformation digraph.

5 Development of a Problem Solver

A *problem solver* is a component of some intelligent service which processes information resources and which encapsulates business logic for problem solving. It is a set of agents, each of them solves some subproblem(s) and interacts with others by message exchange. A lifecycle of a message starts from its creation by some agent, followed by it being sent to another agent which receives and processes it. Then a message ceases to exist.

The proposed approach for development of agent communication means is a multilanguage one. Messages must be represented in some language(s) which syntax and semantics must be understood by interacting agents. Each language can have an arbitrary complex syntax structure (represented by metainformation digraph), and contents of messages (represented by digraphs of information) are formed in accordance with it.

There are two agents within the solver (in general case) which have particular roles:

- *root agent* – an agent to which an *initializing message* is sent by utility agent *System agent* when a service starts to run after its launch (meaning that this agent runs first among all agents of problem solver);
- *interface controller agent* – an agent whose interaction with the utility agent *View agent* (see Sect. 8) provides coupling of UI with problem solver (in case when a service with UI is developed).

The mentioned *initializing message* is represented in the communication language which belongs to the class of utility ones. Another such distinguished languages are used for interacting with utility agents and for stopping the work of the problem solver.

During the process of service execution agents which are parts of the problem solver connect with each other dynamically. In case of a service without UI this interaction starts from the *root agent*. In the case of a service with a UI it usually starts from the *interface controller agent* – for processing the events which are generated in the UI (the *root agent* may do no work at all in that case).

In order for a problem solver to become usable for various services at the stage of their assembly the information resource which represents the declarative specification of this problem solver must be created. It is formed in two stages:

1. creation of a new information resource of "problem solver" type with setting of its name and *Problem solver structure* information resource as metainformation;

2. formation of content of this new information resource (problem solver assembly) with the use of *Editor for digraphs of information* where the process of editing is controlled by the set metainformation and consists of setting of the following:

   – information about the purpose of the problem solver,
   – a link to its *root agent,*
   – links to *formal parameters* (in case when services should process information resources, i.e. must have actual parameters at runtime),
   – a *UI* which includes a link to *interface controller agent* (in case when a service with the UI is being developed),
   – links to own information resources (shared among all running instances of the problem solver).

The described organization of a problem solver (which implies dedication of a special *interface controller agent* among others) gives an opportunity to separate development and maintenance of problem solver business-logic from same work on UI. This leads to the possibility of involving independent appropriate specialists to these types of work.

6   Development of an Agent

An *agent* is a (possibly reusable) software component which interacts with other agents with the use of message reception/sending. It is capable of processing (reading and modification) information resources. Reusability means that an agent can become a part of various problem solvers with no modification. Data processing is organized in form of productions which are grouped into one or several production blocks – by the amount of message templates that an agent can process.

An agent consists of two parts: a declarative one and a procedural one. Declarative part of an agent consists of two sections: agent's documentation (which is presented by a set of descriptions: for an agent itself and for each of its production block, written in natural language) and formal specification for its set of production blocks (which comprise an agent). The declarative part is used as a basis for the support of automation of agent's documented source code development and maintenance. A digraph 2-level model of information resources representation allows storing of declarative description and code of an agent (procedural part) in a single information resource which represents this agent.

Development of an agent consists of the following stages:

1. creation of new information resource of "agent" type with setting of its name and *Agent structure* information resource as metainformation;
2. formation of content of this new information resource with the use of *Editor for digraphs of information* (with extensions) where the process of editing is controlled by the set metainformation and consists of setting of the following initial data: agent name, agent class name, description, local data structure

and production blocks specification (description, templates of incoming messages and corresponding templates of outgoing messages)[1];

3. acquiring agent source code (by generating its sketch using its declarative description or using pre-saved source code) and executable code of used message templates;

4. writing (modifying) the source code of an agent (code for its production blocks in particular) and forming its executable code (as a result of compilation of its source code);

5. uploading source code and executable code into the correspondent information resource (thus extending agent's declarative specification);

6. agent testing (optional).

Acquiring agent source code and executable code of reused message templates must be done with extended functionality of the *Editor for digraphs of information*. For agent source code it provides downloading of either sketch of source code which is generated on the basis of new agent declarative description or downloading of the stored source code of modified agent.

Writing the source code of an agent must be done using some modern programming language powerful enough for solving intelligent problems. A suitable IDE can be used or such functionality can be implemented within the toolkit (within some extension of the *Editor for digraphs of information*). The source code of agent's production block implements the whole of part of the ontology-based algorithm for knowledge-based processing using toolkit API methods for: incoming message data reading, knowledge base traversing, outgoing message creation. Note that an agent can make an arbitrary number of messages to be sent to a set of other agents (including system ones and itself).

After the source code of an agent is ready it is necessary to form its ready-to-run version (e.g. bytecode) and load it into the information resource which represents an agent. In order to achieve this a compilation of the source code must be committed either locally or online (if the toolkit has such support). While code uploading and/or compilation it is checked for correctness and safety.

Agent testing is carried out by a separate tool which performs multiple start and execution of the set of its production blocks on a provided set of tests (formed as information resources with metainformation *Agent tests structure* by use of the *Editor for digraphs of information*). Reports are saved with results of test executions. A single test generally includes the information resource representing incoming message, a set of information resources representing expected outgoing messages, and tuples of information resources which act as input, output (initial and final states) actual parameters and own ones (initial and ending states). A test is considered to be passed if the amount and the contents of the outgoing messages and of processed information resources are as expected. Formed sets of tests can be used for regressive testing during the stage of agent maintenance.

---

[1] Different production blocks of the same agent must have different incoming message templates.

7   Development of a Message Template

A *message* in multi-agent systems is a mechanism for coordinated interaction of agents which provides exchange of information between them and transfer of requests [21]. Agents communicate in different languages whose amount is extensible (by means of creating new message templates and adding new production blocks into agents or extending existing ones) and is limited only by the total amount of message templates. Specific languages of agent interaction (message templates) are set at the level of separate production blocks.

As messages are object information resources so languages for sets of messages are represented by information resources that are metainformation – *Message templates*. They not only contain the structure for a set of messages but may also hold a set of methods for processing these messages. Thus, like an agent, a message template consists of two parts – a declarative one and a procedural one. Its structure is simpler though: name, class name, description, message structure, source code and executable code.

Development of the message template consists generally of the same stages as of an agent. The differences appear at the stages of creation (when the *Message template structure* information resource is set as metainformation) and of writing the source code (due to differences in the structure of declarative specifications of agents and message templates).

Message template testing can be done only through testing of an agent (see Sect. 6).

8   Development of a User Interface

Development of an interface for an intelligent cloud service is a development of web-interface (as services are available online and are accessed via web-browsers). The interface consists of interface controller agent (development described in Sect. 6) and a set of web-pages (with one selected as the starting one). Each *web-page* has a name and data which can be of *content* or *design* type:

- *content* – a mixture of text, *ui tags* and a set of names of *design web-pages* (of the same problem solver);
- *design* – a description of CSS classes (a set of CSS rules). Such separation allows:
- to apply various CSS to the same content of the interface and vice versa – to use the same CSS for interface of various services, which leads to increase of flexibility and adaptability of developed interfaces and to simplification of their maintenance;
- to divide the processes of development and maintenance (thus, to make them independent) of these parts and to involve independent appropriate specialists to these types of work (their only interaction would lie in setting/using same names for classes in CSS).

The *ui tags* of a *web-page* are processed as *ui requests* (one request per tag) sent through *View agent* to agents which act as *interface controllers* within solvers at the initial *web-page* display. Further interactions of user with web-page elements produce other *ui requests* (determined by those elements). Each *ui request* is a set of pairs: *parameter = value*. After the request is passed to solver agent, the *View agent* waits for result and in case it is a fragment of UI – puts it into the shown web-page content in place of the processed *ui tag*.

A detailed scheme of interaction of the *View agent* with Web-server and *interface controller agent* (which is a part of some problem solver) is shown in Fig. 2. A process of interaction consists of request transferring from browser to agents and returning of result to browser. A processing of a request is performed in between. Numeration of arrows in Fig. 2 sets the order of interaction.

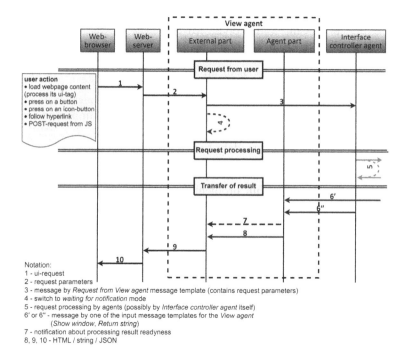

Fig. 2. A scheme of interaction of the *View agent* with Web-server and *interface controller agent*.

The basis of the UI presentation model is an "MVC" (Model-View-Controller) pattern [22]. Its projection on the proposed interface model is as follows.

1. Model. This component includes:

– *Model of abstract user interface* – an information resource which represents metainformation and holds a description of structure for standard interface elements of WIMP-interfaces and a way of their organization into a single nested structure.

– *Abstract interface generation API* – a set of high-level functions for creation of fragments of abstract interfaces. Performing calls of these functions (with necessary arguments) significantly increases the level of abstraction at which the information resource that represents some abstract interface is formed. To form a description for some fragment of an abstract interface one has to construct a superposition of function calls of this API.

2. View. This component is presented by the utility agent *View agent*, which is a "hybrid" one. It is divided into two parts so that it can mediate between the two:

– Web-server – it interacts with external part of the *View agent*,
– *interface controller agents* of problem solvers – they interact with agent part by receiving, processing and replying to messages created by *Request from View agent* utility message template.

The other tasks of the *View agent* are the following:

– the production of specific interface (HTML-code) on the basis of its abstract model (with the use of built-in mapping rules for all supported interface elements);
– uploading/downloading binary data to/from Web-server.

3. Controller. This component is represented by agents which play a role of *interface controller agent* (within problem solvers). These agents interact with the *View agent* by message exchange. Such messages are created by particular message templates. Agents implement (possibly by interaction with other agents) logic for processing *ui requests* of the following origins: *ui tags* (from web-pages content data) and ui events (generated by interface elements in response to user actions).

A result of processing a *ui request* is either an information resource (which represents a description of an abstract interface which is passed to the agent part of the *View agent*) or an arbitrary string of characters.

The development of UI consists of the following steps:

1. creation of a set of *web-pages* within the declarative specification of the used problem solver – with formation of content for each page;
2. development of *interface controller agent*, which must implement the logic for processing *ui requests*.

9 IACPaaS Cloud Platform

The proposed technology is implemented on the IACPaaS platform – a cloud computing system for support of development, control and remote use of multi-agent services. Thus, it provides not only users with remote access to applied intelligent systems but also developers with remote access to appropriate tools for creation of such systems and their components which make this process more automated. Conceptual 4-level architecture of the IACPaaS platform (Fig. 3) consists of:

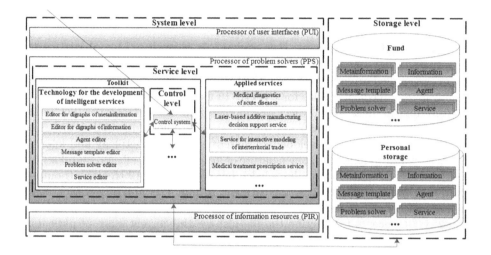

Fig. 3. Conceptual 4-level architecture of the IACPaaS platform.

The System Level. The Virtual machine of the IACPaaS platform consists of three processors: processor of information resources (PIR), processor of problem solvers (PPS), processor of user interfaces (PUI). Each processor is meant for support of the correspondent components of intelligent systems. An access to information resources of the IACPaaS platform (by means of PIR), a launch and execution of services (by means of PPS) and an interaction of services with users (by means of PUI) are provided at this level.

The Storage Level. The Fund and personal user storages of the IACPaaS platform are sets of storage units of various types and levels of abstraction (data, knowledge, ontology, problem solver, agent, etc.). Each storage unit is represented by an information resource which can be either metainformation or information or their mixture. The Fund is structurally divided into sections. Fund sections and Personal storages are divided into folders. A folder holds information resources and subfolders. The Fund is where reusable information resources are placed.

The Service Level. This level is represented by a collection of running services. Each service includes a problem solver, which is represented by a set of interacting agents that process information resources and exchange messages.

The Control Level. This level is represented by a basic system service of the platform – the Control system. It provides a controlled access to functional capabilities of the IACPaaS platform.

An intelligent service of the IACPaaS platform is a cloud KBS for solving some applied problems which belong to some domain. Representation of all components (architectural model of KBS) that provide a solution to the problem, based on knowledge bases, is as follows (in its most general form): a set of knowledge bases; software problem solver; components that provide the UI.

10   Medical Treatment Prescription Service Development

One of the applied services created on the IACPaaS platform using the described technology is a medical service for COVID-19 treatment prescription.

According to the service project, the following ontologies (together they form the ontology of the problem being solved) and the knowledge and data bases formed on their basis are developed or reused[2]: formulary ontology and knowledge base (for describing the nomenclature of drugs and their effects); ontology of disease treatment prescription; knowledge base on COVID-19 treatment; ontology of the report on the prescribed treatment; terminology and observation base ontology and the base itself (both are reused, the base already contains more than 25,000 concepts to describe the life history, the current state of patients, laboratory and instrumental studies); case record ontology.

The new ontologies are created in the developer's Personal storage using the *Control system* and are formed using the IACPaaS platform tool *Editor for digraphs of metainformation*. The new correspondent bases are also created using the *Control system* (with specification of the necessary ontologies) and are formed using the tool *Editor for digraphs of information*. Ontologies control the editing process and UI generation, which provides a human-computer interaction with experts in pharmacology and the treatment of COVID-19 in their professional terms. So, the development of knowledge bases is carried out without involving mediators, e.g. knowledge engineers. A fragment of the knowledge base on COVID-19 treatment is shown in Fig. 4.

In parallel with the formation of bases, the software is developed. An ontological solver is being created to generate hypotheses about solving the problem (in the form of the prescribed treatment). The entire process of hypothesis generation and testing is implemented by a single agent that processes input information according to the ontology. The result of its work is stored in an information resource with a report, where hypotheses about solutions and explanation of their adoption (taking into account the characteristics of the organism and existing symptoms) are represented. The structure of the recommended treatment report is pre-consistent with specialists (potential users).

The information resource of the agent being developed consists of the following components: "treatment prescription agent" (agent name); "MedicalTreatmentAgent" (agent class name); "agent for treatment hypothesis generation and testing" (agent description) and one production block. The message templates

---

[2] This and other resources are retrieved for reuse from the Medical knowledge portal (section of the Fund) of the IACPaaS platform.

of the production block are system ones (they are present in the platform Fund) and are reused. Agent source code is not given in this example.

Fig. 4. UI fragment of *Editor for digraphs of information* running with the COVID-19 treatment knowledge base.

The declarative specification of a problem solver is formed by specifying this agent as the *root* one. This specification also integrates the problem solver named "treatment prescription" with information resources representing ontologies as follows (see Sect. 5). The "treatment prescription agent" is set as solver's *root agent*. Formulary ontology, ontology of disease treatment regimens, terminology and observation base ontology and case record ontology are set as solver's *input formal parameters*. Ontology of the report on the prescribed treatment is set as solver's *output formal parameter*.

The COVID-19 treatment prescription service is created for user from this solver and actual parameters – knowledge bases, case record and an empty report information resources. It is done just by creation and filling of the information resource of the service type, called "COVID-19 treatment". (Same information resources can also be created by developers - for debugging the problem solver.) Before that it is necessary to create an information resource for case record description and, using the *Editor for digraphs of information*, fill it with observations (based on the base of terminology and observations) and diagnosis

(COVID-19). It is also necessary to create an information resource in which the report will be stored. Then the integration of the solver with bases of knowledge and data (service declarative specification) is performed as follows (see Sect. 3). The "treatment prescription" solver is set as service's *problem solver*. Formulary, knowledge base on COVID-19 treatment, base of terminology and observations and case record database are set as service's *input actual parameters*. Base with a report on the work is set as service's *output actual parameter*.

The created service is used via the *Control system* – by launching it from the user's Personal storage. The report on the tested treatment hypotheses can be viewed using the *Editor for digraphs of information* (Fig. 5) where the report is represented by a hierarchical graph structure with possibility to unfold and fold its parts for convenient reading.

Fig. 5. UI fragment of *Editor for digraphs of information* running with the report on the prescribed treatment.

11   Discussion and Future Work

Let's highlight the main features that distinguish the described technology for the development of cloud services and their components from other available solutions.

The Possibility to Include Domain Experts in the Process of Developing Knowledge Bases and Databases. The proposed technology supports a two-level ontological approach to the formation of information resources. Its feature is a clear separation between the ontology and the knowledge base (database) formed on its basis. The ontology (metainformation) sets not only the structure and terminology for a knowledge base, but also the rules for its formation, control of the integrity and completeness. The ontology is formed by a knowledge engineer (possibly in cooperation with domain expert) with the use of the ontology editor. On its basis, a UI is automatically generated that allows domain experts to create (form) knowledge bases and databases without involving professional intermediaries. All information resources have a semantic representation that is understandable to domain experts.

Providing Reuse of Ontologies and Problem Solvers. A clear separation between ontology and knowledge bases (databases) also provides another significant advantage. When an ontology is formed – the solver is designed in its terms. Then using this ontology, an arbitrary number of knowledge bases can be developed and their binding with the solver (which is integrated with UI and plays the role of KBS shell) makes the new KBS. So this moves us from developing of specific KBSs each time from a scratch to developing of shells first which can then be used with different knowledge bases to comprise different KBSs. Thus, the ontology and the solver are reused for a whole class of problems.

Modification of Knowledge Bases Without Changing the Problem Solver's Code. This is also provided by the separation between the knowledge base and its ontology, the lack of domain knowledge in the solver. The ontological solver is implemented not as an inference in calculus, but as an algorithm that traverses the knowledge base in accordance with its ontology to match statements in the knowledge base with the input data and, thus, consistently confirming or refuting elements of knowledge.

Transparency and Maintainability of Problem Solvers. The development of KBS solvers is based on the processing of hierarchical graphs of concepts, which makes it possible to create a set of common APIs (application programming interfaces) for working with such graphs. Based on the specifics of the problem, the expected repeatability of their smaller subproblem, the developer can choose software components that will provide a more transparent architecture of solvers. The use of an agent-based approach provides the possibilities to parallelize the execution of subtasks, which is important for problems with high solvation speed requirements.

It is important that the model (metainformation) of each software component is hard-set and allows one to create them using the common editor or its appropriate specialized adaptations (Fig. 6). This increases components' transparency and maintainability, as it is known from software engineering [23] that declarative components are easier to maintain than procedural ones. A unified declarative representation of agents, as well as message templates made it possible to automate the process of code templates generation for them.

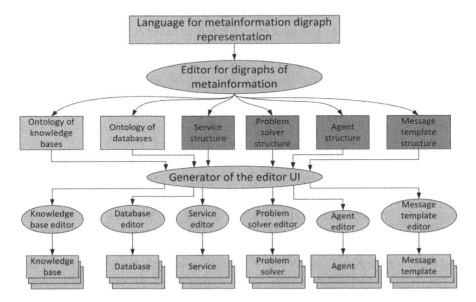

Fig. 6. Usage of the development toolkit for creating information and software components of intelligent services.

Currently, the IACPaaS platform has several hundreds of users who, using the proposed technology, have created ontologies, knowledge bases, tools and problem solvers for various domains: a set of tools for developing professional virtual cloud environments [24], services for interactive verification of intuitive mathematical proofs, underwater robotics, practical psychology, agriculture and others. In particular, the formed portal of medical knowledge includes a wide range of medical ontologies, complex knowledge bases formed on their basis (for example, the knowledge base for medical diagnosis of diseases of various nosologies contains more than 130 000 concepts) and problem solvers (computer-based training simulator using classical research methods in ophthalmology, diagnosis of diseases [25], differential diagnosis of acute and chronic diseases: infectious diseases, gastro-intestinal diseases, hereditary diseases, diseases of the cardiovascular and respiratory systems, etc.), the prescription of personalized medical and rehabilitation treatment, etc.). Also, a knowledge portal for laser-based additive manufacturing (LBAM) was created [26]. It is intended for development of technological modes of cladding processes suitable for practical use. The information components of the knowledge portal are a set of databases and reference books used in LBAM, a case database, a knowledge base on the settings of LBAM modes, as well as a set of ontologies required for their formation. The software components include editors for developing databases and the knowledge base (driven by the corresponding ontologies), as well as a decision support service based on both knowledge base and case database. To date, a number of information and software components of the knowledge portal have been developed.

By now, users of the platform have created more than 2 thousands of resources, rough numbers are: almost 1750 information resources (ontologies – 650, knowledge and data bases – 1100) and 500 software components (problem solvers – 180, agents – 250, message templates – 70). So we can say that the active use of the platform demonstrates that the technology proposed by the authors meets modern requirements for the development of viable KBS and fits the needs of users.

However, we continue to work on improving the platform and the technology for KBS development. Our main efforts are aimed at creating tools for generating adaptive interfaces, tools for intelligent user support and design automation. Special attention is paid to the creation of specialized technologies for developing classes of KBS and increasing the level of instrumental support. Important tasks are the improvement of tools for security of the platform, of the common APIs for processing the storage units and creation of high level abstraction operations for information resources.

References

1. Gensym G2: The World's Leading Software Platform for Real-Time Expert System Application. https://ignitetech.com/softwarelibrary/gensym. Accessed 7 Oct 2021
2. Golenkov, V.V., Gulyakina, N.A., Davydenko, I.T., Shunkevich, D.V.: Semantic technologies of intelligent systems design and semantic associative computers. Doklady BGUIR **3**, 42–50 (2019)
3. Musen, M.A.: The Protégé project: a look back and a look forward. AI Matters **4**, 4–12 (2015)
4. Rybina, G.V.: Intellektual'nye sistemy: ot A do YA. Seriya monografij v trekh knigah. Kn. 3. Problemno-specializirovannye intellektual'nye sistemy. Instrumental'nye sredstva postroeniya intellektual'nyh system (Intelligent systems: A to Z. A series of monographs in three books. Book 3. Problem-specialized intelligent systems. Tools for building intelligent systems), M. Nauchtekhlitizdat (2015). (in Russian)
5. Rodríguez, G., Soria, Á., Campo, M.: Artificial intelligence in service-oriented software design. Eng. App. Artif. Intell. **53**, 86–104 (2016)
6. Gupta, I., Nagpal, G.: Artificial Intelligence and Expert Systems. Mercury Learning & Information. CRC Press, Boston (2020)
7. Tecuci, G., Marcu, D., Boicu, M., Schum, D.: Knowledge Engineering: Building Cognitive Assistants for Evidence-Based Reasoning. Cambridge University Press, Cambridge (2016)
8. Grant, C.E., Wang, D.Z.: A challenge for long-term knowledge base maintenance. J. Data Inf. Qual. **6**(2–3), 7 (2015)
9. Pressman, R.S., Maxim, B.G.: Software Engineering: Practitioner's Approach. 9th edn. McGraw-Hill, New York (2019)

10. Torreño, A., Sapena, Ó., Onaindia, E.: FMAP: a platform for the development of distributed multi-agent planning systems. Knowl. Based Syst. **145**, 166–168 (2018)
11. Gholamian, M., Fatemi, G., Ghazanfari, M.: A hybrid system for multiobjective problems - a case study in NP-hard problems. Knowl. Based Syst. **20**(4), 426–436 (2007)
12. Gribova, V.V., et al.: A cloud computing platform for lifecycle support of intelligent multi-agent internet-services. In: Proceedings of International Conference on Power Electronics and Energy Engineering (PEEE-2015), Hong Kong, pp. 231–235 (2015)
13. AI portal. Agent classification. https://www.aiportal.ru/articles/multiagent-systems/agent-classification.html. Accessed 7 Oct 2021
14. Gribova, V., Moskalenko, P., Timchenko, V., Shalfeeva, E.: The technology for the development of viable intelligent services. Open Semant. Technol. Intell. Syst. **5**, 25–32 (2021)
15. Khoroshevsky, V.F.: Proyektirovaniye sistem programmnogo obespecheniya pod upravleniyem ontologiy: modeli, metody, realizatsii [Ontol. Driven Softw. Engi. Models, Methods, Implement.], Ontologiya proyektirovaniya [Ontol. Des.]. **9**(4), 429–448 (2019). (in Russian)
16. Gribova, V.V., Kleshchev, A.S., Moskalenko, F.M., Timchenko, V.A.: Implementation of a model of a metainformation controlled editor of information units with a complex structure. Autom. Doc. Math. Linguist. **1**, 14–25 (2016)
17. Taentzer, G., et al.: Model transformation by graph transformation: a comparative study. In: Proceedings Workshop Model Transformation in Practice, Montego Bay, Jamaica, pp. 1–48 (2005)
18. Atkinson, C., Kuhne, T.: Model-driven development: a metamodeling foundation. IEEE Softw. **5**, 36–41 (2003)
19. Kleppe, A., Warmer, S., Bast, W.: MDA Explained. Practice and Promise. The Model Driven Architecture. Addison-Wesley Professional, Boston (2003)
20. Gribova, V.V., Kleshchev, A.S., Moskalenko, F.M., Timchenko, V.A.: A two-level model of information units with complex structure that correspond to the questioning metaphor. Autom. Doc. Math. Linguist. **49**(5), 172–181 (2015). https://doi.org/10.3103/S0005105515050052
21. Dyundyukov, V.S., Tarasov, V.B.: Goal-resource networks and their application to agents communication and co-ordination in virtual enterprises. IFAC Proc. Vol. **46**(9), 347–352 (2013)
22. R. Trygve, MVC. Xerox PARC 1978–79. https://folk.universitetetioslo.no/trygver/themes/mvc/mvc-index.html. Accessed 7 Oct 2021
23. Sommerville, I.: Software Engineering. 10th edn. Pearson (2015)
24. Gribova, V.V., Fedorischev, L.A.: Software toolset for development of cloud virtual environments. Softw. Syst. **2**, 60–64 (2015). (in Russian)
25. Gribova, V., Moskalenko, Ph., Petryaeva, M., Okun, D.: Cloud environment for development and use of software systems for clinical medicine and education. Adv. Intell. Syst. Res. **166**, 225–229 (2019)
26. Gribova, V., Kulchin, Y., Nikitin, A., Timchenko, V.: The concept of support for laser-based additive manufacturing on the basis of artificial intelligence methods. In: Kuznetsov, S.O., Panov, A.I., Yakovlev, K.S. (eds.) RCAI 2020. LNCS (LNAI), vol. 12412, pp. 403–415. Springer, Cham (2020). https://doi.org/10.1007/978-3-030-59535-7_30

Measuring Protocol Consistency in Cohesive Hybrid Intelligent Multi-agent Systems

Igor Kirikov[iD] and Sergey Listopad[✉][iD]

Kaliningrad Branch of the Federal Research Center "Computer Science and Control"
of the Russian Academy of Sciences, Kaliningrad 236022, Russian Federation
ser-list-post@yandex.ru

Abstract. The paper develops research in the field of building distributed artificial intelligent systems for computer modeling of collective problem solving by specialists "at a round table", in particular, cohesive hybrid intelligent multi-agent systems. The main feature of such systems is the presence of mechanisms for automatic coordination of goals, ontologies and versions of the problem-solving protocols by its agents. These mechanisms are especially relevant, if the system is assembled from agents, developed by various independent teams, and were not initially adapted to each other to work together efficiently within a single system. This paper considers the issues of constructing one of the methods of cohesive hybrid intelligent multi-agent systems, namely, measuring the consistency of versions of the problem-solving protocol, built by the agents of the system.

Keywords: Cohesion · Hybrid intelligent multi-agent system · Team of specialists · Protocol consistency

1 Introduction

One of the critical points in the construction of artificial intelligent systems, capable of solving practical problems without significantly simplifying them, is modeling the teamwork of specialists. The need for such modeling is caused by both the inherent features of the problem (opacity, heterogeneity, polypersonality, etc.) [26,29], and the impossibility of building an omniscient centralized intelligent system with all the necessary resources, knowledge and tools to solve various problems [9].

In order to simulate the work of a team of specialists in solving problems "at a round table", an approach based on hybrid intelligent multi-agent systems (HIMAS) is proposed in [11]. The elements of such systems are agents, i.e. relatively autonomous software entities, characterized by proactivity, reactivity and social behavior [7,31]. The distinctive features of HIMAS's agents

The reported study was funded by RFBR according to the research project No. 20-07-00104A.

are goal-setting mechanisms, and developed domain models necessary to imitate the intelligent activity of specialists in solving a problem and its parts, as well as methods of various intelligent technologies. Thus, HIMAS combines the advantages of two technologies: hybrid intelligent systems (HIS) [11] and multi-agent systems (MAS) [7,31]. HIMAS, by analogy with HIS, makes it possible to integrate methods for solving problems of various intelligent technologies into a single system, synthesizing from them a hybrid method that is relevant to the complexity of the problem posed. As in MAS, in HIMAS, the general behavior of the system is determined by the interaction of relatively autonomous agents, the interaction protocol and the roles of which are determined during the problem-solving, allowing to model group macro-level processes.

The HIMAS agents proposed in [11] had a common domain model and communication protocol, and their goals were determined by the developers at the design stage and did not change while solving the problem. This approach is relevant to a situation, when all HIMAS agents are designed by one development team to solve a relatively simple, "model" problem. If the problem is so complex that it is required to gather agents built by different developers, it takes significant labor to combine them into a single system. To simplify this procedure, cohesive hybrid intelligent multi-agent systems (CHIMAS) are proposed in [15], agents of which independently agree on their goals, domain model and version of the problem-solving protocol. The presence of these coordination mechanisms makes the system more relevant to a team of specialists, who, in the course of long-term joint work, develop an agreed point of view on the problem, learn to take into account each other's goals, and develop norms of interaction in the process of solving problems. In this paper, one of the methods necessary for implementation of CHIMAS is considered, namely, measuring the consistency of versions of the problem-solving protocol, independently built by the different agents. This paper expands and complements the work [10], presented at XI International Scientific and Technical Conference "Open Semantic Technologies for Intelligent Systems" (OSTIS-2021).

2   Cohesion Phenomenon

The phenomenon of group cohesion, among other macro-level group processes, is studied in group dynamics, a direction of social psychology, created by K. Levin. According to the stratometric concept (SC) of cohesion by A.V. Petrovsky [23], team cohesion could be considered at three layers (strata), which correspond to three levels of group evolution:

- external level, at which cohesion is caused by emotional interpersonal relationships [3,8,30];
- value-orientational unity (VOU), which considers cohesion as the unity of members' basic values, arising as a result of joint activities [1,23,28,30];
- core, at which common values causing cohesion arise because members share the team goals [20,24,30].

Comprehensive reviews of the current state of group cohesion research are given in [20, 25, 27]. According to them, the phenomenon of group cohesion corresponds to the emergence of a socio-psychological community and group properties, which prevent its destruction [30]. A study of different types of groups, for example, sports teams, military units, working groups for solving business problems, demonstrates an increase in the effectiveness of the group with an increase of its cohesion [5]. It should be noted, however, that the processes that ensure group cohesion can also lead to undesirable effects such as conformal behavior and groupthink, so it is important to avoid too high level of cohesion, especially based on emotional interpersonal relationships [2]. In this regard, cohesion modeling in CHIMAS is limited to VOU and core levels.

3 Cohesive Hybrid Intelligent Multi-agent System Model

The CHIMAS model is the HIMAS model [11], extended with the elements necessary to model cohesion in accordance with A.V. Petrovsky's SC [23]:

$$chimas = <AG, env, INT, ORG, MLP>, \tag{1}$$

where AG represents the set of system's agents, which includes the subset of agents-specialists AG^{sp}, the agent-facilitator (AF) ag^{fc}, and the decision-making agent ag^{dm} [15]; env is the conceptual model describing environment of the CHIMAS; INT is the set of the elements that formalizes interaction of agents (2); ORG is the set of architectures, i.e. possible states of the system with established relationships between CHIMAS agents; MLP is the three-element set of macro-level processes' models

$$MLP = \{glng, \ ontng, protng\},$$

where $glng$ represents agents' goal negotiation model, ensuring cohesion at the core level of the SC; $ontng$ is the model describing negotiation of the agents' ontologies that corresponds to the exchange of knowledge in the team of specialists and models processes of the VOU strata; $protng$ is the model of problem-solving protocol negotiation simulating interaction norms coordination in the real teams of specialists at the VOU level of the SC.

The set INT of the elements formalizing interactions (1) is denoted as follows:

$$INT = \{prot_{bsc}, PRC, LANG, ont_{bsc}, chn\}, \tag{2}$$

where $prot_{bsc}$ denotes basic interaction protocol describing communication acts necessary to develop a cohesive problem-solving protocol; PRC is the set of blocks (elements) used to construct problem-solving protocol by agents; $LANG$ are the languages used by agents for coding transmitted messages; ont_{bsc} is the basic ontology (4) providing agents' interpretation of messages' semantics during negotiation their ontologies, goals, and protocols, as well as defining basic concepts for agents' domain specific ontologies; chn is key characteristic of the CHIMAS's state, namely the degree of its agents' cohesion, described as follows:

$$chn = <gls, onts, protc>, gls, onts, protc \in [0,1],$$

where gls, and $onts$ are the degrees of similarity of agents' goals [16] and ontologies [18] respectively; $protc$ is the degree of consistency of the problem-solving protocol, evaluation of which is considered in the following section. The cohesion value $chn_{i\ j}^{ag}$ between agents $ag_i, ag_j \in (AG^{sp} \cup \{ag^{dm}\})$ is determined by its components: $gls_{i\ j}^{ag}$, $onts_{i\ j}^{ag}$ and $protc_{i\ j}^{ag}$. Agents, when negotiating goals, ontologies, and versions of problem-solving protocol, use this value as an optimality criterion. Cohesion of CHIMAS as a whole is calculated as arithmetic mean of cohesion values $chn_{i\ j}^{ag}$ between all pairs of CHIMAS agents. This value is used by AF's fuzzy inference model to estimate CHIMAS's state and to choose methods of collective problem-solving relevant to it. AF tends to choose methods, increasing cohesion, when its value low, which means that CHIMAS's agents have incompatible goals, ontologies and versions of the problem-solving protocol, and decreasing it if its value is too high to prevent conformal behavior.

The common model of an agent $ag \in AG$ (1) is defined by the expression:

$$ag = <id^{ag}, gl^{ag}, LANG^{ag}, ont^{ag}, OCM^{ag}, ACT^{ag}, prot^{ag}>, \qquad (3)$$

where id^{ag} is name or identifier of the agent; gl^{ag} is the fuzzy set defining goal of the agent; $LANG^{ag} \subseteq LANG$ is the subset of available languages; ont^{ag} is the domain specific ontology of the agent (4); OCM^{ag} is the set of mappings of ontology concepts; ACT^{ag} is the set of agent's actions or functions, which contains, among others, goal, ontology and protocol negotiation; $prot^{ag}$ is the model of the agent's version of the problem-solving protocol (5), which defines a scheme for information and knowledge exchange between agents [6].

The common ontology model, which describes both basic ont_{bsc} (2) and agent ont^{ag} (3) ontologies, is represented by the following expression [12]:

$$ont = <L, C, R, AT, FC, FR, FA, H^c, H^r, INST>, \qquad (4)$$

where L is the set of lexemes subdivided into subsets of lexemes which denote concepts L^c, relations L^r, attributes L^{at}, and their values L^{va}; C is the set of concepts; $R : C \times C$ are relations, established between concepts; $AT : C \times L^{va}$ is the set of attributes of concepts C; $FC : 2^{L^c} \to 2^C$ is the function that links lexemes from L and concepts from C; $FR : 2^{L^r} \to 2^R$ is the function linking lexemes with relations; $FA : L^{at} \to AT$ is the function, which links lexemes with attributes; $H^c = C \times C$ is the taxonomic hierarchy of concepts; $H^r = R \times R$ is the hierarchy of relations; $INST$ is the set of instances, which are "ground-level", specific elements of a concepts [4].

The problem-solving protocol $prot^{ag}$ from (3) is described by the expression

$$prot^{ag} = <ROL, MTP, MRC, sch>, \qquad (5)$$

where $ROL \subseteq C$, and $MTP \subseteq C$ are the sets of ontology concepts, which describe the agent roles of and message types respectively; MRC is the correspondence between pairs of agent roles and admissible message types; sch is the message exchange scheme model, determining the expected reaction of the agent taking the role to messages of each type.

Description of the message exchange scheme model sch (5) uses the formalism of Petri nets [22]. Petri net is a tuple, defined by the following expression:

$$pn = <PL, TR, IR>,$$

where $PL \subseteq C$, and $TR \subseteq C$ are the sets of places and transitions respectively; $IR \subseteq (PL \times TR) \cup (TR \times PL)$ is the incidence relation between places and transitions. The message exchange scheme model is a multi-agent interaction protocol net (MIP-net), consisting of a set of synchronized Petri nets, which can be divided into two types: agent workflows net an (A-net) and interaction protocol net ipn (IP-net) [14]. A-net is a connected Petri net, in which there is a source-place, indicating the beginning of the process, and a sink-place, denoting the end of the process. IP-net is a Petri net, containing an input transition, before which there are no other elements of the network, a set of output transitions, after which there are no other elements of the network, as well as two disjoint subsets, the transitions of each of which are connected by synchronous communication elements $tr^{SC} \in TR^{SC}$ with transitions of the A-net, corresponding to the subset, based on multiple synchronization relations R^{SC}.

Thus, the message exchange scheme model sch is a multi-agent interaction protocol net (MIP-net), defined by the expression [14]

$$sch^{ag} = <AN, IPN, TR^{SC}, R^{SC}, RAC, MRIPC>,$$

where $RAC \subseteq ROL \times AN$ is the mapping of the set of agent roles to the set of A-nets; $MRIPC \subseteq MRC \times IPN$ is the mapping of the correspondence of pairs of agent roles and admissible types of messages for each pair to a set of IP-nets.

4   Protocol Consistency Evaluation Model

To evaluate the consistency of versions of the problem-solving protocol, developed by different agents, the similarity of the components of the tuples (5) describing them have to be calculated. For this purpose, the similarity measure of concepts have to be introduced

$$S^C(c_k, c_m) = \sqrt{LSC(c_k, c_m)TS(c_k, c_m)}, \tag{6}$$

where LSC, and TS are the lexicographic (7) and taxonomic (9) similarity of concepts.

The lexicographic similarity of two concepts is described as follows:

$$LSC(c_k, c_m) = LSL(FC^{-1}(c_k), FC^{-1}(c_m)), \tag{7}$$

where $FC^{-1} : C \to L^c$ is the function, inverse to FC, which maps a concept to corresponding lexeme; LSL is the lexeme similarity, described as follows

$$LSL(l_k, l_m) = \max(0, \ 1 - ed(l_k, l_m)\min(|l_k|, |l_m|)^{-1}), \tag{8}$$

where ed is Levenshtein's editorial distance [13], i.e. the number of characters, which have to be changed, added or removed to make lexemes equal.

The taxonomic similarity of the concepts is the ratio of the number of common superconcepts of both concepts to the number of all their superconcepts

$$TS(c_k, c_m, H_k^c, H_m^c) = \frac{|FC^{-1}(UC(c_k, H_k^c)) \cap FC^{-1}(UC(c_m, H_m^c))|}{|FC^{-1}(UC(c_k, H_k^c)) \cup FC^{-1}(UC(c_m, H_m^c))|}, \tag{9}$$

where UC is the upper cotopy [19], which is defined as follows:

$$UC(c, H^c) = \{c_k \in C | H^c(c, c_k) \vee (c = c_k)\}.$$

To evaluate the similarity of the sets of agent roles ROL_i^{ag}, ROL_j^{ag}, a concept correspondence is formed based on the similarity measure of concepts (6) according to the following rule:

$$MRL_{i\ j} = \{(u, v) | (u, v) \in ROL_i^{ag} \times ROL_j^{ag} \wedge v = \arg\max_{v' \in C_j} S^C(u, v')$$
$$\wedge u = \arg\max_{u' \in C_i} S^C(u', v)\}. \tag{10}$$

Using (10), the similarity of the sets ROL_i^{ag}, ROL_j^{ag} is determined as follows

$$ROLS(ROL_i^{ag}, ROL_j^{ag})$$
$$= |(ROL_i^{ag})|^{-1} \sum_{mrl \in MRL_{i\ j}} S^C(proj_1(mrl), \ proj_2(mrl)). \tag{11}$$

By analogy with (10), to evaluate the similarity of the sets of message types MTP_i^{ag}, MTP_j^{ag}, the correspondence between them is introduced, based on the measure of similarity of concepts (6), in accordance with the expression

$$MMT_{i\ j} = \{(u, v) | (u, v) \in MTP_i^{ag} \times MTP_j^{ag} \wedge v = \arg\max_{v' \in C_j} S^C(u, v')$$
$$\wedge u = \arg\max_{u' \in C_i} S^C(u', v)\}. \tag{12}$$

Using the correspondence (12), the similarity of the sets MTP_i^{ag}, MTP_j^{ag} is determined by the following expression:

$$MTPS(MTP_i^{ag}, MTP_j^{ag}) = |(MMT_i^{ag})^{-1}|$$
$$* \sum_{mmt \in MMT_{i\ j}} S^C(proj_1(mmt), \ proj_2(mmt)). \tag{13}$$

To evaluate the similarity the third components of the tuples (5), i.e. correspondences MRC_i^{ag}, MRC_j^{ag}, abbreviated correspondences have to be constructed between compatible pairs of agent roles and message types

$$MRC_i^* = \{(t,u,v)|(t,u,v) \in MRC_i^{ag} \wedge t \in proj_1(MRL_{i\ j})$$
$$\wedge u \in proj_1(MRL_{i\ j}) \wedge v \in proj_1(MMT_{i\ j})\}, \tag{14}$$

$$MRC_j^{**} = \{(MRL_{i\ j}^{-1}(t), MRL_{i\ j}^{-1}(u), MMT_{i\ j}^{-1}(v))|(t,u,v) \in MRC_j^{ag}$$
$$\wedge t \in proj_2(MRL_{i\ j}) \wedge u \in proj_2(MRL_{i\ j}) \wedge v \in proj_2(MMT_{i\ j})\}. \tag{15}$$

Using (14), (15), the similarity of correspondences MRC_i^{ag}, MRC_j^{ag} between pairs of agent roles and admissible types of messages for each pair is calculated

$$MRCS(MRC_i^{ag}, MRC_j^{ag}) = \frac{|MRC_i^* \cap MRC_j^{**}|}{|MRC_i| + |MRC_j| - |MRC_i^* \cap MRC_j^{**}|}. \tag{16}$$

The similarity of the message exchange scheme is determined on the basis of the notion of the transition adjacency relation (TAR) [21]. The TAR in a Petri net defines a set TAR of ordered pairs $<tr_i, tr_j>$ of transitions that can be performed one after another. As shown in [32], the similarity of two Petri nets pn_i, pn_j with TARs TAR_i, TAR_j is determined by the expression

$$PS(pn_i, pn_j) = |TAR_i \cap TAR_j||TAR_i \cup TAR_j|^{-1}.$$

Extension of this measure to the case, when the transitions of the compared Petri nets are defined on different ontologies, is described as follows:

$$PNS(pn_k^i, pn_l^j) = |TR_{t\ k}^i|^{-1} \sum_{mtr \in MTR_{t\ l\ k}^{j\ i}} S^C(proj_1(mtr), proj_2(mtr))$$
$$* \left|TAR_{t\ k}^i \cap F_{j\ i}^{tr}(TAR_{t\ l}^j, pn_k^i)\right|\left|TAR_{t\ k}^i \cup F_{j\ i}^{tr}(TAR_{t\ l}^j, pn_k^i)\right|^{-1}, \tag{17}$$

where $F_{j\ i}^{tr}(TAR_{t\ l}^j, pn_k^i)$ is the function that replaces, if possible, transitions in $TAR_{t\ l}^j$ to the corresponding transitions from pn_k^i. It is defined by the expression

$$F_{j\ i}^{tr}(TAR_{t\ l}^j, pn_k^i) = \{<q,w> | <u,v> \in TAR_{t\ l}^j \wedge ((q = MTR_{t\ l\ k}^{j\ i}(u)$$
$$\wedge q \in proj_1(MTR_{t\ l\ k}^{j\ i})) \vee (q = u \wedge q \notin proj_1(MTR_{t\ l\ k}^{j\ i})))$$
$$\wedge((w = MTR_{t\ l\ k}^{j\ i}(v) \wedge w \in proj_1(MTR_{t\ l\ k}^{j\ i}))$$
$$\vee(w = v \wedge w \notin proj_1(MTR_{t\ l\ k}^{j\ i})))\},$$

where $MTR_{t\ l\ k}^{j\ i}$ is the correspondence between transitions of the nets pn_l^j and pn_k^i, described by the expression

$$MTR_{t\ l\ k}^{j\ i} = \{(u,v)|(u,v) \in proj_2(pn_l^j) \times proj_2(pn_k^i) \wedge ((t = \text{"}a\text{"}$$
$$\wedge pn_k^i = an_k^i \wedge pn_l^j = an_l^j) \vee (t = \text{"}ip\text{"} \wedge pn_k^i = ipn_k^i \wedge pn_l^j = ipn_l^j))$$
$$\wedge v = \underset{v' \in C_i}{\arg\max}\, S^C(u,v') \wedge u = \underset{u' \in C_j}{\arg\max}\, S^C(u',v)\}.$$

Using expression (17), the similarity of the message exchange schemes could be evaluated as follows:

$$SCHS(sch_i^{ag}, sch_j^{ag}) = (|MRL_{i\ j}||MRC_i^*|)^{-1/2}$$

$$* \sqrt{\sum_{mrl \in MRL_{i\ j}} PNS(RAC_i(proj_1(mrl)),\ RAC_j(proj_2(mrl)))}$$

$$* \sqrt{\sum_{mrc \in MRC_i^*} PNS(MRIPC_i(mrc), MRIPC_j(F_{i\ j}^{MRC}(mrc)))},$$

(18)

where $F_{i\ j}^{MRC}$ is the function, intended to express elements of correspondence (14) of the agent ag_i through concepts of ag_j agent's ontology, and defined as follows:

$$F_{i\ j}^{MRC}(mrc) = (MRL_{i\ j}(proj_1(mrc)), MRL_{i\ j}(proj_2(mrc)),$$
$$MMT_{i\ j}(proj_3(mrc))).$$

Thus, the consistency of two problem-solving protocols could be evaluated as the geometric mean of similarities of their components (5) using expressions (11), (13), (16), and (18)

$$prots_{i\ j}^{ag} = \sqrt[4]{ROLS(prot_i^{ag}, prot_j^{ag})MTPS(prot_i^{ag}, prot_j^{ag})}$$
$$* \sqrt[4]{MRCS(prot_i^{ag}, prot_j^{ag})SCHS(prot_i^{ag}, prot_j^{ag})}.$$

(19)

5   An Example of the Protocol Consistency Evaluation

Let us consider the use of the proposed method for evaluating the similarity of the problem-solving protocols on the example of two maximally simplified protocols (the number of agent roles and transmitted messages is reduced) of agents for planning the restoration of the power grid (Fig. 1) [17]. These protocols provide data exchange on the predicted energy consumption between the agent of operational modes, which solves the subproblem of optimizing the switching in the power grid during its recovery, and the agent of consumption prediction. The protocol $prot_1^{agsp}$ assumes unconditional transmission of the results of predicting the energy consumption of nodes in a given grid configuration from the agent of consumption prediction to the agent of operational modes upon its request. The protocol $prot_2^{agsp}$ assumes that the prediction is performed by the agent of consumption prediction for a reward that it sets depending on the complexity of the task, while the agents can bargain for no more than one round.

To describe the considered protocols, ontologies ont_1^{agsp} and ont_2^{agsp} of agents ag_1^{sp} and ag_2^{sp}, respectively, have been developed. For simplicity of presentation, the indices of lexemes and their corresponding concepts in these ontologies coincide. In addition, since this work is devoted to evaluating the consistency of protocols, not ontologies, they were pre-aligned. As a result, each concept of

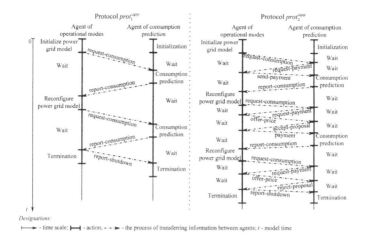

Fig. 1. Messaging schemes in the considered problem-solving protocols

ontology ont_1^{agsp} corresponds to strictly one concept of ontology ont_2^{agsp}. The ontology of agent ag_1^{sp} is described by the following expression:

$$ont_1^{agsp} = <L_1, C_1, R_1, AT_1, FC_1, FR_1, FA_1, H_1^c, H_1^r, INST_1>,$$

where $L_1^c = \{\ l_{1\ 0}^c =$ "concept", $l_{1\ 1}^c =$ "agent", $l_{1\ 2}^c =$ "message", $l_{1\ 3}^c =$ "action", $l_{1\ 4}^c =$ "state", $l_{1\ 5}^c =$ "Agent of operational modes", $l_{1\ 6}^c =$ "Agent of consumption prediction", $l_{1\ 7}^c =$ "request-consumption", $l_{1\ 8}^c =$ "report-consumption", $l_{1\ 9}^c =$ "report-shutdown", $l_{1\ 10}^c =$ "Initialize power grid model", $l_{1\ 11}^c =$ "Send request-consumption", $l_{1\ 12}^c =$ "Receive report-consumption", $l_{1\ 13}^c =$ "Faults detection", $l_{1\ 14}^c =$ "Reconfigure power grid model", $l_{1\ 15}^c =$ "No faults detection", $l_{1\ 16}^c =$ "Send report-shutdown", $l_{1\ 17}^c =$ "Initialization", $l_{1\ 18}^c =$ "Receive request-consumption", $l_{1\ 19}^c =$ "Consumption prediction", $l_{1\ 20}^c =$ "Send report-consumption", $l_{1\ 21}^c =$ "Receive report-shutdown", $l_{1\ 22}^c =$ "in_aom", $l_{1\ 23}^c =$ "out_aom", $l_{1\ 24}^c =$ "in_acp", $l_{1\ 25}^c =$ "out_acp", $l_{1\ 26}^c =$ "Need to update consumption", $l_{1\ 27}^c =$ "Wait for solution", $l_{1\ 28}^c =$ "Need to check faults", $l_{1\ 29}^c =$ "Grid have to be reconfigured", $l_{1\ 30}^c =$ "Grid is functional", $l_{1\ 31}^c =$ "Wait", $l_{1\ 32}^c =$ "Wait for request-consumption", $l_{1\ 33}^c =$ "Got consumption prediction request", $l_{1\ 34}^c =$ "Prediction results are obtained", $l_{1\ 35}^c =$ "fusion"$\}$, $L_1^r = \{l_{1\ 1}^r =$ "type of"$\}$, $C_1 = \{c_{1\ 0},...,c_{1\ 35}\}$, $R_1 = \{r_{1\ 1} = \{(c_{1\ 1}, c_{1\ 0}), ..., (c_{1\ 4}, c_{1\ 0}), (c_{1\ 5}, c_{1\ 1}), (c_{1\ 6}, c_{1\ 1}), (c_{1\ 7}, c_{1\ 2}), (c_{1\ 8}, c_{1\ 2}), (c_{1\ 9}, c_{1\ 2}), (c_{1\ 10}, c_{1\ 3}), ..., (c_{1\ 21}, c_{1\ 3}), (c_{1\ 22}, c_{1\ 4}), ..., (c_{1\ 34}, c_{1\ 4}), (c_{1\ 35}, c_{1\ 0})\}\}$, $AT_1 = \emptyset$, $FC_1 = \{(l_{1\ 0}^c, c_{1\ 0}), ..., (l_{1\ 35}^c, c_{1\ 35})\}$, $FR_1 = \{(l_{1\ 1}^r, r_{1\ 1})\}$, $FA_1 = \emptyset$, $H_1^c = r_{1\ 1}$, $H_1^r = \emptyset$, $INST_1 = \emptyset$.

The ontology of agent ag_2^{sp} is represented by the tuple

$$ont_2^{agsp} = <L_2, C_2, R_2, AT_2, FC_2, FR_2, FA_2, H_2^c, H_2^r, INST_2>,$$

where $L_2^c = \{l_{2\ 0}^c =$ "concept", $l_{2\ 1}^c =$ "agent", $l_{2\ 2}^c =$ "message", $l_{2\ 3}^c =$ "action", $l_{2\ 4}^c =$ "state", $l_{2\ 5}^c =$ "Agent of operational modes", $l_{2\ 6}^c =$ "Agent of consumption prediction", $l_{2\ 7}^c$ = "request-consumption", $l_{2\ 8}^c$ = "report-consumption", $l_{2\ 9}^c$ = "report-shutdown", $l_{2\ 10}^c$ = "request-payment", $l_{2\ 11}^c$ = "payment", $l_{2\ 12}^c$ = "offer-price", $l_{2\ 13}^c$ = "accept-proposal", $l_{2\ 14}^c$ = "reject-proposal", $l_{2\ 15}^c$ = "Initialize power grid model", $l_{2\ 16}^c$ = "Send request-consumption", $l_{2\ 17}^c$ = "Receive report-consumption", $l_{2\ 18}^c$ = "Faults detection", $l_{2\ 19}^c$ = "Reconfigure power grid model", $l_{2\ 20}^c$ = "No faults detection", $l_{2\ 21}^c$ = "Send report-shutdown", $l_{2\ 22}^c$ = "Initialization", $l_{2\ 23}^c$ = "Receive request-consumption", $l_{2\ 24}^c$ = "Consumption prediction", $l_{2\ 25}^c$ = "Send report-consumption", $l_{2\ 26}^c$ = "Receive report-shutdown", $l_{2\ 27}^c$ = "Receive request-payment", $l_{2\ 28}^c$ = "Check if price is acceptable", $l_{2\ 29}^c$ = "Send payment", $l_{2\ 30}^c$ = "Check if price is not acceptable", $l_{2\ 31}^c$ = "Send price offer", $l_{2\ 32}^c$ = "Receive accept-proposal", $l_{2\ 33}^c$ = "Receive reject-proposal", $l_{2\ 34}^c$ = "Price estimation", $l_{2\ 35}^c$ = "Send request-payment", $l_{2\ 36}^c$ = "Receive payment", $l_{2\ 37}^c$ = "Receive price offer", $l_{2\ 38}^c$ = "Send accept-proposal", $l_{2\ 39}^c$ = "Send reject-proposal", $l_{2\ 40}^c$ = "in_aom", $l_{2\ 41}^c$ = "out_aom", $l_{2\ 42}^c$ = "in_acp", $l_{2\ 43}^c$ = "out_acp", $l_{2\ 44}^c$ = "Need to update consumption", $l_{2\ 45}^c$ = "Wait for solution", $l_{2\ 46}^c$ = "Need to check faults", $l_{2\ 47}^c$ = "Grid have to be reconfigured", $l_{2\ 48}^c$ = "Grid is functional", $l_{2\ 49}^c$ = "Wait", $l_{2\ 50}^c$ = "Wait for request-consumption", $l_{2\ 51}^c$ = "Got consumption prediction request", $l_{2\ 52}^c$ = "Prediction results are obtained", $l_{2\ 53}^c$ = "Wait for payment request", $l_{2\ 54}^c$ = "Got payment request", $l_{2\ 55}^c$ = "Price negotiated", $l_{2\ 56}^c$ = "Price offer prepared", $l_{2\ 57}^c$ = "Wait for response to the offer", $l_{2\ 58}^c$ = "Price not agreed", $l_{2\ 59}^c$ = "Price estimated", $l_{2\ 60}^c$ = "Wait for message", $l_{2\ 61}^c$ = "Consumption prediction request is paid", $l_{2\ 62}^c$ = "Got price offer", $l_{2\ 63}^c$ = "Price accepted", $l_{2\ 64}^c$ = "Price rejected", $l_{2\ 65}^c$ = "fusion"}, $L_2^r = \{l_{2\ 1}^r$ = "type of"}, $C_2 = \{c_{2\ 0}, ..., c_{2\ 65}\}$, $R_2 = \{r_{2\ 1} = \{(c_{2\ 1}, c_{2\ 0}), ..., (c_{2\ 4}, c_{2\ 0}), (c_{2\ 5}, c_{2\ 1}),$ $(c_{2\ 6}, c_{2\ 1}), (c_{2\ 7}, c_{2\ 2}), ..., (c_{2\ 14}, c_{2\ 2}), (c_{2\ 15}, c_{2\ 3}), ..., (c_{2\ 39}, c_{2\ 3}), (c_{2\ 40}, c_{2\ 4}), ...,$ $(c_{2\ 64}, c_{2\ 4}), (c_{2\ 65}, c_{2\ 0})\}\}$, $AT_2 = \emptyset$, $FR_2 = \{(l_{2\ 1}^r, r_{2\ 1})\}$, $FA_2 = \emptyset$, $H_2^c = r_{2\ 1}$, $H_2^r = \emptyset$, $INST_2 = \emptyset$.

The protocol $prot_1^{agsp}$ (Fig. 1) is defined using ontology ont_1^{agsp} concepts by the following expression:

$$prot_1^{agsp} = <ROL^1, MTP^1, MRC^1, sch^1>,$$

where $ROL^1 = \{rol_1^1 = c_{1\ 5}, rol_2^1 = c_{1\ 6}\}$, $MTP^1 = \{mtp_1^1 = c_{1\ 7}, mtp_2^1 = c_{1\ 8}, mtp_3^1 = c_{1\ 9}\}$, $MRC^1 = \{((rol_1^1, rol_2^1), mtp_1^1), ((rol_1^1, rol_2^1), mtp_2^1), ((rol_1^1, rol_2^1), mtp_3^1)\}$, and scheme sch^1, graphically shown in Fig. 2, is formally defined by the expression

$$sch^1 = <AN^1, IPN^1, TR^{SC1}, R^{SC1}, RAC^1, MRIPC^1>,$$

where $AN^1 = \{an_1^1, an_2^1\}$, $IPN^1 = \{ipn_1^1\}$, $TR^{SC1} = \{tr_1^{SC1} = c_{1\ 35}\}$, $R^{SC1} = \{(tr_1^{SC1}, tr_{i1\ 1}^1, tr_{a1\ 2}^1), (tr_1^{SC1\ 1}, tr_{i1\ 2}^1, tr_{a2\ 2}^1), (tr_1^{SC1\ 1}, tr_{i1\ 3}^1, tr_{a2\ 4}^1), (tr_1^{SC1\ 1}, tr_{i1\ 4}^1, tr_{a1\ 3}^1), (tr_1^{SC1\ 1}, tr_{i1\ 5}^1, tr_{a1\ 7}^1), (tr_1^{SC1\ 1}, tr_{i1\ 6}^1, tr_{a2\ 5}^1)\}$, $RAC^1 = \{(rol_1^1, an_1^1), (rol_2^1, an_2^1)\}$, $MRIPC^1 = \{(((rol_1^1, rol_2^1), mrc_1^1), ipn_1^1), (((rol_1^1, rol_2^1), mrc_2^1), ipn_1^1), (((rol_1^1, rol_2^1), mrc_3^1), ipn_1^1)\}$.

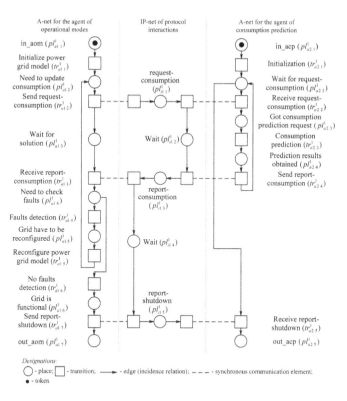

Fig. 2. Multi-agent interaction protocol $prot_1^{agsp}$ net

A-net $an_1^1 \in AN^1$ corresponding to the role rol_1^1 of agent of operational modes in the protocol $prot_1^{agsp}$ is defined by the expression

$$an_1^1 = <PL_{a1}^1, TR_{a1}^1, IR_{a1}^1>,$$

where $PL_{a1}^1 = \{pl_{a1\,1}^1 = c_{1\,22},\ pl_{a1\,2}^1 = c_{1\,26},\ pl_{a1\,3}^1 = c_{1\,27},\ pl_{a1\,4}^1 = c_{1\,28},\ pl_{a1\,5}^1 = c_{1\,29},\ pl_{a1\,6}^1 = c_{1\,30},\ pl_{a1\,7}^1 = c_{1\,23}\}$, $TR_{a1}^1 = \{tr_{a1\,1}^1 = c_{1\,10},\ tr_{a1\,2}^1 = c_{1\,11},\ tr_{a1\,3}^1 = c_{1\,12},\ tr_{a1\,4}^1 = c_{1\,13},\ tr_{a1\,5}^1 = c_{1\,14},\ tr_{a1\,6}^1 = c_{1\,15},\ tr_{a1\,7}^1 = c_{1\,16}\}, IR_{a1}^1 = \{(pl_{a1\,1}^1, tr_{a1\,1}^1),\ (tr_{a1\,1}^1, pl_{a1\,2}^1),\ (pl_{a1\,2}^1, tr_{a1\,2}^1),\ (tr_{a1\,2}^1, pl_{a1\,3}^1),\ (pl_{a1\,3}^1, tr_{a1\,3}^1),\ (tr_{a1\,3}^1, pl_{a1\,4}^1),\ (pl_{a1\,4}^1, tr_{a1\,4}^1),\ (tr_{a1\,4}^1, pl_{a1\,5}^1),\ (pl_{a1\,5}^1, tr_{a1\,5}^1),\ (tr_{a1\,5}^1, pl_{a1\,2}^1),\ (pl_{a1\,4}^1, tr_{a1\,6}^1),\ (tr_{a1\,6}^1, pl_{a1\,6}^1),\ (pl_{a1\,6}^1, tr_{a1\,7}^1),\ (tr_{a1\,7}^1, pl_{a1\,7}^1)\}$.

A-net $an_2^1 \in AN^1$ corresponding to the role rol_2^1 of agent of consumption prediction in the protocol $prot_1^{agsp}$ is defined by the expression

$$an_2^1 = <PL_{a2}^1, TR_{a2}^1, IR_{a2}^1>,$$

where $PL_{a2}^1 = \{pl_{a2\,1}^1 = c_{1\,24},\ pl_{a2\,2}^1 = c_{1\,32},\ pl_{a2\,3}^1 = c_{1\,33},\ pl_{a2\,4}^1 = c_{1\,34},\ pl_{a2\,5}^1 = c_{1\,25}\}$, $TR_{a2}^1 = \{tr_{a2\,1}^1 = c_{1\,17},\ tr_{a2\,2}^1 = c_{1\,18},\ tr_{a2\,3}^1 = c_{1\,19},\ tr_{a2\,4}^1 = c_{1\,20},\ tr_{a2\,5}^1 = c_{1\,21}\}$, $IR_{a2}^1 = \{(pl_{a2\,1}^1, tr_{a2\,1}^1),\ (tr_{a2\,1}^1, pl_{a2\,2}^1),\ (pl_{a2\,2}^1, tr_{a2\,2}^1),\ (tr_{a2\,2}^1, pl_{a2\,3}^1),\ (pl_{a2\,3}^1, tr_{a2\,3}^1),\ (tr_{a2\,3}^1, pl_{a2\,4}^1),\ (pl_{a2\,4}^1, tr_{a2\,4}^1),\ (tr_{a2\,4}^1, pl_{a2\,2}^1),$

$(pl^1_{a2\ 2}, tr^1_{a2\ 5})$, $(tr^1_{a2\ 5}, pl^1_{a2\ 5})$}. IP-net $ipn^1_1 \in IPN^1$ in the protocol $prot^{agsp}_1$ is defined by the expression

$$ipn^1_1 = <PL^1_{i1}, TR^1_{i1}, IR^1_{i1}>,$$

where $PL^1_{i1} = \{pl^1_{i1\ 1} = c_{1\ 7},\ pl^1_{i1\ 2} = c_{1\ 31},\ pl^1_{i1\ 3} = c_{1\ 8},\ pl^1_{i1\ 4} = c_{1\ 31},\ pl^1_{i1\ 5} = c_{1\ 9}\}$, $TR^1_{i1} = \{tr^1_{i1\ 1} = c_{1\ 11},\ tr^1_{i1\ 2} = c_{1\ 18},\ tr^1_{i1\ 3} = c_{1\ 20},\ tr^1_{i1\ 4} = c_{1\ 12},\ tr^1_{i1\ 5} = c_{1\ 16},\ tr^1_{i1\ 6} = c_{1\ 21}\}$, $IR^1_{i1} = \{(tr^1_{i1\ 1}, pl^1_{i1\ 1}),\ (pl^1_{i1\ 1}, tr^1_{i1\ 2}),\ (tr^1_{i1\ 2}, pl^1_{i1\ 2}),$ $(pl^1_{i1\ 2}, tr^1_{i1\ 3}),\ (tr^1_{i1\ 3}, pl^1_{i1\ 3}),\ (pl^1_{i1\ 3}, tr^1_{i1\ 4}),\ (tr^1_{i1\ 4}, pl^1_{i1\ 4}),\ (pl^1_{i1\ 4}, tr^1_{i1\ 5}),\ (tr^1_{i1\ 5}, pl^1_{i1\ 5}),\ (pl^1_{i1\ 5}, tr^1_{i1\ 6})\}$

The protocol $prot^{agsp}_2$ (Fig. 1) is defined using ontology ont^{agsp}_2 concepts by the following expression:

$$prot^{agsp}_2 = <ROL^2, MTP^2, MRC^2, sch^2>,$$

where $ROL^2 = \{rol^2_1 = c_{2\ 5}, rol^2_2 = c_{2\ 6}\}$, $MTP^2 = \{mtp^2_1 = c_{2\ 7},\ mtp^2_2 = c_{2\ 8},\ mtp^2_3 = c_{2\ 9},\ mtp^2_4 = c_{2\ 10},\ mtp^2_5 = c_{2\ 11},\ mtp^2_6 = c_{2\ 12},\ mtp^2_7 = c_{2\ 13},\ mtp^2_8 = c_{2\ 14}\}$, $MRC^2 = \{((rol^2_1, rol^2_2), mtp^2_1),\ ((rol^2_1, rol^2_2), mtp^2_2),\ ((rol^2_1, rol^2_2), mtp^2_3),$ $((rol^2_1, rol^2_2), mtp^2_4),\ ((rol^2_1, rol^2_2), mtp^2_5),\ ((rol^2_1, rol^2_2), mtp^2_6),\ ((rol^2_1, rol^2_2), mtp^2_7),$ $((rol^2_1, rol^2_2), mtp^2_8)\}$, and scheme sch^2 [1], graphically shown in Fig. 3, is formally defined by the expression

$$sch^2 = <AN^2, IPN^2, TR^{SC2}, R^{SC2}, RAC^2, MRIPC^2>,$$

where $AN^2 = \{an^2_1, an^2_2\}$, $IPN^2 = \{ipn^2_1\}$, $TR^{SC2} = \{c_{2\ 65}\}$, $R^{SC2} = \{(tr^{SC2}_1, tr^2_{i1\ 1}, tr^2_{a1\ 2}),\ (tr^{SC2}_1, tr^2_{i1\ 2}, tr^2_{a2\ 2}),\ (tr^{SC2}_1, tr^2_{i1\ 3}, tr^2_{a2\ 4}),\ (tr^{SC2}_1, tr^2_{i1\ 4}, tr^2_{a1\ 3}),$ $(tr^{SC2}_1, tr^2_{i1\ 5}, tr^2_{a1\ 5}),\ (tr^{SC2}_1, tr^2_{i1\ 6}, tr^2_{a2\ 5}),\ (tr^{SC2}_1, tr^2_{i1\ 7}, tr^2_{a1\ 7}),\ (tr^{SC2}_1, tr^2_{i1\ 8}, tr^2_{a2\ 6}),\ (tr^{SC2}_1, tr^2_{i1\ 9}, tr^2_{a2\ 8}),\ (tr^{SC2}_1, tr^2_{i1\ 10}, tr^2_{a1\ 8}),\ (tr^{SC2}_1, tr^2_{i1\ 11}, tr^2_{a2\ 10}),$ $(tr^{SC2}_1, tr^2_{i1\ 12}, tr^2_{a1\ 9}),\ (tr^{SC2}_1, tr^2_{i1\ 13}, tr^2_{a2\ 12}),\ (tr^{SC2}_1, tr^2_{i1\ 14}, tr^2_{a1\ 10}),\ (tr^{SC2}_1, tr^2_{i1\ 15}, tr^2_{a2\ 14}),\ (tr^{SC2}_1, tr^2_{i1\ 16}, tr^2_{a2\ 13})\}$, $RAC^2 = \{(rol^2_1, an^2_1), (rol^2_2, an^2_2)\}$, $MRIPC^2 = \{(((rol^2_1, rol^2_2), mrc^2_1), ipn^2_1),\ ...,\ (((rol^2_1, rol^2_2), mrc^2_8), ipn^2_1)\}$.

A-net $an^2_1 \in AN^2$ corresponding to the role rol^2_1 of agent of operational modes in the protocol $prot^{agsp}_{2\ 1}$ is defined by the expression

$$an^2_1 = <PL^2_{a1}, TR^2_{a1}, IR^2_{a1}>,$$

where $PL^2_{a1} = \{pl^2_{a1\ 1} = c_{2\ 40},\ pl^2_{a1\ 2} = c_{2\ 44},\ pl^2_{a1\ 3} = c_{2\ 53},\ pl^2_{a1\ 4} = c_{2\ 54},\ pl^2_{a1\ 5} = c_{2\ 55},\ pl^2_{a1\ 6} = c_{2\ 56},\ pl^2_{a1\ 7} = c_{2\ 57},\ pl^2_{a1\ 8} = c_{2\ 58},\ pl^2_{a1\ 9} = c_{2\ 45},\ pl^2_{a1\ 10} = c_{2\ 46},\ pl^2_{a1\ 11} = c_{2\ 47},\ pl^2_{a1\ 12} = c_{2\ 48},\ pl^2_{a1\ 13} = c_{2\ 41}\}$, $TR^2_{a1} = \{tr^2_{a1\ 1} = c_{2\ 15},\ tr^2_{a1\ 2} = c_{2\ 16},\ tr^2_{a1\ 3} = c_{2\ 27},\ tr^2_{a1\ 4} = c_{2\ 28},\ tr^2_{a1\ 5} = c_{2\ 29},\ tr^2_{a1\ 6} = c_{2\ 30},\ tr^2_{a1\ 7} = c_{2\ 31},\ tr^2_{a1\ 8} = c_{2\ 32},\ tr^2_{a1\ 9} = c_{2\ 33},\ tr^2_{a1\ 10} = c_{2\ 17},\ tr^2_{a1\ 11} = c_{2\ 18},\ tr^2_{a1\ 12} = c_{2\ 19},\ tr^2_{a1\ 13} = c_{2\ 20},\ tr^2_{a1\ 14} = c_{2\ 21}\}$, $IR^2_{a1} = \{(pl^2_{a1\ 1}, tr^2_{a1\ 1}),\ (tr^2_{a1\ 1}, pl^2_{a1\ 2}),\ (pl^2_{a1\ 2}, tr^2_{a1\ 2}),$ $(tr^2_{a1\ 2}, pl^2_{a1\ 3}),\ (pl^2_{a1\ 3}, tr^2_{a1\ 3}),\ (tr^2_{a1\ 3}, pl^2_{a1\ 4}),\ (pl^2_{a1\ 4}, tr^2_{a1\ 4}),\ (tr^2_{a1\ 4}, pl^2_{a1\ 5}),$ $(pl^2_{a1\ 5}, tr^2_{a1\ 5}),\ (tr^2_{a1\ 5}, pl^2_{a1\ 9}),\ (pl^2_{a1\ 9}, tr^2_{a1\ 10}),\ (tr^2_{a1\ 10}, pl^2_{a1\ 10}),\ (pl^2_{a1\ 10}, tr^2_{a1\ 11}),$ $(tr^2_{a1\ 11}, pl^2_{a1\ 11}),\ (pl^2_{a1\ 11}, tr^2_{a1\ 12}),\ (tr^2_{a1\ 12}, pl^2_{a1\ 2}),\ (pl^2_{a1\ 10}, tr^2_{a1\ 13}),$ $(tr^2_{a1\ 13}, pl^2_{a1\ 12}),\ (pl^2_{a1\ 12}, tr^2_{a1\ 14}),\ (pl^2_{a1\ 4}, tr^2_{a1\ 6}),\ (tr^2_{a1\ 6}, pl^2_{a1\ 6}),\ (pl^2_{a1\ 6}, tr^2_{a1\ 7}),$

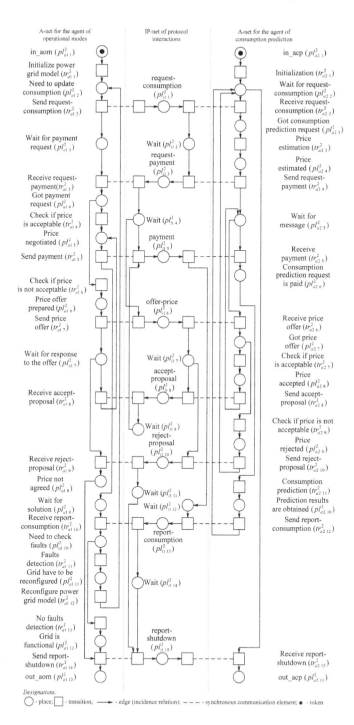

Fig. 3. Multi-agent interaction protocol $prot_2^{agsp}$ net

$(tr^2_{a1\ 7}, pl^2_{a1\ 7})$, $(pl^2_{a1\ 7}, tr^2_{a1\ 8})$, $(tr^2_{a1\ 8}, pl^2_{a1\ 5})$, $(pl^2_{a1\ 7}, tr^2_{a1\ 9})$, $(tr^2_{a1\ 9}, pl^2_{a1\ 8})$, $(pl^2_{a1\ 8}, tr^2_{a1\ 14})$, $(tr^2_{a1\ 14}, pl^2_{a1\ 13})\}$.

A-net $an^2_2 \in AN^2$ corresponding to the role rol^2_2 of agent of consumption prediction in the protocol $prot^{agsp}_{2\ 1}$ is defined by the expression

$$an^2_2 = <PL^2_{a2}, TR^2_{a2}, IR^2_{a2}>,$$

where $PL^2_{a2} = \{pl^2_{a2\ 1} = c_{2\ 42},\ pl^2_{a2\ 2} = c_{2\ 50},\ pl^2_{a2\ 3} = c_{2\ 51},\ pl^2_{a2\ 4} = c_{2\ 59}$, $pl^2_{a2\ 5} = c_{2\ 60},\ pl^2_{a2\ 6} = c_{2\ 61},\ pl^2_{a2\ 7} = c_{2\ 62},\ pl^2_{a2\ 8} = c_{2\ 63},\ pl^2_{a2\ 9} = c_{2\ 64}$, $pl^2_{a2\ 10} = c_{2\ 52},\ pl^2_{a2\ 11} = c_{2\ 43}\}$, $TR^2_{a2} = \{tr^2_{a2\ 1} = c_{2\ 22},\ tr^2_{a2\ 2} = c_{2\ 23}$, $tr^2_{a2\ 3} = c_{2\ 34},\ tr^2_{a2\ 4} = c_{2\ 35},\ tr^2_{a2\ 5} = c_{2\ 36},\ tr^2_{a2\ 6} = c_{2\ 37},\ tr^2_{a2\ 7} = c_{2\ 28}$, $tr^2_{a2\ 8} = c_{2\ 38},\ tr^2_{a2\ 9} = c_{2\ 30},\ tr^2_{a2\ 10} = c_{2\ 39},\ tr^2_{a2\ 11} = c_{2\ 24},\ tr^2_{a2\ 12} = c_{2\ 25},\ tr^2_{a2\ 13} = c_{2\ 26}\}$, $IR^2_{a2} = \{(pl^2_{a2\ 1}, tr^2_{a2\ 1})$, $(tr^2_{a2\ 1}, pl^2_{a2\ 2})$, $(pl^2_{a2\ 2}, tr^2_{a2\ 2})$, $(tr^2_{a2\ 2}, pl^2_{a2\ 3})$, $(pl^2_{a2\ 3}, tr^2_{a2\ 3})$, $(tr^2_{a2\ 3}, pl^2_{a2\ 4})$, $(pl^2_{a2\ 4}, tr^2_{a2\ 4})$, $(tr^2_{a2\ 4}, pl^2_{a2\ 5})$, $(pl^2_{a2\ 5}, tr^2_{a2\ 5})$, $(tr^2_{a2\ 5}, pl^2_{a2\ 6})$, $(pl^2_{a2\ 6}, tr^2_{a2\ 11})$, $(tr^2_{a2\ 11}, pl^2_{a2\ 10})$, $(pl^2_{a2\ 10}, tr^2_{a2\ 12})$, $(tr^2_{a2\ 12}, pl^2_{a2\ 2})$, $(pl^2_{a2\ 2}, tr^2_{a2\ 13})$, $(tr^2_{a2\ 13}, pl^2_{a2\ 11})$, $(pl^2_{a2\ 5}, tr^2_{a2\ 6})$, $(tr^2_{a2\ 6}, pl^2_{a2\ 7})$, $(pl^2_{a2\ 7}, tr^2_{a2\ 7})$, $(tr^2_{a2\ 7}, pl^2_{a2\ 8})$, $(pl^2_{a2\ 8}, tr^2_{a2\ 8})$, $(tr^2_{a2\ 8}, pl^2_{a2\ 5})$, $(pl^2_{a2\ 7}, tr^2_{a2\ 9})$, $(tr^2_{a2\ 9}, pl^2_{a2\ 9})$, $(pl^2_{a2\ 9}, tr^2_{a2\ 10})$, $(tr^2_{a2\ 10}, pl^2_{a2\ 2})\}$.

IP-net $ipn^2_1 \in IPN^2$ in the protocol $prot^{agsp}_2$ is defined by the expression

$$ipn^2_2 = <PL^2_{i1}, TR^2_{i1}, IR^2_{i1}>,$$

where $PL^2_{i1} = \{pl^2_{i1\ 1} = c_{2\ 7},\ pl^2_{i1\ 2} = c_{2\ 49},\ pl^2_{i1\ 3} = c_{2\ 10},\ pl^2_{i1\ 4} = c_{2\ 49}$, $pl^2_{i1\ 5} = c_{2\ 11},\ pl^2_{i1\ 6} = c_{2\ 12},\ pl^2_{i1\ 7} = c_{2\ 49},\ pl^2_{i1\ 8} = c_{2\ 13},\ pl^2_{i1\ 9} = c_{2\ 49}$, $pl^2_{i1\ 10} = c_{2\ 14},\ pl^2_{i1\ 11} = c_{2\ 49},\ pl^2_{i1\ 12} = c_{2\ 49},\ pl^2_{i1\ 13} = c_{2\ 8},\ pl^2_{i1\ 14} = c_{2\ 49}$, $pl^2_{i1\ 15} = c_{2\ 9}\}$, $TR^2_{i1} = \{tr^2_{i1\ 1} = c_{2\ 16},\ tr^2_{i1\ 2} = c_{2\ 23},\ tr^2_{i1\ 3} = c_{2\ 35}$, $tr^2_{i1\ 4} = c_{2\ 27}, tr^2_{i1\ 5} = c_{2\ 29},\ tr^2_{i1\ 6} = c_{2\ 36},\ tr^2_{i1\ 7} = c_{2\ 31},\ tr^2_{i1\ 8} = c_{2\ 37}$, $tr^2_{i1\ 9} = c_{2\ 38},\ tr^2_{i1\ 10} = c_{2\ 32},\ tr^2_{i1\ 11} = c_{2\ 39},\ tr^2_{i1\ 12} = c_{2\ 33},\ tr^2_{i1\ 13} = c_{2\ 25}$, $tr^2_{i1\ 14} = c_{2\ 17},\ tr^2_{i1\ 15} = c_{2\ 21},\ tr^2_{i1\ 16} = c_{2\ 26}\}$, $IR^2_{i1} = \{(tr^2_{i1\ 1}, pl^2_{i1\ 1})$, $(pl^2_{i1\ 1}, tr^2_{i1\ 2})$, $(tr^2_{i1\ 2}, pl^2_{i1\ 2})$, $(pl^2_{i1\ 2}, tr^2_{i1\ 3})$, $(tr^2_{i1\ 3}, pl^2_{i1\ 3})$, $(pl^2_{i1\ 3}, tr^2_{i1\ 4})$, $(tr^2_{i1\ 4}, pl^2_{i1\ 4})$, $(pl^2_{i1\ 4}, tr^2_{i1\ 5})$, $(tr^2_{i1\ 5}, pl^2_{i1\ 5})$, $(pl^2_{i1\ 5}, tr^2_{i1\ 6})$, $(tr^2_{i1\ 6}, pl^2_{i1\ 12})$, $(pl^2_{i1\ 12}, tr^2_{i1\ 13})$, $(tr^2_{i1\ 13}, pl^2_{i1\ 13})$, $(pl^2_{i1\ 13}, tr^2_{i1\ 14})$, $(tr^2_{i1\ 14}, pl^2_{i1\ 14})$, $(pl^2_{i1\ 14}, tr^2_{i1\ 15})$, $(tr^2_{i1\ 15}, pl^2_{i1\ 15})$, $(pl^2_{i1\ 15}, tr^2_{i1\ 16})$, $(pl^2_{i1\ 4}, tr^2_{i1\ 7})$, $(tr^2_{i1\ 7}, pl^2_{i1\ 6})$, $(pl^2_{i1\ 6}, tr^2_{i1\ 8})$, $(tr^2_{i1\ 8}, pl^2_{i1\ 7})$, $(pl^2_{i1\ 7}, tr^2_{i1\ 9})$, $(tr^2_{i1\ 9}, pl^2_{i1\ 8})$, $(pl^2_{i1\ 8}, tr^2_{i1\ 10})$, $(tr^2_{i1\ 10}, pl^2_{i1\ 9})$, $(pl^2_{i1\ 9}, tr^2_{i1\ 5})$, $(pl^2_{i1\ 7}, tr^2_{i1\ 11})$, $(tr^2_{i1\ 11}, pl^2_{i1\ 10})$, $(pl^2_{i1\ 10}, tr^2_{i1\ 12})$, $(tr^2_{i1\ 12}, pl^2_{i1\ 11})$, $(pl^2_{i1\ 11}, tr^2_{i1\ 15})\}$.

Before considering directly the process of evaluating the similarity of the protocols for solving the problem, let us give an example of estimation the similarity of two concepts $c_{1\ 12}$ and $c_{2\ 25}$ in accordance with the expressions (6)–(8). The lexicographic similarity of concepts LSC is determined by the expression

$$LSC(c_{1\ 12}, c_{2\ 25}) = LSL(FC^{-1}(c_{1\ 12}), FC^{-1}(c_{2\ 25})) = LSL(l^c_{1\ 12}, l^c_{2\ 25})$$

$$= \max(0,\ 1 - \frac{ed(l^c_{1\ 12}, l^c_{2\ 25})}{\min(|l^c_{1\ 12}|, |l^c_{2\ 25}|)}) = \max(0,\ 1 - \frac{6}{\min(26, 23)}) = 0,74.$$

The taxonomic similarity of concepts $c_{1\ 12}$ and $c_{2\ 25}$, using their upper cotopy values $UC(c_{1\ 12}, H_1^c) = \{c_{1\ 12}, c_{1\ 2}, c_{1\ 0}\}$, $UC(c_{2\ 25}, H_2^c) = \{c_{2\ 25}, c_{2\ 2}, c_{2\ 0}\}$ is determined by expression:

$$TS(c_{1\ 12}, c_{2\ 25}, H_1^c, H_2^c) = \frac{|FC^{-1}(UC(c_{1\ 12}, H_1^c) \cap FC^{-1}(UC(c_{2\ 25}, H_2^c))|}{|FC^{-1}(UC(c_{1\ 12}, H_1^c) \cup FC^{-1}(UC(c_{2\ 25}, H_2^c))|}$$

$$= \frac{|\{l_{1\ 12}^c, l_{1\ 2}^c, l_{1\ 0}^c\} \cap \{l_{2\ 25}^c, l_{2\ 2}^c, l_{2\ 0}^c\}|}{|\{l_{1\ 12}^c, l_{1\ 2}^c, l_{1\ 0}^c\} \cup \{l_{2\ 25}^c, l_{2\ 2}^c, l_{2\ 0}^c\}|} = \frac{2}{4} = 0,5.$$

As a result the of similarity of two concepts is

$$S^C(c_{1\ 12}, c_{2\ 25}) = \sqrt{LSC(c_{1\ 12}, c_{2\ 25})TS(c_{1\ 12}, c_{2\ 25})} = 0,6.$$

This similarity measure of concepts from different ontologies makes it possible to form correspondence between the roles, used in the description of the protocol by each agent, using expression (10), as follows:

$$MRL_{1\ 2} = \{(u, v)|(u, v) \in ROL_1^{ag} \times ROL_2^{ag} \wedge v = \arg\max_{v' \in C_2} S^C(u, v')$$

$$\wedge u = \arg\max_{u' \in C_1} S^C(u', v)\} = \{(c_{1\ 5}, c_{2\ 5}), (c_{1\ 6}, c_{2\ 6})\},$$

based on which the similarity of the sets of concept-roles is calculated according to (11) as follows

$$ROLS(ROL_1^{ag}, ROL_2^{ag})$$

$$= |ROL_1^{ag}|^{-1} \sum_{mrl \in MRL_{1\ 2}} S^C(proj_1(mrl), proj_2(mrl))$$

$$= |ROL_1^{ag}|^{-1}(S^C(c_{1\ 5}, c_{2\ 5}) + S^C(c_{1\ 6}, c_{2\ 6})) = 1.$$

In the considered example $ROLS(ROL_2^{ag}, ROL_1^{ag}) = 1$ also, as the agent roles sets are equal. The similarity of the sets MTP_1^{ag}, MTP_2^{ag} is calculated similarly, using expressions (12), (13):

$$MMT_{1\ 2} = \{(c_{1\ 7}, c_{2\ 7}), (c_{1\ 8}, c_{2\ 8}), (c_{1\ 9}, c_{2\ 9})\},$$

$$MTPS(MTP_1^{ag}, MTP_2^{ag})$$

$$= |MTP_1^{ag}|^{-1} \sum_{mmt \in MMT_{1\ 2}} S^C(proj_1(mmt), proj_2(mmt))$$

$$= |MTP_1^{ag}|^{-1}(S^C(c_{1\ 7}, c_{2\ 7}) + S^C(c_{1\ 8}, c_{2\ 8}) + S^C(c_{1\ 9}, c_{2\ 9})) = 1,$$

$$MTPS(MTP_2^{ag}, MTP_1^{ag}) = 0,375.$$

As can be seen in this case $MTPS(MTP_1^{ag}, MTP_2^{ag}) \neq MTPS(MTP_2^{ag}, MTP_1^{ag})$, since, in fact, MTP_2^{ag} includes MTP_1^{ag}.

To evaluate the degree of similarity of correspondences MRC_1^{ag}, MRC_2^{ag} the abbreviated correspondences using expressions (14), (15) should be formed as follows:

$$MRC_1^* = \{(t, u, v) | (t, u, v) \in MRC_1^{ag} \wedge t \in proj_1(MRL_{1\ 2})$$
$$\wedge u \in proj_1(MRL_{1\ 2}) \wedge v \in proj_1(MMT_{1\ 2})\}$$
$$= \{((c_{1\ 5}, c_{1\ 6}), c_{1\ 7}), ((c_{1\ 5}, c_{1\ 6}), c_{1\ 8}), ((c_{1\ 5}, c_{1\ 6}), c_{1\ 9})\},$$
$$MRC_2^{**} = \{((MRL_{1\ 2}^{-1}(t), MRL_{1\ 2}^{-1}(u), MMT_{1\ 2}^{-1}(v))) | (t, u, v) \in MRC_2^{ag}$$
$$\wedge t \in proj_2(MRL_{1\ 2}) \wedge u \in proj_2(MRL_{1\ 2}) \wedge v \in proj_2(MMT_{1\ 2})\}$$
$$= \{((c_{1\ 5}, c_{1\ 6}), c_{1\ 7}), ((c_{1\ 5}, c_{1\ 6}), c_{1\ 8}), ((c_{1\ 5}, c_{1\ 6}), c_{1\ 9})\}.$$

Thus, using expression (16), the similarity of correspondences MRC_1^{ag}, MRC_2^{ag} is calculated in accordance with the expression

$$MRCS(MRC_1^{ag}, MRC_2^{ag})$$
$$= \frac{|MRC_1^* \cap MRC_2^{**}|}{|MRC_1| + |MRC_2| - |MRC_1^* \cap MRC_2^{**}|} = 0,375,$$
$$MRCS(MRC_2^{ag}, MRC_1^{ag}) = 0,375.$$

Before considering the computation of the similarity of the message exchange schemes, let us demonstrate the computation of the similarity of two Petri nets, defined on the concepts of different ontologies using the example of nets an_1^1 and an_1^2. At the first stage, a TAR should be formed based on the corresponding incidence relations IR_{a1}^1 and IR_{a1}^2, as well as the sets of concepts C_1 and C_2

$$TAR_{a\ 1}^1 = \{(tr_{a1\ 1}^1, tr_{a1\ 2}^1), (tr_{a1\ 2}^1, tr_{a1\ 3}^1), (tr_{a1\ 3}^1, tr_{a1\ 4}^1), (tr_{a1\ 4}^1, tr_{a1\ 5}^1),$$
$$(tr_{a1\ 3}^1, tr_{a1\ 6}^1), (tr_{a1\ 5}^1, tr_{a1\ 2}^1), (tr_{a1\ 6}^1, tr_{a1\ 7}^1)\}$$
$$= \{(c_{1\ 10}, c_{1\ 11}), (c_{1\ 11}, c_{1\ 12}), (c_{1\ 12}, c_{1\ 13}), (c_{1\ 13}, c_{1\ 14}), (c_{1\ 12}, c_{1\ 15}),$$
$$(c_{1\ 14}, c_{1\ 11}), (c_{1\ 15}, c_{1\ 16})\},$$
$$TAR_{a\ 1}^2 = \{(tr_{a1\ 1}^2, tr_{a1\ 2}^2), (tr_{a1\ 2}^2, tr_{a1\ 3}^2), (tr_{a1\ 3}^2, tr_{a1\ 4}^2), (tr_{a1\ 4}^2, tr_{a1\ 5}^2),$$
$$(tr_{a1\ 5}^2, tr_{a1\ 10}^2), (tr_{a1\ 10}^2, tr_{a1\ 11}^2), (tr_{a1\ 11}^2, tr_{a1\ 12}^2), (tr_{a1\ 12}^2, tr_{a1\ 2}^2),$$
$$(tr_{a1\ 10}^2, tr_{a1\ 13}^2), (tr_{a1\ 13}^2, tr_{a1\ 14}^2), (tr_{a1\ 3}^2, tr_{a1\ 6}^2), (tr_{a1\ 6}^2, tr_{a1\ 7}^2),$$
$$(tr_{a1\ 7}^2, tr_{a1\ 8}^2), (tr_{a1\ 8}^2, tr_{a1\ 5}^2), (tr_{a1\ 7}^2, tr_{a1\ 9}^2), (tr_{a1\ 9}^2, tr_{a1\ 14}^2)\}$$
$$= \{(c_{2\ 15}, c_{2\ 16}), (c_{2\ 16}, c_{2\ 27}), (c_{2\ 27}, c_{2\ 28}), (c_{2\ 28}, c_{2\ 29}), (c_{2\ 29}, c_{2\ 17}),$$
$$(c_{2\ 17}, c_{2\ 18}), (c_{2\ 18}, c_{2\ 19}), (c_{2\ 19}, c_{2\ 16}), (c_{2\ 17}, c_{2\ 20}), (c_{2\ 20}, c_{2\ 21}),$$
$$(c_{2\ 27}, c_{2\ 30}), (c_{2\ 30}, c_{2\ 31}), (c_{2\ 31}, c_{2\ 32}), (c_{2\ 32}, c_{2\ 29}),$$
$$(c_{2\ 31}, c_{2\ 33}), (c_{2\ 33}, c_{2\ 21})\}.$$

In the next step, a correspondence is established between sets of transitions TR_{a1}^1 and TR_{a1}^2 as follows:

$$MTR_{a\ 1\ 1}^{2\ 1} = \{(u,v)|(u,v) \in proj_2(pn_1^2) \times proj_2(pn_1^1) \wedge \wedge pn_1^1 = an_1^1$$
$$\wedge pn_1^2 = an_1^2 \wedge v = \underset{v' \in C_1}{\arg\max}\, S^C(u,v') \wedge u = \underset{u' \in C_2}{\arg\max}\, S^C(u',v)\}$$
$$= \{(c_2\ _{15}, c_1\ _{10}), (c_2\ _{16}, c_1\ _{11}), (c_2\ _{17}, c_1\ _{12}), (c_2\ _{18}, c_1\ _{13}), (c_2\ _{19}, c_1\ _{14}),$$
$$(c_2\ _{20}, c_1\ _{14}), (c_2\ _{21}, c_1\ _{15})\},$$

after which some of the concepts in TAR_{a1}^2 can be replaced by the corresponding concepts of the ag_1 agent's ontology

$$F_{2\ 1}^{tr}(TAR_{a\ 1}^2, an_1^1) = \{<q,w> \,|\, <u,v> \in TAR_{a\ 1}^2 \wedge ((q = MTR_{a\ 1\ 1}^{2\ 1}(u)$$
$$\wedge q \in proj_1(MTR_{a\ 1\ 1}^{2\ 1})) \vee (q = u \wedge q \notin proj_1(MTR_{a\ 1\ 1}^{2\ 1})))$$
$$\wedge ((w = MTR_{a\ 1\ 1}^{2\ 1}(v) \wedge w \in proj_1(MTR_{a\ 1\ 1}^{2\ 1}))$$
$$\vee (w = v \wedge w \notin proj_1(MTR_{a\ 1\ 1}^{2\ 1})))\}$$
$$= \{(c_1\ _{10}, c_1\ _{11}), (c_1\ _{11}, c_2\ _{27}), (c_2\ _{27}, c_2\ _{28}), (c_2\ _{28}, c_2\ _{29}), (c_2\ _{29}, c_1\ _{12}),$$
$$(c_1\ _{12}, c_1\ _{13}), (c_1\ _{13}, c_1\ _{14}), (c_1\ _{14}, c_1\ _{11}), (c_1\ _{12}, c_1\ _{15}), (c_1\ _{15}, c_1\ _{16}),$$
$$(c_2\ _{27}, c_2\ _{30}), (c_2\ _{30}, c_2\ _{31}), (c_2\ _{31}, c_2\ _{32}), (c_2\ _{32}, c_2\ _{29}), (c_2\ _{31}, c_2\ _{33}),$$
$$(c_2\ _{33}, c_1\ _{16})\}.$$

Thus, the following elements of the expression (17) can be evaluated:

$$TAR_{a\ 1}^1 \cap F_{2\ 1}^{tr}(TAR_{a\ 1}^2, an_1^1) = \{(c_1\ _{10}, c_1\ _{11}), (c_1\ _{12}, c_1\ _{13}), (c_1\ _{13}, c_1\ _{14}),$$
$$(c_1\ _{12}, c_1\ _{15}), (c_1\ _{14}, c_1\ _{11}), (c_1\ _{15}, c_1\ _{16})\},$$
$$TAR_{a\ 1}^1 \cup F_{2\ 1}^{tr}(TAR_{a\ 1}^2, an_1^1) = \{(c_1\ _{10}, c_1\ _{11}), (c_1\ _{11}, c_1\ _{12}), (c_1\ _{12}, c_1\ _{13}),$$
$$(c_1\ _{13}, c_1\ _{14}), (c_1\ _{12}, c_1\ _{15}), (c_1\ _{14}, c_1\ _{11}), (c_1\ _{15}, c_1\ _{16}), (c_1\ _{11}, c_2\ _{27}),$$
$$(c_2\ _{27}, c_2\ _{28}), (c_2\ _{28}, c_2\ _{29}), (c_2\ _{29}, c_1\ _{12}), (c_2\ _{27}, c_2\ _{30}), (c_2\ _{30}, c_2\ _{31}),$$
$$(c_2\ _{31}, c_2\ _{32}), (c_2\ _{32}, c_2\ _{29}), (c_2\ _{31}, c_2\ _{33}), (c_2\ _{33}, c_1\ _{16})\},$$

as well as the expression (17) as a whole

$$PNS(an_1^1, an_1^2) = |TR_{a\ 1}^1|^{-1} \sum_{mtr \in MTR_{a\ 1\ 1}^{2\ 1}} S^C(proj_1(mtr), proj_2(mtr))$$

$$* \frac{|TAR_{a\ 1}^1 \cap F_{2\ 1}^{tr}(TAR_{a\ 1}^2, pn_1^1)|}{|TAR_{a\ 1}^1 \cup F_{2\ 1}^{tr}(TAR_{a\ 1}^2, pn_1^1)|} = \frac{7}{7} \cdot \frac{6}{17} = 0,35.$$

Using this value, as well as the similarity values $PNS(an_2^1, an_2^2) = 0,26$ and $PNS(ipn_1^1, ipn_1^2) = 0,22$ calculated in a similar way, the similarity of the message exchange schemes sch_i^{ag} and sch_j^{ag} is evaluated in accordance with the expression (18)

$$SCHS(sch_1^{ag}, sch_2^{ag}) = (|MRL_{1\ 2}||MRC_1^*|)^{-1/2}$$
$$* ((PNS(an_1^1, an_1^2) + PNS(an_2^1, an_2^2)) \, (3 * PNS(ipn_1^1, ipn_1^2)))^{1/2}$$
$$= \left(|2|^{-1}|3|^{-1} (0,35 + 0,26) (3 \cdot 0,22)\right)^{1/2} = 0,26.$$

The similarity of the message exchange schemes $SCHS(sch_j^{ag}, sch_i^{ag}) = 0,11$ using the similarity values of Petri nets $PNS(an_1^2, an_1^1) = 0,18$, $PNS(an_2^2, an_2^1) = 0,1$, and $PNS(ipn_1^2, ipn_1^1) = 0,08$ is calculated analogically. Thus, the consistency of the problem-solving protocol $prot_1^{ag}$ with $prot_2^{ag}$ can be evaluated using expression (19)

$$prots_{1}^{ag}{}_{2} = \sqrt[4]{ROLS(prot_1^{ag}, prot_2^{ag})MTPS(prot_1^{ag}, prot_2^{ag})}$$
$$* \sqrt[4]{MRCS(prot_1^{ag}, prot_2^{ag})SCHS(prot_1^{ag}, prot_2^{ag})} = \sqrt[4]{1 \cdot 1 \cdot 0,375 \cdot 0,26}$$
$$= 0,56.$$

Similarly the consistency of the problem-solving protocol $prot_2^{ag}$ with $prot_1^{ag}$ is $prots_{2}^{ag}{}_{1} = 0,35$. Consistency of two copies of the same problem-solving protocol is expectedly equal to one.

Thus, despite the fact that the roles of agents in the protocols under consideration completely coincide, as well as lexemes describing the same types of messages, the proposed measure of protocol consistency demonstrates that the protocols are seriously different and need to be negotiated before starting joint work on solving the problem. In addition, this measure can be used as an indirect indicator of the relative "complexity" (the number of actions, agent roles, and interactions between them) of protocols in a pair of agents: the consistency of a more complex protocol with a less complex one is lower than vice versa.

6   Conclusion

The paper discusses the features of building hybrid intelligent multi-agent systems for solving practical problems and difficulties arising from the integration of intelligent agents created by various developers. The necessity of modeling the mechanisms of cohesion of teams of specialists and the transition to CHIMAS is shown. The formal CHIMAS model is considered, and one of the methods necessary for its implementation is described in detail, namely the evaluation of the consistency of problem-solving protocols developed by the agents. Modeling cohesion mechanisms allows to overcome disagreements caused by differences in the agents' goals, problem's models, and ways of its solution. As a result, CHIMAS relevantly model the problem-solving by long-existing teams of specialists.

References

1. Al-Yaaribi, A., Kavussanu, M.: Teammate prosocial and antisocial behaviors predict task cohesion and burnout: the mediating role of affect. J. Sport Exerc. Psychol. **39**(3), 199–208 (2017)
2. Bernthal, P., Insko, C.: Cohesiveness without groupthink: the interactive effects of social and task cohesion. Group Organ. Manag. **18**(1), 66–87 (1993)

3. Brisimis, E., Bebetsos, E., Krommidas, C.: Does group cohesion predict team sport athletes' satisfaction? Hell. J. Psychol. **15**, 108–124 (2018)
4. Dubielewicz, I., Hnatkowska, B., Huzar, Z., Tuzinkiewicz, L.: Domain modeling in the context of ontology. Found. Comput. Decis. Sci. **40**(1), 3–15 (2015)
5. Forsyth, D.: Group Dynamics. Wadsworth, Cengage Learning, Belmont (2010)
6. Gorodetskii, V.: Self-organization and multiagent systems: I. Models of multiagent self-organization. J. Comput. Syst. Sci. Int. **51**, 256–281 (2012)
7. Hajduk, M., Sukop, M., Haun, M.: Cognitive Multi-agent Systems. SSDC, vol. 138. Springer, Cham (2019). https://doi.org/10.1007/978-3-319-93687-1
8. Karimova, A., Khasanova, O., Shemshurenko, O., Ganieva, A.: The problem of raising group cohesiveness in the EFL classroom. In: Valeeva, R. (ed.) V International Forum on Teacher Education. ARPHA Proceedings, vol. 1, pp. 1025–1035. Pensoft Publishers, Sofia (2019). https://doi.org/10.3897/ap.1.e0972
9. Karpov, V.E., Tarassov, V.B.: Synergetic artificial intelligence and social robotics. In: Abraham, A., Kovalev, S., Tarassov, V., Snasel, V., Vasileva, M., Sukhanov, A. (eds.) IITI 2017. AISC, vol. 679, pp. 3–15. Springer, Cham (2018). https://doi.org/10.1007/978-3-319-68321-8_1
10. Kirikov, I., Listopad, S.: Method for evaluating the hybrid intelligent multi-agent system's cohesion: consistency of the problem-solving protocol. In: Open Semantic Technologies for Intelligent Systems: Research Papers Collection, vol. 5, pp. 33–38. Belarusian State University of Informatics and Radioelectronics, Minsk (2021)
11. Kolesnikov, A., Kirikov, I., Listopad, S.: Gibridnye intellektual'nye sistemy s samoorganizatsiey: koordinatsiya, soglasovannost', spor [Hybrid intelligent systems with self-organization: coordination, consistency, dispute]. IPI RAN, Moscow (2014). (in Russian)
12. Kryukov, K., Pankova, L., Pronina, V., Sukhovev, V., Shipilina, L.: Mery semanticheskoy blizosti v ontologii [Measures of semantic similarity in ontology]. Problemy upravleniya [Control Problems] **5**, 2–14 (2010). (in Russian)
13. Levenshtein, I.: Binary codes capable of correcting deletions, insertions, and reversals. Cybern. Control Theory **10**(8), 707–710 (1966)
14. Ling, S., Loke, S.W.: MIP-nets: a compositional model of multiagent interaction. In: Mařík, V., Pěchouček, M., Müller, J. (eds.) CEEMAS 2003. LNCS (LNAI), vol. 2691, pp. 61–72. Springer, Heidelberg (2003). https://doi.org/10.1007/3-540-45023-8_8
15. Listopad, S.: Cohesive hybrid intelligent multi-agent system architecture. In: Balandin, S., Paramonov, I., Tyutina, T. (eds.) Proceeding of the 26th Conference of FRUCT Association, pp. 262–269. FRUCT Oy, Helsinki (2020). https://doi.org/10.23919/FRUCT48808.2020.9087438
16. Listopad, S.: Estimating of the similarity of agents' goals in cohesive hybrid intelligent multi-agent system. In: Proceedings of the 8th International conference Fuzzy Systems, Soft Computing and Intelligent Technologies (FSSCIT-2020), pp. 180–185. CEUR Workshop Proceedings, Smolensk (2020)
17. Listopad, S.: Hybrid intelligent multi-agent system for power restoration. In: Golenkov, V., Krasnoproshin, V., Golovko, V., Azarov, E. (eds.) OSTIS 2020. CCIS, vol. 1282, pp. 245–260. Springer, Cham (2020). https://doi.org/10.1007/978-3-030-60447-9_16
18. Listopad, S., Kirikov, I.: Similarity measure of agents' ontologies in cohesive hybrid intelligent multi-agent system. J. Phys. Conf. Ser. **1679**(3), 032061 (2020)

19. Maedche, A., Zacharias, V.: Clustering ontology-based metadata in the semantic web. In: Elomaa, T., Mannila, H., Toivonen, H. (eds.) PKDD 2002. LNCS, vol. 2431, pp. 348–360. Springer, Heidelberg (2002). https://doi.org/10.1007/3-540-45681-3_29

20. McLeod, J., von Treuer, K.: Towards a cohesive theory of cohesion. Int. J. Bus. Soc. Res. **3**(12), 1–11 (2013)

21. Pei, J., Wen, L., Ye, X., Kumar, A.: Efficient transition adjacency relation computation for process model similarity. IEEE Trans. Serv. Comput. (2020). https://doi.org/10.1109/TSC.2020.2984605

22. Peterson, J.: Petri nets. Comput. Surv. **9**(3), 223–252 (1977)

23. Petrovskiy, A.: Opyt postroeniya sotsial'no-psikhologicheskoy kontseptsii gruppovoy aktivnosti [The experience of building a socio-psychological concept of group activity]. Voprosy psikhologii [Psychology Issues] **5**, 3–17 (1973). (in Russian)

24. Pochebut, L., Chiker, V.: Organizatsionnaya sotsial'naya psikhologiya. Uchebnoe posobie [Organizational social psychology. Tutorial]. Rech', Saint-Petersburg (2002). (in Russian)

25. Savinkina, A.: A test to express diagnostic cohesion of football team. Int. Sch. Sci. Res. Innov. **11**(5), 1089–1092 (2017)

26. Seel, N.: Problems: definition, types, and evidence. In: Seel, N. (ed.) Encyclopedia of the Sciences of Learning, pp. 2690–2693. Springer, Boston (2012). https://doi.org/10.1007/978-1-4419-1428-6_914

27. Severt, J., Estrada, A.: On the function and structure of group cohesion. In: Salas, E., Vessey, W., A.X., E. (eds.) Team Cohesion: Advances in Psychological Theory, Methods and Practice, Research on Managing Groups and Teams, vol. 17, pp. 3–24. Emerald Group Publishing Limited, Bingley (2015)

28. Sidorenkov, A., Pavlenko, R.: GROUP PROFILE computer technique: a tool for complex study of small groups. SAGE Open **5**(1), 1–13 (2015). https://doi.org/10.1177/2158244015569418

29. Spiridonov, V.: Psikhologiya myshleniya: Resheniye zadach i problem: Uchebnoye posobiye [Psychology of thinking: Solving tasks and problems]. Genezis, Moscow (2006). (in Russian)

30. von Treuer, K., McLeod, J., Fuller-Tyszkiewicz, M., Scott, G.: Determining the components of cohesion using the repertory grid technique. Group Dyn. Theory Res. Pract. **22**(2), 108–128 (2018)

31. Wooldridge, M., Jennings, N.: Intelligent agents: theory and practice. Knowl. Eng. Rev. **10**(2), 115–152 (1995)

32. Zha, H., Wang, J., Wen, L., Wang, C., Sun, J.: A workflow net similarity measure based on transition adjacency relations. Comput. Ind. **61**(5), 463–471 (2010)

Concepts and Models of Semantic Technologies

Julia Rogushina[✉][iD]

Institute of Software Systems, National Academy of Sciences of Ukraine,
Kyiv, Ukraine
ladamandraka2010@gmail.com
http://www.isofts.kiev.ua

Abstract. The paper discusses the main distinctions of semantic information systems from other types of intelligent software. We analyse conceptual aspects of semantic technologies realised by semantic applications with use of semantic resources and knowledge bases and try to define terminology used in this sphere. Ontological analysis is used as an instrument for representation of domain knowledge and formalisation of relations between main components of semantic technologies. Examples of semantic software designed by us are used for testing of proposed approach.

Keywords: Ontology · Semantic technology · Semantic Web · semantic information resource

1 Introduction

Now use of semantics in development of intelligent information systems (IISs) is one of the most promising directions of information technologies (IT) that has both a broad theoretical basis and significant practical results related to the development of intelligent applications in various fields. Such IISs use semantics represented by domain ontologies, organizational ontologies, task thesauri and ontologies, etc. These ontologies can be integrated with the help of top-level ontologies. Knowledge stored in these ontologies is renewed with use of the Web information resources (IRs).

Ontology-based semantic technologies (STs) allow to build powerful applied IISs aimed on analysis and modeling of complex objects and processes of different nature. STs are oriented on knowledge processing from open environment without changes of IIS software.

IIS effectiveness depends on level of problem solving automation that is based on knowledge about users, their current problem and adapting the problem solutions to the current state of the information environment and needs of specific user.

Ontology-based semantic IISs (SIISs) of independent developers can be integrated by mapping and alignment of ontologies that they use in their work for data exchange: relationships can be established directly between elements of individual

© The Author(s), under exclusive license to Springer Nature Switzerland AG 2022
V. Golenkov et al. (Eds.): OSTIS 2021, CCIS 1625, pp. 59–76, 2022.
https://doi.org/10.1007/978-3-031-15882-7_4

ontologies or through some top-level ontology. Results generated by one SIIS can be used by another SIIS as input data. For example, different SIISs can add information to user profile - about his/her learning outcomes, qualifications, interests, etc. Processing of information by SIIS is based on semantic computing (SC). Software realizations of SIISs are named semantic applications (SAs).

Another important problem of STs deals with integration of IRs used by SIISs because open information environment such as the Web can contain inconsistent and fuzzy data that connect with different situations and moments of environment. Integration of semantic IRs (SIRs) can be based also on matching of ontologies that represent their structure and semantics.

Integration of non-structured and non-semantic IR such as plain natural language (NL) documents needs in considerably more complex processing with use of external knowledge bases (KBs). Therefore the aim of this work is to differ SIISs from other kinds of IISs and SIRs from variety of the Web IRs.

The quality of integration depends on the proximity of ontologies used by SIISs and SIRs (matching of ontologies of non-intersected domains can not generate usable result) and on quality of their mapping that is determined by the presence or absence of links, primarily information ones, between ontological classes and instances. Establishing such links is a separate complex problem based on the use of background knowledge acquired from various external information sources and from domain experts, and on evaluation and normalization of the obtained results.

Development of SIIS needs in standards, knowledge representation languages and tools that support them. One of the most well-known projects in this sphere of STs is the Semantic Web that provides a large number of standards and tools for representation and processing of information at the meaning level based on ontologies, Web-services and software agents.

Unfortunately, the popularity of STs causes a rather incorrect use of terminology from this area: such concepts as "artificial intelligence", "knowledge processing", "semantics" are applied to various types of software and information processing methods that are not use the Semantic Web approach and where processing of semantics is not a significant part of IIS. For example, some IISs use logical inference on their internal data representation or realize some intelligent tasks such as planning but if they are not use knowledge from external IRs they can non be consider as semantic ones.

This determines the necessity to determine more formally criteria that allow to define SIIS. Formulation of these criteria needs in corresponding unambiguous terminology base than can be used for development of general ST model. Such model defines means of knowledge representation and processing used in ST, requirements to semantic IRs that can be analysed as a source of information, etc.

Now much attention is paid by many researchers specialized in various subarias of artificial intelligence (AI) and knowledge management (KM) to this problem [1] such as NL processing or image recognition. But at present a single generally accepted point of view on the basic concepts of semantic information processing that satisfy for all direction is not defined.

2   Task Definition

Development of semantic applications oriented on the Web needs in more accurately defined terminology that provide possibility of comparison and integration of various methods, resources and services. On base of analysis of existing approaches to classification of the main components used in STs and of experience of development ontology-based applications we try to define main elements of STs (such concepts as semantic IRs, semantic applications and semantic computing) and relations between them.

These definitions are aimed on differentiation of semantic-based elements of IIS from the all spectrum of intelligent software and methods of intellectualizing for considering of their specifics.

We propose to integrate these definitions in general model of STs represented by ST ontology for it's unambiguous interpretation by various researchers. This model can be increased by ontologies of various directions of AI by specific algorithms and knowledge representations.

3   Semantics in Information Technologies

Semantics is a part of several scientific disciplines such as Knowledge Representation, Knowledge Acquisition, Information Retrieval, Computational Linguistics, Artificial Intelligence and Knowledge Management. Specifics of every scientific direction causes different approaches to the set of the main ST concepts and their meanings. Usually, efforts related to formal semantics have involved limiting expressiveness to allow for acceptable computational characteristics.

Various syntactic structures are used in heterogeneous IRs for knowledge representation because IR structures depends on type of represented information. For example, structure of NL document differs from structure of DB or multimedia IR. Some names used in these structures can be identical but their meanings are different. Such situation causes problems in semantic interpretations of data associated with these names.

Semantics is a section of logic devoted to the study of the meaning of concepts and statements, as well as their formal analogues – expressions (terms and formulas) represented by means of different formal systems [3]. The tasks of semantics, first of all, include the clarification of the most important general concepts such as "meaning", "truth", "interpretation", "model", etc. – up to general concepts such as "set", "subject", "correspondence".

A number of important semantic problems are grouped around the difference between the meanings and denotations of concepts and between the meaning and significance (truth) of statements. Properties related to the meaning of concepts and statements are called intensional, and properties related to the scope of concepts and the truth values of statements are called extensional.

Semantics can be classified into formal (explicit) and informal (implicit) semantics. Formal semantics operate on formal notation; informal one is described and transmitted by NL constructions. The result of cognition of an abstract object is semantics; and the consequence of behavior is the semantics of execution. Implicit semantics is either present in most the Web IRs or can be extracted from them with the help of Data Mining and Machine Learning methods that provide acquisition of structured knowledge or enrichment of existing structured formal representations. Such semantics can be transformed into formal one with human involvement.

Formal semantics definite meaningful interpretation of data for their machine processing [2] and has unique was of its interpretation.

We can see that a lot of AI tasks are not semantic and don't use open information environment. They work with the fixed set of rules that are represented by internal KB of appropriate IIS. For example, various logical games such as chess, mahjong or kakuro can be solved by AI methods but don't involve external knowledge. These tasks are solved by fixed rules and don't use external information about context of situation. Their solving don't need in some knowledge about world and is based only on logical inference.

From other hand, some other simple intelligent games such as crosswords are semantic because they need in matching of NL definitions or pictures with words that satisfy some restrictions. For more complex tasks these distinction are less evident and in some cased of applications can depend on their software realizations.

In [4] semantic applications are defined as software tools that explicitly or implicitly use domain semantics to improve usability and completeness. An example of a semantic application in this understanding is information retrieval systems that use synonyms, super-classes and sub-classes of domain terms from the relevant domain ontology to enrich the user request by additional keywords and inspect search result on presence of these terms.

But it should be noted that almost all software uses the knowledge of developers about domain, but these knowledge usually can be not formalized and represented explicitly. This knowledge is a part of internal data base of IIS, therefore user can not change or even view elements of this knowledge. Such situation don't allow IIS to use more actual or relevant to user needs information.

The main advantage of semantic knowledge-based systems is the separation of knowledge from means of their processing. SIIS allows to change background KB by more adequate and actual set of knowledge from external IRs. This external knowledge for the Web-oriented applications is usually represented by ontologies.

4   Use of Ontological Analysis in Semantic Technologies

Most authors associate STs with creation, use and processing of ontologies in semantic applications (SAs) [4] because ontologies are widely used for interoperable representation of distributed knowledge. The knowledge contained into the relevant ontologies should ensure the processing of NL information, data integration and information retrieval. Ontologies that can be used for these purposes differ significantly in expressiveness, volume, level of abstraction and means of representation. In the most general form all ontologies contain the finite non-empty set of concepts (they can be represented by classes and individuals of classes), the finite set of relations between concepts and the finite set of rules or restrictions that deals with combinations of concepts and their relations. Semantics of data is defined in ontology by connection with element of description of domain knowledge and meaning of this connection.

Ontologies are usually divided into: 1) top-level ontologies that represent common knowledge of different domains; 2) domain ontologies that describe the specific features of some subject area; 3) ontologies of tasks that contain the knowledge required to run a particular software aimed on solving of some task. But such division is quite conditional because domain scope depends on the problem specifics and real application are based usually not on one ontology but on some complex hierarchy of ontologies.

Use of external ontologies is one of the distinguishing characteristic of SIISs. Various SIISs use ontologies to integrate data and knowledge and to interact wit other SIISs. Ontologies can also become the basis for a more intelligent user interface of IIS - for example, users can communicate with software through NL queries interpreted with the help of ontology knowledge. However, the NL interface is not a mandatory feature of the SIISs.

Source of ontologies for semantic application is one of important questions of STs. Retrieval or generation of pertinent ontology is a task for domain experts but it's technical features and restrictions on such ontology are defined by SIIS developers.

An important issue in the application of STs is retrieval the pertinent domain ontology [5]. For some important domains such as medicine, domain ontologies are recognized universally, but for many specialized business and science sectors fitting ontologies do not yet exist and need to be created. Although a number of ontology engineering methodologies developed in an academic context are widely used for various practical problems and are tested in the context of real-world or corporate applications.

More often we have situation that some ontology is developed for sufficiently near domain but it can be used by SIIS after some reduction or expansion. The main problem deals with accurate definition of task domain borders to change existing ontology according to them. This aim can be achieved by matching the NL or semi-structured description of user task solved by IIS and a set of existing ontologies or SIRs (for example, IRs with semantic markup). Selected SIRs that can be used for generation of new domain ontologies or for replenishment of existing ones.

5   Semantic Information Resources

Now the main part of information for IISs is provided by the Web. The current Web is primarily a very large number of hyperlinked documents. Part of them designed for human reading is represented in HTML or more controlled XHTML formats. But much of information relating to real-world or abstract notions and the relationships between them is stored in relational and quasi-relational SQL databases. Information processed by IIS can be trusted, dynamic, transparent, user-friendly [6].

Volume of information available by the Web is very large, and this fact causes transformation of retrieval problem to filtering problem: SIIS has to choose such relevant IRs that are more appropriate for automatic processing at semantic level.

Effectiveness of STs depends of quality, relevance and actuality of information into IRs processed by SIISs. Processing of structured information requires less time of calculation, and availability of semantic markup that connect parts of the IR content with some concepts of domain ontology provides more correct and unambiguous acquisition of IR knowledge that can be used by SIISs.

Structuring and semantic markup are important factors of selection IRs into results of retrieval into the Web. SIRs are more efficient for processing then non-semantic IRs. Additional desirable properties of IRs are use of generally accepted standards and languages, open access, actuality, etc. Therefore we try to define distinctions of SIRs.

Every IR is a set of one ore more documents that can be stored and used by information systems. IR contains some information (at least its name and size) that can be interpreted into some meaning. SIRs correspond to some non-empty subset of all available data and IRs.

SIRs can use various terminological and lexical resources, KBs, ontologies and other SRs. Such SIRs include some formal semantic components that define relations between content and formal semantic representation. The paper [7] analyzes the approach to information processing at the semantic level oriented on NL processing. Various researchers combine term "semantic resources" with lexics, annotations, thesauri, etc.

Different types of IRs such as taxonomies, vocabularies, thesauri or ontologies can be used as SIRs if they have means of their simultaneous use [8], and their semantic interoperability consists in preventing problems of misunderstandings between users by taking into account the semantics associated to the data, and ensuring exchanged information share the same meaning. SIRs can be heterogeneous and their analysis can be implemented at different levels. For NL such levels are syntax (representation format), structure (data organization) and semantics (different points of view).

In our research we consider IISs that process various types of information objects (IOs) with different levels of complexity, where NL-entities represent only one of the elements along with multimedia IOs and structured IOs. The set of IOs used in some SIIS is defined by solved problem, structure of processed information and particular information model realized by software. Usually SIIS developers select some ontology (or other knowledge representation) to define structure of IOs but population of individuals is executed in process of interaction of SIIS with users by acquisition of appropriate values of IO attributes from the Web SIRs.

This information about individuals of IOs them can be contained into heterogeneous IRs – SIRs, NL texts, multimedia (video, audio, images), structured and semi-structured components and links between them. Knowledge about IO structure and relations can be represented by ontologies too but we can consider other representations (for example, rules, decision trees or semantic networks).

6   Main Components of Information Sources in SIISs

Researchers analyse semantics of NL entities on base of NL documents and single out such three components of ST:

1) ontologies;
2) models of NL entities;
3) semantic IRs.

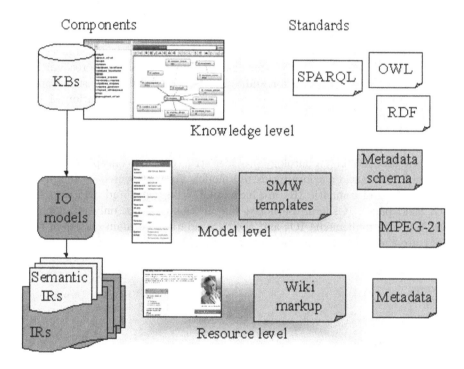

Fig. 1. Main components and standards of semantic technologies.

In general IRs used by STs in general can be described by combination of three main components (see Fig. 1):

– KBs (external and internal) that define main concepts, their features and relations (usually this KBs are represented by ontologies);

– IO models that define structure of typical elements processed by application;
– IRs that contain information about these IOs (explicitly or implicitly) (SIRs are the subset of these IRs).

KBs represent the upper level of abstraction of the application knowledge structure. For example, domain ontology define the set of concepts that are used by application, their possible and illegal relations, their attributes and types of attribute values. Expressiveness of knowledge representation is defined by selected formal language.

IO models represents the structure and elements of typical elements that are processed by application in terms of selected KB. For example, ontology classes can become the base of corresponding typical IOs, and ontology relations can b used for formalized definition of link semantics between IO individuals. Complexity level of IO model and means of it's representation determines the expressiveness of domain description.

Level of IRs identifies what types of sources can process IIS to take information about individuals of IOs. For SIRs such information can be extracted automatically. Structures but not semantic IRs need in explicit linking of data fields with IO properties. Non-structured IRs require various specialized means of processing that depend on IR data (for example, methods of image recognition for pictures, speech recognition for audio and text recognition for scan copies of text documents, NL processing for text documents). Semantization of IRs reduces the computational complexity of algorithms used by SAs and provides processing of the task-specific aspects of data only.

If we consider these ST components on the example of Wiki resource based on Semantic MediaWiki, an ontology provides structure and concepts of domain knowledge for semantic markup terms, IO models are represented by templates of typical IOs, and semantic IRs are individual Wiki pages and arbitrary sets of such Wiki pages. It should be noted that in this case not only NL content is used, but also multimedia IOs and their metadata. The main classes of this ontology are such semantic components (see Fig. 2):

– ontologies,
– services,
– tools,
– models,
– standards,
– methods,
– applications,
– information resources,
– information objects.

Object relations of this ontology define possible links between individuals of these classes and their sub-classes; data relations define possible values of class attributes; and characteristics of classes provide possibilities of logic inference (by such properties of relations as transitivity, symmetry, etc.)

Different types of IRs such as taxonomies, vocabularies, thesauri or ontologies can be used as SRs if they have means of their simultaneous use [8], and their semantic interoperability consists in preventing problems of misunderstandings between users by taking into account the semantics associated to the data, and ensuring exchanged information share the same meaning. SRs can be heterogeneous and their analysis can be implemented at different levels. For NL such levels are syntax (representation format), structure (data organization) and semantics (different points of view).

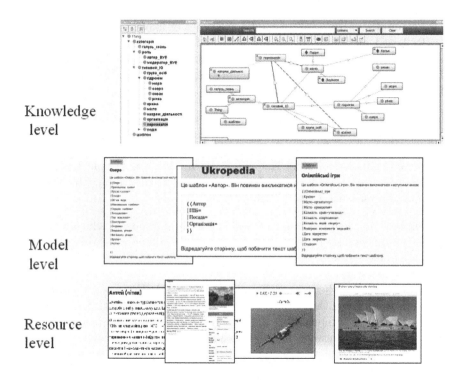

Fig. 2. Three levels of semantic technologies (on example of the Wiki).

7 Semantic Technologies and the Semantic Web

The main aim of the Semantic Web is to provide automated processing of the Web IRs and software on the knowledge level. These technologies are used to formally represent metadata by Extensible Markup Language (XML) [9]. XML defines a set of rules for encoding documents in a format that is both human-readable and machine-readable. Various types of semantic markup of IRs are based usually on XML syntax.

The Semantic Web project proposes a set of languages for knowledge representation such as Resource Description Framework (RDF) [10], RDF Schema

[11] and Web Ontology Language (OWL) [12]. Every IR specified by means of RDF or OWL is SIR.

SPARQL [13] is an RDF query language that provides requests to SIRs that use RDF. The definition of a formal semantics for SPARQL plays a key role in the standardization of this query language.

Some researchers base definition of SIRs on context [14] where context of IO (i.e. an object, an event or a process) is considered as a collection of semantic situational information that characterizes features of this IO and its relations with other IOs. Contextual information can include metadata of IRs, links with other knowledge descriptions, models of IOs, etc.

Some examples of SIRs that use different types of knowledge are considered in [7]: IRs based on the Wiki technology and the Web resources accessed by information retrieval systems (IRS). But this work does not propose definition of SIRs. In this study, we distinguish the following types of IRs that can be used by STs:

- SIRs are IRs with elements (content and/or metadata) that contain semantic markup for clear connection of the IR fragments with domain concepts formalized by some knowledge representation means;
- non-semantic IRs are all other IRs where information is not explicitly related to domain concepts (but such relationships can be determined by various means of analysis such as Text Mining [15]).

NL text data is a good example of unstructured information, which is one of the simplest forms of data that can be generated in most scenarios. Unstructured IRs is easily processed and perceived by humans, but is significantly harder for machines to understand.

The main difference between SIRs and non-semantic IRs deals with unambiguous interpretation of their semantics with the help of external standards and KBs. SIRs have clear references to the formally described knowledge about the semantics of their structuring – ontology, taxonomy, thesaurus. Examples of SIRs are metadata of the Dublin Core standard [16], semantic Wiki resources based on Semantic MediaWiki [17], multimedia IRs with metadata in the MPEG-21 standard [18], etc.

On base of above analysis we propose following definition: SIR as IR where elements of content or IR in whole are connected explicitly with elements of some formalized representation of knowledge with unambiguous semantic interpretation. Examples of such SIRs are: 1) IRs with semantic markup where ontology classes are used as markup tags; 2) documents with metadata based on standards defined by ontologies.

8   Models of Semantics

Models of semantics (MSs) depend on IO and IR specifics and on modelling approaches used in STs. Various models are oriented on some type of information (NL text, multimedia, images, structured data, etc.). Such models reflect the specific features of information type. Models of semantics of NL-entities in [7] contain models of semantic primitives, texts and their comparison. They have various expressiveness that depends on IIS purposes. For example, NL text can be represented as a semantic net that connect all words for every simple or complex sentence on base of syntax analysis but the same text can be represented as a set of links between sentences.

Now a lot of standards are developed for representation of metadata for various types of IRs. They can be used as MSs directly and as elements of SIR semantic markup. For example, Dublin Core is an example of a lightweight ontology that is used to specify the characteristics of electronic documents. Now this ontology is most widely applied for metadata semantization.

The examples of these standards are DCMI has several elements for defining different categories (roles) of users with respect to a document (Dublin Core Metadata Initiative [16] and FOAF (Friend of a Friend) [20] – an RDF-based general-purpose model for description of users on the Web. Many of them use ontological representation of knowledge. For example, There is an example of lightweight ontology aimed at creating an annotated network of homepages for people, groups, companies, etc. FOAF is implemented in RDF Schema and contains such basic classes as agent, person, organization, group, project, document, image, as well as some basic properties of instances of these classes.

Other MSs are oriented on some fixed type of IOs (or group of connected IOs). Examples of such MSs are user profiles used by learning SAs that can be exported from one SIIS to another by matching of corresponding ontologies [19]. Even the most typical characteristics of the users can be modelled by user profiles with different terms and categories that causes need in standardization of user profiling.

An other example of universal MSs are templates from Semantic MediaWiki that formalize the structure, categories and semantic properties of Wiki page with arbitrary content. Such Wiki templates can be developed for various IOs described by Wiki content. Expressiveness of these templates is very low: developer can define types of attributes and their possible values but can't fix relations and restrictions for them or possible categories of values. Therefore in practice template developers Use ontologies to formalize MSs of IOs. It makes them more interoperable and simplifies integration of different modelling approaches.

To model IOs with complex structure we can use models of simple and complex IOs (CIO), as well as methods of CIO. CIOs are formed by the meaningful relations between simpler IOs. For example, CIO "Family" can be formed by relations "child-parent" and "married" applied to CIOs "Person" and by relation "address" for CIO "place of residence". The set of related CIO can be exported from the Semantic Wiki environment and be used as a SM of task domain for external SIISs.

9   Algorithms Used in Semantic Technologies

Structuring of information is one of the ST tasks that helps in selection of important for user attributes. Such attributes can be considered as information factors acquired from data by various machine learning (ML) algorithms, means of Data Mining and other elements of AI such as pattern recognition and logical inference.

We analyse various methods and approaches uses in ST in [21]. Great attention was paid to methods of Data Mining, Text Mining, Web Mining and specifics of their use in various spheres. In this work we also consider service-oriented architecture used by the Web applications, intelligent software agents and multi-agent systems, instrumental tools of ontological engineering, Semantic Web technologies and their use in Business Intelligence, expressiveness of different Ontological languages, various models of the Web content semantization, etc. Results of this research work become the basis of this article.

Instruments that are used for analysis of SR content from the point of view of Data mining depend on specifics of these resources, means of their semantization and goals of analysis. For example, NL documents can be processed by Text Mining methods.

10   Semantic Computing and Semantic Applications

SC is a term used to describe a set of methods, algorithms and software used to process data based on their semantics, which are uniquely defined and interpreted.

This research direction is based on success in three areas:

– methods and means of practical engineering of ontologies as structures for integration and representation of heterogeneous distributed knowledge and data that make them equally accessible to humans and software;
– retrieval and processing of the Web IRs with varying degrees of structuring as universal sources of knowledge about the meaning of concepts, IOs, words and other entities;
– methods, algorithms and tools for processing and analysis of large amounts of data (Big Data technologies) [22].

SC combines different disciplines – multimedia computing, Semantic Web, soft computing [23], cognitive calculations, computational intelligence, computational linguistics, semantic information retrieval, etc. The use of SC allows to link informal intentions of people with content that may contain structured and semi-structured data, multimedia, natural language text, software, services, etc. SC is an instrument to disseminate traditional IT of character processing and content syntax in the direction of knowledge processing.

SAs are those software tools where the components of formal models at the conceptual level are described by formal knowledge representation, for example, by set of concepts and relations of pertinent ontology, and data transformation processes are performed with use of semantic computing. Some authors associate SC only with NL processing, for example, in semantic clustering and classification problems. However, although methods for establishing the semantics of text entities, their comparison with the use of semantic proximity measures are used in many SAs, but there is a large number of other SAs that process structured information, multimedia, etc.

In [7] SAs are defined as software that explicitly or implicitly use the domain semantics. But such definition does not make it possible to divide arbitrary software into semantic and non-semantic because implicit domain semantics is used in some way by almost any software. The main criterion for identifying software as SA is a separation of KB from the means of knowledge processing, i.e. clear representation of both semantics. Therefore, we propose to use the term "semantic application" only for software where domain knowledge is separated from the built-in knowledge of IIS and can be changed independently of the IIS itself.

Applications designed to solve problems that traditionally belong to the field of AI but with knowledge that fully integrated into IIS and can not be changed without software transformation, can be considered intelligent or intellectualized, but are beyond the scope of this research and are not considered as semantic ones. The central component of any SA is KB that contains knowledge about task. Interpretation of this knowledge allows to obtain results that the user needs and that can not be obtained without the use of this knowledge (or which lack requires much more time and calculations).

The goal of the "Semantic Web Challenge" project is to use Semantic Web technologies to build applications that integrate, connect and logically process information required by the user.

This project defines some basic requirements to software that can be named the Semantic Web application:

1. Values of data plays a key role.
   - Values of data have be represented with use of formal definitions.
   - Data should be processed in non-trivial ways in order to obtain useful information.
   - Processing of semantic information should play a central role in achieving results that cannot be obtained with alternative technologies at the same level or at all.
2. IRs used in the application
   - Should have different owners (i.e. there is no possibility to control IR change),
   - Should be heterogeneous (syntactically, structurally and semantically),
   - Should contain real-world data (not toy examples).
3. The search of IRs is carried out in the real information space of the Web

It is necessary that all applications perceive the open world, i.e. they have to take into account that information about world is never complete.

Applications are also assumed to use RDF, RDF Schema, or OWL in some way, although this is not required. Most importantly, if semantic technology is used, it plays a key role in reaching new levels of functionality or presentation.

In addition to these minimum requirements, a number of other wishes can be formulated. Most desirable:

– Exact transformations of information demonstrate the benefits of semantic technologies or evaluating the results obtained;
– The application has to be scalable (in terms of used data volume and in terms of distributed components working together);
– Functionality of application is different from usual information retrieval;
– The application has clear commercial potential Contextual information is used to rank or order the results of processing;
– Multimedia documents are used;
– Dynamic workflows are used, possibly in combination with static information;
– Various languages are supported.

All these requirements are actual for definition of SAs. Proposed ontology (see Fig. 3) represents main components of semantic technologies and relations between these components. Ontology can be expanded by links to external ontologies that define more precisely some particular aspects of this research sphere. For example, "inductive inference" can be specified by ontology of inductive modeling algorithms that by-turn can be supplemented with ontology of by The Group Method of Data Handling (GMDH) linked with individuals of methods, their properties and software realizations [31].

11   Use of the Semantic Web for Semantics Applications

Recently, developers of distributed IISs exhibit a tendency to transition from the use of relational databases to ontological knowledge bases (KBs). This process causes semantization of IISs and their transformation to SAs with differentiation of interoperable knowledge and formally described means of their processing on base of common standards.

The Semantic Web [24] is a project that aims to transform the Web information space into a distributed KB and to ensure the interoperability of knowledge representation. These goals require the use of generally accepted standards in SAs for the languages of knowledge representation and requests for them. For example, semantic search can use ontologies that characterize the user's area of interest or describe his profile, and such ontologies can be selected (by the user or developers) regardless of the implementation of search and mapping algorithms from any external repositories of ontologies. Main components of the Semantic Web

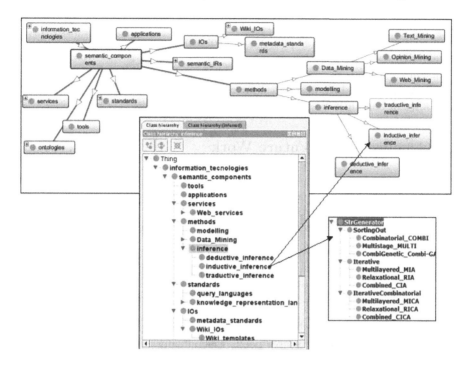

Fig. 3. Ontology of semantic technology components.

The Semantic Web conception is based on tree main elements:

– ontologies [25] for knowledge representation;
– Web-services [26] for representation of knowledge processing means;
– software agents [27] that can activate Web-services for knowledge processing for the benefit of users.

In SAs ontologies are used for formal modeling of the system structure, i.e. they define the relevant objects, subjects of domain and relations between them. Now domain ontologies are usually represented by the OWL [12] language developed by the Semantic Web initiative that is an add-on to the RDF language [14]. RDF provides information in the form of an oriented marked graph. The basic elements of RDF are triplets <subject, predicate, object>.

However, SAs are not equivalent to IISs based on the Semantic Web standards: now many IISs use ontologies as KBs but their usage is not a prerequisite for IIS semantization. IIS can be based on other formalisms of knowledge representation which for some reasons better meet the domain needs or already are accumulated in previously created IISs and KBs. But in practice the main part of SCs uses the Semantic Web technologies and satisfy the conditions formulated by the Semantic Web Challenges. The major challenges of the Semantic Web are [28]:

– the availability of content;
– ontology availability, development and evolution;
– scalability;
– multilinguality;
– visualization to reduce information overload;
– stability of Semantic Web languages.

12   Conclusion and Future Work

To test the correctness of proposed definitions we apply them to various ISSs and IRs that we develop. Such decision is explained by reason that we don't know exactly all characteristics of IRs and ISS of other developers and don't sure of meanings of concepts in their manuals. We consider three IISs:

– e-learning system M(e)L for distant control of student skills by formal model of domain knowledge [32];
– information retrieval system MAIPS [33] oriented on personified user needs;
– advisory system AdvisOnt [34].

All these IISs use external ontologies (in OWL) that can be changed by any others according to changes of user needs without any changes of software and apply ontological knowledge for processing of user requests. Therefore we can designate them SAs. We also consider some IRs on base of Semantic MediaWiki (for example, portal version of Great Ukrainian Encyclopedia e-VUE) where we take part in development of the KB structure [35]. Markup of Wiki-pages is based on terms from pertinent ontology, and content elements are connected explicitly with ontology classes by semantic properties connected with ontology relations. Therefore we can consider this IRs as SIRs.

On base of this practical testing of definitions formulates to main components of STs we propose to use tam as criteria to differ semantic elements of AI from all other results in this sphere it has to simplify comparison and selection of models, methods and tools for solving of specific user tasks.

References

1. Lassila, O., McGuinness, D.: The role of frame-based representation on the semantic web. Linköping Electron. Articles Comput. Inf. Sci. **6**(5) (2001)
2. Sheth, A., Ramakrishnan, C., Thomas, C.: Semantics for the semantic web: the implicit, the formal and the powerful. Int. J. Semant. Web Inf. Syst. (IJSWIS) **1**(1), 1–18 (2005)
3. Palagin, O.V., Petrenko, M.G.: Explanatory ontographic dictionary on knowledge engineering. LLC NVP Interservice, Kyiv (2017). (in Ukrainian)
4. Bartussek, W., et al.: Introduction to semantic applications. In: Hoppe, T., Humm, B., Reibold, A. (eds.) Semantic Applications, pp. 1–12. Springer, Heidelberg (2018). https://doi.org/10.1007/978-3-662-55433-3_1

5. Hoppe, T., Humm, B.G., Reibold, A.: Semantic Applications - Methodology, Technology, Corporate Use. Springer, Heidelberg (2018). https://doi.org/10.1007/978-3-662-55433-3

6. Sheth, A., Lytras, M.D.: Semantic Web-Based Information Systems: State-of-the-Art. IGI Global (2006)

7. Gorodetsky, V.I., Tushkanova, O.N.: Semantic technologies for semantic applications. Part 1. Basic components of semantic technologies. Artif. Intell. Decis. Making (4), 61–71 (2018)

8. Da Silva, C.F., Médini, L., Ghafour, S.A., Hoffmann, P., Ghodous, P., Lima, C.: Semantic interoperability of heterogeneous semantic resources. Electron. Notes Theor. Comput. Sci. **150**(2), 71–85 (2006)

9. Bray, T., Paoli, J., Sperberg-McQueen, C.M., Maler, E., Yergeau, F., Cowan, J.: Extensible markup language (XML) 1.0. W3C Recommendation (2000). https://www.w3.org/TR/REC-xml. Accessed 23 Feb 2021

10. Lassila, O., Swick, R.: Resource Description Framework (RDF) Model and Syntax Specification, W3C. https://www.w3.org/TR/REC-rdf-syntax. Accessed 4 Feb 2021

11. Brickley, D., Guha, R.V.: Resource Description Framework (RDF) Schema Specification. W3C Proposed Recommendation. https://www.w3.org/TR/PR-rdf-schema. Accessed 14 Feb 2021

12. OWL Web Ontology Language. Overview, W3C Recommendation: W3C (2009). https://www.w3.org/TR/owl-features/

13. Perez, J., Arenas, M., Gutierrez, C.: Semantics and complexity of SPARQL (2009). https://marceloarenas.cl/publications/tods09a.pdf. Accessed 4 Feb 2021

14. Huang, W., Webster, D.: Enabling context-aware agents to understand semantic resources on the WWW and the semantic web. In: IEEE/WIC/ACM International Conference on Web Intelligence (WI 2004), pp. 138–144 (2004)

15. Allahyari, M., et al.: A brief survey of text mining: classification, clustering and extraction techniques (2017). https://arxiv.org/pdf/1707.02919.pdf

16. Dublin Core Metadata Initiative. https://dublincore.org/. Accessed 22 Feb 2021

17. Vrandecic, D., Krotzsch, M.: Semantic MediaWiki. In: Davies, J., Grobelnik, M., Mladenić, D. (eds.) Semantic Knowledge Management, pp. 171–179. Springer, Heidelberg (2009). https://doi.org/10.1007/978-3-540-88845-1_13

18. Burnett, I., Van de Walle, R., Hill, K., Bormans, J., Pereira, F.: MPEG-21: goals and achievements. IEEE MultiMedia **10**(4), 60–70 (2003)

19. Rogushina, J.: User profile ontological modelling by wiki-based semantic similarity. In: Golenkov, V., Krasnoproshin, V., Golovko, V., Azarov, E. (eds.) OSTIS 2020. CCIS, vol. 1282, pp. 198–211. Springer, Cham (2020). https://doi.org/10.1007/978-3-030-60447-9_12

20. Golbeck, J., Rothstein, M.: Linking social networks on the web with FOAF: a semantic web case study. In: AAAI, vol. 8, pp. 1138–1143 (2008)

21. Gladun, A., Rogushina, J.: Semantic technologies: principles and practices. ADEF-Ukraine, Kyiv (2016). (in Ukrainian)

22. Wang, Y.: On formal and cognitive semantics for semantic computing. Int. J. Semant. Comput. **4**(02), 203–237 (2010)

23. Zadeh, L.A.: Some reflections on soft computing, granular computing and their roles in the conception, design and utilization of information/intelligent systems. Soft Comput. **2**(1), 23–25 (1998)

24. Davies, J., Fensel, D., van Harmelen, F.: Towards the Semantic Web: Ontology-Driven Knowledge Management. John Wiley Sons Ltd, England (2002)

25. Obrst, L., Ceusters, W., Mani, I., Ray, S., Smith, B.: The evaluation of ontologies. In: Baker, C.J.O., Cheung, K.H. (eds.) Semantic Web, pp. 139–158. Springer, Boston (2007). https://doi.org/10.1007/978-0-387-48438-9_8
26. Studer, R., Grimm, S., Abecker, A.: Semantic Web Services. Springer, Heidelberg (2007). https://doi.org/10.1007/3-540-70894-4
27. Hendler, J.: Agents and the semantic web. IEEE Intell. Syst. **16**(2), 30–37 (2001)
28. Benjamins, V.R., Contreras, J., Corcho, O., Gomez-Porez, A.: Six Challenges for the Semantic Web (2014). https://oa.upm.es/5668/1/Workshop06.KRR2002.pdf. Accessed 16 Feb 2021
29. Sheu, P.C.: Semantic computing. In: Semantic Computing, pp. 1–9 (2010)
30. Wang, Y.: Software Engineering Foundations: A Software Science Perspective. CRC Press, Boca Raton (2007)
31. Pidnebesna, H., Stepashko, V.: On construction of inductive modeling ontology as a metamodel of the subject field. In: ACIT 2018 (2018)
32. Gladun, A., Rogushina, J.: Distant control of student skills by formal model of domain knowledge. Int. J. Innov. Learn. **7**(4), 394–411 (2010)
33. Gladun, A., Rogushina, J.: Use of semantic web technologies in design of informational retrieval systems. In: Building and Environment, pp. 89–103. Nova Scientific Publishing, New-York (2009)
34. Pryima, S.M., Strokan, O.V., Rogushina, J.V., Gladun, A.Y., Lubko, D.V., Malkina, V.M.: Ontological analysis of outcomes of non-formal and informal learning for Agro-advisory system AdvisOnt. In: Valencia-García, R., Alcaraz-Marmol, G., Del Cioppo-Morstadt, J., Vera-Lucio, N., Bucaram-Leverone, M. (eds.) CITI 2020. CCIS, vol. 1309, pp. 3–17. Springer, Cham (2020). https://doi.org/10.1007/978-3-030-62015-8_1
35. Rogushina, J.: Semantic Wiki resources and their use for the construction of personalized ontologies. In: CEUR Workshop Proceedings, vol. 1631, pp. 188–195 (2016)

Semantic Aspects of the Experts' Communication Problem in Relation to the Conceptual Design of Complex Systems

Alexandre Kourbatski⬡ and Konstantin Mulyarchik$^{(\boxtimes)}$⬡

Belarusian State University, Minsk, Belarus
kurb@unibel.by, k.mulyarchik@gmail.com

Abstract. This article discusses several world-wide problems in the communication between the experts, such as harmonization of conceptual apparatus and translation between traditional languages as major barriers for effective and rapid complex systems' design process. The authors of the article state that in modern, especially post-covid world has been formed the conditions that encourage the development of a new planned language of international communication for experts, which, on one hand, would help to overcome the problems of translation, coordination of the conceptual apparatus, raising the effectiveness of communication between experts, and on the other hand, to make a breakthrough in the evolution of software development. The authors consider the initiative in the creation of such a language may come from experts and the business environment, especially from the global innovative IT companies, for which such language would greatly simplify the writing of software as would replace or simultaneously play a role the programming language.

Keywords: Conceptual design · Desing of complex systems · Intelligent symantic systems · Communication language

1 Introduction

This paper develops the main ideas presented in the paper "New language for conceptual design of complex systems in the era of post-covid and mass digitalization" [1]. In particular, the concepts of complex systems design have been clarified based on traditional and new semantic technologies, context of the emergence of the new language of experts' communication have been developed and specified, the conditions for fast adoption of the new language and possible stakeholders have been identified.

Widespread automation, the integration of digital solutions and cyber-physical systems, and artificial intelligence technologies are rapidly changing the landscape of human life, leading to a radical change in management technologies, the nature of communication, processes in the society and economy, making

V. Golenkov et al. (Eds.): OSTIS 2021, CCIS 1625, pp. 77–88, 2022.
https://doi.org/10.1007/978-3-031-15882-7_5

the modern world extremely dynamic and complex. Digitalization, in addition to the mass of positive aspects, generates more and more new risks and threats not only for countries, business, but for every individual as well. With the help of modern cyber weapons, one can "kill" the economy of a certain country, the business of a particular company, depending on the degree of digitalization.

Literally over the past 10 years, all of us in person have practically moved into cyberspace. There is a rapid "digitization of a person" most commonly without his consent. We can say that a digital shell is being created around each of us, or, even more simply, a "digital twin". And how this information is used - for good or for bad - is another question. The rules that would regulate these nuances are still not stated clearly.

The rapid development of computer technologies that combine high computing power and low costs has led to the penetration of these technologies into all spheres of human activity and thus led to widespread digitalization. This, in turn, creates a demand for the development of technologies, approaches and methods that allow faster design and development of software systems, with lower costs and with a higher degree of reliability. A number of technologies have been developed for the design of classic software systems in which both the data model and business logic are hard- coded into the system itself. The technologies for design and development of intelligent computer systems, including their semantic compatibility, are becoming more widespread.

With the increasing complexity and scale of the systems being created, more and more people should be involved in these projects and ensure their coordinated activities. This is undoubtedly facilitated to a large extent by the developed technologies for design of solutions, which, however, focus primarily on the system being developed. From the point of view of the actors involved in the process, the process itself as a whole remained unchanged - this is communication in one of the classical languages, discussion of certain issues, coordination, achievement of a common understanding of the problem being solved. And in this sense, this process is filled with difficulties in mutual understanding, establishing contact, communicating a particular point of view so that others can understand it, not to mention the need to translate from one language into another, if there is such.

2   Software Systems' Desing Methodologies

Over the past 30 years, the world expert community has developed a number of notations, modeling tools and software systems design. The main groups of modeling standards are: descriptive models (IDEF0, OPM, SysML and others), analytical models and simulations (DIS, HLA, UML and others); data exchange standards, transformation models, general modeling standards and other modeling standards for specific areas: software development models, equipment design models, business process models [3]. The languages of system modeling are distinguished separately. The rapid development of cyber-physical systems, in particular such paradigms as the Internet of Things and Industry 4.0, in which technical systems and humans are combined, reveals the limitations in the ability of classical technologies and modeling notations to meet the new emerging requirements of these new paradigms. The reason for this is the universality of these models and their focus on universal applicability, in which a number of details specific to a specific subject area are ignored. This also implies the duration of their update cycle, which does not meet modern technology development requirements.

Thus, one of the topical areas of research in the field of designing computer and information systems is the study of new languages of conceptual modeling and the development of tools for their active and widespread use [4] It is discussed that the basis of domain-based conceptual modeling is metamodeling, which allows combining BPMN [5], ERD [6], EPC [7], UML [8] and Petri Nets [9,10], within one tool.

Many from the above-mentioned technologies can be used for standardization and unification in solving a number of other tasks: design of a domain, design of business and organizational systems, design of a knowledge system, etc. Despite this, they are little used by the international expert community for such purposes, probably, because of their focus primarily on computer systems, and secondly, because of their contextual dependence and the need to harmonize basic terms and concepts in natural languages anyway. Amongst such design technologies one can mention business analysis, systems engineering, the theory of inventive problem solving, and others, directly aimed at the consistent analysis of problems and the search for solutions.

3   Complex Systems' Design Methodologies Based on the Technologies for Intelligent Semantic Systems

It is necessary to pay attention to a number of breakthrough developments in the field of semantically compatible intelligent systems that provide fast and high-quality design of intelligent systems of various scales and complexity. Within the framework of this direction, the world expert community is solving a number of problems: standardization of intelligent systems, unification of the principles of building knowledge bases, problem solvers and interfaces of intelligent systems, semantic compatibility of various types of knowledge, various models for solving problems, intelligent systems among themselves and intelligent systems with their users. On the one hand, these technologies are characterized by a strict formalization of their apparatus and rules of use, which makes it possible to quickly computerize and automate the corresponding models. On the other hand, they are quite close to how people communicate with each other, if an attempt is made to formalize such a communication.

We believe that there is a real need for unification, on the one hand, the design technologies and conceptual design of computer systems, including intelligent systems, and on the other hand, the ways of communication between experts, coordination of tasks to be solved, which may result in the creation of a new language of international communication.

With the development of computer and computing technology, the increase in complexity of the problems being solved, the requirements for design and development technologies in terms of their flexibility and efficiency of modeling began to increase as well. A whole class of information systems has appeared, called semantic systems, in which, unlike classical systems, the data structure is determined by the data itself, and the algorithms for its processing are described by a number of statements, and not rigidly fixed in the program code of the information system. Since such systems are universal in relation to subject areas, their integral part is the presence of a structured description of the subject area - ontology.

There are significant achievements [2,13–15] in the development of flexible semantically compatible intelligent systems, which have great potential for solving the problem of coordinated communication between experts and the problem of conceptual design. The cornerstone of these studies is the idea of developing a universal language for representing the meaning of knowledge. It is noted that such a language should have the property of nonlinearity.

At the applied level, such a universal language describes not only the knowledge itself, but also its meaning through the definition of both information and meta-information. Due to such property it can cover a number of types of information content: specifications and descriptions of various entities, documentation and requirements for systems and their evolution, descriptions of domain areas, definition of tasks and classes of tasks, description of problems, description of solutions to these problems, description of ways to solve various typical problems, description of projects and concepts. If necessary, this language has the ability to expand the description of new types of knowledge, thus allowing it to be widely distributed for solving problems in various applied areas of computer systems. Semantic code SC-code (Semantic Code), presented in [16], refers to such a language.

4   Harmonization of Conceptual Apparatus and Translation Between Traditional Languages as Major Barriers in Experts' Communication and Complex Systems' Design Process

Moving to an earlier stage of the software development life cycle - to the level of conceptual design, problem statement, it should be noted that the traditional language (English, Russian, etc.) is still the means of design and coordination. Concepts are drawn up in the form of text documents in traditional languages, using certain schemes, or elements of notation. Traditional language, carrying both communicative and cognitive functions, has one drawback: all languages that exist today are linear, they are directly connected with time so that the information is revealed sequentially. All this leads to several problems in their use.

First of all, the effective work of the expert group is conditioned by the presence of an agreed conceptual apparatus and context among all its members. This includes not only the terms and meanings that stand behind them, but also the interrelationships of the terms with each other.

Especially when innovative things are discussed in an expert environment, it is necessary to form a conceptual apparatus ab initio, since it simply does not exist. This takes a long time due to the ineffectiveness of natural language, no matter what language to consider.

It should be emphasized that even experts who speak the same language do not always understand each other, especially if they are discussing new problems or innovative approaches. For example, in a discussion there may be situations when they use the same term, but each understands it differently. The worst case scenario is when the concepts of these terms do not intersect at all.

The face of the matter is that at the initial stage of its development, the traditional language was a simple means of communication in everyday life. But over time, languages have become a working tool of the expert layer. The level of complexity of the tasks being solved has increased significantly, but the main tool for solving them - the means of communication - has remained the same, which leads to the slow work of experts, the slow work of the government, and business, especially large ones, contrasted with the extreme dynamics of the modern world [11].

Another problem of using traditional languages at an expert level, closely related to the first one, is the need to translate from one language to another. In this case, a partial loss and replacement of meaning inevitably occurs, which also leads to a loss of the effectiveness of the work of experts. Unfortunately, there are only a few qualified translators in the world who not only know both languages but also know the specifics of the subject area, thus able to convey not only the text, but also the specific meaning. At the same time, at the everyday level, the problem of translation from language into language can very soon be solved with the help of automatic translation systems. They have achieved quite acceptable results, are progressing rapidly, and the role of human translators will diminish.

Until recently, during the period of globalization, the world community used English as the language of international communication. However, the coronavirus pandemic that came in 2020 led to some reduction in global international communication and created the preconditions for the emergence of independent regional economic zones with their own civilizational model, relying on norms, ideas and traditions familiar to the most. Within each zone, the dominant national language common to the zone and the national languages of other peoples who have joined the zone will be used [12].

Since the economic and cultural interaction between the zones will be preserved, the need for international communication in the new world will remain. Cultural exchanges, tourist trips, joint scientific research, especially of a fundamental nature, and joint projects will remain. It will also be necessary to solve problems common to human civilization, for example, in the field of ecology.

English, which is now used as a means of international communication, is not suitable in this sense. It seems unlikely that all countries will officially and forever recognize the language of one of the zones as a means of international communication. Therefore, in the world of regional zones, English, like any other national language, is likely to be used as the main international language of communication for only a limited, albeit, possibly quite long, time.

5 Environment for Experts' Communication

Linguists note that the language is directly connected with the environment of communication and its distribution. For natural languages such environment is human community; for programming languages - this is a particular software development environment. Unsuccessful attempts to create an artificial language before are associated primarily with the lack of a proper environment for its dissemination, since we had only natural ways to communicate.

Today the Internet is such an environment for the whole world. Now any person has at least something: a smartphone, tablet or computer. The new communication medium is able to very quickly conquer the audience. If a new language could be attached to a computer program, then the entire population of the globe would be immediately covered. As an example, we can cite software from Microsoft, which is imposed all over the world.

We believe that the stage of conceptual design and problem setting in the software development can be used as a reference point. In addition to solving the abovementioned problems of aligning the conceptual apparatus and translation, this language can automatically become a means of the conceptual software design.

When programming was born, the task was set to use separate programming languages as languages understandable by the machine. The implication was that in the future, the computer will learn to understand natural language. And when they say "high-level programming language", they mean that it comes close to a natural language. We haven't made much progress, but the goal remains. It seemed that if a computer began to understand a language close to natural, both the programming process itself and the formulation of the problem would be simplified. But now we have come to understanding that natural language is not very effective. There are many ambiguities that are difficult for a computer to understand.

6 Preceding Attempts to Create an Artificial Language

Earlier in world history, several attempts were made to create an artificial (planned) language of international communication. As conceived by their authors, such a language should be more logical, simpler and, accordingly, easier to learn than any "foreign" language. It should allow one to get rid of the burden of ineffective historical layers inherent in any modern language. They hoped that it would be accepted by representatives of different countries as the second language of educated people. In the future, this will make their language international, and then universal.

The most famous and widespread planned language is Esperanto, created by the Warsaw linguist and optometrist Ludwik Zamenhof in 1887. According to various estimates, today it is spoken by from one hundred thousand to two million people - in the best case, only 0.03% of the world's inhabitants. Nevertheless, only Esperanto can be considered an established planned language. The rest are linguistic projects, mostly within the ownership of small groups of enthusiasts. For more than two thousand years of described human history, linguists have counted about 1000 of such projects.

It is also necessary to pay attention to Latin. The Latin alphabet is the basis of writing in many modern languages. Throughout history, Latin has been used in conversations between diplomats because the parties did not speak their partner's language. Latin is known not only as the language spoken in the Roman Empire, but also the language that has long served as a source for the formation of international socio-political and scientific terminology.

In 1956, Noam Chomsky described a theory of universal grammar, based on the generalization of the Standard Average European languages. The main idea of this theory was that there is a number of pre-built patterns in the human brain, according to which one or another language is constructed. However, the gradual extension of this theory to languages "more distant" from European languages began to reveal the limitations of his theory. This later led to the emergence of a set of Chomsky principles and parameters, and subsequently one principle - the principle of recursion. However, it was not applicable to some of the languages of the tribes of South America.

Chomsky's universal grammar was replaced by the conventional theory of language acquisition, mentioned by researchers Paul Ibbotson and Michael Tomasello.

Its main idea is that language acquisition occurs in the process of social interactions due to a set of a number of cognitive mechanisms, such as: categorization, construction of analogies, the ability to "read" the speaker's communicative intention, schematization, addiction, decontextualization, automation. Such tools help to reconstruct grammatical categories and rules from the language that a person hears around him.

It should be noted that in the process of creating a new language of communication, it is necessary to take into account and be based on these cognitive mechanisms, since they will ensure the wide and rapid spread of this language.

However, one cannot fail to note the idea that underlies Chomsky's universal grammar - to create a universal open theory that will allow creating or explaining the existence of any language on the planet. Such an open theory should be simple enough to explain in advance what it itself does not include, but at the same time it should not be so simple as not to be able to explain the things that it is intended to explain.

7 Principles of Visualization of Information as the Basis for the New Language

The new language may inherit some principles of visualization of information. We have carried out research on various diagrams, graphs and other visual representations of information with the aim of identifying several classes of visual forms and compiling a dictionary of visual forms.

First of all, it is worth dividing visual forms into simple and complex ones. Simple visual forms reflect information that answers one question. Reflects one type of information. Simple visual forms can be divided into several types depending on how they reflect information.

Maps. A visual form that reflects the position of an object in space. The coordinates for the space can be any parameters, the reflection of which is necessary. Thus, the map reflects the state of the object at some point in time, and we see this as the location of points in certain coordinates. If we reflect the state at each moment in time, then we will see a regular graph. Therefore, graphs can be attributed to this type of visual form.

Networks. Visual forms that reflect relationships between objects. This classification also includes visual forms that do not initially look like a network.

Visual comparisons. Visual comparison most often reflects the numerical characteristics of an object in comparison with other objects. These can be images of objects located side by side at different time periods to compare their appearance, there can be histograms to reflect the number. For example, the number of active users of social networks. Everywhere we visually compare several objects.

Object images. Pictures or portraits to clarify the appearance or characteristics of the described object. A set of objects. In the visual form, the characteristics of both one object and several that have some kind of connection can be reflected.

Complex visual forms are made up of a combination of several basic forms. Moreover, they can consist of several of the same types of simple forms or from a set of different types of visual forms. Thus, we can use several basic visual techniques one or more times, combining them with each other, we reflect the data or semantic sequence we need.

To display certain semantic sequences, it is necessary to develop a dictionary of visual forms, relying on the above classification. However, to use the full range of possibilities and bring various visual forms, it is necessary to have ready-made algorithms available, and based on their work and the result provided, this information can be presented in a structured and user-friendly form. Since at the moment the study of the possibilities of constructing such forms is being conducted to a greater extent, at the moment they will be presented in a simple form.

To begin with, let's analyze the main features of the speech or text presentation of information. In any text there are objects that have their own characteristics and the importance for the entire text also varies. Thus, we can select entities along with any description of these entities.

The selection of such objects is valuable, for example, in the automatic analysis of documents. It is especially important in this case to highlight named entities. The selection of such objects can allow, for example, automatic classification of documents by who are the parties to the contract, extracting them as named entities. We are conducting a general analysis of the possibilities, therefore, both ordinary objects in the text and named entities are important for us.

The second feature, which is based on what was described above, is that although both ordinary and named objects are equally important to us, we still need to distinguish between them, so for this we will use the technique of visual comparison.

Also, if there are objects, then there are connections between them. For example, in the sentence "London is the capital" there is a relationship between the named entity "London" and the object "capital". And "is" is the connecting ring. Thus, we can extract the data of the connection and represent it in the form of a network.

From the above features, you can see that many of the elements from the classification of visual forms that were given earlier can be used. It would also be possible to use an object image to reflect the appearance or related images for named entities, which would make them easier to define. But it would also clutter up the image if there are a lot of named entities in the text, so for now this will be an unnecessary element.

As a result, when constructing a visual form of a speech or text presentation of information, it is advisable to strive for a kind of graph, the nodes of which will be objects of various types, and the edges of the connection between them.

8 Creation of a New Language for Experts' Communication Based on the Achievements in Computer Technologies

Another idea of basing a new language on the principles from the field of software development might be interesting for discussion.

A certain breakthrough in the development of software solutions was made by No-code and Low-code technologies. They allow to create software using visual development platforms with little or no programming in classical sense. Isn't it a prototype for a new language? The emergence of this trend was supported by the development of cloud systems technologies, the need in the shortening the time of product development, which can be easily upgraded or reformatted, the need in quick testing of hypotheses, and the development of flexibility of large companies.

The rapid development of computer technologies over the past half century has led to the emergence of many different notations, approaches, algorithms and languages for designing software systems, complex integrated systems, and intelligent computer systems. These include the world-famous graphical description language for object modeling UML, the concept of process management of an organization based on business processes, BPM and the notations widely known in the world practice BPMN, EPC, IDEF0. These languages were originally developed for the purpose of unifying approaches to software design, in fact, they can be used to solve a number of other problems: design of a subject area, design of business and organizational systems, knowledge systems.

Separately, we shall single out a whole area of development of flexible and compatible technologies that provide fast and high-quality construction of intelligent systems for various purposes. Within the framework of this direction, the world expert community is solving a number of problems: standardization of intelligent systems, unification of the principles of building knowledge bases, problem solvers and interfaces of intelligent systems, semantic compatibility of various types of knowledge, various models for solving problems, intelligent systems among themselves and intelligent systems with their users.

Thus if we can create a new language, which on the first stage would be the language of communication between experts, and then becomes clear for the computer, we will be able to make breakthrough in software development. As a process, it will become more natural, because a programmer does not need to learn a separate programming language, it is enough for him to conduct a dialogue with a customer in a new language. Indeed, the lack of such a language especially in the IT environment is obvious, considering the fact that the production of software in the world has become a massive process. The language could help solve many problems in the era of mass digitalization.

9   Initiatives for Creation of a New Language

In order that a new planned language for international communication avoids the fate of its unpopular predecessors, the initiative for its development must be properly framed. It is not so important who will be the creator. Creating a planned language is an understandable task that does not require huge resources. The key question is who will be the customer in the first place. The initiative should come from those who are ready to subsequently implement it among the broad masses.

A country or a large world-class company can become such a customer, if it sees own interest in it.

For the first time, the need for a planned language for international communication may be formed not by the wishes of enthusiastic linguists, not by the theoretical reflections of great scientists, but by the interests of experts and the business environment. For the first time, powerful and real competitors of planned languages - national languages - are ready to step aside in advance and leave the field of international linguistic communication to their artificial counterparts.

IT companies, by definition, must be innovative, otherwise they will not survive long. With the advent of a new language, the programming process itself may change. Universal digitalization led to the fact that almost everyone needed software or, in common parlance, software. We digitize almost everything - industry, transport, healthcare, education and much more. And a man to boot. Therefore, the need for programmers has increased dramatically. Since the advent of computers, it has been considered that you need to strive for a programming language to be close to natural. And if the communication language coincided with the programming language, it would greatly simplify the writing of software. Even without professional education, people would be able to program for themselves.

10   Conclusion

On the agenda is the task of creating, in the future, a new language of international communication, which, on the one hand, would be the language of communication for the expert layer, and on the other hand, would allow to effectively solve the problems of conceptual design of systems [1].

A number of open questions arise that need to be resolved when developing such a language. What well-known technologies, best practices and know-hows can the new language rely on? To what extent should existing artificial intelligence and machine learning technologies be taken into account and used in the development of this language? For example, the previously mentioned open semantic technologies for the design of intelligent systems. Or UML notations, IDEF0, No-code and Low-code technologies mentioned earlier in the article. To what extent the approaches that have shown their viability in the development of programming languages should there be used? Programming languages, keeping their basic corpus unchanged, are developing due to constantly updated libraries.

What alphabet to take as a basis? Use one of the existing languages as a prototype or start from scratch? Perhaps the eastern hieroglyphic writing could be taken into account. For example, Chinese characters may be closer to a new language of communication - they are already inherent in great visualization. Hieroglyphs are more like visual objects that are used in modern programming than words in English or Russian. Should the new language effectively use the elements of visualization?

In addition to applied issues, the conceptual questions arise too. What should be the methodological foundations for building a new language? For example, this could be systematization, systems thinking, the apparatus of models, the theory of business analysis, the theory of inventive problem solving, etc. What should be the contribution of other knowledge areas to the new language?

References

1. Kourbatski, A., Mulyarchik, K.: New language for conceptual design of complex systems in the era of post-covid and mass digitalization. Otkrytye semanticheskie tekhnologii proektirovaniya intellektual'nykh system [Open semantic technologies for intelligent systems], pp. 55–58 (2021)
2. Golenkov, V., Golovko, V., Guliakina, N., Krasnoproshin, V.: The standardization of intelligent computer systems as a key challenge of the current stage of development of artificial intelligence technologies. Otkrytye semanticheskie tekhnologii proektirovaniya intellektual'nykh system [Open semantic technologies for intelligent systems], pp. 73–88 (2020)

3. Enin, S., Gerasimuk, Y.: Effektivnoe upravlenie tsifrovizatsiei: arkhitekturnyi podkhod [Effective digital governance: an architectural approach]. Razvitie informatizatsii i gosudarstvennoi sistemy nauchno-tekhnicheskoi informatsii RINTI-2020 [Development of informatization and the state system of scientific and technical information RINTY-2020], pp. 33–40 (2020)

4. Bork, D.: An open platform for modeling method conceptualization: the OMiLAB digital ecosystem. Communications of the Association for Information Systems, pp. 673–679 (2019)

5. OMG: The BPMN specification page. http://www.bpmn.org. Accessed May 2021

6. Chen, P.: The entity-relationship model-toward a unified view of data. ACM Trans. Database Syst. **1**, 9–36 (1976)

7. Software AG: ARIS-the community page. http://www.ariscommunity.com. Accessed May 2021

8. OMG: The UML resource page. http://www.uml.org. Accessed May 2021

9. Reisig, W.: Understanding Petri Nets. Springer, Heidelberg (2013). https://doi.org/10.1007/978-3-642-33278-4

10. Petri, C.A., Reisig, W.: Petri net. Scholarpedia, p. 6477 (2008)

11. Kourbatski, A.: Novaya semantika yazyka IT - eto vam ne angliiskii... [The new semantics of the IT language - this is not English...]. Vesnik suvyazi [Herald of Communication], vol. 6, pp. 30–33 (2020)

12. Kourbatski, A., Zekov, M.: Yazyk obshcheniya v mire, kotorogo nikto ne zhdal [The language of communication in the world that no one expected]. Mezhdunarodnaya zhizn [International Affairs]. https://interaffairs.ru/news/show/27236. Accessed May 2021

13. Golenkov, V., Shunkevich, D., Davydenko, I., Grakova, N.: Principles of organization and automation of the semantic computer systems development. Otkrytye semanticheskie tekhnologii proektirovaniya intellektual'nykh system [Open semantic technologies for intelligent systems], pp. 53–90 (2019)

14. Listopad, S.: Agent interaction protocol of hybrid intelligent multi-agent system of heterogeneous thinking. Otkrytye semanticheskie tekhnologii proektirovaniya intellektual'nykh system [Open semantic technologies for intelligent systems], pp. 51–56 (2020)

15. Kolesnikov, A., Jasinski, E., Rumovskaya, S.: Predicative representations of relations and links of the intellectual operational-technological control in complex dynamic systems. Otkrytye semanticheskie tekhnologii proektirovaniya intellektual'nykh system [Open semantic technologies for intelligent systems], pp. 43–50 (2020)

16. Golenkov, V., Guliakina, N.: Principles of building mass semantic technology-component design of intelligent systems. Otkrytye semanticheskie tekhnologii proektirovaniya intellektual'nykh system [Open semantic technologies for intelligent systems], pp. 21–58 (2011)

Knowledge Ecosystems: An Intelligent Agent for Knowledge Discovery

Viktor Krasnoproshin[1] , Vadim Rodchenko[2] , and Anna Karkanitsa[2]($\boxtimes$)

[1] Belarusian State University, Minsk, Belarus
krasnoproshin@bsu.by
[2] Yanka Kupala State University of Grodno, Grodno, Belarus
{rovar,a.karkanica}@grsu.by

Abstract. One of the major objectives of any knowledge ecosystem is the effective management of its main resource - knowledge. As a general rule, this is to be achieved through developing an environment for interaction between system participants, simplifying the decision-making process and stimulating innovation. The fundamental elements of the knowledge ecosystem are software agents. Located in the ecosystem environment, agents receive data about internal events, interpret them and execute commands that affect the environment. The paper proposes one of the possible implementations of an intelligent agent for knowledge discovery (KD-agent). The input for such an agent is a priori dictionary of features and a training set. As the outcome of the KD-agent activity previously unknown patterns are revealed and can be interpreted within the subject domain. The effectiveness of the proposed approach is demonstrated on the example of model data analysis.

Keywords: Knowledge Ecosystem · Data Mining · Supervised Learning · Training Set

1 Introduction

Any ecosystem is a complex integration project involving a large number of participants. As for the Digital Ecosystem (DE), it is a software and information system that is like a biological ecosystem has the properties of reliability, scalability and self-organization [1]. DE combines various elements of a digital platform, ensures the interaction of these elements and their connection with the world around [2]. The elements of the system include a unified account, digital services for solving various problems, server infrastructure, developer teams, engineers, customers and other stakeholders [3].

The knowledge ecosystem is a complex adaptive system including a database, a knowledge base and experts [4]. The development and implementation of such systems is one of the priority courses of information technologies growth and usage [5].

The knowledge ecosystem is intended to provide high-quality interaction between its various elements for the effective implementation of the decision-making process [6]. The basic elements of the ecosystem are the technology core, critical interdependencies, knowledge agents and performative actions [7].

V. Golenkov et al. (Eds.): OSTIS 2021, CCIS 1625, pp. 89–100, 2022.
https://doi.org/10.1007/978-3-031-15882-7_6

Knowledge agents, while in the ecosystem, receive and interpret data about internal events, and execute commands that have impact on the environment. The most important agents' properties are autonomy, social ability, reactivity and proactivity [8].

The paper proposes one of the possible approaches to building an intelligent agent. The results of its practical use for knowledge discovery are presented. In automatic mode, based on the a priori dictionary of features and the training set, the KD-agent forms a set of informative ensembles of features that ensure classes separation.

2   Agents and Their Properties

The core idea of the Knowledge Ecosystem (KE) is to implement such a knowledge management mechanism when:

- the development of interactions between the participants of the exchange is ensured (see Fig. 1);
- the decision-making process is simplified;
- fostering innovation is ensured through the evolution of collaboration between agents.

Instead of directive management methods, the ecological approach proposes strategies that are based on self-organization in response to external changes.

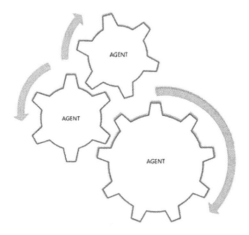

Fig. 1. Interaction of agents.

The development of artificial agent technology in the context of the implementation of multi-agent systems (MAS) and knowledge ecosystems is one of the most important current development trends of information technology [9].

The approaches and requirements for agents in information systems are changing. Within the classical approach, an intelligent agent was considered as a powerful system that has a global vision of the problem and all the necessary abilities, knowledge and resources to solve the problem [10].

Currently, a different approach dominates in MAS. In fact, agents are highly specialized. An individual agent provides a solution to only a certain subproblem, while solving a complex problem requires the interaction of agents within MAS [11]. Agents are considered as complex objects that are able to manipulate other objects. They have the developed tools of interaction with the environment and their own kind.

Each agent is a software- or hardware-based computer system that enjoys the following properties:

- autonomy (or semi-autonomy) is the ability to function without outside interference and at the same time exercise self-control over agent actions and internal states;
- social ability is the ability to interact with other agents by messages exchange using communication tools;
- reactivity is the ability to perceive the state of the external environment;
- proactivity is the ability of agent not only to respond to environment incentives, but also to initiate its own goal-directed behaviors [12].

3   Knowledge Discovery Based on the Analysis of the Feature Ensembles Properties

The development and introduction of new data mining methods and technologies is currently one of the priorities in the growth and practical application of knowledge ecosystems.

The ongoing progress in the development of artificial intelligence technologies is largely due to the wide implementation of machine learning methods based on identifying empirical patterns in datasets [13].

For the learning process an intelligent system is commonly provided with a set of positive and negative examples connected by a previously unknown regularity. As an output, an algorithm that separates examples into two classes (positive and negative) is being generated [14].

The essence of machine learning, therefore, actually is reduced to building decision rules that implicitly express empirical patterns [15]. For example, the result of Supervised Learning is a classification algorithm that is practically useful "black box" [16]. Unfortunately, the algorithm defies interpretation in terms of the subject domain.

Knowledge Discovery in Databases (KDD) is a process of discovering in the initial datasets a previously unknown, useful and interpretable patterns, which are further necessary for effective decision-making [17]. Unfortunately, machine learning methods do not fully satisfy all the KDD requirements. As a rule, they do not allow to interpret the discovered patterns.

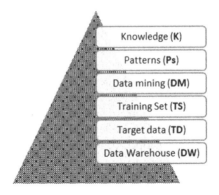

Fig. 2. Patterns detection circuit.

Formally, the process of Knowledge Discovery in Databases can be represented as a sequential execution of the following major stages (see Fig. 2):

$$DW \xrightarrow{S1} TD \xrightarrow{S2} TS \xrightarrow{S3} DM \xrightarrow{S4} Ps \xrightarrow{S5} K,$$

where:
DW – data warehouse;
TD – target dataset;
TS – training set;
DM – Data Mining procedure;
Ps – resulting set of patterns;
K – knowledge;
S1 (Stage 1) – the stage of formulating the goal and objectives of the KDD process and the formation of a target dataset on which the search for patterns will be carried out;
S2 (Stage 2) – the stage of data preprocessing and formation of a training set;
S3 (Stage 3) – execution of the Data Mining procedure;
S4 (Stage 4) – building class patterns;
S5 (Stage 5) – patterns interpretation in terms of the subject domain.

The KDD process begins with the definition of a classes alphabet, the formation of a set of observable characteristics, and the construction of an a priori dictionary of features (PDF). Using the constructed features, the observed objects are described and, on their basis, a training set is formed. Then, for each subset (ensemble) of features from the PDF, estimates of their informativeness (suitability) are calculated for the correct separation of the stated classes.

After that, domains of classes (class patterns) for each combination of features are constructed. And on the results of the analysis of the mutual placement of class patterns, the informativeness of the corresponding ensembles of features are estimated.

The output of KDD process is previously unknown knowledge about the informative value of feature ensembles. The knowledge thus acquired can be interpreted in terms of the subject domain, since each feature in any combination carries a specific semantic load.

4 Knowledge Discovery in Dataset

In Machine Learning, the result of Supervised Learning is a classification algorithm called decision rule.

Traditionally, the learning process is reduced to the construction of decision rules that deliver the extremum of some functional. The families of decision rules are selected a priori with accuracy up to some parameters. And then in the learning process, specific values of the parameters which provide the extremum of the pre-set functional are determined. The dictionary of features is used not only for constructing a training sample. It also defines the feature space where surfaces separating classes are built.

Currently, the Machine Learning methods allows to solve a large number of applied problems that were not trivial until recently. In particular, impressive results have been obtained using artificial neural networks. The latter make it possible to ensure not only a high quality of learning, but also provide for the almost automatic implementation of the Supervised Learning procedure.

However, it should be noted that a significant disadvantage of artificial neural networks and other Machine Learning methods is their narrow focus on building a classification algorithm (classifier). Resulting, it turns out that a useful but modest output of the entire resource-intensive process of preparation (about 80% of all costs) and processing of the training set is only a classifier, which in fact is a "black box".

Thus, the goal-setting of machine learning methods mainly on building classification algorithms turns out to be a weakness of the approach described above. As a result of its implementation, it is possible to learn how to separate class patterns, but at the same time there is no information of any kind about the properties of the classes themselves.

An alternative to the data analysis of the training set can be an approach based on the idea of extracting from PDF some subsets that would provide the separation of classes in a feature subspaces.

Indeed, features themselves and their combinations have varying informativity extent about classes properties. Suppose the a priori dictionary contains n features. Obviously, $2^n - 1$ of every possible combinations (ensembles) of features can be constructed [18]. If we find ensembles by which the classes are well separating in the corresponding feature subspaces, then it can be stated that:

1. Previously unknown patterns of classes properties are discovered;
2. These patterns can be interpreted in the subject domain terms;
3. Based on the revealed properties, the problem of constructing a classifier becomes trivial.

To detect the described ensembles, it is proposed, initially, to build the domains of class definitions based on the data of the training set. Thereafter, in this subspace, we can calculate the estimates of their mutual placement.

In fact, the process described above implements a typical procedure of knowledge discovery in dataset. On its basis, it is proposed to build an intelligent KD-agent that gets as an input a priori dictionary of features and a training set. This agent will automatically process the data and form the patterns it discovers.

5   Algorithm of the Agent

In machine learning, the classification problem has the following statement:

Problem 1. Let the objects descriptions X and the acceptable answers Y for objects classification are given. Suppose there is an unknown target dependency $y^* : X \to Y$, which values $X^m = \{(x_1, y_1), ..., (x_m, y_m)\}$ are known only for the training set objects. It is necessary to construct an algorithm $a : X \to Y$ that would approximate this target dependency not only on the objects of the finite set, but also on the entire set X [19].

The solution to this problem is carried out in two main stages. At first, a certain family of algorithms is specified up to parameters. Then (in the learning process) the values of the parameters are determined providing the extremum of the preselected functional.

The selection of algorithms model (family) $A = \{a : X \to Y\}$ is a far from trivial task. This requires the participation of a qualified specialist. It means that learning is only carried out in an automated mode, but not automatic mode. The following fact is also a serious disadvantage. Resulting algorithm $a : X \to Y$ is a "black box" whose outcomes cannot be interpreted.

An alternative approach to the learning phase which eliminates the indicated disadvantages is proposed. Let's consider the following statement of the above-mentioned problem:

Problem 2. Let the objects descriptions X and the acceptable answers of objects classification Y are given. Supposing there is an unknown target dependency $y^* : X \to Y$, which values $X^m = \{(x_1, y_1), ..., (x_m, y_m)\}$ are only known for the training set objects. It is required to find feature subspaces where patterns do not intersect [20].

Suppose that the training set $X^m = \{(x_1, y_1), ..., (x_m, y_m)\}$ be formed on the basis of the dictionary of features $F = \{f_1, ..., f_n\}$. Let $V = \{v_1, ..., v_q\}$ denote the set of all possible combinations (ensembles) of features from F. Obviously, V contains $q = \sum_{i=1}^{n} C_n^i = 2^n - 1$ subsets.

The algorithm of constructing feature subspaces $V^* = \{v_1^*, ..., v_k^*\}$, where class patterns do not intersect is as follows:

Step 1. In the set V, n combinations $V^+ = \{v_1^+, ..., v_n^+\}$, that contain one feature are being selected. For each individual feature, class patterns are built and their mutual placement is estimated [21]. If the patterns do not intersect, then the feature is included in the resulting set V^* The combinations that contain this feature are excluded from the set V. If the patterns intersect, then the feature is excluded from V.

Step 2. Let $V^\Delta = \{v_1^\Delta, ..., v_p^\Delta\}$ denote by the subset obtained as a result of the set V transformation at the previous step. For each individual combination from V^Δ, class patterns are built and their mutual placement is estimated.

If the patterns do not intersect, then the combination of features is included in the resulting set V^*. And all elements that contain this combination are being excluded from V.

If the patterns intersect, then the combination is excluded from V^Δ. The process is repeated until V^Δ becomes empty.

As a result of the analysis of all elements from $V = \{v_1, ..., v_q\}$ (possible combinations of features from the dictionary $F = \{f_1, ..., f_n\}$) a set $V^* = \{v_1^*, ..., v_t^*\}$ will be constructed, where $0 \leq t \leq q$.

Based on each individual ensemble of features $v_i^* \in V^*$, we formulate a previously unknown, empirically revealed pattern: *in the feature space of the subset v_i^* the classes do not intersect*. It should be noted that within a specific applied problem, each combination of features v_i^* can be interpreted by a subject domain expert [22].

Thus as an input, the KD-agent receives an a priory dictionary of features $F = \{f_1, ..., f_n\}$ and the training set $X^m = \{(x_1, y_1), ..., (x_m, y_m)\}$. Based on the above algorithm, agent forms the set $V^* = \{v_1^*, ..., v_t^*\}$, where $0 \leq t \leq q$ (see Fig. 3).

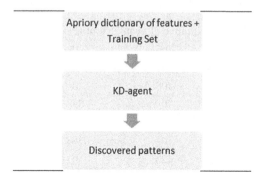

Fig. 3. KD-agent workflow.

It is worth to mention that the so constructed KD-agent satisfies all major characteristics subjecting to agents in multi-agent systems (autonomy, local views, decentralization).

6   The Outcomes of the Intelligent Agent's Usage

Let's demonstrate the efficiency of the KD-agent by the example of analyzing the training set data aiming to reveal hidden patterns. Let the given:

– number classes - *even* and *odd*;
– a priori dictionary of features F = {units, tens, hundreds, thousands, tens of thousands, hundreds of thousands, millions};

– training set of seven-bit integers, which contains 2000 even and 2000 odd numbers.

Table 1 shows the results of researching the intersection of class patterns based on the feature *units*, where

$$NE_i = Number\ of\ even_i$$
$$NO_i = Number\ of\ odd_i$$

$$a_i = \begin{cases} NE_i + NO_i, NE_i = 0 \vee NO_i = 0 \\ 0, NE_i > 0 \wedge NO_i > 0 \end{cases}$$

$$Intersection = \frac{\sum_{i=0}^{9} NE_i + \sum_{i=0}^{9} NO_i - \sum_{i=0}^{9} a_i}{\sum_{i=0}^{9} NE_i + \sum_{i=0}^{9} NO_i} * 100\%$$

Table 1 shows that even numbers are lack of 1, 3, 5, 7, 9 in the unit's digit, and odd numbers are lack of 0, 2, 4, 6, 8. In addition, the *units* feature provides an absolute separation of the classes *even* and *odd* since the *Intersection = 0%*.

Table 1. Experiment results for the feature *units*.

Digit	Number of even	Number of odd
0	405	0
1	0	415
2	408	0
3	0	398
4	373	0
5	0	383
6	423	0
7	0	404
8	391	0
9	0	400

Table 2 shows the analysis results for the feature *tens*. It could be seen therefore that this feature has no the property of class separation since *Intersection = 100.0%*.

Table 3 shows the analysis results for the feature *hundreds*. It could be seen that this feature has no the property of class separation since *Intersection = 100.0%*. Tables 4, 5, 6 present the analysis results for the features *thousands, tens of thousands, hundreds of thousands, millions*. The tables show that these features do not have the property of class separation neither, since *Intersection = 100.0%*. The feature *millions* has no the property of class separation as well. It could be seen from the Table 7.

Table 2. Experiment results for the feature *tens*.

Digit	Number of even	Number of odd
0	204	192
1	201	204
2	205	190
3	190	216
4	203	191
5	183	216
6	200	192
7	216	194
8	197	195
9	201	210

Table 3. Experiment results for the feature *hundreds*.

Digit	Number of even	Number of odd
0	196	218
1	186	181
2	206	193
3	191	215
4	208	217
5	189	177
6	211	219
7	183	191
8	216	181
9	214	208

Table 4. Experiment results for the feature *thousands*.

Digit	Number of even	Number of odd
0	194	205
1	198	202
2	217	201
3	193	217
4	216	184
5	181	185
6	192	194
7	192	201
8	214	214
9	203	188

Table 5. Experiment results for the feature *tens of thousands*.

Digit	Number of even	Number of odd
0	196	226
1	211	176
2	204	211
3	182	177
4	202	208
5	192	190
6	218	199
7	204	210
8	189	192
9	202	211

Table 6. Experiment results for the feature *hundreds of thousands*.

Digit	Number of even	Number of odd
0	192	213
1	229	178
2	173	206
3	192	202
4	216	190
5	194	208
6	185	196
7	219	212
8	194	198
9	206	197

Table 7. Experiment results for the feature *millions*.

Digit	Number of even	Number of odd
0	201	211
1	212	211
2	193	187
3	174	190
4	189	191
5	210	181
6	208	204
7	196	210
8	218	212
9	199	203

Table 8. Experiment results for all features.

Feature name	Intersection (%)
units	0.0
tens	100.0
hundreds	100.0
thousands	100.0
tens of thousands	100.0
hundreds of thousands	100.0
millions	100.0

Table 8 shows the results of the analysis for all features from the a priori dictionary. Let's note that the algorithm running time spent on solving this problem was only 0.09 s.

7 Conclusion

The paper presents one of the possible options for implementing an intelligent agent for knowledge discovery. The input for such an agent is the a priori dictionary of features and the training set. In automatic mode, the intelligent agent detects previously unknown patterns that can be interpreted in terms of the corresponding subject domain.

The results of the KD-agent's activity can later be used by other ecosystem agents. The effectiveness of the proposed approach is demonstrated by the example of the model data analysis when solving a nontrivial mathematical problem.

References

1. Kumar, P., Jain, V., Ponnusamy, V.: The Smart Cyber Ecosystem for Sustainable Development. Wiley-Scrivener Publishing, Hoboken (2021)
2. Curry, E., Metzger, A., Zillner, S., Pazzaglia, J.-C., Robles, A.C.: The Elements of Big Data Value: Foundations of the Research and Innovation Ecosystem. Springer, Cham (2021). https://doi.org/10.1007/978-3-030-68176-0
3. Jahankhani, H., O'Dell, L., Bowen, G., Hagan, D., Jamal, A.: Strategy, Leadership, and AI in the Cyber Ecosystem: The Role of Digital Societies in Information Governance and Decision Making. Academic Press, Cambridge (2021)
4. Szoniecky, S.: Ecosystems Knowledge: Modeling and Analysis Method for Information and Communication. Wiley, Hoboken (2018)
5. Knowledge ecosystem. https://en.wikipedia.org/wiki/Knowledge_ecosystem. Accessed 15 Oct 2021
6. Choo, C.W., Bontis, N.: The Strategic Management of Intellectual Capital and Organizational Knowledge. Oxford University Press, Oxford (2002)
7. Russel, S., Norving, P.: Artificial Intelligence: A Modern Approach. Williams Publishing House, Moscow (2006)

8. AIportal. http://www.aiportal.ru/articles/multiagent-systems/weak-and-strong-intelligent-agent.html. Accessed 15 Oct 2021
9. Luger, G.F.: Artificial Intelligence: Structures and Strategies for Complex Problem Solving. Williams Publishing House, Moscow (2003)
10. Multi-agent system. https://en.wikipedia.org/wiki/Multi-agent_system. Accessed 15 Oct 2021
11. Wooldridge, M.: An Introduction to MultiAgent Systems, 2nd edn. Wiley, Hoboken (2009)
12. Tarasov, V.: Artificial meta-intelligence: a key to enterprise reengineering. In: Proceedings of the 2nd Joint Conference on Knowledge-Based Software Engineering (JCKBSE 1996), Sozopol, Bulgaria, 21–22 September 1996, pp. 15–24. Sofia BAIA (1996)
13. Flach, P.: Machine Learning: The Art and Science of Algorithms that Make Sense of Data. DMK Press, Moscow (2015)
14. Machine Learning. https://en.wikipedia.org/wiki/Machine_learning. Accessed 15 Oct 2021
15. Krasnoproshin, V.V., Rodchanka, V.G.: Learning by precedents based on the analysis of the features properties. Doklady BGUIR **108**(6), 35–41 (2017)
16. Krasnoproshin, V.V., Rodchenko, V.G.: Analiz prostranstv reshenij v zadachah obucheniya po precedentam. Vestnik Brestskogo gosudarstvennogo tekhnicheskogo universiteta. Seriya: Fizika matematika informatika **107**(5), 20–23 (2017)
17. Data mining. https://en.wikipedia.org/wiki/Data_mining. Accessed 15 Oct 2021
18. Vadim, R.: Pattern recognition: supervised learning on the basis of cluster structures. In: Krasnoproshin, V.V., Ablameyko, S.V. (eds.) PRIP 2016. CCIS, vol. 673, pp. 106–113. Springer, Cham (2017). https://doi.org/10.1007/978-3-319-54220-1_11
19. Supervised learning. https://en.wikipedia.org/wiki/Supervised_learning. Accessed 15 Oct 2021
20. Rodchenko, V.: Automatic detection of hidden regularities based on the study of class properties. Pattern Recognit. Image Anal. **30**(2), 224–229 (2020). https://doi.org/10.1134/S1054661820020145
21. Krasnoproshin, V.V., Rodchanka, V.G.: Cluster structures and their applications in data mining. Informatics (2), 71–77 (2016)
22. Krasnoproshin, V.V., Rodchanka, V.G.: Classification based on decision spaces. Doklady BGUIR (6), 20–25 (2019)

Ontology-Based Design of Hybrid Problem Solvers

Daniil Shunkevich[(✉)] [iD]

Belarusian State University of Informatics and Radioelectronics,
Minsk, Republic of Belarus
shunkevich@bsuir.by

Abstract. The creation of problem solvers for intelligent computer systems based on the OSTIS Technology is discussed from an ontological perspective in this study. It is now possible to describe the ideas of a problem-solving model and a problem solver on the basis of the formal interpretation of terms like action, problem, class of actions, class of problems, method, and skill. The collected results will increase the effectiveness of the component approach to problem solving and automation tools for problem solving.

Keywords: OSTIS · problem solver · multiagent system · problem-solving model · ontological approach

1 Introduction

The results presented in this work complement and expand the results considered in the work [27].

An intelligent system's capacity to solve a variety of problems depends heavily on the problem solver (together with the knowledge base). When compared to other modern software systems, intelligent system problem solvers are unique in that they must find information based on a variety of criteria when the information needed is not explicitly localized in the intelligent system's knowledge base [26].

A special problem solver is currently being developed for each unique intelligent system, the composition of which is determined by a set of classes of problems that the appropriate intelligent system should solve. In contrast to the early days of the development of artificial intelligence technologies, when scientists searched for a long time for some universal mechanism that would allow solving any problem, today's problem solvers are being developed specifically for each unique intelligent system. Each category of problems typically has a *problem-solving model* that it matches to. Many of these models have been created recently in the field of artificial intelligence, some of which are regarded as traditional (for instance, classical algorithms, procedural programs, and object-oriented programming), and others of which are regarded as intelligent (neural network models, logical models, genetic algorithms).

Supported by the BRFFR (BRFFR-RFFR No. F21RM-139).

The expansion of the scope of intelligent systems requires such systems to be able to solve complex problems, the solution of each of which involves the joint usage of many different knowledge representation models and various problem-solving models. In addition, the solution of complex problems implies the usage of common informational resources (in the limiting case – of the entire knowledge base of an intelligent system) by various components of the solver focused on solving various subproblems. Since the solver of complex problems integrates various problem-solving models, we will call it a *hybrid problem solver* [26].

Making sure that there is a chance to gain project experience in the creation of problem solvers and that the solver's components can be reused, together with the ability to integrate several problem solving models within a single solver, is a crucial responsibility.

The compatibility of the components of software systems at the semantic level is ensured by coordinating the systems of concepts used within such components, which in turn implies the development of appropriate ontologies common to a certain family of components.

Back in the 1990s, a series of papers was published devoted to the ontological approach to the integration of problem solving methods and the formation of libraries of reusable problem solving methods [3–5,7,11,12,17,24,28,31], important practical results in this direction were obtained within the CLEPE [17] and PROTEGE II [25] systems.

Unfortunately, the level of development of technical means at that time did not allow to fully implement all the ideas expressed by the authors of mentioned works, and since the 2000s, work in the development of problem solvers has mainly focused on the development of new methods for solving problems, and not on accumulation and systematization of already existing implementations. Possible reasons for this were, on the one hand, an objective decrease in the labor intensity of developing software systems and their components by increasing the level of programming languages and related tools, including subprograms libraries, and on the other hand, a sharp increase in the variety of possible ways to implement the same software component, which greatly complicates the integration of components, not even at the semantic, but at the syntactic level.

In addition, the disadvantages of early works devoted to the ontological approach to unifying methods for solving problems and accumulating the corresponding components include the following:

– Despite the fact that the issue of integration of methods for solving problems is being considered, as a rule, we mean similar methods, for example, deductive inference according to different sets of rules. Integration of such heterogeneous methods of solving problems as, for example, logical methods (including fuzzy, temporal, non-binary and other non-classical logical methods), neural network methods, genetic algorithms and other methods widely used at present is not considered. In fairness, it is worth noting that many of the listed methods at that time were either generally unknown or not so widely used. Thus, the developed solvers cannot be considered fully hybrid, taking into account the requirements put forward, for example, in [26].

- The problem solver is considered in a narrow sense, that is, as a system component designed only for solving certain classes of problems related to the direct functionality of the system, while an intelligent system is forced to face the need to solve a large number of problems related to ensuring its stable work, in particular, analyzing and maintaining the quality of its components, for example, the knowledge base. A problem solver that implements all of these features will be called a *combined problem solver* [13];
- There is no common formal basis (standard) for the development of ontologies, which leads to the fact that ontologies of tasks and methods for their solution are developed separately within each project and, thus, their compatibility is also guaranteed only within a single project;
- The principles of integration of various problem solving methods within the framework of one solver are not detailed and it is not specified what such integration actually boils down to and how it is carried out;
- As a continuation of the previous point, there is no general methodology for developing solver components and the solvers themselves based on these components. At the same time, it should be noted that tools for developing solvers are proposed, so we can say that within the framework of such tools there is implicitly a certain methodology, which, nevertheless, is not considered in isolation from the tools and is not formalized itself;
- Basic concepts such as *problem solver, problem, problem solving method, problem solving model, problem solving strategy* and others are not specified formally (ontologically).

Modern approaches to the construction of hybrid problem solvers, as a rule, involve a combination of heterogeneous problem-solving models without any single basis, for example, using specialized software interfaces between different components of the system, which leads to considerable overhead costs when developing such a system and especially when its modifying, including when adding a new problem-solving model to the system [26].

Nevertheless, modern works also consider attempts to unify the classes of problems and tasks and methods for their solution based on ontologies, at least within the framework of specific applied systems [2,9,29].

An approach to hybrid solver development that addresses existing problems in solver design, and in particular, allows them to be modifiable is proposed within the framework of the OSTIS Technology [13,14].

Within the framework of this approach, the problem solver is interpreted as a hierarchical system of agents (sc-agents) that work on shared semantic memory (sc-memory) and interact by the specification of the actions they perform within this memory. It is assumed that each problem-solving model corresponds to some sc-agent (most often – a non-atomic one that could be decomposed into simpler sc-agents). Thus, it becomes possible to combine different problem-solving models when solving the same complex problem as well as to add new problem-solving models to the solver or exclude them without having to make modifications in its other components.

However, the further development of this approach and, in particular, its usage when developing various applied intelligent systems has shown that the capabilities of the problem solver are also in large part determined by the quality of the knowledge base of the appropriate intelligent system. It may safely be said that the approach to the development of solvers discussed above is connected with the description of the *operational semantics* of the solver, that is, interpreters of the appropriate problem-solving models, while it is obvious that for solving problems it is also necessary to describe the *declarative semantics* of the problem-solving model, that is, the texts of programs itself (not the programs of sc-agents but higher-level programs interpreted by the corresponding set of sc-agents), logical statements, certain configurations of artificial neural networks, etc.

Within the framework of the OSTIS Technology, powerful tools have been developed that allow describing any type of knowledge in a unified form, structuring the knowledge base according to various criteria as well as verifying its quality and editing the knowledge base directly in its use [8].

Nevertheless, even in the case of unification of the representation of the processed knowledge, the capabilities of the problem solver largely depend on the knowledge base:

- concepts used in sc-agent programs should be described in an appropriate set of ontologies, these descriptions should be "supplied" with the problem solver;
- the same collective of sc-agents, depending on the body of knowledge presented in the knowledge base at the current moment, can solve problems of completely different classes or problems of the same class but in different ways;
- it is advisable to be able to solve problems of the same class in different ways and accumulate the corresponding components (and entire solvers) that would have the corresponding specification.

The basis of the knowledge base created using the OSTIS Technology is a hierarchical system of subject domains and the corresponding ontologies. An ontology is interpreted as a specification of the system of concepts of the corresponding subject domain, while various types of ontologies are distinguished, each of which reflects a certain set of the concept features of the subject domain, for example, *terminological ontology, logical ontology, set-theoretic ontology*, etc. Speaking about ontologies in the context of this paper, we will have in mind an integrated ontology, which is a combination of ontologies of all types that correspond to a specific subject domain.

2 Proposed Approach

Within the framework of this paper, it is proposed to take as a basis the approaches to the development of hybrid problem solvers and hybrid knowledge bases proposed within the context of the OSTIS Technology, to formally clarify and coordinate the interpretation of such concepts as *problem, problem-solving model, problem solver, skill* and others within the appropriate set of ontologies and on the basis of the results obtained to clarify the actual model of the hybrid problem solver, which would allow taking into account the above-mentioned aspects.

The systems developed on the basis of the OSTIS Technology are called *ostis-systems*. The *OSTIS Technology* is based on a universal method of semantic representation (encoding) of information in memory of intelligent computer systems called *SC-code*. Texts of the *SC-code* (sc-texts) are unified semantic networks with a basic set-theoretic interpretation. The elements of such semantic networks are called *sc-elements* (*sc-nodes* and *sc-connectors*, which, in turn, can be *sc-arcs* or *sc-edges*, depending on the directivity). The *SC-code Alphabet* consists of five main elements, on the basis of which SC-code constructs of any complexity are built as well as more particular types of sc-elements (for example, new concepts) are introduced. Memory that stores the SC-code constructs is called semantic memory or *sc-memory*.

Within the framework of the technology, several universal variants of visualization of the *SC-code* constructs are also proposed, such as *SCg-code* (graphic version), *SCn-code* (non-linear hypertextual version), *SCs-code* (linear string version).

As it was mentioned earlier, the basis of the knowledge base within the framework of the OSTIS Technology is a hierarchical system of subject domains and ontologies. From there, to solve the problems set within the framework of this paper, it is proposed to develop a complex *Subject domain of actions and problems and the corresponding ontology of problem-solving methods and models*.

Within the framework of this paper, fragments of structured texts in the SCn-code [1] will often be used, which are simultaneously fragments of source texts of the knowledge base, which are understandable both to a human and to a machine. This allows making the text more structured and formalized while maintaining its readability. The symbol ":=" in such texts indicates alternative (synonymous) names of the described entity, which reveal in more detail some of its features.

The development of the specified family of sc-models of subject domains and ontologies will allow:

- relating the class of problems and the approach (method) used to solve them explicitly;
- Since the appropriate component combined with the group of sc-agents will also include the necessary fragments of the knowledge base, which are a priori squared with the specified group of sc-agents, this will enable the accumulation of more complex solver components and greatly simplify their integration;
- As a result, it will be possible to increase the intelligence of the automation tools for developing solvers, namely by automating the process of choosing solver components based on the specification of classes of problems that the developed intelligent system should be able to solve;
- in the future, this will allow the intelligent system to independently access the library of problem solver components and select components based on new classes of problems that the system has encountered, that is, it will allow the intelligent system to independently learn new *skills*;
- however, this method will enable the intelligent system to choose a combination of problem-solving models on its own for solving problems of a specific

class (more exactly, since the solver is based on a multiagent approach, a group of sc-agents that interpret different problem-solving models will be able to determine better, which of the sc-agents and in what order should work when solving a specific complex problem).

The subject areas and ontologies discribed in this work were developed on the basis of the theory of subject-object influences proposed in the work of V. Martynov and his colleagues [15, 16, 19–21], and also taking into account the ontologies of actions, considered in detail in the works [18, 30].

In addition, since the concepts of a very high level of abstraction are researched within the framework of the *Subject domain and ontology of actions and tasks*, its development takes into account the results considered in related works from the field of philosophy [6, 22, 23].

Consider next in more detail fragments of sc-models of specified subject domains and ontologies. The full version of the considered *Subject domain of actions and tasks and the corresponding ontology of methods for problem solving* is presented within the framework of the current version of the OSTIS Standard [13].

3   Concept of an Action and the Classification of Actions

It is required to formally define the concepts of a problem and an action intended to solve a specific problem or its subproblems before moving on to problem-solving models and the problem solver.

Within the framework of the *OSTIS Technology*, we will interpret the problem as a formal specification of some action, so it is reasonable at first to clarify the concept of an *action*. Let us consider the specification of the concept *action* in the SCn-code.

action
:=   [a purposeful process performed by one or more subjects (cybernetical systems) with the possible usage of certain tools]
:=   [a process of influencing some (possibly shared) entity (the subject of influence) on one or several entities (objects of influence – source objects (arguments) or target (created or modified) objects)]
:=   [an act]
:=   [an operation]
:=   [an actio]
:=   [an active influence]
:=   [a conscious influence]
⊂   *influence*
      ⊂   *process*
      :=   [a process, in which at least one influencing entity (the subject of influence ′) and at least one entity that is being influenced (the object of influence ′) can be clearly distinguished)]

:=   [a purposeful ("conscious") process performed (managed, implemented)
        by some subject]

:=   [a process of solving some problem]

:=   [a purposeful process managed by some subject]

⇒   *subdividing**:

functional complexity of the action ˆ

=   {•   *elementary action*

      :=   [action performed by an individual cybernetic sys-
          tem]

      ⇒   *explanation**:

      [An elementary action is performed by one individ-
      ual subject and is either an elementary action per-
      formed in the memory of this subject (an elemen-
      tary action of his "processor"), or an elementary
      action of one of his effectors.]

  •   *complex action*

      :=   [non-atomic action]

      :=   [non-elementary action]

      :=   [an action whose execution requires the decomposi-
          tion of this action into a set of its <u>sub-actions</u>, i.e.
          private actions of a lower level]

      ⇒   *cover**:

      {•   *easily accomplished complex action*

          :=   [complex action, for the execution of
              which the corresponding *method* and
              the source data corresponding to this
              method are known, as well as (for
              actions performed in the external
              environment) all the necessary source
              objects (consumables and equipment)
              are available, as well as the tools.]

        •   *intelligent action*

          :=   [difficult to perform complex action]

          :=   [a complex action, for the execution
              of which either the corresponding
              method is unknown, or the possible
              methods are known, but there are no
              conditions for their application.]

          ⊃   *an action for which the goal is known
              is not entirely accurate*

          ⊃   *an action for which a method is not
              known a priori that ensures its
              execution*

      }

  }

⇒   *subdividing*:*
    location of the action ˆ
    =   {•   *action, performed in the memory of the subject of
             the action*
             :=   [information action]
        •   *action, performed in the external environment of
             the subject of action*
             :=   [behavioral action]
        •   *effector action*
        •   *receptor action*
    }
⇒   *subdividing*:*
    multi-agent action execution ˆ
    =   {•   *individual action*
             ⊃   *individual action performed by a computer
                  system*
             ⊃   *individual action performed by a person*
        •   *collective action*
             ⊃   *action performed by a collective of individual
                  computer systems*
             ⊃   *action performed by a team of people*
             ⊃   *action performed by a collective of people
                  and individual computer systems*
    }
⇒   *subdividing*:*
    current state of the action ˆ
    =   {•   *planned action*
        •   *triggered action*
        •   *action in progress*
        •   *interrupted action*
        •   *completed action*
             ⇒   *subdividing*:*
                  {•   *unsuccessfully completed action*
                       ⊃   *action, completed with an error*
                   •   *successfully completed action*
                  }
        •   *cancelled action*
    }

Decomposition of a complex action into sub-actions can have a very complex hierarchical form with a large number of hierarchical levels, i.e. *complex action* sub-actions can also be *complex action.* The overall number of sub-actions in an action and the number of levels in the hierarchy of those sub-actions both contribute to its complexity.

Another illustration is developing the same procedural program in two different programming languages, one at a higher and one at a lower level. In this instance, the language level tightly defines the elementary nature of acts.

The temporal relationships between *sub-actions* of a complex *action* can be very different, but in the simplest case *complex action* is a strict sequence of *actions* at a lower level of the hierarchy.

A *complex action* may include not only *actually sub-actions* of this *complex action*, but also special *sub-actions* that <u>control</u> the process of *complex action*, and, in particular, *sub-actions*, which initiate sub-actions, transfer control to *sub-actions*.

The result of performing an **action, performed in the memory of the subject of the action** is generically a certain new state of information system memory (not necessarily of *sc-memory*) achieved only by transforming the information stored in system memory, that is, either by generating new knowledge based on existing ones or by deleting knowledge that has become unnecessary for whatever reason. It should be noted that if the question is about changing the state of *sc-memory*, then any transformation of information can be reduced to some atomic actions of generating, deleting or changing the incidence of *sc-elements* relative to each other.

In the case of a **action, performed in the external environment of the subject of action**, the result of its performance will be a new state of the environment. It is crucial to keep in mind that the environment in this context also refers to system components that are external from the perspective of memory, meaning they are not information structures that are kept there. The behavior of a robot's mechanical limb can be changed, or information can be displayed directly on the screen for the user's experience, as examples of such components include various manipulators and other ways of affecting the system on the outside environment.

From the point of view of the problem solving formulated in this paper, the informational actions performed in memory of the ostis-system, that is, *actions in sc-memory*, promote outstanding interest. The classification of *actions in sc-memory* is presented in the knowledge base of the *IMS. ostis Metasystem* that describes the documentation of the current state of the *OSTIS Technology* [1,13].

4 Concept of a Problem and the Classification of Problems

Within the framework of this work, the terms *task* and *problem* will be considered synonymous (equivalent).

A *problem* will be interpreted as a specification of some action, within which, depending on the situation, the context of the action performance, the way of its performance, the performer, the customer, the planned result, etc. can be specified in advance using the relations listed above.

Let us consider the specification of the concept *problem* in the SCn-code.

problem
:=   [a description of some desirable state or event either in the knowledge base or in the environment]
:=   [a problem situation]
:=   [a problem definition]
:=   [a problem description]
:=   [a task for performing some action]
:=   [a specification of some action that has sufficient completeness to perform this action]

Each **problem** is a specification of an action that either has already been performed, or is currently being performed, or is planned (should) be performed, or can be performed (but not necessarily). Depending on the specific class of problems, both the internal state of the intelligent system itself and the required state of the environment can be described.

Within each subject domain, classification of problems can be done on a didactic basis. Examples include triangle problems, problems involving sets of equations, etc.

Each *problem* can include:

- the fact that an *action* belongs to some particular class of *actions* (for example, *action. form a complete semantic neighborhood of the specified entity*), including the state of the *action* from the point of view of the life cycle (initiated, performed, etc.);
- a description of the *purpose** (*result**) of the *action*, if it is exactly known;
- specifying the action *customer**;
- specifying the action *performer** (including a collective one);
- specifying a tool or mediator of the *action*;
- specifying the *action argument(-s)'*;
- a description of the *action decomposition**;
- specifying a *sequence of actions** within the *action decomposition**, i.e., construction of a procedural plan for solving the problem. In other words, the construction of a solution plan is a decomposition of the corresponding *action* into a system of interconnected sub-actions;
- specifying the condition for initiating the *action*;
- specifying the domain of the *action*;
- the moment of the starting and ending the *action*, including the planned and actual ones, the expected and/or actual duration of the performance.

The context, or additional details regarding the entities taken into account in the problem definition, i.e., a description of what is given and what is known about these things, might help clarify some problems.

In addition, a *problem* can include any additional information about the action, for example:

- the limitation of information that can be applied to a particular problem, for instance, solving an algebra problem must only employ statements covered in the school curriculum up to and including the seventh grade and not high school-level statements;

- a list of the means and resources that should be employed to solve the problem, such as a list of performers, deadlines, money sources, etc.;
- the restriction of the domain, in which the *action* is performed, for example, one *sc-construct* must be replaced by another according to some rule but only within some *knowledge base section*;
- etc.

As in the case of actions solved by the system, it is possible to classify *informational problems* and *behavioral problems*.

On the other hand, from the point of view of the problem definition, *declarative problem definitions* and *procedural problem definitions* can be distinguished. It should be noted that these classes of problems are not opposed to each other and there may be problem definitions that use both approaches.

problem
⊂   *knowledge*
⊃   *question*
⊃   *command*
⊃   *initiated problem*
    :=   [a problem definition to be performed]
⊃   *procedural problem definition*
⊃   *declarative problem definition*
⊃   *declarative-procedural problem definition*
    :=   [a problem, in the definition of which there are both declarative (target) and procedural aspects]
⊃   *problem solved in memory of a cybernetical system*
    ⊃   *problem solved in memory of an individual cybernetical system*
    ⊃   *problem solved in shared memory of a multiagent system*
    :=   [an informational problem]
    :=   [a problem aimed either at <u>generation</u> or search for information that meets the specified requirements or at some <u>transformation</u> of the specified information]
    ⊃   *mathematical problem*

The *problem* definition may not contain an indication of the context (solution domain) of the *problem* (in this case, the *problem* solution domain is either the entire *knowledge base* or its compliant part) and may also not contain either a description of the underlying situation or a description of the target situation. For example, a description of the target situation for an explicitly specified contradiction found in a *knowledge base* is not required.

Declarative problem definition is a description of the underlying (initial) situation, which is a condition for performing the corresponding action, and the target (final) situation, which is the result of performing this action, that is, a description of the situation (state) that would be produced if the intended action was carried out. In other words, such a problem definition has a description, whether explicit or implicit, of:

– what is <u>given</u> – the source data, conditions for performing a specified action;
– what is <u>required</u> – the definition of the purpose and the result of performing the specified action.

In the case of the **_procedural problem definition_**, the characteristic of the action specified by this problem is explicitly indicated, namely, for example:

– a subject or subjects that perform this action;
– objects, on which the action is performed – arguments of the action;
– tools that are used to perform the action;
– the time and any other circumstances that may apply for initiating and terminating the action;
– a class or classes that each *action* belongs to (including sub-actions) are explicitly specified.

However, it is not made clear what the outcome of doing the associated action should be.

Let us note that, if necessary, the *procedural problem definition* can be reduced to the *declarative problem definition* by translating based on some rule, for example, of the definition of the class of actions through a more general class.

Particular types of problems are a *question* and a *command*.

question
:=   [a request]
⊂   *problem solved in memory of a cybernetical system*
:=   [a non-procedural problem definition for searching (in the current state of the knowledge base) or for generating knowledge that meets the specified requirements]
⊃   *question – what is it*
⊃   *question – how*
⊃   *question – wherefore*
⊃   *question – why*
　　　　:=   [a request for a method (way) for solving a given (specified) type of problems or class of problems or a plan for solving a particular specified problem]
:=   [a problem aimed at satisfying the information needs of a certain subject-customer]

command
:=   [an initiated problem]
:=   [a specification of the initiated action]

It should be noted that there should be a classification of problems from the point of view of their semantics, or in terms of the essence of the specified action, in addition to the given extremely general classification of problems, which inherently reflects the classes of problems from the point of view of their definition. This classification can be based on the classification presented in [10].

Within the framework of this paper, as already mentioned, the problems solved in sc-memory promote outstanding interest.

5   Relations Defined on Actions and Concept of Complex Action Plan

On the set of actions a number of relations are defined [1,13]. Let's take a closer look at some of them.

relation defined on the set*(action)
$\ni$ *sub-action**
  $\Leftrightarrow$ *inverse relation*:*
        superaction*
$\ni$ *problem**
  $\Rightarrow$ *subdividing*:*
        {•   *procedural problem definition**
            $\Rightarrow$ *second domain*:*
                procedural problem definition
          •   *declarative problem definition**
            $\Rightarrow$ *second domain*:*
                declarative problem definition
        }
$\ni$ *plan**
$\ni$ *action initial situation**
$\ni$ *action context**
  :=   [information resource required to perform a given action*]
$\ni$ *target**
$\ni$ *set of used methods**
  :=   [operational (functional) resource required to perform a given action*]
$\ni$ *declarative specification for performing an action**
$\ni$ *protocol**
$\ni$ *effective part of the protocol**

As already noted, complex or intelligent actions are of the greatest interest for intelligent systems. The implementation of such actions involves the construction of a **plan** for their implementation based on some criteria.

complex action plan
$\subset$ *knowledge*
:=   [specification of the associated action, specifying <u>how</u> the action is supposed to be performed]
:=   [plan]
$\Rightarrow$ *subdividing*:*

{•   *complex action procedural plan*
       :=   [decomposition of a *complex action* into a set of sequentially
              and/or parallel *sub actions*]
 •   *complex action non-procedural plan*
       :=   [decomposition of the original *problem* corresponding to the
              given *complex action* into a hierarchical system and/or sub-
              problems]
}

Each *plan* is a *semantic neighborhood*, the key sc-element' of which is *action*,
for which the proposed process of its execution is additionally detailed. The main
task of such detailing is to localize the area of the knowledge base in which it is
supposed to work, as well as the set of agents required to perform the described
action. At the same time, detailing does not necessarily have to be brought to
the level of elementary actions, the purpose of drawing up a plan is to clarify an
approach to solving a particular problem, which does not always involve drawing
up a detailed step-by-step solution.

When describing the *plan*, both procedural and declarative approaches can
be used. In the case of a procedural approach, for the corresponding *action* indicates its decomposition into more particular sub-actions, as well as the necessary
specification of these sub-actions. In the case of a declarative approach, a set of
subgoals is indicated (for example, using logical statements), the achievement of
which is necessary to perform the considered *action*. In practice, both considered
approaches can be combined.

In general, *plan* can also contain variables, for example, in the case when
a part of the plan is specified in the form of a cycle (multiple repetitions of a
set of actions). Also, the plan may contain constants, the value of which is not
currently set and will become known, for example, only after the execution of
the preceding *actions*.

Each *plan* can be predefined as part of the *action* specification, i.e. *tasks*, or
subjects can be formed already in the process of *actions* performing, for example,
in the case of using the strategy of splitting a task into subtasks. In the first case,
the *plan* is *included** in the *task* corresponding to the same action.

In the *complex action procedural plan*, the corresponding *sub-actions** of the
complex action being decomposed are represented by their specifying *tasks*. But,
in addition to this kind of *tasks*, *complex action procedural plan* also includes
tasks, which specify *actions* that provide:

□ synchronization of execution of *sub-actions** of a given *complex action*
□ transfer of control to the specified *sub-actions** (more precisely, to the
corresponding *tasks*), i.e. initiation of the specified *sub-actions** (and the
corresponding *tasks*).

action to control the interpretation of a complex action procedural plan
⊃   *unconditional transfer of control from one sub-action to another*
⊃   *initiation of a given sub-action when a situation or event of a given type occurs in the knowledge base*
⊃   *initiation of a given set of sub-actions upon successful completion of <u>at least one</u> sub-action of another given set*
⊃   *initiation of a given set of sub-actions upon successful completion of <u>all</u> sub-actions of another given set*

6   Concepts of a Class of Actions and a Class of Problems

From the point of view of the organization of the problem-solving process, the concepts of an *action* and a *problem* are not more important than the concepts of a *class of actions* and a *class of problems*, since it is for them that the appropriate performance algorithms and solution methods are being developed.

Let us define a **class of actions** as a <u>maximal</u> set of coincident (similar in a certain way) actions, for which there is (but is not necessarily currently known) at least one **method** (or mean) that provides the performance of <u>any</u> action from the specified set of actions.

class of actions
⇐   *family of subclasses**:
     action
:=   [a set of similar actions]
⊃   *class of atomic actions*
⊃   *class of easily performable complex actions*

Each distinguished *class of actions* corresponds to at least one common *method* for performing these *actions*. It means that the question is about <u>semantic</u> "clustering" of a set of *actions*, i.e., about the allocation of *classes of actions* on the basis of the <u>semantic similarity</u> (coincidence) of *actions* that are part of the selected *class of actions*. In this case, first of all, the coincidence (similarity) of *underlying situations* and *target situations* of the *actions* being considered, i.e., the coincidence of *problems* solved as a result of performing the corresponding *actions*, is taken into account. Since one and the same *problem* can be solved as a result of performing several <u>different</u> *actions* that belong to <u>different</u> *classes of actions*, we should talk not only about *classes of actions* (sets of similar actions) but also about **classes of problems** (sets of similar problems) solved by these *actions*. For example, the following *relations* are set on the set of *classes of actions*:

– a *relation*, each bunding of which connects two different (disjoint) *classes of actions* that solve one and the same *class of problems*;
– a *relation*, each bunding of which connects two different *classes of actions* that solve different *classes of problems*, one of which is a *superset* of the other.

In addition to the class of actions, the concept of a **class of atomic actions** is also distinguished, that is, the set of atomic actions, the indication of belonging to which is a necessary and sufficient condition for performing this action. The set of all possible atomic actions performed by each subject should be divided into classes of atomic actions.

Belonging of some *class of actions* to the set of the **classes of atomic actions** fixes the fact that, when all the necessary arguments are specified, belonging of *action* to this class is sufficient for some subject to start performing this action.

At the same time, even if the *class of actions* belongs to the set of the **class of atomic actions**, it is not forbidden to introduce more particular *classes of actions*, for which, for example, one of the arguments is fixed in advance.

If a specified **class of atomic actions** is more particular in relation to *actions in sc-memory*, this indicates that there is at least one *sc-agent* in the current version of the system that is focused on performing actions of this class.

In addition, it is also reasonable to introduce the concept of a *class of easily performable complex actions*, that is, a set of *complex actions*, for which at least one **method** is known and available, the interpretation of which allows performing a complete (final, ending with atomic actions) decomposition into sub-actions of each complex action from the above set.

Belonging of some *class of actions* to the set of the **class of easily performable complex actions** fixes the fact that, even when specifying all the necessary arguments of belonging the *action* to this class, it is unsufficient for some *subject* to start performing this action, and additional clarifications are required.

In turn, by the **class of problems** we will mean the set of problems, for which it is possible to construct a generalized definition of problems that corresponds to the whole set of problems. Each *generalized definition of the problems of the corresponding class* is in fact nothing more than a strict logical definition of the specified class of problems.

class of problems
⇐   *family of subsets**:
    problem

A specific class of actions can be defined in at least two ways.

class of actions
⇒   *subdividing**:
        {•   **class of actions that is precisely defined by the class of problems being solved**
           ≔   [a *class of actions* that provide a solution of the corresponding *class of problems* and at the same time use a wide variety of *methods* for solving problems of this class]

- *class of actions that is precisely defined by the used method of solving problems*

}

Further, let us consider in more detail the formal interpretation of the concept of a *method*.

7 Concept of a Method

By the method we will mean a description of <u>how</u> any or almost any (with explicit exceptions) action that belongs to the corresponding class of actions can be performed.

method
:= [a way]
⊂ *knowledge*
⇐ *second domain**:
 method*
:= [a program for solving problems of the corresponding class, which can be both procedural and declarative (non-procedural) ones]
:= [a method for solving the corresponding class of problems that provides a solution of any or most of the problems of the specified class]
:= [a knowledge of how it is necessary to solve problems of the corresponding class of problems (a set of equivalent (similar) problems)]
:= [a method (way) for solving a certain (corresponding) class of problems]
:= [an information (knowledge) sufficient to solve any *problem* that belongs to the corresponding *class of problems* using the corresponding *problem-solving model*]

The specification of each *class of problems* includes a description of how to "bind" a *method* to the source data of a specific *problem* that is being solved using this *method*. The description of such a method of "binding" includes:

– a set of variables that are included both in the *method* and in the *generalized definition of problems of the corresponding class* and whose values are the corresponding elements of the source data of each specific problem being solved;
– a part of the *generalized definition of problems* of the class, to which the *method* being considered corresponds, which are a description of the <u>conditions of usage</u> of this *method*.

The very "binding" of the *method* to a specific *problem* being solved using this *method* is carried out by <u>searching</u> in the *knowledge base* for such a fragment that satisfies the conditions for using the specified *method*. One of the results of such a search is to establish a correspondence between the abovementioned variables of the used *method* and the values of these variables within the framework of a specific *problem* being solved.

Another option for establishing the correspondence being considered is an explicit appeal (call) of the corresponding *method* (program) with the explicit transmission of the corresponding parameters. But this is not always possible, because, when performing the process of solving a specific *problem* based on the declarative specification of performing this action, it is not possible to set:

– when it is necessary to initiate the call (use) of the required *method*;
– which specific *method* should be used;
– what parameters that correspond to the specific initiated *problem* should be transmitted for "binding" the used *method* to this *problem*.

The process of "binding" the *method* of solving *problems* to a specific *problem* solved using this *method* can also be represented as a process that consists of the following stages:

– construction of a copy of the used *method*;
– binding the main (key) variables of the used *method* with the main parameters of the specific *problem* being solved.

As a result, on the basis of the considered *method* used as a sample (template), a specification of the process for solving a specific problem – a procedural specification (*plan*) or a declarative one – is built.

Let us note that *methods* can be used even when constructing *plans* for solving specific *problems*, in the case when there is a need for multiple repetition of certain chains of *actions* with an a priori unknown number of such repetitions. It is question about various types of **cycles**, which are the simplest type of procedural *methods* for solving problems that are repeatedly used when implementing *plans* for solving some *problems*.

It is also obvious that several *methods* can correspond to one *class of actions*.

Thus, we assume that the term "method" is with the term "program" synonymous in the generalized sense of this term.

method
:=   [a program]
:=   [a program for performing actions of a certain class]
⊃   *procedural program*
    ⊂   *algorithm*
    :=   [a generalized plan for solving a certain class of problems]
    :=   [a generalized plan]
    :=   [a generalized plan for performing a certain class of actions]
    :=   [a generalized specification of the decomposition of any action that belongs to a given class of actions]

Let us consider in more detail the concept of a procedural program (procedural method). Each **procedural program** is a generalized plan for performing *actions* that belong to a certain class, that is, it is a *semantic neighborhood; the key sc-element ′* is a *class of actions*, for the elements of which the process of their performance is additionally detailed.

The input parameters of the *procedural program* in the traditional sense correspond to the arguments that correspond to each *action* from the *class of actions* described by this *procedural program*. When generating a specific *plan* of performing a specific *action* from this class based on this program, these arguments take specific values.

Each *procedural program* is a system of described actions with an additional indication for the action:

- or a *sequence of actions** (transmission of initiation) when the condition for performing (initiating) actions is the performance of one of the specified or all of the specified actions;
- or an event in the knowledge base or the environment that is a condition for its initiation;
- or a situation in the knowledge base or the environment that is a condition for its initiation.

The concept of a method allows determining the relation *problem equivalence** on a set of problems. Problems are equivalent if and only if they can be solved by interpreting one and the same *method* (way) stored in memory of a cybernetical system.

Some *problems* can be solved by different *methods*, one of which, for example, is a generalization of the other. Thus, some relations can also be set on a set of methods.

Let's take note of the fact that the concept of a *method* enables localizing the domain of solving problems of the corresponding class, that is, restricting the set of information necessary to answer problems of this class in a particular manner. By reducing the number of pointless actions, this in turn enables enhancing the system's overall efficiency.

relation defined on a set of methods
∋   *submethod**
    :=   [a subprogram*]
    :=   [to be a method that is supposed to be used (accessed) when implementing a given method*]
    ⇔   *it is important to distinguish**:
       particular method*
          :=   [to be a method that provides a solution to a class of problems, which is a subclass of problems being solved using a given method*]

In the literature dedicated to the construction of problem solvers, the concept of a **problem-solving strategy** is found. Let us define it as a meta-method for solving problems that provides either the search for one relevant known method or the synthesis of a purposeful sequence of actions using various known methods in the general case.

problem-solving strategy
⊏   *method*

It can be said about a universal meta-method (universal strategy) for solving problems that explains all kinds of particular strategies.

We can specifically discuss a number of global strategies for solving informational problems in knowledge bases. Assume for the moment that the knowledge base has shown evidence of a started activity with the definition of the proper informational purpose, i.e., a purpose limited to altering the state of the knowledge base. Because there is now no context (source material) in the knowledge base that is sufficient to accomplish the aforementioned goal-that is, a context for which there is a method (program) in the package (set) of methods (programs) available-the aforementioned goal cannot be accomplished. There are three methods (three strategies) to accomplish such a goal, for which the context (source data) is insufficient:

- Decomposition is the reduction of an initial purpose to a hierarchy and/or subpurposes (and/or subproblems), based on an examination of the knowledge base's current state and an analysis of what is lacking in the knowledge base for employing a certain method.
  The approaches that take the least amount of work to set up the conditions for using them, however, receive the most attention. Ultimately, we must get at subpurposes (at the base of the hierarchy), whose context is suitable for using one of the programs (methods) accessible for problem-solving;
- creation of new knowledge in the semantic neighborhood surrounding the definition of the initial purpose using any methods available in the hope of achieving a state of the knowledge base that will contain the necessary context (sufficient source data) to achieve the initial purpose using any methods for resolving problems that are currently available;
- combination of the first and second approaches.

Similar approaches can be used to identify solutions to environmental problems.

8   Specification of Methods and the Concept of a Skill

Each specific *method* is considered by us not only as an important type of specification of the corresponding class of problems but also as an object that itself needs a specification that provides direct usage of this method. In other words, the method is not only a specification (the specification of the corresponding class of problems) but also an object of the specification. The most important type of such specification is the indication of the different types of **the method semantics**.

method specification*
∋   *declarative semantics of the method**
      :=   [a description of the system of concepts that are used within the framework of this method*]

∋   *denotative semantics of the method**
    :=   [generalized formulation of the class of problems solved using this method*]
∋   *operational semantics of the method**
    :=   [a family of methods that provide interpretation of a given method*]
    :=   [a formal description of the interpreter of a given method*]

The relation *declarative semantics of the method** connects the *method* and the formal description of the system of concepts (a fragment of the *logical ontology* of the corresponding *subject domain*) that are used (mentioned) within this method. This is necessary for ensuring that one and the same concept is interpreted unambiguously within the framework of the method and the rest of the knowledge base, which is especially important when borrowing a method from a library of reusable components of problem solvers. It is important to note that the fact that any concepts are used within the framework of the method does not mean that the formal record of their definitions is part of this method. For example, a method that allows solving problems for calculating the area of a triangle will include various formulas for calculating the area of a triangle but will not include the definitions of the concepts "area", "triangle", etc., since if there are a priori correct formulas, these definitions will not be used directly in the process of solving the problem. At the same time, the formal definitions of these concepts will be part of the declarative semantics of this method.

It is important to note that a special case of the method is the program of an atomic sc-agent. In this case, a collective of lower-level agents interpreting the corresponding program acts as the operational semantics of the method (in the limiting case, these will be agents that are part of the platform for interpreting models of computer systems, including hardware).

Thus:

– we can talk about the hierarchy of methods and about the methods of interpreting other methods;
– we can say that the concept of a method generalizes the concept of an sc-agent program for non-atomic sc-agents.

Combining the *method* and its operational semantics, that is, information about how this *method* should be interpreted, we will call a *skill*.

skill
:=   [an ability]
:=   [a combination of a *method* with its comprehensive specification – a *complex representation of the operational semantics of the method*]
:=   [a method + a method of its interpretation]
:=   [an ability to solve the corresponding class of equivalent problems]
:=   [a method plus its operational semantics, which describes how this method is interpreted (performed, implemented) and is at the same time the operational semantics of the corresponding problem-solving model]

⇒   *subdividing**:
      { •   *passive skill*
        •   *active skill*
            :=   [a self-initiating skill]
      }

Thus, the concept of a *skill* is the most important concept from the point of view of constructing problem solvers, since it combines not only the declarative part of the description of the method of solving a class of problems but also the operational one.

Skills can be *passive skills*, that is, such *skills*, the usage of which must be explicitly initiated by some agent, or *active skills*, which are initiated independently when a corresponding situation occurs in the knowledge base. To do this, in addition to the *method* and its operational semantics, the *sc-agent*, which responds to the appearance of a corresponding situation in the knowledge base and initiates the interpretation of the *method* of this *skill*, is also included in the *active skill*.

This separation allows implementing and combining different approaches for solving problems, in particular, *passive skills* can be considered as a way to implement the concept of a smart software package.

9   Concepts of a Class of Methods and a Language for Representing Methods

Like actions and problems, methods can be classified into different classes. We will define a set of methods, for which it is possible to unify the representation (specification) of these methods, as a **class of methods**.

class of methods
⇐   *family of subclasses**:
      method
:=   [a set of methods, for which the representation language of these methods
      is set]
∋   *procedural method for solving problems*
      ⊃   *algorithmic method for solving problems*
∋   *logical method for solving problems*
      ⊃   *functional method for solving problems*
      ⊃   *productional method for solving problems*
∋   *artificial neutral network*
      :=   [a class of methods for solving problems based on artificial neural
      networks]
∋   *genetic "algorithm"*
:=   [a set of methods represented in the same language]
:=   [a set of methods based on a common ontology]
:=   [a set of methods that corresponds to a separate problem-solving model]

:=   [a set of methods for solving problems, which corresponds to a special language (for example, an sc-language) that provides a representation of methods from this set]

Each specific *class of methods* mutually identically corresponds to a *language for representing methods* that belong to this (specified) *class of methods*. Thus, the specification of each *class of methods* is reduced to the specification of the corresponding *language for representing methods*, i.e., to the description of its syntactic, denotational and operational semantics.

Examples of *languages for representing methods* are all *programming languages*, which mainly belong to the subclass of *languages for representing methods* – to *languages for representing methods for information processing*. But now the need to create effective formal languages for representing methods for performing actions in the environment of cybernetical systems is becoming increasingly relevant. Complex automation, in particular, in the industrial sphere, is impossible without this.

Such specialized languages can be numerous, and each one will correspond to a certain model of problem solving (i.e., to its own interpreter).

language for representing methods
:=   [a method language]
:=   [a language for representing methods that correspond to a specific class of methods]
⊂   *language*
:=   [a programming language]
⊃   *language for representing methods for information processing*
        :=   [a language of representing methods for solving problems in memory of cybernetical systems]
⊃   *language of representing methods for solving problems in the environment of cybernetical systems*
        :=   [a programming language for external actions of cybernetical systems]

10   Concept of a Problem-Solving Model

By analogy with the concept of a problem-solving strategy, we introduce the concept of a **problem-solving model**, which we will interpret as a meta-method for interpreting the corresponding class of methods.

problem-solving model
⊂   *method*
:=   [a meta-method]
:=   [an abstract machine for interpreting the corresponding class of methods]

:=   [a hierarchical system of "microprograms" that provide interpretation of the corresponding class of methods]
⊃   *algorithmic problem-solving model*
⊃   *procedural parallel asynchronous problem-solving model*
⊃   *procedural parallel synchronous problem-solving model*
⊃   *productional problem-solving model*
⊃   *logical problem-solving model*
⊃   *functional problem-solving model*
    ⊃   *strict logical problem-solving model*
    ⊃   *fuzzy logical problem-solving model*
⊃   *"genetic" problem-solving model*
⊃   *"neural network" problem-solving model*

Each *problem-solving model* is defined by:

- the corresponding class of methods for solving problems, i.e., the language of representing methods of this class;
- the subject domain of this class of methods;
- the ontology of this class of methods (i.e., the denotational semantics of the language of representing these methods);
- the operational semantics of the specified class of methods.

It is important to note that for the interpretation of all problem-solving models, an agent-oriented approach considered in [26] can be used.

problem-solving model*

=   *narrowing the relation by the first domain(specification*; class of methods)**
:=   [a specification of the *class of methods**]
:=   [a specification of the *language for representing methods**]
⇐   *generalized union**:
    {•   *syntax of the language for representing methods of the corresponding class**
    •   *denotational semantics of the language for representing methods of the corresponding class**
    •   *operational semantics of the language for representing methods of the corresponding class**
    }

Each specific *class of methods* has a one-to-one correspondence with the *method representation languages* belonging to this (specified) *class of methods*. Thus, the specification of each *class of methods* is reduced to the specification of the corresponding *method representation language*, i.e. to the description of its syntactic, denotational semantics and operational semantics. Examples of *method representation languages* are all *programming languages*, which mainly belong to the *method representation languages* subclass – *information processing methods representation languages.* But now the need to create effective formal languages for representing methods of performing actions in the external environment of cybernetic systems is becoming increasingly important. Without this, complex automation, in particular in the industrial sector, is impossible.

denotational semantics of the language for representing methods of the corresponding class
:=   [an ontology of the corresponding class of methods]
:=   [the denotational semantics of the corresponding class of methods]
:=   [the denotational semantics of a language (an sc-language) that provides
       a representation of methods of the corresponding class]
:=   [the denotational semantics of the corresponding problem-solving model]
⇒   *note*:*
       [If the question is about a language that provides an internal representation of the methods of the corresponding class in the ostis-system, the
       syntax of this language coincides with the syntax of the SC-code]
⊂   *ontology*

operational semantics of the language for representing methods of the corresponding class
:=   [a meta-method of interpretation of the corresponding class of methods]
:=   [a family of agents that provide interpretation (usage) of any method that
       belongs to the corresponding class of methods]
:=   [the operational semantics of the corresponding problem-solving model]

Since each *method* corresponds to a *generalized definition of problems* solved using this *method*, then each *class of methods* must correspond not only to a certain *language of representing methods* that belong to the specified *class of methods* but also to a certain *language of representation of generalized definitions of problems for various classes of problems* that are solved using *methods* that belong to the specified *class of methods*.

11 Concepts of a Problem Solver and a Knowledge Processing Machine

Taking into account the system of concepts discussed above, we will define the problem solver of an intelligent computer system as a set of *skills* that allow the system to solve problems of a particular class.

problem solver
:=   [a problem solver of an intelligent computer system]
:=   [a set of all the skills (abilities) acquired by the computer system by now]
⊃   *combined problem solver*
⊃   *hybrid problem solver*

By the **combined problem solver** we will mean a solver that provides all the functionality of an intelligent system, that is, the solution of all problems that are related to the direct purpose of the system and ensure the efficiency of its work. Thus, for example, a solver that implements some variant of logical inference cannot be considered as combined, since to use a system that contains such a solver it is necessary to have at least basic information search tools that allow localizing the received answer as well as means that ensure the translation of a question from the user to the system and an answer from the system to the user.

In general, the *combined problem solver*, in contrast to the *problem solver* in a general sense, solves problems related to:

- ensuring the main functionality of the system (solving explicitly defined problems on demand);
- ensuring the correctness and optimization of the system (permanently throughout the system life cycle);
- ensuring the automation of the development of an intelligent system.

By the **hybrid problem solver** we will mean a *problem solver*, within which several different *problem-solving models* are used. It is obvious that the *combined problem solver* is predominantly a *hybrid problem solver*, since for the functioning of even a fairly simple intelligent system it is necessary to solve problems of fundamentally different classes discussed above.

In turn, by a *knowledge processing machine* we will mean the set of interpreters of all skills that build some *problem solver*. Taking into account the approach to information processing used within the framework of the OSTIS Technology and discussed in [13], a *knowledge processing machine* is a *sc-agent* (most often – a *non-atomic sc-agent*), which includes simpler sc-agents that provide interpretation of the corresponding set of *methods*.

Thus, we can talk, for example, about a *deductive logical inference machine* or an *information search machine*.

12   Example of the Usage of the Developed Ontologies

Let us consider the usage of the abovementioned fragments of ontology on the example of the description in the knowledge base of ways to solve a simple problem – the problem of finding roots of a quadratic equation.

As it is known from the school course in mathematics, the problems of this class can be solved in at least two ways – through the discriminant and the Vieta formulas for the quadratic equation.

On the other hand, from the point of view of implementation in the ostis-system, both of these options can also be implemented in two ways:

- in a particular way when an *abstract sc-agent* designed to solve problems of a specific class in a specific way is being developed;

– in a more general way when the corresponding formulas are written in the form of logical rules, which are further interpreted by a group of domain-independent sc-agents. This option is worse in terms of performance but much better in terms of flexibility and extensibility of the system.

Figure 1 shows an example of implementing the solution of problems of the considered class in both ways (through the discriminant and Vieta formulas) in a more particular way in the form of active skills. In this variant, it is assumed that the sc-agent programs are implemented in the SCP language, which is the basic language for processing SC-code texts and whose programs are also written in the SC-code. Based on this, the operational semantics of the methods is an *Abstract scp-machine*, that is, an interpreter of SCP programs.

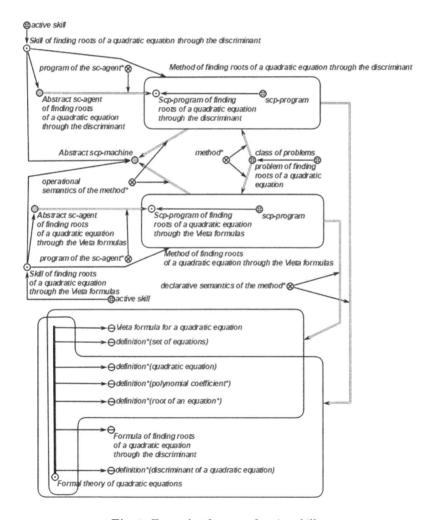

Fig. 1. Example of usage of active skills

In turn, Fig. 2 shows an example of the implementation of the same skills but in a more general way and in the form of passive skills. In this case, the operational semantics of the methods is a *Non-atomic abstract sc-agent of logical inference*, which allows using logical statements and, if necessary, calculating mathematical expressions that are obtained as a result of using a logical statement.

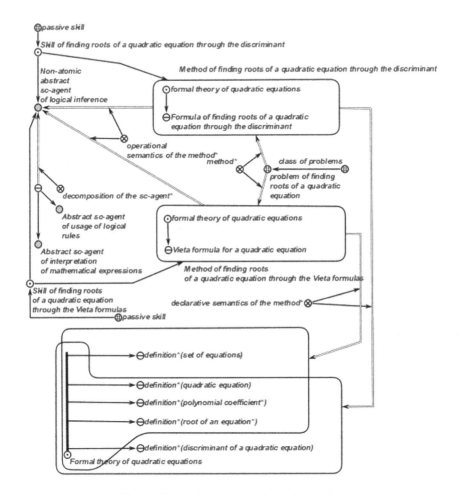

Fig. 2. Example of usage of passive skills

The presented figures also show how the declarative semantics of the corresponding methods are set.

13   Conclusion

The paper considers an ontological approach to the development of problem solvers for intelligent computer systems based on the OSTIS Technology.

The *Ontology of actions and tasks and the corresponding ontology of methods for problems solving* have been developed.

The model of the hybrid problem solver has been refined, which makes it possible to more effectively implement the component approach to the development of solvers. The OSTIS Standard contains a more thorough description of each of the outcomes that were presented [13].

Examples of describing skills that allow solving one and the same class of problems in different ways are given.

The results achieved will improve the effectiveness of the component approach to problem solving and automation tools for problem solving in the future. They will also give the intelligent system and the developer the opportunity to choose solutions to a given problem automatically.

Acknowledgment. The author would like to thank the research groups of the Departments of Intelligent Information Technologies of the Belarusian State University of Informatics and Radioelectronics and the Brest State Technical University for their help in the work and valuable comments.

References

1. IMS.ostis Metasystem, October 2021. https://doi.org/ims.ostis.net
2. Ansari, F., Khobreh, M., Seidenberg, U., Sihn, W.: A problem-solving ontology for human-centered cyber physical production systems. CIRP J. Manuf. Sci. Technol. **22**, 91–106 (2018). https://doi.org/10.1016/j.cirpj.2018.06.002. https://www.sciencedirect.com/science/article/pii/S1755581718300324
3. Benjamins, V.R., Gomez-Perez, A.: Knowledge-system technology: ontologies and problem-solving methods (1999)
4. Chandrasekaran, B., Josephson, J., Benjamins, V.R.: Ontology of tasks and methods (1999)
5. Coelho, E., Lapalme, G.: Describing reusable problem-solving methods with a method ontology. In: University of Calgary, pp. 3–1. SRDG Publications (1996)
6. Crowther, T.: Temporal ontology and joint action. Inquiry 1–23 (2020). https://doi.org/10.1080/0020174X.2020.1731592
7. Crubézy, M., Musen, M.A.: Ontologies in support of problem solving. In: Staab, S., Studer, R. (eds.) Handbook on Ontologies, pp. 321–341. Springer, Heidelberg (2004). https://doi.org/10.1007/978-3-540-24750-0_16
8. Davydenko, I.: Semantic models, method and tools of knowledge bases coordinated development based on reusable components. In: Golenkov, V. (ed.) Otkrytye semanticheskie tehnologii proektirovanija intellektual'nyh sistem [Open semantic technologies for intelligent systems], pp. 99–118. BSUIR, Minsk, BSUIR (2018)
9. Fang, K., Lin, S.: An integrated approach for modeling ontology-based task knowledge on an incident command system. Sustainability **11**(12), 3484 (2019). https://doi.org/10.3390/su11123484
10. Fayans, A., Kneller, V.: About the ontology of task types and methods of their solution. Ontol. Des. **10**(3), 273–295 (2020). https://doi.org/10.18287/2223-9537-2020-10-3-273-295

11. Fensel, D., Motta, E., Decker, S., Zdrahal, Z.: Using ontologies for defining tasks, problem-solving methods and their mappings. In: Plaza, E., Benjamins, R. (eds.) EKAW 1997. LNCS, vol. 1319, pp. 113–128. Springer, Heidelberg (1997). https://doi.org/10.1007/BFb0026781

12. Fensel, D., Benjamins, V.R.: Key issues for automated problem-solving methods reuse. In: 13th European Conference on Artificial Intelligence, ECAI 1998. Wiley (1998)

13. Golenkov, V., Guliakina, N., Shunkevich, D.: Otkrytaja tehnologija ontologicheskogo proektirovanija, proizvodstva i jekspluatacii semanticheski sovmestimyh gibridnyh intellektual'nyh komp'juternyh sistem [Open technology of ontological design, production and operation of semantically compatible hybrid intelligent computer systems]. Bestprint [Bestprint], Minsk (2021)

14. Golenkov, V., Gulyakina, N., Davydenko, I., Shunkevich, D.: Semanticheskie tekhnologii proektirovaniya intellektual'nyh sistem i semanticheskie associativnye komp'yutery [Semantic technologies of intelligent systems design and semantic associative computers]. Otkrytye semanticheskie tehnologii proektirovanija intellektual'nyh sistem [Open semantic technologies for intelligent systems], pp. 42–50 (2019)

15. Hardzei, A.: Theory for Automatic Generation of Knowledge Architecture: TAPAZ-2. Transl. from Rus. I. M. Boyko. Rev. English edn. The Republican Institute of Higher School Publ., Minsk (2017)

16. Hardzei, A.: Plagiarism problem solving based on combinatory semantics. In: Golenkov, V., Krasnoproshin, V., Golovko, V., Azarov, E. (eds.) OSTIS 2020. CCIS, vol. 1282, pp. 176–197. Springer, Cham (2020). https://doi.org/10.1007/978-3-030-60447-9_11

17. Ikeda, M., Seta, K., Kakusho, O., Mizoguchi, R.: Task ontology: ontology for building conceptual problem solving models, pp. 126–133 (1998)

18. Kemke, C.: About the Ontology of Actions. No. Technical Report MCCS-01-328 (2001)

19. Martynov, V.: Semiologicheskie osnovy informatiki [Semiological Foundations of Informatics]. Nauka i tekhnika [Science and technics], Minsk (1974)

20. Martynov, V.: Universal'nyi semanticheskii kod (Grammatika. Slovar'. Teksty) [Universal Semantic Code (Grammar. Dictionary. Texts). Nauka i tekhnika [Science and technics], Minsk (1977)

21. Martynov, V.: Universal'nyi semanticheskii kod: USK-3 [Universal Semantic Code: USC-3]. Nauka i tekhnika [Science and technics], Minsk (1984)

22. McBride, R., Packard, M.D.: On the ontology of action: actors are not "abstractions". Acad. Manag. Rev. **46**(1), 211–214 (2021). https://doi.org/10.5465/amr.2020.0093

23. McCann, H.J.: The Works of Agency. Cornell University Press, Ithaca (1998). https://doi.org/10.7591/9781501737176

24. Perkuhn, R.: Reuse of problem-solving methods and family resemblances. In: Plaza, E., Benjamins, R. (eds.) EKAW 1997. LNCS, vol. 1319, pp. 174–189. Springer, Heidelberg (1997). https://doi.org/10.1007/BFb0026785

25. Puerta, A.R., Egar, J.W., Tu, S.W., Musen, M.A.: A multiple-method knowledge-acquisition shell for the automatic generation of knowledge-acquisition tools. Knowl. Acquis. **4**, 171–196 (1992)

26. Shunkevich, D.: Agentno-orientirovannye reshateli zadach intellektual'nyh sistem [Agent-oriented models, method and tools of compatible problem solvers development for intelligent systems]. In: Golenkov, V. (ed.) Otkrytye semanticheskie tekhnologii proektirovaniya intellektual'nykh system [Open semantic technologies for intelligent systems], pp. 119–132. BSUIR, Minsk (2018)
27. Shunkevich, D.: Ontological approach to the development of hybrid problem solvers for intelligent computer systems. In: Golenkov, V. (ed.) Otkrytye semanticheskie tekhnologii proektirovaniya intellektual'nykh system [Open semantic technologies for intelligent systems], pp. 63–74. BSUIR, Minsk (2021)
28. Studer, R., Eriksson, H., Gennari, J., Tu, S., Fensel, D., Musen, M.: Ontologies and the configuration of problem-solving methods (1996)
29. Taranchuk, V.: Tools and examples of intelligent processing, visualization and interpretation of GEODATA. J. Phys. Conf. Ser. **1425**(1), 012160 (2019). https://doi.org/10.1088/1742-6596/1425/1/012160
30. Trypuz, R.: Formal ontology of action: a unifying approach. Ph.D. thesis (2007)
31. Tu, S.W., Eriksson, H., Gennari, J.H., Shahar, Y., Musen, M.A.: Ontology-based configuration of problem-solving methods and generation of knowledge-acquisition tools: application of PROTégé-II to protocol-based decision support. Artif. Intell. Med. **7**(3), 257–289 (1995). https://doi.org/10.1016/0933-3657(95)00006-r

Ontology-Based Representation of an Artificial Neural Networks

Mikhail Kovalev$^{(\boxtimes)}$

Belarusian State University of Informatics and Radioelectronics,
Minsk, Republic of Belarus
michail.kovalev7@gmail.com

Abstract. The paper considers a method for combining knowledge bases and artificial neural networks to solve complicated problems. A model for artificial neural networks (ANN) representation and actions for their processing in the knowledge base is required and is justified. The subject domains and associated ontologies for the following concepts are used to represent this model: a) ANN; b) actions for ANN processing. This page describes these subject domains and ontologies.

Keywords: neuro-symbolic AI · ANN · knowledge base

1 Introduction

Intelligent systems are increasingly required to tackle difficult problems using a variety of conventional and modern problem-solving techniques inside a single information resource (in the limit – in a single knowledge base) [10].

Artificial neural networks are one of the most widely utilized intelligent problem-solving techniques. This popularity is primarily due to the advancement of ANN theory and the hardware capabilities of the machines used to train them.

When working with unstructured data, neural network models produce outstanding results, but their main drawback has historically been the absence of input that is understood by humans, or what is sometimes called a "reasoning chain." Therefore, the majority of neural network models operate in a "black box" [3].

However, in order to communicate the evaluation and optimization of the activity of ANN, it is necessary to monitor, explain, and comprehend the mechanics of modern intelligent systems that employ neural network models due to their complexity and the vast amounts of data they process.

The necessity to tackle complicated problems using ANN and the need to describe how these problems were solved are therefore mutually exclusive. The development of neuro-symbolic methods—in particular, methods for the integration of artificial neural networks (ANN) with knowledge bases that make use of ontologies—becomes pertinent in such situation [2,5]. Such systems can incorporate the following:

© The Author(s), under exclusive license to Springer Nature Switzerland AG 2022
V. Golenkov et al. (Eds.): OSTIS 2021, CCIS 1625, pp. 132–151, 2022.
https://doi.org/10.1007/978-3-031-15882-7_8

- the capacity for semantic interpretation of the processed data, employing both the specification of the input and output data for the ANN as well as the representation of the applied problems being handled;
- with a depiction of the ANN structure itself, a description of its attributes, and states that simplify comprehension of how it functions [7].

There are two main directions of integration of ANN with knowledge bases:

- the creation of intelligent systems that can solve complicated issues using a combination of internal and external methods, including neural network techniques. Such systems will be able to take into consideration the problems' semantics at a higher level, which will result in more structured and visible solutions to these challenges;
- the establishment of an intelligent environment for the depiction of ANN with the aid of ontological structures and their interpretation utilizing knowledge representation, allowing for the development, training, and integration of diverse ANN compatible with knowledge bases. A closer examination of an ANN's operation will be possible in such a setting since it will be possible to save the states of the ANN after training and network reconfiguration. Additionally, a formalized definition of the information contained in the ANN topic domain will assist in lowering the barrier for developers to enter the field of ANN-based problem-solving techniques.

The evolution of both directions suggests that the knowledge base has information about the neural network models it contains, how they are internally structured, the challenges they can address, and other topics, to varying degrees of complexity. The creation of a model for the representation of artificial neural networks and procedures for their processing in the knowledge base serves as the foundation for the growth of both directions. This article's goal is to create such a model.

2   Proposed Approach

The basis of the proposed approach is the usage of the OSTIS Technology and its basic principles for building a knowledge base [6].

Within the framework of the OSTIS Technology, powerful tools have been developed. Its allow describing any type of knowledge in a unified form, structuring the knowledge base according to various criteria as well as verifying its quality and editing the knowledge base directly while in operation [4].

A hierarchical system of subject domains and the related ontologies forms the foundation of the knowledge base constructed using the OSTIS Technology. An ontology is seen as a description of the associated subject domain's conceptual framework.

Additionally, any subject domain and ontology development will refer to the creation of a subject domain and ontology using the language of the OSTIS Technology.

Knowledge in knowledge bases built using the OSTIS Technology is represented using an SC-code. To record formalized texts, in the article, the variants of the external display of SC-code constructions are used – SCg (graphic version) and SCn (hypertext version). It is possible to examine in detail the representation of knowledge with the help of the SC-code here [1].

As a result, the stated issue of creating a model for the representation of artificial neural networks in the knowledge base and steps for their processing within the context of the OSTIS Technology is reduced to creating:

– the subject domain and the corresponding ontology of artificial neural networks;
– the subject domain and the corresponding ontology of actions for processing artificial neural networks.

3   Subject Domain and the Corresponding Ontology of Artificial Neural Networks

The subject domain of artificial neural networks contains a formal description of knowledge about particular artificial neural networks. The corresponding ontology contains a formal description of the concepts that are necessary for the representation of such knowledge.

The maximum class of objects of research in the subject domain of artificial neural networks is the *artificial neural network*. This concept denotes a class, to which all entities that denote specific ANN belong.

An *artificial neural network* is a set of neural elements and connections between them [8]. The ANN consists of *formal neurons*, which are interconnected by *synaptic connections*. Neurons are organized in *layers*. Each neuron of the layer receives signals from the synaptic connections that come in it, processes them in a single way using the *activation function* prescribed for it or for the entire layer, and transmits the result to the synaptic connections that go out of it.

Figure 1 shows the general scheme of the ANN.

We will call a set of information, which denotes data about the structure of ANN layers, formal neurons, synaptic connections, and activation functions, i.e., something that can be trained and used to solve problems, the ANN architecture.

In accordance with the ANN architecture, it is possible to distinguish the following hierarchy of classes of ANN. Let us consider this hierarchy in the SCn-code.

artificial neural network
⇒   *subdividing**:
       *Typology of ANN on the basis of the directivity of connections*ˆ
       =   {•   *ANN with direct connections*
                      ⇒   *decomposition**:
                      {•   *perceptron*
                              ⇒   *decomposition**:

{•   *Rozenblatt perceptron*
   •   *autoencoder ANN*
}
   •   *support vector machine*
   •   *ANN of radial-basis functions*
}
•   *ANN with inverse connections*
⇒   *decomposition**:
     {•   *Hopfield ANN*
     •   *Hamming ANN*
     }
•   *recurrent artificial neural network*
⇒   *decomposition**:
     {•   *Jordan ANN*
     •   *Elman ANN*
     •   *multi-recurrent ANN*
     •   *LSTM-element*
     •   *GRU-element*
     }
}
⇒   *subdividing**:
Typology of ANN on the basis of completeness of connections ˆ
=   {•   *fully connected ANN*
     •   *weakly connected ANN*
     }

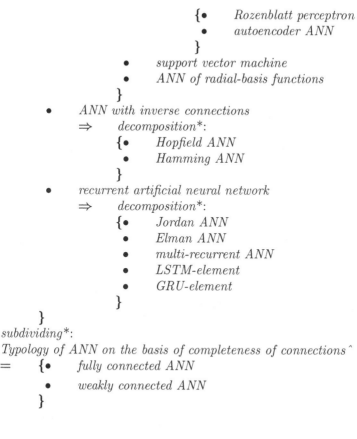

Fig. 1. The general scheme of the artificial neural network [8]

Next, the key elements of the ontology of ANN, the concepts used to formalize the ANN architecture will be described.

A **formal neuron** is the main element of the *artificial neural network*, which applies its *activation function* to the sum of the products of input signals by weight coefficients [8]:

$$y = F\left(\sum_{i=1}^{n} w_i x_i - T\right) = F(WX - -T)$$

where $X = (x_1, x_2, ..., x_n)^T$ is an input signal vector; $W - -(w_1, w_2, ..., w_n)$ – a vector of weight coefficients; T – a threshold value; F – an activation function.

Formal neurons can have a complete set of connections with neurons of the previous layer or an incomplete (discharged) set of connections.

The role relation *formal neuron'* is used to denote the belonging of a particular formal neuron to any ANN.

A separate formal neuron is an artificial neural network with one neuron in a single layer.

formal neuron
:=　　[an artificial neuron]
:=　　[a neuron]
⊂　　*artificial neural network*
⇒　　*subdividing**:
　　　　{•　　*fully connected formal neuron*
　　　　　　:=　　[a neuron that has a complete set of connections with the neurons of the previous layer]
　　　　•　　*convolutional formal neuron*
　　　　　　⇒　　*explanation**:
　　　　　　　　[A separate processing element of the ANN, which performs a functional transformation of the result of the operation of convolution of the matrix of input values using the activation function.]
　　　　　　⇒　　*explanation**:
　　　　　　　　[A convolutional formal neuron can be represented by a fully connected formal neuron.]
　　　　•　　*recurrent formal neuron*
　　　　　　⇒　　*explanation**:
　　　　　　　　[A formal neuron that has an inverse connection with itself or with other neurons of the ANN.]
　　　}

Figure 2 shows the general scheme of a formal neuron.

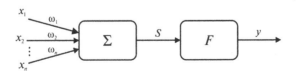

Fig. 2. The general scheme of a formal neuron of the ANN [8]

A ***threshold formal neuron'*** is a role relation that connects an artificial neural network with such a neuron, the output value of which is always equal to -1. The weight coefficient of the synaptic connection that goes out of such a neuron is the threshold for the neuron in which this synaptic connection comes.

A ***synaptic connection*** is a set of oriented pairs, the first components of which are the neurons, out of which the signal goes, and the second components are the neurons that receive this signal. When denoting the belonging of a particular synaptic connection to any ANN, the role relation *synaptic connection'* is used.

A ***weight coefficient of the synaptic connection*** is a numerical factor that is assigned to each synapse of the neural network and that changes during training. If the force of the synaptic connection is negative, then it is called an *inhibitory* one. Otherwise, it is *reinforcing.*

A ***pattern of the ANN input activity*** is an oriented multiset of numerical values of some object's features, which can act as input values of neurons. At this stage, it is assumed that the pattern of the input activity contains only prepro-cessed data, that is, data reduced to a numerical form and, possibly, transformed using known statistical methods (for example, normalizing).

A ***feature*** is a set of role relations, each of which connects a certain pattern of the input activity with a numerical value that characterizes this pattern of the input activity from any side.

An ***input value of a formal neuron**** is a non-role relation that connects the neuron of the input layer with the feature value of the pattern of the input activity, which is input to the neural network. Using a set as a form of represent-ing input data is a serious assumption since in real terms the input data is more complexly structured – in multidimensional arrays. The closest theoretical ana-log is a tensor. Unfortunately, the description of the theory of neural networks using tensor calculus is missing from the literature in principle but is actively used in practice: for example, in many neural network frameworks that are being developed. The formalization of neural networks using tensors is considered by the author as the most possible area of work.

The ***weighted sum**** is a non-role relation that connects a formal neuron with a number that is the sum of the products of input signals by the weight coefficients of the synaptic connections that come in the neuron.

Formula:

$$S = \sum_{i=1}^{n} w_i x_i - T$$

where n is the dimension of the vector of input values, w_i is the i-th element of the vector of weight coefficients, x_i is the i-th element of the vector of input values, T is the threshold value.

The ***activation function**** is a non-role relation that connects a formal neuron with a function, the result of applying which to the weighted sum of the neuron determines its output value. To describe such functions, in the knowl-edge base, classes of such functions (threshold one, sigmoid, ReLU, etc.) and information about the cases, in which they are usually used, are described.

activation function*

:=   [neuron activation function*]

⇒   *explanation**:

[an **activation function*** is a non-role relation that connects the formal neuron with the function, the result of appliance of which to the **weighted sum of the neuron** determines its **output value.**]

⇒   *decomposition**:

{•   *linear function*

⇒   *formula**:

[

$$y = kS$$

where k is the coefficient of the slope of line, S is the weighted sum]

•   *threshold function*

⇒   *formula**:

[

$$y = sign(S) = \begin{cases} 1, S > 0, \\ 0, S \leq 0 \end{cases}$$

]

•   *sigmoid function*

⇒   *formula**:

[

$$y = \frac{1}{1 + e^{-cS}}$$

where $c > 0$ is a coefficient that characterizes the width of the sigmoid function at the x-axis, S is a weighted sum.]

•   *hyperbolic tangent function*

⇒   *formula**:

[

$$y = \frac{e^{cS} - e^{-cS}}{e^{cs} + e^{-cS}}$$

where $c > 0$ is a coefficient that characterizes the width of the sigmoid function at the x-axis, S is a weighted sum.]

•   *softmax function*

⇒   *formula**:

[

$$y_j = softmax(S_j) = \frac{e^{S_j}}{\sum_j e^{S_j}}$$

where S_j is the weighted sum of the j-th output neuron.]

•   *function ReLU*

⇒   *formula**:

[

$$y = F(S) = \begin{cases} S, S > 0, \\ kS, S \leq 0 \end{cases}$$

where $k = 0$ or a small value, such as 0.01 or 0.001.]

}

The **ANN layer** is a set of neural elements that receive information from other neural elements of the network in parallel at each clock period [8]. The activation function of a layer is the activation function of all the formal neurons of this layer. The description of the sequence of ANN layers with the configuration of each layer sets the ANN architecture. The configuration of the layer is set by the type, the number of formal neurons, the activation function. The description of the sequence of ANN layers with the configuration of each layer sets the ANN architecture. A separate layer is an artificial neural network with a single layer.

ANN layer
:=   [layer]
:=   [set of layers of artificial neural networks]
⊂   *artificial neural network*
⇒   *decomposition*:*
    {•   *fully connected ANN layer*
        :=   [a layer, in which each neuron has a connection with each neuron of the previous layer]
    •   *convolutional ANN layer*
        :=   [a layer, in which each neuron is convolutional]
    •   *nonlinear transformation ANN layer*
        :=   [a layer that performs nonlinear transformation of input data]
        ⇒   *explanation*:*
        [As a rule, they are allocated into separate layers only in software implementations. In fact, they are considered as the final stage of calculating the output activity of any neuron – the application of the activation function.]
    •   *dropout ANN layer*
        :=   [a layer that implements the dropout regularization technique]
        ⇒   *explanation*:*
        [This type of layer functions only during training the ANN.]
        ⇒   *explanation*:*
        [Since fully connected layers have a large number of configurable parameters, they are subject to the effect of overtraining. One of the ways to eliminate this negative effect is to perform partial exclusion of results at the output of a fully connected layer. During the training phase, the dropout technique allows discarding the output activity of some neurons with a certain, specified probability. Output activity of the "discarded" neurons is assumed as equal to zero.]

- *pooling ANN layer*
  :=   [subsampling layer]
  :=   [pooling layer]
  :=   [a layer that reduces the dimensionality of the input data]
- *ANN layer of the butch-normalization*
}

The layers are connected with the ANN by the following non-role relations:

- a **distribution layer*** is a non-role relation that connects the artificial neural network with its layer, whose neurons take input values of the entire neural network;
- a **processing layer*** is a non-role relation that connects the ANN with its layer, whose neurons take as input the output values of the neurons of the previous layer;
- an **output layer*** is a non-role relation that connects the ANN with its layer, the output values of neurons of which are the output values of the entire neural network.

Also, within the subject domain, the hierarchy of ANN parameters is formalized.

ANN parameter
⊂   *parameter*
⇒   *decomposition**:
    {•   *configurable ANN parameter*
       :=   [an ANN parameter, the value of which changes during training]
       ⇒   *decomposition**:
          {•   *weight coefficient of the synaptic connection*
          •   *threshold value*
          •   *convolution kernel*
          }
    •   *architectural ANN parameter*
       ⇒   *explanation**:
       [The ANN parameter that defines its architecture.]
       ⇒   *decomposition**:
          {•   *number of layers*
          •   *number of neurons*
          •   *number of synaptic connections*
          }
}

With the help of the allocated concepts, it becomes possible to formalize the architecture of a particular ANN in the knowledge base. Figure 3 shows an example of the formalization of a fully connected two-layer ANN with two neurons on the input layer and one neuron on the processing layer.

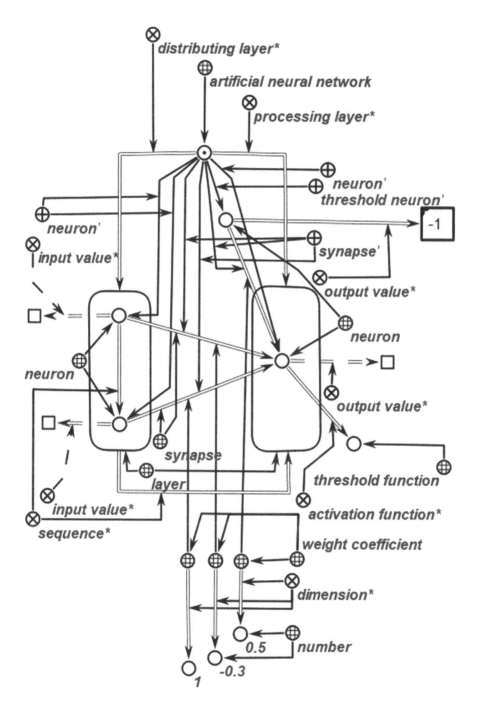

Fig. 3. An example of the formalization of the architecture of an artificial neural network in the knowledge base

It should be noted that within the subject domain, it is possible to formalize knowledge about the ANN without formalizing knowledge about the ANN architecture. This is possible when the ANN is a sign of an external entity in relation to the knowledge base, for example, the ANN is implemented and works on a third-party service. In this case, it is sufficient to formalize the specification of such an ANN that includes:

- the ANN class;
- the ANN parameters;
- the type of problem being solved;
- the types of input and output data;
- the identifier, by which the specification of the ANN in the knowledge base can be correlated with the model in a third-party service;
- other knowledge that will help the system decide whether to use ANN as a method for solving a specific problem.

The description of each knowledge about ANN will allow the system that uses the subject domain under consideration to decide to use one or another ANN to solve a specific problem or to help the developer make such a decision when choosing an ANN to train for solving such a problem. For the same purposes, for each particular ANN, it is necessary to specify the problem that it can solve. The following classes of problems are identified, which can be solved with the help of the ANN with acceptable accuracy:

- the *classification problem*. The problem of creating a classifier, i.e., displaying $\tilde{c} : X \rightarrow C$, where $X \in \mathbb{R}^m$ is the attribute space of the input pattern, $C = C_1, C_2, ...C_k$ – a finite and usually small set of class labels.
- the *regression problem*. The problem of constructing an evaluation function based on examples $(x_i, f(x_i))$, where $f(x)$ is an unknown function. The *evaluation function* is the display of the form $\tilde{f} : X \rightarrow \mathbb{R}$, where $X \in \mathbb{R}^m$ is the attribute space of the input pattern.
- the *clustering problem*. The problem of dividing the set of input patterns into groups (clusters) according to some similarity metric.
- the *problem of reducing the dimensionality of the feature space*;
- the *control problem*;
- the *filtering problem*;
- the *detection problem*. It is a special case of a classification problem and a regression problem.
- the *problem with associative memory*.

4   Subject Domain and Ontology of Actions for Processing Artificial Neural Networks

In the previous section, we considered the subject domain and the corresponding ontology of ANN, within which the ANN architecture is described. However, the formalization of the ANN architecture is not enough to use ANN as a method of solving problems; the system should perform some *actions* on the configuration of the architecture, training, and usage (interpretation) of ANN.

4.1   Action for Processing the ANN

An ***action for processing the ANN*** is the maximum class of objects of research of the subject domain of actions for processing artificial neural networks. This concept denotes a class, to which all entities that denote specific actions for processing the ANN belong.

Within the framework of the *OSTIS Technology*, an *action* is defined as a purposeful *process* performed by one or more subjects (cybernetic systems) with the possible usage of certain tools [10].

Therefore, the *action for processing the ANN* is an action, the object of which is some ANN, the subject of which is an intelligent system, in the knowledge base of which this ANN is described.

Actions for processing the ANN are carried out by the appropriate group of agents [10].

Depending on whether the ANN is a sign of an entity external to the system memory, the elements of the set of the actions for processing the ANN are either elements of the set *action performed by a cybernetic system in its environment* or an element of the set *action performed by a cybernetic system in its memory*.

Let us consider the hierarchy of classes of actions for processing the ANN in the SCn-code.

action for processing the artificial neural network
:=   [action for processing the ANN]
:=   [action with the artificial neural network]
⊂   *action*
⇒   *decomposition**:
         {•   *action for configuring the ANN*
          •   *action for configuring the weight coefficients of the ANN*
          •   *action for interpreting the ANN*
         }

action for configuring the ANN
⊂   *action for processing the ANN*
⇒   *decomposition**:
         {•   *action for creating the ANN*
          •   *action for editing the ANN*
          •   *action for deleting the ANN*
          •   *action for configuring the ANN layer*
              ⇒   *decomposition**:
                      {•   *action for adding a layer to the ANN*
                       •   *action for editing a layer of the ANN*

- *action for deleting a layer of the ANN*
- *action for setting the activation function of the neurons of the ANN layer*
- *action for configuring a neuron in the ANN layer*
  ⇒   *decomposition*:*
  {•   *action for adding a neuron to the ANN layer*
  •   *action for editing a neuron in the ANN layer*
  •   *action for deleting a neuron from the ANN layer*
  •   *action for setting the activation function of a neuron in the ANN layer*
  }
  }
  }

action for configuring the weight coefficients of the ANN
⊂   *action for processing the ANN*
⊃   *action for training the ANN*
⊃   *action for initializing the weights of the ANN*
    ⊃   *action for initializing the weights of neurons of the ANN layer*
        ⊃   *action for initializing the weights of the neuron of the ANN*

Since as a result of the actions for processing the ANN, the object of these actions, a particular ANN, can change significantly (the configuration of the network, its weight coefficients change), the ANN is represented in the knowledge base as a temporal union of all its versions. Each version is the ANN and a temporal entity. On the set of these temporal entities, a temporal sequence is set with the indication of the first and last versions. Specific knowledge is described for each version. The knowledge common to all versions is described for the ANN, which is a temporal union of all versions.

Figure 4 shows an example of the representation of the ANN as a temporal union of all its versions.

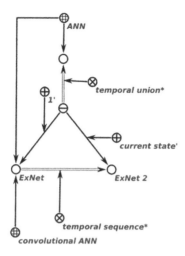

Fig. 4. The representation of the artificial neural network as a temporal union of all its versions

4.2 Action for Training the ANN

Special attention should be paid to the description of the ***action for training the ANN*** as a basic action, as a result of which it is possible to obtain an ANN suitable for usage as a method for solving problems.

An ***action for training the ANN*** is an action, during which a certain *method of training the ANN* is implemented with the specified *parameters of training the ANN*, *optimization method*, and *loss function* on a given set of input data – a *training dataset*.

Known training issues are:

– Overtraining is a problem that arises when training an ANN, which lies in the fact that the network adapts well to the pattern of the input activity from the training dataset while losing the ability to generalize. Overtraining is a result of using an unreasonably complex model while the training of an ANN. This happens when the number of configurable ANN parameters is much larger than the training dataset size. Possible solutions to the problem are to simplify the model, increase the dataset, and use regularization (regularization parameter, dropout technique, etc.).
  To detect overtraining is more difficult than to detect undertraining. As a rule, to do this, cross-validation on a validation set is used, which makes it possible to estimate the moment of completion of the training process. The ideal option is to strike a balance between overtraining and undertraining.

– Undertraining is a problem that arises when training an ANN, which lies in the fact that the network gives equally bad results on training and control datasets. Most often, this kind of problem occurs when there is not enough time spent on training the model. However, this can also be caused by a too simple architecture of the model or small size of the training dataset. In accordance with that, a decision that can be made by an ML engineer is to eliminate these disadvantages: to increase the training time, use a model with a large number of configurable parameters, increase the size of the training dataset as well as decrease regularization and select features for training examples more carefully.

Let us consider the key concepts used to describe the action for training.

The **method of training the ANN** is a method of iterative search for optimal values of the configurable parameters of the ANN, which minimize some given loss function. It is worth noting that although the purpose of using the method of training is to minimize the loss function, the "utility" of the model obtained after training can be assessed only by the achieved level of its generalizing ability. The role relation *method of training'* is used to indicate the belonging of a particular method of training to any action for training the ANN.

Let us consider the hierarchy of methods of training the ANN in the SCn-code.

method of training the ANN
⊂   *method*
⊃   *method of training with a teacher*
    ⇒   *explanation**:
        [A **method of training with a teacher** is a method of training using the set target variables.]
    ⊃   *method of backward propagation of the error*
    :=   [MBPE]
    ⇒   *explanation**:
        [MBPE uses a certain optimization method and a certain loss function to implement the phase of backward propagation of the error and change the configurable ANN parameters. One of the most common optimization methods is the method of stochastic gradient descent.]
    ⇒   *explanation**:
        [It should also be noted that despite the fact that the method is classified as one of the methods of training with a teacher, in the case of using MBPE for training autoencoders, in classical publications, it is considered as a method of training without a teacher, since in this case there is no marked data.]
⊃   *method of training without a teacher*
    ⇒   *explanation**:

[The **method of training without a teacher** is the method
of training without using the set target variables (in the self-
organization mode)]

⇒   *explanation**:

[During the performance of the algorithm of the method of training without a teacher, useful structural properties of the set are
revealed. Informally, it is understood as a method for extracting
information from a distribution, the dataset for which was not
manually annotated by a human [9].]

An **optimization method** is a method for minimizing the target loss function during training the ANN. When denoting the belonging of a particular
optimization method to any method of training the ANN, the role relation *optimization method'* is used.

optimization method

⊂   *method*

⇒   *explanation**:

[The **optimization method** is a method for minimizing the target loss
function during training the ANN]

⇒   *inclusion**:

- *SGD*
  - :=   [stochastic gradient descent]
  - :=   [SGD]
- *Nesterov method*
- *AdaGrad*
  - :=   [adaptive gradient]
- *RMSProp*
  - :=   [root mean square propagation]
- *Adam*
  - :=   [adaptive moments]

The **loss function** is a function used to calculate the error, which is calculated as the difference between the factual reference value and the predicted
value being obtained by the ANN. When denoting the belonging of a particular
loss function to any method of training the ANN, the role relation *loss function'*
is used.

loss function

⊂   *function*

⇒   *inclusion**:

{• *MSE*
  - :=   [mean square error]
- *BCE*

$:=$ [binary cross entropy]

- *MCE*

$:=$ [multi-class cross entropy]

}

To solve the classification problem, it is recommended to use a binary or multiclass cross-entropy loss function. To solve the regression problem, it is advisable to use the mean square error.

A *parameter of training the ANN* is a group of the most general parameters of the method of training the ANN. The following parameters of training the ANN are distinguished:

- the *learning rate* is a parameter that determines the rate of change in the weight coefficients of synaptic connections of the ANN in the training process.
- The *moment parameter* is a parameter used in the training process to eliminate the problem of the "blocking" of the training algorithm in the local minima of the minimized loss function. When training the ANN, the situation of stopping of the process at a certain point of the local minimum without achieving the desired level of generalizing ability of the ANN is frequent. To eliminate such an undesirable phenomenon, an additional parameter (moment) is introduced, which allows the training algorithm to "jump" through the local minimum and continue the process.
- The *regularization parameter* is a parameter used to control the level of overtraining the ANN. *Regularization* is the addition of extra restrictions to the rules for changing the configurable ANN parameters to avoid overtraining.
- The *size of the training group* is the size of the group from the dataset that is used to change the weight coefficients of synaptic connections at each elementary step of training.
- The *training epoch* is one iteration of the training algorithm, during which all the images from the training dataset were used once.

With the help of the concepts highlighted in the subject domain under consideration, it becomes possible to formalize a specific action for processing the ANN in the knowledge base. Figure 5 shows an example of the formalization of the action for training the ANN.

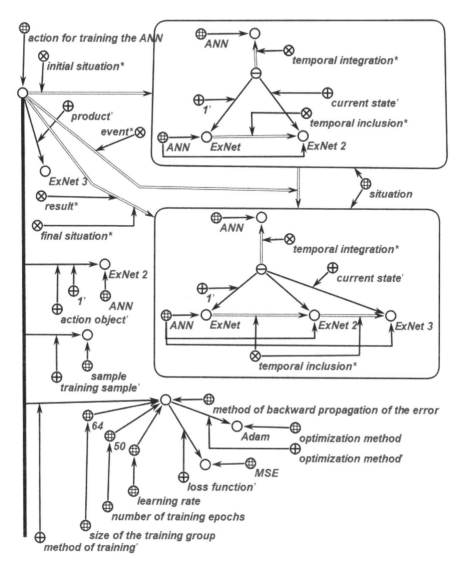

Fig. 5. An example of the formalization of the action for training the artificial neural network in the knowledge base

Conclusion

In the knowledge base built on the foundation of the OSTIS Technology, a model for the modeling of artificial neural networks and actions for their processing has been constructed. The model is offered as subject domains, associated ontologies for artificial neural networks, and processing operations for those networks.

It is possible to describe ANN in the knowledge base with all the variety of their architectures, classes, methods of training, etc. within the framework of the stated subject domains with the aid of their ontologies.

The presence of such a possibility allows creating intelligent systems that can:

- use neural network methods along with other methods available in the system to solve complex problems in a common memory;
- configure, train, and interpret ANN within the knowledge base for the purpose of their introspection and a deeper analysis of their work.

The described model creates the basis for further research in the field of developing:

- universal integration with the knowledge base of any neural network models, whose architecture is not formalized directly in the knowledge base itself;
- a group of agents capable of performing the described actions for processing ANN;
- an approach to automatic decision-making on the usage of a particular neural network model for solving system problems;
- an approach to using the knowledge base to improve the training results of artificial neural networks.

Acknowledgment. The author appreciates the assistance and insightful criticism provided by the research teams at the Departments of Intelligent Information Technologies at the Brest State Technical University and the Belarusian State University of Informatics and Radioelectronics. Particularly, Aleksandr Aleksandrovich Kroshchenko, Danil Vyacheslavovich Shunkevich, Vladimir Adamovich Golovko, and Egor Vladimirovich Mikhno.

References

1. IMS.ostis Metasystem, June 2021. https://ims.ostis.net. Accessed 10 June 2021
2. Besold, T.R., et al.: Neural-symbolic learning and reasoning: a survey and interpretation, November 2017. https://arxiv.org/pdf/1711.03902.pdf. Accessed 10 June 2021
3. Castelvecchi, D.: Can we open the black box of AI? Nat. News **538**(7623), 20–23 (2016)
4. Davydenko, I.: Semantic models, method and tools of knowledge bases coordinated development based on reusable components. In: Golenkov, V. (ed.) Open Semantic Technologies for Intelligent Systems, pp. 99–118. Belarusian State University of Informatics and Radioelectronics Publ., Minsk (2018)
5. Garcez, A.D., et al.: Neural-symbolic learning and reasoning: contributions and challenges. In: Proceedings of the AAAI 2015 Propositional Rule Extraction Under Background Knowledge 11 Spring Symposium on Knowledge Representation and Reasoning: Integrating Symbolic and Neural Approaches. AAAI Press Technical report SS-15-03 (2015)

6. Golenkov, V., Gulyakina, N., Davydenko, I., Shunkevich, D.: Semantic technologies of intelligent systems design and semantic associative computers. In: Golenkov, V. (ed.) Open Semantic Technologies for Intelligent Systems, pp. 42–50. Belarusian State University of Informatics and Radioelectronics Publ., Minsk (2019)
7. Golovko, V.A., et al.: Integration of artificial neural networks and knowledge bases. In: Golenkov, V. (ed.) Open Semantic Technologies for Intelligent Systems, vol. 2, pp. 133–145. Belarusian State University of Informatics and Radioelectronics Publ., Minsk (2018)
8. Golovko, V.A., Krasnoproshin, V.V.: Neural Network Technologies for Data Processing. BSU Publishing House, Minsk (2017)
9. Goodfellow, J., Benjio, I., Courville, A.: Deep Learning. DMK Press, Moscow (2017)
10. Shunkevich, D.: Agent-oriented models, method and tools of compatible problem solvers development for intelligent systems. In: Golenkov, V. (ed.) Open Semantic Technologies for Intelligent Systems, vol. 2, pp. 119–132. Belarusian State University of Informatics and Radioelectronics Publ., Minsk (2018)

The Software System for Calculating the Aggregated Forecast of Time Series

Vadim Moshkin$^{(\boxtimes)}$, Irina Moshkina, and Nadezhda Yarushkina

Ulyanovsk State Technical University, Ulyanovsk, Russia
{v.moshkin,i.timina,jng}@ulstu.ru
http://www.ulstu.ru

Abstract. The paper presents a general algorithm for computing an aggregated time series forecast (TS), within which machine learning methods are used to adjust the parameters of a hybrid combined forecasting model. Also presented are the results of experiments on the application of the developed algorithm using the TS competition "Computational Intelligence in Forecasting" (CIF). The use of a neural network for choosing forecasting methods allowed, on average, for all experiments to reduce the error by 7.225%, as can be seen from the results of the experiments. The average error for the eight prediction methods chosen by the neural network turned out to be lower than the average error for all methods in 47 cases out of 50 (94%).

Keywords: Time series · forecasting · aggregated forecast · machine learning

1 Introduction

The state of their technical systems is often described by time series (TS) during their design. It is necessary to predict the state of the design object for making a design decision. The developed approach uses machine learning methods to tune the parameters of a hybrid combined time series forecasting model. According to the developed predictive approach, it is necessary to determine a set of significant characteristics of time series. These characteristics should fully describe the dynamics of the time series [1].

There are many methods for predicting vehicles. Combined models are used to take advantage of several methods at once. According to [2], a combined forecasting model is a forecasting model consisting of several individual models, called a base set.

In [3], a number of factors are highlighted that emphasize the effectiveness of the combined model:

– Impossibility of choosing a single model based on experimental data, according to the theory of multiple models [4].

Supported by the RFBR. Projects No. 20-07-00672, No. 19-07-00999.

- An attempt to choose the only best model leads to the need to choose from a group of models with similar statistical characteristics [5].
- The choice of a forecasting model for a vehicle with a pronounced dynamic of level and properties leads to the choice of an averaged model [2]. It is impossible to quickly replace one forecasting model with another by analyzing its dynamics.
- Each forecasting model considers only one side of the dynamics of the analyzed process. The set of models allows a more detailed description of the dynamics. Any forecast rejected due to non-optimality contains information important for modeling [5].

According to [5], combined forecasting models are divided into selective and hybrid ones.

In the selective model, the current predicted value is calculated from the selected value according to the selective criterion of the model from the base set.

The selective criterion can be:

- the minimum of the absolute value of the forecast error of the current member of the series;
- minimum of the absolute value of the error for the last K observations (K-test);
- the minimum of the exponentially smoothed squared deviation error (B-criterion).

Thus, when using a selective model, at each moment in time, the forecast is built according to a single method selected from the basic set, hybrid models, in turn, make it possible to build a forecast using several models at once, using the advantages of their joint application.

In a hybrid model, the predicted value is obtained by aggregating the predicted results from several models from the base set. As a rule, the final forecast is a weighted sum of individual forecasts.

In [6], for the first time, the idea of creating a hybrid model based on combining forecasts of several statistical models was substantiated; in [[7]], this idea was developed, and it was proposed to use the arithmetic mean of forecasting results of the models included in the base set [3] as the final forecast.

According to [5], the main problem of constructing hybrid forecasting models is to determine the optimal weights of individual forecasting models from the base set.

In [3], the following main directions of development of hybrid forecasting models are identified:

1. inclusion in the basic set of new (emerging) forecasting models
2. development of new methods for combining forecasts.

There are 7 main groups of methods for combining forecasts [8]:

1. Methods based on the arithmetic mean of particular predictions [6,9,10]. However, the presence of anomalous forecasts as part of a combined forecast significantly reduces its accuracy [11]. It is proposed to exclude anomalous predictions by using a truncated arithmetic mean [12,13].

2. Methods based on minimizing the final forecast error by the least squares method [14].
3. Methods based on minimizing the variance of the combined forecast error (works by Bates and Granger [6], Ershov [15], Baltrushevich [16]).
4. Methods based on retrospective forecasts. This group includes the AFTER method [17]. The weights of the private forecasts are calculated based on their own past values, conditional variance, and the past values of the private forecasts. The weights are updated after each new observation.

   The following disadvantages of the AFTER method were noted in [8]:
   - difficult applicability in practice;
   - strong dependence of the weights on the first set value.

   This group includes the following methods:
   - ARM, developed by Yang [18];
   - the Bunn method [19], which assumes finding the distribution function for the weight coefficient through the beta distribution;
   - an adaptive method based on exponential smoothing [2, 20].
5. Methods based on factor analysis. These methods were proposed by Frenkel [21] and Gorelik and Frenkel [5]. The idea of using factor analysis is based on the fact that particular forecast results using a separate forecasting method are an external expression of some really existing but immeasurable forecast value, which is taken as a combined forecast [8].
6. The method of Gupta and Wilton, based on finding the optimal weights of the coefficients of particular predictions using a matrix of pairwise preferences, has been placed in a separate group [22].
7. Methods based on quadratic programming. The paper [23] describes a method for calculating the weights of particular predictions by minimizing the retrospective relative errors of particular predictions using quadratic programming methods.

The main advantage of the method is efficiency and ease of implementation. The main disadvantage is the obligatory preliminary selection of particular forecasting methods in order to comply with the requirement of error independence [8].

Most of the methods for combining forecasts are based on the assumptions about the independence of the absolute forecast errors and their distribution in accordance with the normal law with zero mathematical expectation and unknown variance. However, these assumptions are often not met [3], and therefore, methods based on fuzzy logic and stable statistical estimates are currently being actively developed, for example:

1. method of combining forecasts by Kovalev [24] based on a system of fuzzy rules;
2. the Davydov union method [25], based on the use of a robust M-estimate;
3. Methods for combining particular forecasts by Vasiliev [26] based on the robust Huber estimate of the truncated mean type and on the basis of the Hodges-Lehmann R-estimate.

Thus, despite a significant number of publications on the topics of forecasting methods for time series and methods for aggregating individual forecasts, the question of choosing the most appropriate aggregating method and its constituent forecasting models for the predicted time series remains.

2 Developed Algorithm for Calculating the Aggregated Forecast of Time Series

Figure 1 shows a schematic description of the developed algorithm for calculating the aggregated forecast of time series.

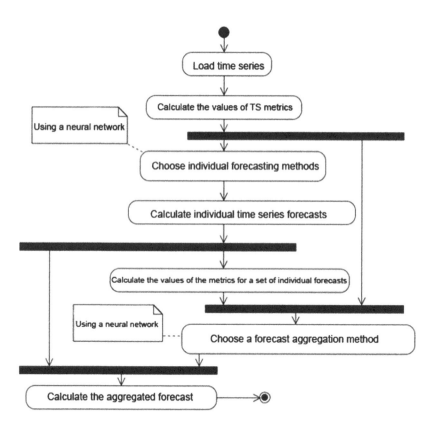

Fig. 1. Algorithm for calculating the aggregated forecast of time series

In this paper, 2 methods of setting the forecast weights are considered:

- the first method is based on the values of the prediction error on the control part of the time series;
- the second method is based on the error values assumed by the neural network for choosing a prediction method.

The structure of the neural network for choosing the aggregating method is close to the structure of the neural network for choosing individual prediction methods, but it includes more input neurons corresponding to the metrics. Neurons corresponding to individual prediction methods have been replaced with neurons corresponding to aggregation methods. The structure of the neural network of the aggregating method is shown in Fig. 2.

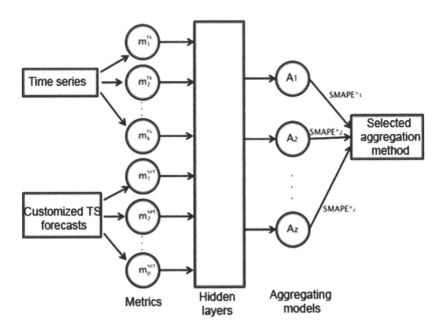

Fig. 2. The structure of the neural network for choosing the aggregating method

Input neurons $m_1^{ts}, \ldots, m_k^{ts}$ correspond to time series metrics. Neurons $m_1^{set}, \ldots, m_p^{set}$ set correspond to the metrics of the aggregated set of individual predictions. The output values correspond to the estimated prediction error (SMAPE) values calculated by the neural network for each aggregator $(A_1, \ldots, A_z)$ from the base set. The aggregator from the base set of the combined model with the lowest estimated error value is used to obtain the final forecast.

The following main reasons for choosing just such a set of metrics for the input layer of the neural network can be distinguished:

– it is difficult to correctly train a neural network if the input neurons correspond to individual forecasting methods, since different individual methods will be selected for each time series. This means that the values of the signals arriving at the input of the neural network under consideration will be equal to zero for the unselected methods;
– the choice of the aggregator depends on the values of the time series metrics, but transitively;

- the direct dependence of the choice of an aggregator based on particular forecasting results is implemented through the metrics of a set of individual forecasts.

An error backpropagation algorithm with a logistic activation function is used to train the neural network. The training sample file contains the metric values and prediction errors (SMAPE) for each time series included in the set for each aggregation method.

This method of setting the weights includes dividing the time series into training and control parts, followed by forecasting by each individual method using the training part of the control values and calculating the prediction error. The weights of individual forecasts as part of the aggregator are set in inverse proportion to the magnitude of the error of each method.

3 Software System and Experimental Results

The developed program is designed to solve the problem of obtaining an aggregated forecast for the time series of the states of a technical system.

The software product is developed on the .NET Framework 4.6.1 platform in the C # language. The development environment was Microsoft Visual Studio 2015.

The "neuralnet" library [27] for the R language was used to work with neural networks. It made it possible to create neural networks with the structure of a multilayer preceptron, trained by the method of back propagation of the error (ordinary or elastic propagation). This library has a user-friendly interface and a high degree of configuration flexibility, allowing you to select the activation function and the error function.

The R library "ForecastComb" was used to compute the aggregated forecast. This library contains more than 12 aggregation methods (Fig. 3).

3.1 Experiment №1

Time series from the Computational Intelligence in Forecasting (CIF) competition [28] were selected to test the effectiveness of the developed solution.

- The first CIF benchmark contains 91 time series of different lengths (from 12 to 1089 observations) and different frequency of observations: day, month, quarter, year.
- The second CIF benchmark includes 72 time series with a frequency of a month and a length of 28 to 120 observations.

Five experiments with identical algorithm were carried out. The averaged final result was obtained for them.

1. A set of 152 time series of the benchmark was randomly divided into training (142 time series) and control parts (10 time series) during each experiment.

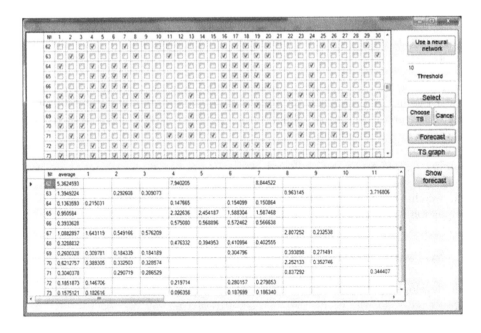

Fig. 3. Forecast aggregation system form

2. The time series of the control part were excluded from the general table of the training sample.
3. The neural network for choosing prediction methods (with automatic selection of the optimal number of neurons) was trained using the remaining data.
4. The resulting neural network was used to select the 8 best forecasting methods from the base set for the time series of the control part of the general table [29] (Table 1).

Figure 4 is a diagram showing, for each of the five experiments, the average SMAPE error for best practices and SMAPE for all methods.

The use of a neural network for choosing forecasting methods allowed, on average, for all experiments to reduce the error by 7.225%, as can be seen from the results of the experiments. The average error for the eight prediction methods chosen by the neural network turned out to be lower than the average error for all methods in 47 cases out of 50 (94%).

3.2   Experiment №2

The effectiveness of the developed solution was tested on time series containing information about downtime of new, modernized and old CNC equipment connected to the monitoring system.

Table 1. Experiment №1 results.

Experiment No.	Time series No.	Average SMAPE by best methods,%	Average SMAPE for all 30 methods,%	Absolute increase in accuracy,%	Average absolute increase in accuracy for the experiment,%
1	7	4,635	16,176	11,541	9,424
	18	4,002	9,583	5,582	
	49	4,298	12,274	7,976	
	58	8,778	39,305	30,526	
	69	0,279	0,906	0,627	
	70	0,662	3,828	3,166	
	92	0,881	5,399	4,518	
	99	0,812	6,348	5,536	
	120	3,804	11,208	7,404	
	136	10,966	28,326	17,360	
2	23	2,243	6,216	3,973	5,793
	33	0,265	1,549	1,284	
	47	2,943	6,428	3,484	
	68	0,348	0,999	0,651	
	95	5,081	12,659	7,578	
	114	4,097	16,337	12,240	
	139	3,374	12,872	9,498	
	140	5,286	15,163	9,877	
	145	2,981	7,432	4,450	
	149	3,923	8,812	4,888	
3	23	8,191	6,216	-1,975	5,015
	29	5,653	15,455	9,802	
	36	0,406	4,062	3,656	
	42	2,445	12,397	9,952	
	43	6,082	15,849	9,768	
	59	4,122	17,053	12,931	
	68	0,352	0,999	0,647	
	99	0,812	6,348	5,536	
	121	4,606	13,619	9,013	
	141	25,472	16,288	-9,183	
4	26	8,586	23,249	14,663	9,373
	31	2,253	15,323	13,070	
	55	7,104	28,786	21,682	
	61	2,523	10,022	7,499	
	62	3,471	13,814	10,343	
	70	0,127	3,828	3,701	
	85	2,004	4,575	2,570	
	96	3,463	4,782	1,319	
	122	11,088	28,805	17,717	
	130	0,538	1,707	1,168	
5	22	3,879	23,479	19,600	6,520
	46	10,839	21,934	11,096	
	49	1,478	12,274	10,796	
	61	2,127	10,022	7,896	
	63	20,157	6,374	-13,783	
	73	0,145	0,328	0,183	
	80	0,192	3,073	2,881	
	101	9,735	26,690	16,954	
	135	0,121	0,293	0,173	
	140	5,754	15,163	9,409	

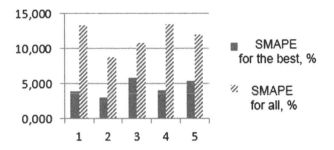

Fig. 4. Results of the conducted experiments

Data were received from JSC Aviastar-SP (Ulyanovsk, Russia) on 11 machines of shop 255 for the period from April to December 2020. The time series was formed based on data on the following reasons for downtime:

– the machine is turned off;
– the machine is stopped;
– emergency repair;
– control of the technical control bureau;
– operator control;
– regulated break;
– replacement tool;
– adjustment of control programs;
– revision of control programs;
– service by the operator;
– replacement of cutting fluids;
– unreasonable downtime;
– non-compliance with the regulations.

Thus, a set of 143 time series was obtained: data for 11 machines for 13 reasons of downtime. The resulting time series are difficult to predict for the following reasons:

– the time series are short (9 values);
– they contain null values;
– in most cases do not have a visible pattern.

For the experiments, 23 time series containing more than two zero observations were excluded from the set. A series of experiments similar to the above was carried out. However, when calculating forecasts for all methods (for constructing a training sample table) for some of the 120 time series, most forecasting methods from the base set failed to calculate the forecast. In this regard, these time series were excluded from the experiment.

Time series for which only less than 30% of the methods could not calculate the forecast were left in the training sample table, but the error value for them was set as 100%. Also, all calculated errors of more than 100% for the table were reduced to this value (in order to prevent a large scatter of the output values in the training set of the neural network).

The general table of the training sample was randomly divided five times into the training (94 time series) and control (7 time series) parts.

In all experiments for time series from the control part of the training table for solving the problem of choosing forecasting methods, the effectiveness of a neural network trained on benchmark time series was tested.

According to the results of the experiments, the use of a neural network of method selection made it possible to reduce the average error by 29.419% if a network trained on enterprise data was used, and by 13.397% if a network trained on a benchmark time series was used. The experimental results are shown in more detail in Fig. 5 and Table 2. It was suggested that the significant difference in the efficiency of a neural network trained on enterprise data and a network trained on benchmark data is due to the specifics of the enterprise time series. Some of the baseline methods either do not work with enterprise time series or provide predictions of poor accuracy. At the same time, a neural network trained on enterprise data recognizes these situations and does not choose non-working or ineffective methods, in contrast to a neural network trained on a benchmark, where all methods gave acceptable results.

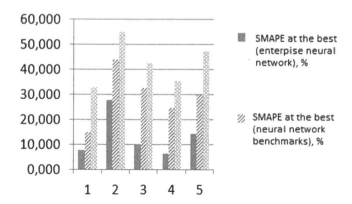

Fig. 5. An experiment to select individual methods for enterprise TS. SMAPE diagram

Time series were removed from the results of the previous experiment, for which the neural network trained on the benchmark chose non-working methods to test this assumption.

The reduction in error when using this neural network averaged 28.21%. Reducing the error when using neural networks trained on enterprise data -25.122%. In this case, the high efficiency of the network based on the benchmark can be explained by the large variety of the training set (and, as a consequence, the quality) of this network.

Table 2. Experiment №2 results.

Experiment No.	TS Number	Average SMAPE for all methods,%	Average SMAPE by best methods,%		Absolute increase in accuracy,%		Average absolute increase in accuracy for the experiment,%	
			Enterprise neural network	Neural network benchmarks	Enterprise neural network	Neural network benchmarks	Enterprise neural network	Neural network benchmarks
1	4	45,754	26,102	3,232	19,652	42,522	25,138	18,056
	13	19,321	0,004	0,513	19,317	18,808		
	15	18,299	4,050	0,636	14,249	17,663		
	33	50,898	24,605	71,430	26,292	-20,532		
	63	38,447	0,073	1,079	38,374	37,368		
	64	22,246	0,033	0,971	22,214	21,275		
	100	35,885	0,015	26,598	35,870	9,287		
2	11	18,427	0,021	0,268	18,406	18,159	27,317	10,905
	26	92,898	70,787	100,000	22,111	-7,102		
	34	39,758	0,040	0,389	39,718	39,369		
	54	61,824	0,396	71,458	61,428	-9,634		
	58	32,211	0,043	0,267	32,168	31,945		
	72	60,701	60,807	35,500	-0,106	25,201		
	90	78,401	60,909	100,001	17,492	-21,600		
3	16	42,039	11,328	73,687	30,711	-31,648	32,786	10,002
	19	67,745	10,370	50,843	57,374	16,901		
	20	74,718	31,808	85,720	42,910	-11,002		
	28	41,951	6,662	1,260	35,289	40,691		
	45	13,854	0,003	0,439	13,851	13,415		
	76	29,509	7,796	2,262	21,714	27,248		
	91	27,661	0,005	13,253	27,656	14,408		
4	12	25,969	4,018	1,362	21,951	24,606	28,846	10,590
	18	53,780	23,586	83,372	30,195	-29,591		
	31	32,927	3,025	0,483	29,902	32,445		
	35	45,288	0,141	78,719	45,146	-33,432		
	59	29,570	1,320	0,328	28,250	29,241		
	74	28,177	4,548	1,218	23,629	26,959		
	76	30,645	7,796	6,746	22,849	23,899		
5	5	48,269	6,220	0,387	42,049	47,882	33,007	17,432
	16	42,039	14,899	73,687	27,140	-31,648		
	29	35,174	0,006	0,298	35,168	34,876		
	31	36,646	3,025	0,483	33,621	36,163		
	72	62,671	60,807	35,500	1,864	27,171		
	82	71,975	14,486	79,355	57,488	-7,381		
	98	33,771	0,050	18,813	33,720	14,957		

4 Conclusions

Thus, as a result of the project, a general algorithm for computing an aggregated time series forecast (TS) was proposed, within which machine learning methods are used to tune the parameters of a hybrid combined forecasting model. Also presented are the results of experiments on the application of the developed algorithm using the TS competition "Computational Intelligence in Forecasting" (CIF).

The use of a neural network for the choice of forecasting methods allowed, on average, for all experiments to reduce the error by 7.225%, which can be seen from the results of the experiments. The average error for eight prediction methods selected by the neural network was lower than the average error for all methods in 47 cases out of 50 (94%).

The effectiveness of the developed solution was tested on time series containing information about downtime of new, modernized and old CNC equipment connected to the monitoring system. Data were received from JSC Aviastar-SP (Ulyanovsk, Russia) on 11 machines of shop 255.

The reduction in error when using neural network averaged 28.21%. Reducing the error when using neural networks trained on enterprise data -25.122%.

References

1. Averkin, A.N.: Soft computations and measurements. Intell. Syst. **2**(1–4), 93–114 (1997)
2. Lukashin, Y.P.: Adaptive Methods of Short-term Forecasting of Time Series, 416p. Finance and statistics, Moscow (2003)
3. Vasiliev, A.A.: Genesis of hybrid forecasting models based on the combination of forecasts. Bull. TVGU. Ser. Econ. Manage. **23**, 316–331 (2014)
4. Ivakhnenko A.G.: Inductive Method of Self-organization of Models of Complex Systems, 296p. Monograph Naukova Dumka, Kiev (1981)
5. Gorelik, N.A., Frenkel, A.A.: Statistical problems of economic forecasting. Statistical Methods of Analysis of Economic Dynamics: Textbook. Application on Statistics, vol. 46, pp. 9–48. Nauka (1983)
6. Bates, J.M., Granger, C.W.J.: The combination of forecasts. Oper. Reser. Quart. **20**(4), 451–468 (1969)
7. Newbold, P., Granger, C.W.J.: Experience with forecasting univariate time series and combination of forecasts. J. R. Statist. Soc. Ser. A. **137**(2), 131–164 (1974)
8. Frenkel, A.A. Methodological approaches to improving forecasting accuracy by combining forecasts. In: Frenkel, A.A., Surkov, M. (eds.) Questions of Statistics, vol. 8, pp. 17–36 (2015)
9. Barnard, G.A.: New methods of quality control. J. R. Statist. Soc. **126**, 255–259 (1963)
10. Makridakis, S., Winkler, R.L.: Averages of forecasts: some empirical results. Manag. Sci. **9**, 987–996 (1983)
11. Winkler, R.L., Clemen, R.T.: Sensitivity of weights in combining forecasts. Operations Research. **40**, 609–614 (1992)
12. Goodwin, P.: New evidence on the value of combining forecasts. FORESIGHT **12**, 33–35 (2009)

13. Jose, V.R., Winkler, R.L.: Simple robust averages of forecasts: some empirical results. Int. J. Forecast. **24**, 163–169 (2008)
14. Granger, C.W.J., Ramanathan, R.: Improved methods of combining forecasts. J. Forecast. **3**, 197–204 (1984)
15. Ershov E.B.: On one method of combining private forecasts. In: Ershov, E.B. (ed.) Statistical Methods of Analysis of Economic Dynamics. UCHealth App. According to Statistics, pp. 87–105. Nauka, Moscow (1973)
16. Baltrushevich, T.G.: Models and methods for assessing the effectiveness of flexible production systems. Avtoref. Dis. Cand. Econ. Sci. 17–20 (1991)
17. Yang, Y.: Combining forecasting procedures: some theoretical results. Department of Statistics and Statistical Laboratory Iowa State University (2001)
18. Yang, Y.: Adaptive regression by mixing. J. Am. Statist. Assoc. **96**, 574–588 (2001)
19. Bunn, D.W.: A Bayesian approach to the linear combination of forecasts. Oper. Res. Q. **26**, 325–329 (1975)
20. Dubrova T.A. Statistical analysis and forecasting of economic dynamics: problems and approaches. In: Methodology of Statistical Research Of Socio-economic Processes, pp. 129–138. Unity (2012)
21. Frenkel, A.A.: Forecasting labor productivity: methods and models. Economics. 142–154 (1989)
22. Gupta, S., Wilton, P.C.: Combination of forecasts: an extension. Manage. Sci. **3**, 356–371 (1987)
23. Beilinson, Y.E.: Combined forecast models. In: Beilinson, Y.E., Motova, M.A. (eds.) Expert information. Series: Modeling of Socio-economic Processes, pp. 110–121 (1990)
24. Yarushkina, N.G., Filippov, A.A., Romanov, A.A., Moshkin, V.S., Egov, E.N.: Developing a system for time series data mining on the basis of F-transform and the domain-specific ontology. In: Fuzzy Systems Association and 9th International Conference on Soft Computing and Intelligent Systems (IFSA-SCIS), 2017 Joint 17th World Congress of International, pp. 1–6. IEEE (2017)
25. Davydov, A.A.: Forecasting social phenomena using "neural" networks. In: Kryshtanovsky, A.O. (ed.) Sociological Methods in Modern Sociological Practice: Collection of Articles. Materials Vseross. Scientific Conference in Memory. GU-HSE, pp. 41–49 (2008)
26. Vasiliev, A.A. Forecasting in logistics based on stable hybrid models. In: Lukinsky, V.S., Vasiliev, A.A., Kurganov, V.M. (eds.) Logistics: Modern Development Trends: Materials of the X International. Scientific-practical Conference 14–15 April 2011, SPbGIEU, pp. 52–55 (2011)
27. Yashin, D., Moshkina, I., Moshkin, V.: An approach to the selection of a time series analysis method using a neural network. In: Gervasi, O., et al. (eds.) ICCSA 2020. LNCS, vol. 12249, pp. 692–703. Springer, Cham (2020). https://doi.org/10.1007/978-3-030-58799-4_50
28. Ayvazyan, S.A.: Applied statistics and foundations of econometrics. In: Ayvazyan, S.A., Mkhitaryan, V.S. (eds.) UNITI, 1024 p. (1998)
29. Yarushkina, Nadezhda, Andreev, Ilya, Moshkin, Vadim, Moshkina, Irina: Integration of fuzzy owl ontologies and fuzzy time series in the determination of faulty technical units. In: Misra, S., et al. (eds.) ICCSA 2019. LNCS, vol. 11619, pp. 545–555. Springer, Cham (2019). https://doi.org/10.1007/978-3-030-24289-3_40

Semantic-Based Design of an Adaptive User Interface

Mikhail Sadouski$^{(\boxtimes)}$ ⓘ

Department of Intelligent Information Technologies, Belarusian State University
of Informatics and Radioelectronics, Minsk, Republic of Belarus
sadovski@bsuir.by

Abstract. An approach to the building of adaptive user interfaces (UIs)
based on their semantic model (semantic-based design) is described in the
article. A variant of the implementation of a framework for building UIs
is proposed within this approach, which is based on the *OSTIS Technology*. The existing approaches to the building of UIs are also considered;
examples and methods of designing UI components for the proposed
implementation variation are shown.

Keywords: OSTIS · User interface (UI) · Adaptive user interface
(AUI) · Ontological approach · Semantic model · Semantic-based design

1 Introduction

There is a growing need for the usage of computer systems in the modern world,
as well as the daily life of people. The efficiency of their usage largely depends on
the UI, since it is the UI as a component of the system that is a way to interact
with users.

Currently, the UI is the most frequently changed component of the system
and is the part of the application requiring the maximum number of changes.
Approximately 80% of the costs in the development of computer systems are
accounted for by the testing, design, and development of the UI. Meanwhile,
almost all applications change their interface after the release of the first version and the addition of new functionality always affects the already developed
component. Additionally, most modern systems should be cross-platform for the
convenience of users, which implies the development of the web, mobile, and
desktop versions of the interface [1].

When building the UI, the following issues remain relevant:

– in most systems, there is no possibility of changing the UI during running;
– there is a difficulty in usage of the same interface for different platforms;
– in most systems, there is no possibility of flexible adaptation of the UI to the
  needs of a particular user;
– the absence of general principles for building UI limits the possibility to reuse
  already developed components and increases the time required to train the
  user in new UIs, which also increases the development time and the cost of
  supporting and designing UIs.

V. Golenkov et al. (Eds.): OSTIS 2021, CCIS 1625, pp. 165–191, 2022.
https://doi.org/10.1007/978-3-031-15882-7_10

Within this paper, an ontological approach to the building of semantic models of adaptive UIs based on the OSTIS Technology is proposed to solve the problems mentioned above.

AUIs have been promoted as a solution for the context variability due to their ability to automatically adapt to the context-of-use at runtime. An AUI modifies content, structure, and functionality independently to meet the needs of individual users, can edit a display based on user preferences that are obtained as a result of user actions. The development of AUIs involves the development of several sub-components, which are required for supporting the complex representation and inference, that underlie adaptive behaviour. This fact is reflected in all models that have been proposed in the literature for the description of AUIs [13, 29, 30]. The ideas proposed in [12] and [26] are elaborated in this article that is aimed at more detailed consideration of the problem of the UI automatic building, which is a key idea to support the flexibility and simplicity of improving the designed interfaces.

The building of the AUI according to the proposed approach will be carried out on the basis of its full semantic model that contains a precise specification of all the used concepts with the help of a hierarchical system of formal ontologies, which will ensure the integration of various aspects of the UI within a unified system, the ability of the system to analyze the actions performed within the UI, as well as its flexible configuration during the operation. Therefore, the development of the UI will be reduced to the building and improvement of its semantic model.

2   Analysis of Existing Approaches

Nowadays, there are several basic approaches for generating a UI, which consider its various aspects:

- a context-sensitive approach;
- an approach based on specialized description languages;
- an ontological approach;
- a data-based approach.

A particular user interface is assumed to be represented in a platform-independent manner in the approach based on specialized description languages. Interface description languages include **UIML** [9], **UsiXML** [21], **XForms**, [8] and **JavaFX FXML** [4] respectively. The fundamental goal of the depicted languages is to generate dialog models and interface forms independent of the technology being utilized. They also describe visual elements, their relationships, and features to produce a particular UI.

The context-sensitive approach integrates the usage of a structural description of the interface based on description languages with a behavioral specification, that is, the generation of the interface is based on user actions. Transitions between various types of a particular UI are specified within the approach. Examples of the implementation of this approach are **CAP3** [11] and **MARIA** [23].

A model-oriented, or a data-based, approach uses a model of the subject domain as the basis for creating UIs. The implementation includes **JANUS** [10] and **Mecano** [25].

Existing ontological approaches are usually based on the approaches considered earlier and use ontologies as a way of information representation about a particular UI. For example, by analogy with the approach based on specialized description languages, the framework [22] was proposed, which uses an ontology to describe the UI based on concepts stored in the knowledge base (KB). By analogy with the context-dependent approach, within the article [16], the model of the subject domain together with the UI model is used, associated with the ontology of actions. The **ActiveRaUL** [14] project combines a model-oriented approach with UIML. In this project, the ontological model of the subject domain is correlated with the ontological representation of the UI. The approach proposed in [20] combines application data with the UI ontology for the creation of a single description in the KB for the subsequent automatic generation of various interface options for questionnaire applications with ready-made user interaction scerenarios. It is also worth noting the articles [18] and [19], in which a concept is proposed, that simplifies the development of the interface to the level of the information generation for each component of the interface model using editors controlled by the corresponding models of ontologies.

The interface generation principle based on a declarative description lies in the basis of many applied projects. Thus, the **mermaid** [5] project allows automatically generating diagrams based on their description, and the **rjsf** [7] project allows generating forms for user input. Additionally, a main approach to displaying and generating an interface based on its description on the server side of the system can also be found in industrial development under the terms **Server-Driven UI**, or **Backend-Driven UI** [2].

The disadvantages of existing solutions for generating the UI include the following ones:

– solutions that offer a platform-independent description allow generating only simple UIs that are limited in functionality (diagrams, questionnaire applications, etc.);
– as a rule, the created models are specific to a certain platform or a particular implementation of the UI, which hinders their reusage for other purposes.

Among the proposed approaches, the ontological one is the most preferable for the following reasons:

– it allows creating the most complete description of different aspects of the UI. The composition of this description will be discussed in more detail below;
– it simplifies the reusage of the interface by applying a single representation of the interface model for various platforms;
– it allows integrating earlier proposed approaches due to a single way of knowledge representation.

Nevertheless, the problem of compatibility of various ontologies within a unified system remains relevant for existing solutions based on the ontological approach as well as the lack of the ability to adapt to user requests and analyze their actions for independent improvement (the ontology of user actions serves as a basis for such an analysis).

3   Proposed Approach

Based on the conducted analysis, an approach on the basis of an ontological one is proposed, which consists in creating a complete semantic model of the interface, which will eliminate the shortcomings of existing solutions. The key features of the approach are:

- the presence of a complete semantic model of the interface, that contains a "syntactic" interface description (rules for forming full and correct interface from its components), a "lexical" interface description (a description of the components, from which the interface is formed), but also its semantic description (knowledge of which entity the displayed component a sign is). Meanwhile, the semantic description also includes the purpose, a description of the interface user activity, and scope of application of the interface components;
- the fixation of the interface description in the form of an abstraction, regardless of the device and platform;
- the reduction of development costs due to the reusage of interface components;
- the representation of the specification of the interface generation tools and, if necessary, the tools themselves in a common format with a description of the interface through some unified knowledge representation language;
- universality, that is, the possibility of using the approach to build interfaces of any systems, regardless of their purpose. The unified principles of the building of the interface will allow the user to easily switch from using one system to another, significantly reducing the cost of training;
- the reduction of development costs due to the usage of a hierarchical structuring of the UI model, which allows independently developing the components;
- the integration of the semantic model of the interface with other models within a unified system. For example, the integration with the user model (knowledge about the user's behavior within the system, biographical information) will make the interface adaptive. In this case, an interface can adapt to a certain user or category of users (which implies not only a change in the visual component of the interface but also a change in its internal functionality).

Thus, based on the above, the following demands can be made to the technology, on the ground of which this approach can be implemented:

- the technology should support a component approach to creating semantic models;
- the technology should allow the simple integration of various semantic models within a unified system;
- the technology should provide an opportunity to describe different semantic models and their components of various types of knowledge in a single format.

Among the existing system design technologies, the *OSTIS Technology* meets the specified requirements, among the advantages of which it is also possible to additionally highlight the presence of a basic set of ontologies that can serve as the ground for the AUI model being developed.

Thus, within this approach, in the article, an option for implementing a framework for building UIs is proposed, which is based on the *OSTIS Technology*, providing a universal language for the semantic representation (encoding) of information in the memory of intelligent computer systems, called an *SC-code*. Texts of the *SC-code* (sc-texts) are unified semantic networks with a basic set-theoretic interpretation. The elements of such semantic networks are called *sc-elements* (*sc-connectors* and *sc-nodes*, which, in turn, can be *sc-edges* or *sc-arcs*, depending on the directivity). The *SC-code alphabet* consists of five main elements, on the ground of which SC-code constructions of any complexity are built, as well as more particular types of sc-elements (for example, new concepts) are introduced. The memory that stores SC-code constructions is called semantic memory (*sc-memory*) [17].

The architecture of each ostis-system includes a platform for interpreting semantic models of ostis-systems as well as a semantic model of the ostis-system described using the SC-code (sc-model of the ostis-system). In turn, the sc-model of the ostis-system includes the sc-model of the KB, the sc-model of the interface, and the sc-model of the problem solver. The principles of the design and structure of KBs and problem solvers are discussed in more detail in [15] and [28], respectively. Within this article, the sc-model of the UI will be considered, which is included in the sc-model of the interface. Its principles were described in the article [12], the development of which is this paper.

The SC-code representation languages include:

- **SCs-code** – a string (linear) version of the SC-code representation. It is designed to represent sc-graphs (SC-code texts) in the form of sequences of characters;
- **SCn-code** – a string non-linear version of the SC-code representation. The SCn-code is designed to represent sc-graphs in the form of sequences of characters formatted according to given rules, in which basic hypermedia tools, such as graphic images as well as tools of navigation between parts of sc.n-texts, can also be used [12];
- **SCg-code** – one of the possible ways of visual representation of SC-texts. The basic principle that underlies the SCg-code is that each sc-element is assigned a sc.g-element (graphical representation).

Within this article, fragments of SCn- and SCg-codes [3] will be used, which are simultaneously fragments of the source texts of the KB, that are understandable both to a human and to a machine. This allows making the text more formalized and structured while maintaining its readability.

It is also worth noting that ostis-systems allow integrating knowledge from many sources and the amount of knowledge of the system can be significant, which requires the ability to display knowledge in a user-friendly way. Thus, the

usage of an adaptive interface for ostis-systems will allow dynamically changing
the representation of the response grounded on the preferences of a certain user.

4   Problem Definition

The UI within the proposed approach is a specialized ostis-system focused on
solving interface problems and that includes a KB and a problem solver of the
UI. The general architecture of the ostis-system is shown in Fig. 1.

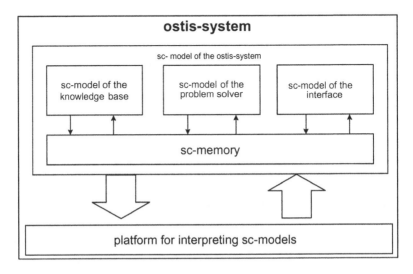

Fig. 1. The architecture of the ostis-system

To build a UI, in the KB, an sc-model of UI components, interface actions
of a user, as well as the classification of UI in general is used, as shown in Fig. 2.
When designing the interface, a component approach is used, which represents
the application interface in the form of unified, specified components. The development, support, and updating of components can occur independently. It is
important to note that as a result of the building, the UI should be both static
(visually formed) and dynamic (capable of performing user actions).

The basis of the *sc-model of the ostis-system knowledge base* is a hierarchical system of subject domains and their corresponding ontologies. Accordingly,
within the proposed approach, it is necessary to develop:

- the Subject domain of user interfaces;
- the Subject domain of user interface components;
- the Subject domain of users;
- the Subject domain of interface user actions.

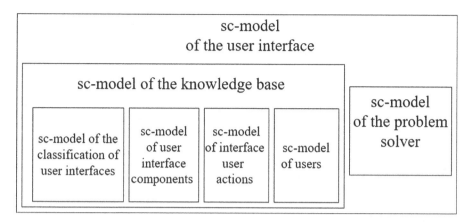

Fig. 2. The structure of the sc-model of the UI

The problem solver is a hierarchical system of agents of knowledge processing in semantic memory (sc-agents), which interact with each other exclusively by specifying the actions they perform in the memory. An sc-agent is a particular subject that can perform actions in sc-memory, which belong to a certain class of autonomous actions. An autonomous action is an action that is performed regardless of whether the specified action is part of the decomposition of a more common action [27]. To build a UI, it is necessary to implement the following agents:

- the Agent of processing of user actions;
- the Agent for interpretation of the sc-model of the user interface knowledge base.

5   SC-Model of the Knowledge Base

5.1   Subject Domain of User Interfaces

The Subject domain of user interfaces includes the classification of user interfaces.

user interface
⊃   *graphical user interface*
    ⊃   *WIMP-interface*
        ⊃   *ostis-system user interface*
⊃   *command-line interface*
⊃   *SILK-interface*
    ⊃   *natural-language interface*
        ⊃   *speech interface*

A *user interface (UI)* is a combination of software and hardware tools that allows the user to interact with the computer system.

A *command-line interface* is a UI, in which interaction between the computer system and the user occurs using commands or text instructions.

A *graphical user interface* is a UI, in which interaction between the computer system and the user occurs using the graphical components of a computer system.

A *WIMP-interface* is a UI, in which interaction between the computer system and the user occurs in the form of a dialog using menus, windows, and other controls.

An *ostis-system user interface* is a specialized ostis-system focused on solving interface problems and that includes a KB and a problem solver of the UI.

SILK-interface is a UI that is the closest to the natural form of human communication. The computer system searches for commands, the results of which are converted into a human-understandable form, for example, into a natural-language text or an image.

A *natural-language interface* is a SILK-interface, in which interaction between a computer system and a user occurs through a dialog in one of the natural languages.

A *speech interface* is a natural-language interface, in which interaction occurs using speech. This type of UI is the closest to natural communication between humans.

5.2   Subject Domain of User Interface Components

The subject domain of user interface components describes the features and the structure of the visual representation of UI components. The Ui2Ont ontology [24] was taken as the ground of this subject domain.

A *user interface component* is a sign of a fragment of the KB, that has a certain form of external representation on the screen.

user interface component
⇒   *subdividing**:
    {•   *atomic user interface component*
      •   *non-atomic user interface component*
    }

An *atomic user interface component* is a UI component that does not contain other UI components in its structure.

A *non-atomic user interface component* is a UI component that includes other UI components.

visual part of the ostis-system user interface
⊂   *non-atomic user interface component*

A *visual part of the ostis-system user interface* is a part of the knowledge base of the ostis-system user interface, which includes the components necessary for displaying the UI.

Below is the classification of user interface components:

- interactive user interface component
  - data input component
    * data input component with direct feedback
      · drawing area
      · slider
      · text input component with direct feedback (single line text field, multi line text field)
      · selection component (selection component with single values, selection component with multiple values)
      · selectable data representation (selectable item, radio button, toggle button, check box)
    * data input component without direct feedback
      · spin button
      · motion input
      · speech input
  - presentation manipulation component
    * activating component
    * continuous manipulation component
      · resizer
      · scrollbar
  - operation trigger component
    * command selection component
      · menu item
      · button
    * command input component
- presentation user interface component
  - output
    * video output
    * sound output
    * image output
    * graphical output
      · progress bar
      · chart
      · map
    * text output
      · message
      · headline
      · paragraph
  - decorative user interface component
    * blank space
    * separator
  - container
    * list container
    * tree container
    * tree node container
    * table row container

  * table cell container
  * tab panel
  * spin panel
  * menu
  * menu bar
  * toolbar
  * status bar
  * scroll pane
  * window
      · modal window
      · non-modal window

A *presentation user interface component* is a component of the UI that does not imply interaction with the user.

A *decorative user interface component* is a UI component designed to style the interface.

A *container* is a UI component, whose task is to place a set of components included in its structure.

A *window* is a separate screen panel that contains various elements of the UI. Windows can be placed on top of each other.

A *modal-window* is a window that blocks the user experience with the application until the user closes the window.

A *non-modal-window* is a window that allows the user to interact with other windows without having to close this window.

An *interactive user interface component* is a UI component that is used to interact with the user.

A *data-input-component* is a UI component designed for input of information.

A *presentation-manipulation-component* is a UI component designed to represent information and interact with the user.

An *operation-trigger-component* is a UI component that asks the user to perform some action.

A non-atomic component is connected to its constituent components using the *decomposition** relation.

The Subject domain of user interface components also contains a description of the component features. As part of the work on the knowledge base of the *IMS.ostis Metasystem* [3], the Subject domain of spatial entities and their forms was created. The *IMS.ostis Metasystem* is an intelligent metasystem built according to the standards of the OSTIS Technology and aimed at usage by ostis-system engineers – at supporting the implementation, design, and updating (reengineering) of ostis-systems – and at developers of the OSTIS Technology – at supporting collective activities for the development of libraries and standards of the OSTIS Technology.

Metasystem IMS.ostis

:=   [Metasystem, which is:
- □ *corporate ostis-system* providing organization (coordination) of *OSTIS Consortium* activities;
- □ implementation representation form and fixation of the current state *Core of OSTIS Technology*;
- □ by a corporate *ostis-system*, interacting with all corporate ostis-systems, each of which coordinates the development of the corresponding *specialized ostis-technology.*

]

Metasystem IMS.ostis

:=   [OSTIS-system for automation of integrated design of ostis-systems]

⇒   *note**:

[During the *Development of the Basic Integrated Technology for Designing Intelligent Computer Systems* (more precisely, ostis-systems), the means of automating this activity is not the entire *Metasystem IMS.ostis*, but only part of it, which is part of the *Metasystems IMS.ostis* typical *Embedded ostis-support system for reengineering of ostis-systems* that supports the activities of the developers of the knowledge base of the Metasystem IMS.ostis. This is due to the fact that all *Development of the Basic Integrated Technology for Designing Intelligent Computer Systems* (ostis-systems) is reduced to the development (engineering) and updating (improvement, reengineering) *Knowledge Bases of the Metasystem IMS.ostis*).]

Metasystem IMS.ostis

:=   [Universal basic (domain-independent) ostis-system for automating the design of ostis-systems (any ostis-systems)]

⇔   *to be distinguished**:
specialized ostis design automation system for ostis systems

∈   *ostis-system*

⇐   *corporate ostis-system**:
OSTIS Consortium

:=   [IMS.ostis]

:=   [An intelligent metasystem built according to *OSTIS* standards and designed (1) for *ostis-systems* engineers – to support design. Implementations and updates (reengineering) *ostis-systems* and for developers *OSTIS Technologies* – to support collective development of standards and libraries *OSTIS Technologies.*]

⇐   *implementation form**:
OSTIS technology

⇐   *product**:
Project IMS.ostis

:=   [Intelligent Metasystem, which is a form (variant) of the implementation (representation, design) of *OSTIS Technologies* in the form of a *ostis-system*]

⇒   *note**:

[The fact that OSTIS Technology is implemented as an ostis-system is very important for the evolution of OSTIS Technology, since the methods and means of evolution (permanent improvement) of OSTIS Technologies become in fact the same as the methods and means of developing any (!) ostis systems at all stages of their life cycle.

In other words, the evolution of the OSTIS Technology is carried out by the methods and means of this technology itself.]

:= [Complex automation system (information and instrumental support) for the design and implementation of ostis systems, which itself is also implemented as an ostis system.]

:= [Portal of knowledge on OSTIS Technology, integrated with OSTIS-system and implemented as an ostis-system.]

∈ *portal of scientific and technical knowledge*

In the Subject domain of spatial entities and their forms, there are descriptions of such concepts as:

- form;
- spatial entity;
- rectangle;
- coordinate system;
- two-dimensional Cartesian coordinate system;
- Cartesian coordinate system;
- point of reference;
- segment;
- point;
- thickness;
- length;
- width;
- height.

The spatial entity is a entity, for which is given position as in borders of some plane as relatively others entities in this plane or space.

On spatial entity may be given next unary relations:

- *By horizontal**;
- *By vertical**.

A number of relationships are also introduced for several spatial entities:

- *Be on the right**
- *Be on the left**
- *Be on the top**
- *Be on the bottom**

The first way to specify the position of a spatial entity is to introduce some coordinate system within which the properties of the spatial entity will be described.

Used coordinate systems:

- *Cartesian coordinate system* – a coordinate system with mutually perpendicular axes on a plane or in space, in which each point is uniquely determined by the distances from the origin of the Cartesian coordinate system to the projections of the determined point on each of the axes.
- Polar coordinate system – a coordinate system in which each point on the plane is uniquely determined by the values of the measure of the polar angle and the length of the polar radius.

The second way to specify the position in the space is layout managers.

The layout manager is a semantic neighborhood, key item of which is a some container, relative to which size and alignment of others UI-components are given.

Types of layout managers:

- border layout manager, which places UI-components in one from five preset regions of container: top, bottom, left, right and center.
- stream layout manager, which places UI-components by order in container orientation direction
- table layout manager, which places UI-components by table rows and columns,
- list layout manager, which places UI-components by vertical and by horizontal

On the coodinate system is given three basic relationships:

- The coordinate – a ternary relationship, which includes some coordinate system, geometric point, which belongs to the border of some spatial entity, and function, which maps each entity in the set of numbers.
- The Origin – a binary relationships, which includes some coordinate system, geometric point, which be used as a starting point for other points.
- The reference point – a binary relationships, whic h includes the sign of a geometric figure, which is the boundary of a spatial entity, the sign of a point used to set the position of a spatial entity relative to some plane or space.

The Subject domain of user interface components intersects with the Subject domain of spatial entities and their forms and adds a set of concepts to describe the features of components, part of which is given below.

Text* is a binary relation that connects a UI component to a file that contains the text of the UI component.

Color is a parameter of the UI component that determines its color.

Text color is a parameter of the UI component that determines the color of its text.

Text size is a parameter of the UI component that determines the size of its text.

Text font is a parameter of the UI component that determines the font of its text.

The *deactivation property* is a logical parameter of a UI component that can be set to inhibit the usage of the component until a particular action is performed.

The *maximum number of characters* is a parameter of the text-input-component-with-direct-feedback component, which sets the maximum number of characters that can be input by the user.

Next, we will give an example of the description of interface component in the knowledge base of the system in the SCg-language and the result of its visualization. The formalization of the "button" component is shown in Fig. 3, the result of its display in the web interface is represented in Fig. 4.

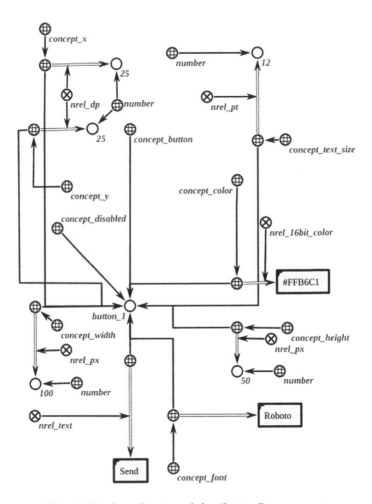

Fig. 3. The formalization of the "button" component

Thus, within this subject domain, both component classes and their instances are described as well as the features of components for visualization, regardless of the platform. At the same time, these properties and components are easily extensible and changeable.

Send

Fig. 4. The result of the display of the "button" component in the UI

5.3 Subject Domain of Interface User Actions

The Subject domain of interface user actions contains a specification of user actions, which can be performed for UI components. The Ui2Ont ontology [24] was used as the ground of this subject domain.

An *interface user action* is a minimally meaningful fragment of some activity of the user, performed through the UI.

Next is the classification of interface user actions.

interface user action
⊃   *speech-action*
⊃   *mouse-action*
 ⊃   *mouse-scroll*
  ⊃   *mouse-scroll-up*
  ⊃   *mouse-scroll-down*
 ⊃   *mouse-hover*
 ⊃   *mouse-drop*
 ⊃   *mouse-click*
  ⊃   *mouse-double-click*
  ⊃   *mouse-single-click*
 ⊃   *mouse-gesture*
 ⊃   *mouse-unhover*
 ⊃   *mouse-drag*
⊃   *keyboard-action*
 ⊃   *press-function-key*
 ⊃   *type-text*
⊃   *tangible-action*
⊃   *pen-base-action*
 ⊃   *touch-function-key*
 ⊃   *draw*
 ⊃   *write-text*
⊃   *touch-action*
 ⊃   *touch-click*
  ⊃   *touch-single-click*
  ⊃   *touch-double-click*
 ⊃   *touch-gesture*
  ⊃   *one-fingure-gesture*
  ⊃   *multiple-finger-gesture*
 ⊃   *touch-drop*
 ⊃   *touch-drag*

A *mouse-hover* is the interface user action, which corresponds to the appearance of the mouse cursor within the UI component.

A *mouse-drop* is the interface user action, which corresponds to dropping some component of the UI within another UI component using the mouse.

A *mouse-gesture* is an interface user action, which corresponds to the performance of a particular gesture through the movement of the mouse.

A *mouse-drag* is an interface user action, which corresponds to dragging a UI component with the mouse.

A *mouse-unhover* is an interface user action, which corresponds to the exit of the mouse cursor outside the frame of the UI component.

A *touch-action* is an interface user action performed using the sensor.

A *tangible-action* is an interface user action performed using taction.

A *touch-gesture* is an interface user action, which corresponds to the performance of a certain gesture with the movement of fingers on the screen of the sensor.

A *multiple-fingure-gesture* is an interface user action, which corresponds to the performance of a particular gesture by moving several fingers on the screen of the sensor.

A *one-fingure-gesture* is an interface user action, which corresponds to the performance of a certain gesture by moving one finger on the screen of the sensor.

A *touch-drop* is an interface user action, which corresponds to dropping a certain component of the UI within another component of the UI using a sensor.

A *touch-drag* is an interface user action, which corresponds to dragging a certain component of the UI using a sensor.

A *touch-function-key* is an interface user action, which corresponds to pressing the function key of the graphics tablet with a pen.

A *pen-base-action* is an interface user action performed using a pen on a graphics tablet.

The above user actions are common to all systems. It should be noted that the interface user action, as a rule, initiates some internal action of the system.

internal action of the system
⊃   *internal action of the ostis-system*

In the case of ostis-systems, as part of the work on the KB of the IMS.ostis Metasystem [3], the *Subject domain and ontology of actions, problems, plans, protocols, and methods implemented by the ostis-system in its memory as well as internal agents that perform these actions* was allocated. A fragment of this subject domain is shown below.

internal action of the ostis-system
:=   [an action in sc-memory]
:=   [an action performed in sc-memory]

Each *internal action of the ostis-system* denotes some transformation performed by some *sc-agent* (or a group of *sc-agents*) and focused on the transformation of *sc-memory*.

action in sc-memory
⊃   *action of interpreting a program stored in sc-memory*
⊃   *action of setting the mode of the ostis-system*
⊃   *action in sc-memory initiated by a question*
⊃   *action of editing a file stored in sc-memory*
⊃   *action of editing the ostis-system knowledge base*

An *action in sc-memory initiated by a question* is an action aimed at forming an answer to the raised question.

To define an action that is initiated when interacting with the UI, the *action initiated by the user interface** relation is used.

action initiated by the user interface*
∈   *quasi-binary relation*
∈   *oriented relation*
⇒   *first domain**:
     user interface component ∪ *user interface action class*
⇒   *second domain**:
     class of internal actions of the system

The first component of the binding of the *action initiated by the user interface** relation is a binding, the elements of which are an element of the set of UI components and an element of the *user interface action class* set. The second component is an element of the *class of internal actions of the system* set. An example of using this relation is shown in Fig. 5.

Thus, within these subject domains, interface user actions and internal actions of the system are described. These actions are basic and can be easily refined and expanded.

5.4   Subject Domain of Users

To represent information about users, an appropriate model of the ontology and the subject domain is created. The structure of this subject domain is shown below:

Subject domain of users
⇒   *private subject domain**:
●   *Subject domain of biography*
⇒   *private subject domain**:
●   *Subject domain of territorial entities*

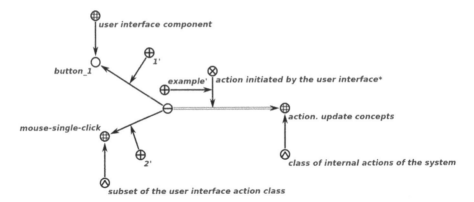

Fig. 5. An example of using the *action initiated by the user interface** relation

- Subject domain of living beings
- Subject domain of awards
- Subject domain of education
- Subject domain of organizations
- Subject domain of personal characteristics

The Subject domain of biography contains means of describing factual data from the biography of the interlocutor, such as:

- relations that connect them with territorial entities (such as the *place of birth**);
- participation in any organizations and their characteristics;
- awards received (including honorary titles);
- educational qualifications;
- information about marital status and relatives.

The Subject domain of personal characteristics contains means of describing the mental state of the interlocutor and their personality type. The need to store this information is due to one of the goals of the system – to maintain a good mood in the interlocutor, which results in the need to take into account their current state during the dialog. Within this subject domain, the following classes of mental states are distinguished:

mental state
⇐ *decomposition**:
{• *short-term mental state*
 • *medium duration mental state*
 • *long-term mental state*
}
⇐ *decomposition**:
{• *conscious mental state*

- *unconscious mental state*
}
⇐ *decomposition**:
{• *personality-related mental state*
- *mental state caused by the situation*
}
⇐ *decomposition**:
{• *superficial mental state*
- *deep mental state*
}
⇐ *decomposition**:
{• *positive mental state*
- *neutral mental state*
- *negative mental state*
}

A fragment of the description in the knowledge base of a certain user known to the system is shown in Fig. 6.

The information about the user in the aforementioned description includes both long-term data (name, gender, etc.), which will be saved after the dialog has ended, and short-term data (mood, last visit date, age, etc.), which can be updated with each new conversation.

Each component of the *beginning* set belongs to a class of temporary entities, or objects with temporal properties such as initial time, duration, final point, etc. They all share a common point at which they first came into existence. This parameter's actual value can either be an exact value or an interval or discrete value.

Each component of the *completion* set belongs to a class of transient objects that all end at the same time (the moment of the end of existence). This parameter's precise value can either be an interval or a discrete value, as indicated by the symbol [31].

Thus, within the Subject domain of users, users known to the system can be described.

The integration of the abovementioned ontologies allows implementing an approach, within which:

- the classification of components allows the further building of the UI taking into account the knowledge about them. For example, the presentation UI component can be highlighted in one color and the interactive UI component – in another;
- all the UI components correspond to a particular fragment of the knowledge base. It allows addressing different questions about these components to the system. As examples of such questions, the following ones can act: "what is the specified component designed for?", "what does the specified component consist of", "what class of components does the specified component belong to?", etc.;

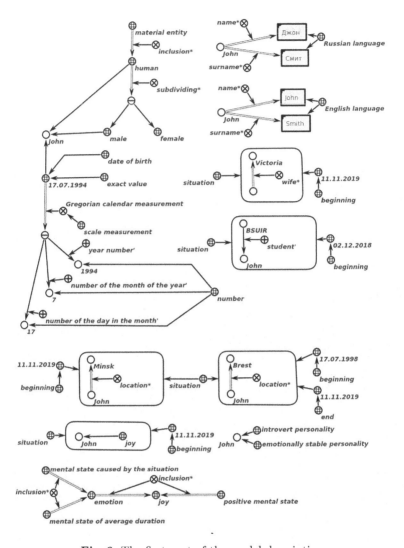

Fig. 6. The first part of the model description

- the user will have the opportunity to receive answers to questions about the organization of interface activities. Examples of such questions include: "what interface actions were performed the most often?", "what interface actions can be performed for the specified component?", etc.;
- it is possible to analyze the efficiency of user actions for further improvement of the interface (for example, several interface actions performed by the user in a row can be replaced by one);
- it is possible to accumulate the results of the interface user activity to further adapt the UI for them. Changing the interface is reduced to changing its sc-model, which can be carried out on the ground of logical rules, which are

also described in the system knowledge base. For example, the system may contain a logical rule for adding the most frequently initiated interface user actions to a separate component;
- the possibility of personalized display of the UI is opened up, depending on the knowledge accumulated about it in the system.

6   SC-Model of the Problem Solver

From the point of view of processing the sc-model of the UI knowledge base, the following problems should be solved:

- the processing of user actions;
- the interpretation of the sc-model of the UI knowledge base (building the UI).

user interface problem solver
⇐ *decomposition of an abstract sc-agent**:
   {• *Agent of processing of user actions*
    • *Agent for interpretation of the sc-model of the user interface knowledge base*
   }

An *Agent for interpretation of the sc-model of the user interface knowledge base* accepts an instance of the UI component for displaying as an input parameter. The component can be either an atomic or non-atomic (a component of the main application window, for example). As a result of work such agent is a graphical representation of the indicated component, taking into account the used implementation of the platform for interpreting semantic models of ostis-systems.

The operation algorithm of this agent is as follows:

- the input component type (atomic or non-atomic) is checked;
- if the component is atomic, then to display its graphical representation based on the features, which are specified for it. If this component is not included in the decomposition of any other component, then complete the performance. Otherwise, to determine the component, the decomposition of which includes the considered component, apply its properties to the current atomic component, and start processing the found non-atomic component, going to the first item;
- if the component is non-atomic, then to check whether the components, into which it was decomposed, were displayed. If these components were displayed, then complete the performance or else determine the component from the decomposition of the non-atomic component being processed and start processing the found component by going to the first item.

An *Agent of processing of user actions* is a non-atomic agent that includes many agents, each of which processes user actions of a particular class (an agent of processing a mouse click action, an agent of processing a mouse drop action, etc.). The agent reacts to the appearance of an instance of an interface user action in the KB of the system, finds an internal action class connected with it, and generates an instance of this internal action for subsequent processing.

7 Implementation of the Proposed Approach

The sc-model interpretation platform is currently implemented as a web-based platform [6]. It is suggested to design the agent for interpretation of the sc-model of the UI knowledge base as a non-atomic agent taking into account the characteristics of the platform and the potential for integrating the proposed method with existing solutions in the field of building UIs. Such an agent is divided into two other agents, one that displays the required format in the graphical representation of the UI and the other that converts the sc-model of the UI knowledge base into a format compatible with existing solutions.

It is proposed to use the JSON format as an intermediate description format for many reasons:

- it is the most popular format for data transmission and storage in modern systems;
- the simplicity of transmission and processing;
- the simplicity of making changes;
- the simple and compact syntax.

Thus, an additional *Agent for translation of the description of the user interface component from the sc-model to the JSON format* is introduced. As an input parameter, this agent accepts an instance of the translation UI component in the JSON format. The JSON description is formed by recursively processing the description of components from non-atomic to atomic ones.

The *Agent of displaying the specified format in the graphical representation of the user interface* is non-atomic and is decomposed into a set of agents that perform displaying for various interpretation platforms (mobile, desktop, web computer platforms, etc.). As input, this agent accepts a description of the UI component in the JSON format. The result of the operation of the agent is a graphical representation of the UI.

For the possibility of changing the sc-model of the UI, editing tools such as the SCn-, SCs-, and SCg-editors are implemented within the OSTIS Technology. So, the framework proposed within the approach contains three key components:

- an sc-model of the UI;
- tools for editing of the sc-model of the UI;
- tools for visualization of the sc-model of the UI.

The general structure of the framework is shown in Fig. 7.

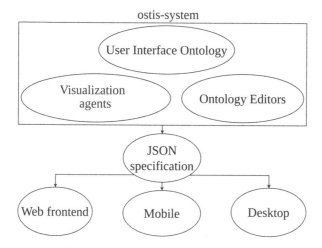

Fig. 7. The structure of the framework for generating the UI

8   Technique of Developing UI Components

One of the advantages of the proposed approach is the accumulation of frequently used components. To do this, it is supposed to create a library of components with specific properties, which is included in the Subject domain of user interface components. The components included in the library are platform-independent (they can be visualized regardless of the used interpretation platform).

The process of creating an instance of a UI component can be described as follows:

– to check whether the class of the necessary component is present in the Subject domain of user interface components;
– if it is not available, it is necessary to create a class of the necessary component, specifying the set of features for it;
– to check whether there is a description of the instance of the required component in the component library;
– if it is missing, it is required to supplement the component library with a description of a new instance of the component with preset properties;
– if necessary, to create a new instance of the class of the required component, setting it certain properties and actions based on the ontology of the subject domain of a particular system;
– to run the agent of visualization of the component instance for the used interpretation platform.

The described process is shown in Fig. 8.

For any UI-component before adding in the components library it is recommended to create component specification.

The description of UI-component specification includes next items:

- the name of a component;
- the type of a component: mapping of set-theoretic connections, which were given on a component;
- the version;
- developers: group of specialists, which have developed such UI-component;
- the description of a component – information about purpose of UI-component and components, which are included in this one.

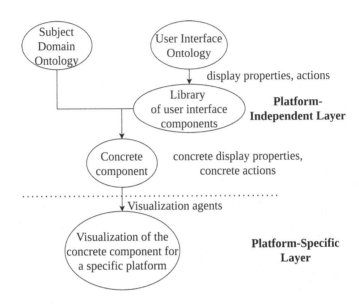

Fig. 8. The process of creating an instance of a UI component

9 Conclusion

In this paper, an ontological approach to the building of semantic models of adaptive UI based on the OSTIS Technology is proposed.

The analysis of existing approaches to the building of UIs is carried out, the technique and structure of building UI components for the framework proposed within the approach are represented.

In contrast to the existing approaches, the proposed one will allow:

- generating questions to the system related to the UI;
- taking into account the semantics of UI components when building it;
- rebuilding the UI by changing its model during the operation of the system;
- taking into account the history of the interface user activity to improve the quality of their work with the system.

At this stage, according to the proposed approach, the following items were implemented:

- a fragment of the Subject domain of interface user actions;
- a fragment of the Subject domain of user interface components;
- an agent of displaying the JSON format in a graphical representation of the UI for a web platform;
- an agent for translation of the description of the UI component from the sc-model to the JSON format.

As part of further work, it is planned to expand specified subject domains and implement visualization agents for other platforms.

References

1. Data-Driven UI: Unlimited Power. https://mobius-piter.ru/en/2018/spb/talks/v96lokugwe8cwggio8ois/. Accessed 21 May 2021
2. Exploring Server-Driven UI. https://betterprogramming.pub/exploring-server-driven-ui-cf67b3da919. Accessed 22 Apr 2021
3. IMS.ostis Metasystem. http://ims.ostis.net/. Accessed 03 June 2021
4. Introduction to FXML. https://openjfx.io/javadoc/12/javafx.fxml/javafx/fxml/doc-files/introduction_to_fxml.html. Accessed 23 May 2021
5. Mermaid Documentation. https://mermaid-js.github.io/mermaid. Accessed 18 Apr 2021
6. OSTIS Web Platform. https://github.com/ostis-dev/ostis-web-platform. Accessed 25 Apr 2021
7. React Json Schema Form. https://rjsf-team.github.io/react-jsonschema-form/. Accessed 20 Apr 2021
8. XForms 1.1. https://www.w3.org/TR/xforms. Accessed 25 May 2021
9. Abrams, M., Phanouriou, C., Batongbacal, A., Williams, S., Shuster, J.: UIML: an appliance-independent XML user interface language. In: Proceedings of the Eighth International Conference on World Wide Web, pp. 1695–1708 (1999)
10. Balzert, H., Hofmann, F., Kruschinski, V., Niemann, C.: The JANUS application development environment - generating more than the user interface. In: Computer Aided Design of User Interfaces, vol. 96, pp. 183–206 (1996)
11. Van den Bergh, J., Luyten, K., Coninx, K.: CAP3: context-sensitive abstract user interface specification. In: Proceedings of the 3rd ACM SIGCHI Symposium on Engineering Interactive Computing Systems - EICS 2011, pp. 31–40 (2011). https://doi.org/10.1145/1996461.1996491
12. Boriskin, A., Sadouski, M., Koronchik, D., Zhukau, I., Khusainov, A.: Ontology-based design of intelligent systems user interface. In: Golenkov, V. (ed.) Open Semantic Technologies for Intelligent Systems (OSTIS), pp. 95–106. Belarusian State University of Informatics and Radioelectronics Publ, Minsk (2017)
13. Brusilovsky, P., Karagiannidis, C., Sampson, D.G.: Adaptive User Interfaces Models and Evaluation (2013)
14. Butt, A.S., Haller, A., Liu, S., Xie, L.: ActiveRaUL: Automatically Generated Web Interfaces for Creating RDF Data (2013)

15. Davydenko, I.: Semantic models, method and tools of knowledge bases coordinated development based on reusable components. In: Golenkov, V. (ed.) Open Semantic Technologies for Intelligent Systems (OSTIS), pp. 99–118. 2, Belarusian State University of Informatics and Radioelectronics Publ., Minsk (2018)
16. Gaulke, W., Ziegler, J.: Using profiled ontologies to leverage model driven user interface generation. In: Proceedings of the 7th ACM SIGCHI Symposium on Engineering Interactive Computing Systems - EICS 2015, pp. 254–259 (2015)
17. Golenkov, V., Guliakina, N., Davydenko, I., Eremeev, A.: Methods and tools for ensuring compatibility of computer systems. In: Golenkov, V. (ed.) Open Semantic Technologies for Intelligent Systems (OSTIS), vol. 3, pp. 25–52. Belarusian State University of Informatics and Radioelectronics Publ, Minsk (2019)
18. Gribova, V., Cherkezishvili, N.: Automating the development of user interfaces with dynamic data. In: Golenkov, V. (ed.) Open Semantic Technologies for Intelligent Systems (OSTIS), pp. 287–292. Belarusian State University of Informatics and Radioelectronics Publ, Minsk (2011)
19. Gribova, V., Tarasov, A.: An ontology-driven user interface code generator. Artif. Intell. **4**, 457–464 (2005)
20. Hitz, M., Kessel, T.: Using application ontologies for the automatic generation of user interfaces for dialog-based applications. In: Research and Practical Issues of Enterprise Information Systems, CONFENIS, vol. 268 (2016). https://doi.org/10.1007/978-3-319-49944-4_2
21. Limbourg, Q., Vanderdonckt, J.: UsiXML: a user interface description language supporting multiple levels of independence. In: Matera, M., Comai, S. (eds.) ICWE Workshops, pp. 325–338. Rinton Press (2004)
22. Liu, B., Chen, H., He, W.: Deriving user interface from ontologies: a model-based approach. In: 17th IEEE International Conference on Tools with Artificial Intelligence (ICTAI 2005), pp. 254–259 (2005)
23. Paternò, F., Santoro, C., Spano, L.: Maria: a universal, declarative, multiple abstraction-level language for service-oriented applications in ubiquitous environments. ACM Trans. Comput.-Hum. Interact. **16**, 1–30 (2009). https://doi.org/10.1145/1614390.1614394
24. Paulheim, H., Probst, F.: Ui2ont - a formal ontology on user interfaces and interactions. In: Semantic Models for Adaptive Interactive Systems, pp. 1–24 (2013). https://doi.org/10.1007/978-1-4471-5301-6_1
25. Puerta, A., Eriksson, H., Gennari, J., Musen, M.: Beyond data models for automated user interface generation. In: Proceedings British HCI 1994, pp. 353–366 (1994)
26. Sadouski, M.: Ontological approach to the building of semantic models of user interfaces. In: Golenkov, V. (ed.) Open Semantic Technologies for Intelligent Systems (OSTIS), pp. 105–116. 5, Belarusian State University of Informatics and Radioelectronics Publ., Minsk (2021)
27. Shunkevich, D.: Ontology-based design of knowledge processing machines. In: Golenkov, V. (ed.) Open Semantic Technologies for Intelligent Systems (OSTIS), pp. 73–94. 2, Belarusian State University of Informatics and Radioelectronics Publ., Minsk (2017)
28. Shunkevich, D.: Agent-oriented models, method and tools of compatible problem solvers development for intelligent systems. In: Golenkov, V. (ed.) Open Semantic Technologies for Intelligent Systems (OSTIS), pp. 119–132. Belarusian State University of Informatics and Radioelectronics Publ, Minsk (2018)
29. Turner, E.K.: Adaptive user interfaces for the semantic web. Ph.D. thesis, Hamilton, New Zealand, doctoral (2018). https://hdl.handle.net/10289/12041

30. Yigitbas, E., Josifovska, K., Jovanovikj, I., Kalinci, F., Anjorin, A., Engels, G.: Component-Based Development of Adaptive User Interfaces (2019). https://doi. org/10.1145/3319499.3328229
31. Zahariev, V., Nikiforov, S., Azarov, E.: Conversational speech analysis based on the formalized representation of the mental lexicon. In: Golenkov, V. (ed.) Open Semantic Technologies for Intelligent Systems (OSTIS), pp. 141–158. Belarusian State University of Informatics and Radioelectronics Publ, Minsk (2021)

Universal Semantic Markup and Top-Level Ontology Representation

Aliaksandr Hardzei[1], Marina Sviatoshchik[1], Liza Bobyor[2], and Sergei Nikiforov[3]([✉])

[1] Minsk State Linguistic University, Minsk, Republic of Belarus
[2] Intelligent Semantic Systems Ltd., Minsk, Republic of Belarus
[3] Belarusian State University of Informatics and Radioelectronics, Minsk, Republic of Belarus
nikiforov.sergei.al@gmail.com

Abstract. The article is dedicated to Natural Language Processing in the Theory for Automatic Generation of Knowledge Architecture (TAPAZ-2) paradigm and the immersion of the obtained semantic formalisms into the software environment through the Open Semantic Technology for Intelligent Systems (OSTIS). A specific feature of the approach is the formalization of natural language semantics based on the World Model and the combination of Semantic Coding with the ontology and taxonomy of semantic networks.

Keywords: Natural Language Processing (NLP) · Natural Language Understanding (NLU) · Open Semantic Technology for Intelligent Systems (OSTIS) · Theory for Automatic Generation of Knowledge Architecture (TAPAZ-2) · SC-code (Semantic Computer Code) · macroprocess · roles of individs · semantic network · Parts of Language · Parts of the Sentence · Combinatory Semantics · ontology · taigens · yogens · taxonomy

1 Introduction

The present research is carried out in the framework of Combinatory Semantics, which studies the linguistic mapping of the dynamics of individs' roles in an event [43, p. 13]. Natural language is understood as a system of figures and signs for decoding the World Model and conscious management of intellectual activity [33, p. 35]. The World Model (hidden knowledge) is the architecture of patterns, i.e., the ordered set of patterns and the ordered set of transformations of some patterns in others [34, p. 226], [44, p. 182]. It is necessary to distinguish between verbal and non-verbal knowledge. Non-verbal knowledge is beyond the rational approach for comprehension of the World, it is beyond any term system, whether it is computer science, mathematics, linguistics, paralinguistics, and semiotics as a whole. It is impossible to explain and show how the imageries of Raphael's paintings came up, therefore, non-verbal knowledge should not be confused with facial expressions and gestures. Sign or finger language (language of the deaf and dumb) is as

V. Golenkov et al. (Eds.): OSTIS 2021, CCIS 1625, pp. 192–221, 2022.
https://doi.org/10.1007/978-3-031-15882-7_11

a natural language as any other hieroglyphic language [29, p. 18]. Verbal knowledge consists of information and fascination. According to Yu. V. Knorozov, the maximum information is contained in mathematics and the maximum fascination is contained in music [53]. Further studies have shown that fascination, along with factuation or factualization, is still a kind of information [64].

In this case, fascination that involves any stylistic nuance, all kinds of emotional and expressive shades and "induced" emotions, including those created with the help of meter, rhythm, pause, chant, representational devices, and other accentological means, are equally covered by declarative and procedural methods of representing knowledge. Due to the fact that language categories as supporting constructions of the metatheory for any natural language are linked to verbal knowledge, only those that are distinguished procedurally, fixed declaratively, and confirmed combinatorially can be determined as relevant [45]. Meanwhile, "The "chunks" of reasoning, memory, language, and "perception" ought to be larger and more structured; their factual and procedural contents must be more intimately connected in order to explain the apparent power and speed of mental activities" [62, p. 1].

The purpose of the article is to demonstrate the possibility of understanding texts in a natural language by computer systems with semantic software that allows creating a problem solver architecture based on a combination of Semantic Coding with the ontology and taxonomy of semantic networks.

To write formalized texts, the variants of the external displaying of SC-code constructions – SCg (graphic version) and SCn (hypertext version) – are used in the article.

2   Problem Definition

The discrepancy of the World Model and the Linguistic Image of the World, indefinite meaning of lexical units, and syntactic incompleteness of sentences are the main stumbling blocks in Natural Language Processing (NLP) [61]. Attempts to remove or circumvent these problems with the help of statistics based on co-occurrence by Z. S. Harris [49] resemble guessing the correct answers by schoolchildren during centralized testing. No matter how sophisticated the methods of statistical processing for structured or unstructured natural language content are, they only imitate the intellectual or inventive activity of a human, guessing the correct answer with more or less certainty, but we do not doubt that neural networks are able to efficiently scale the solutions found by combinatory methods. As for the currently popular combinatory methods, they go back to the semantic cases of Ch. Fillmore [10–20] and Stowell's "theta-grids" [68] and are used, in particular, in the Semantic Web project of T. Berners-Lee [1, 3, 4, 66] and on an international community resource Schema.org of the Microsoft, Google, Yandex, and Yahoo developer communities [65]. The main disadvantage of these methods is their empirical character and the lack of unified algebraic bases of semantic calculus. Because of these reasons, the creators of the Semantic Web, despite titanic efforts to standardize the technology, have not yet managed to reduce various subject ontologies to a top-level ontology, which, as many commentators emphasize, is "critical for the entire concept" [63, p. 94]. The fact is that the top-level ontology cannot be built from below, it, so to speak, "does not grow" from the ontologies of subject domains but must be initially set from above and in an algebraic standard that is suitable for formalizing texts in natural language including sentences, free and stable strings of combinatory variants of lexical items, and lexical items themselves, that make up these texts. In other words, to embed patterns of the World Model in presentation formalisms, a formalized language is required, which is comparable in semantic power to a natural language, as V. V. Martynov pointed out at the time [60]. Otherwise, as a result, we will get, as D. G. Bobrow and T. Winograd wrote, an extremely fragile structure, which often resembles a house of cards and collapses immediately "if swayed in the slightest from the specific domain (often even the specific examples), for which it was built" [5, p. 4].

Let us pay attention one more time: semantics as the relation of language to the World Model is manifested in the dynamics of individs' roles in an event, which is reflected in the content of patterns, the meaning of signs, and the sense of sentences [29, 33, 34, 43]. It is possible to arbitrarily declare any top-level object-oriented programming language, such as C++, C#, Java, or the next version of the OWL language from the Semantic Web project, as a top-level ontology, but until such languages can encode the content of patterns, the meaning of signs, and the sense of sentences and then reduce them to semantic primitives underlying calculus [71], such statements will be only declarations. If the OWL language allowed encoding patterns of the World Model and conjugating the code with natural language semantics, then the Internet would already be turned into the Global Artificial Intelligence through the Semantic Web project. It should be noted that linguistics has only one synthetic (consistently deductive and procedural) language model – Panini grammar that is dated from the 5th century BC, in which, with the help of 3959 short rules (sutras), the generation, construction, and transformation of all Sanskrit units are exhaustively described, starting from the phonetic-phonological level and ending with the semantic-syntactic one [2, 69, 70]. Unfortunately, it has not yet been clarified what formalisms are the basis for such an accurate description of natural language and how it was possible to achieve this in such a long time. From modern methods of encoding language semantics, six versions of Universal Semantic Code (USC) of V. V. Martynov [54–58, 60] and their finalization in the Theory for Automatic Generation of Knowledge Architecture (TAPAZ-2) by A. Hardzei [26–29, 39, 42, 48] are known.

TAPAZ Semantic Classifier as a top-level ontology includes the Set of Macroprocesses as Semantic Primitives (Paradigm of Actions) ordered by TAPAZ-algebra, TAPAZ Knowledge Graph, and Role List of Individs [44].

Taking into account that the calculus of subject domains and the semantics of each subject domain is implemented in TAPAZ-2 separately using a specially oriented knowledge graph, the most effective means of immersing TAPAZ formalisms in the software environment are dynamic graph models, primarily an

SC-code (Semantic Computer Code) of the Open Semantic Technology for Intelligent Systems (OSTIS) developed by the school of V. V. Golenkov [23–25].

We suppose that combining efforts and an organic conjunction of semantic coding with the ontology and taxonomy of semantic networks will solve a number of central problems of automatic data processing in natural language (Natural Language Processing), shifting the emphasis towards machine understanding of natural language (Natural Language Understanding, NLU).

3 Proposed Approach

According to T. N. Domnina and O. A. Khachko, in 2014, the number of scientific peer-reviewed journals was 34,274. If the average amount of articles is at least 50 per year, then 1,713,700 articles are published per year [9]. T. V. Chernigovskaya complains that "the number of articles related to the brain exceeds 10 million – they simply cannot be read" [6]. The average growth in the number of peer-reviewed scientific journals is 4% per year. In 2018, 1.6 million scientific articles were included in the Web of Science database [50]. So, it is essential to use automatic text analysis, artificial intelligent systems for searching and processing information.

In 1994, A. Hardzei, in a group led by V. V. Martynov, for the first time proposed a procedure for calculating semantics in the form of a specially oriented graph for ranking complex strings [26]. Use of the procedure has required the establishment of a one-to-one (vector) transition between actions in basic semantic classifier and has led to the creation of the Theory for Automatic Generation of Knowledge Architecture (TAPAZ), which was founded on the formal theory, the semantic counterpart, the set of macroprocesses (actions) as semantic primitives, the algorithm defining roles of individs, and the graph for searching processes through macroprocesses (knowledge graph) [42, p. 11].

In 2014, the second version of TAPAZ appeared, in which algebraic apparatus, increased number of rules for interpretation of the standard superposition of individs are greatly simplified [39].

At the same time, the problems of unifying the principles for building various components of computer systems were solved within the framework of the OSTIS project [22] aimed at creating an open semantic technology for engineering knowledge-driven systems. This technology allows combining heterogeneous models of problem solving as a universal platform and reducing costs that arise during development and modification, including when adding new components to the system. The OSTIS Technology makes it possible to use both combinatory and statistical methods that operate with knowledge. It is founded on a unified version of information encoding based on semantic networks with a basic set-theoretic interpretation called an SC-code. The architecture of each system built using the OSTIS Technology (ostis-system) includes a platform for interpreting semantic models of ostis-systems as well as a semantic model of the ostis-system described using the SC-code (sc-model of the ostis-system). In turn, the sc-model of the ostis-system includes the sc-model of the knowledge base, the sc-model of the problem solver, and the sc-model of the interface (in particular, the user one).

The foundation of the knowledge base of any ostis-system (sc-model of the knowledge base) is a hierarchical system of subject domains and corresponding ontologies. The upper level of the hierarchy of the knowledge base fragment related directly to natural language processing is shown below.

At the top level, the knowledge base of the natural language processing system consists of the following subject domains:

- Section. Subject domain of lexical analysis;
- Section. Subject domain of syntactic analysis;
- Section. Subject domain of semantic analysis.

The problem solver of any ostis-system (sc-model of the ostis-system problem solver) is a hierarchical system of agents for knowledge processing in semantic memory (sc-agents) that interact with each other solely by specifying the acts they perform in the specified memory.

The problem solver of the natural language processing system is decomposed into the following agents:

- Agent of lexical analysis;
- Agent of syntactic analysis;
- Agent of semantic analysis;
- Agent of merging structures in the knowledge base;
- Agent of logical inference.

In turn, the agent of merging structures in the knowledge base is decomposed into:

- Agent of searching for contradictions;
- Agent of resolving contradictions.

The agent of lexical analysis decomposes the text into lexemes and nominative units (stable strings of combinatory variants of lexemes) based on the dictionary included in the subject domain of lexical analysis. Note that the lexicographic description also presupposes the establishment of the linguistic semantic category for the lexeme, i.e., its belonging to a certain Part of Language [31, 32, 35, 38, 47]. The agent of syntactic analysis builds the syntactic structure of the analyzed text using the specified rules.

The agent of semantic analysis performs the transition from the text specification created by the previous agents to the structure that describes its semantics. The agent of merging structures in the knowledge base compares the structures obtained as a result of the text analysis with the data available in the knowledge base and, if contradictions are detected, resolves them.

The agent of logical inference uses logical rules written by means of the SC-code and interacts with the agents of syntactic and semantic analysis.

A more detailed explanation of the abovementioned subject domains and agents of the proposed approach is given on the example of processing a particular fragment of natural-language text, namely the description of the technological process for production of cottage cheese: «Производство творога кислотным способом включает в себя: приёмку молока, нормализацию молока до жирности 15%, очистку и пастеризацию молока, охлаждение молока до температуры заквашивания, внесение закваски в молоко, сквашивание молока, разрезку сгустка, подогрев и обработку сгустка, отделение сыворотки, охлаждение творога»[1].

From the ostis-system point of view, any text is a file (i.e., an sc-node with content). An example of such a node is shown in Fig. 1.

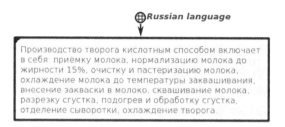

Fig. 1. Representation of natural language text in the system

Automatic processing of such texts can simplify the creation of formal specifications for production processes.

The stages of processing the text are *lexical analysis, syntactic analysis, transition to the construction in terms of TAPAZ-2, and integration into the knowledge base.*

Let us consider each stage of processing this text.

4 Lexical Analysis

Lexical analysis is a decomposition of a text by an agent of lexical analysis into separate lexemes and stable strings of combinatory variants of lexemes (nominative units) based on a dictionary that is part of the Subject domain of lexical analysis. Below is a fragment of the ontology containing knowledge about Parts of Language.

---

[1] "Manufacture of cottage cheese by the acid method includes: acceptance of milk, normalization of milk to 15% fat, purification and pasteurization of milk, cooling of milk to the fermentative temperature, adding sourdough to milk, fermentation of milk, cutting of the clot, heating and processing of the clot, separation of whey, cooling of cottage cheese".

lexeme
⊂   *file*

nominative unit
⊂   *file*

combinatory variant of the lexeme
⊂   *file*

The *lexeme* is a taigen or yogen of a certain natural language [33, p. 35]. A *combinatory variant of lexeme* is a variant of a lexeme in an ordered set of its variants (paradigm) [37, p. 351].

A *nominative unit* is a stable string of combinatory variants of lexemes, in which one variant of the lexeme (modificator) defines another one (actualizator), for example: "записная книжка" = 'note book', "бежать галопом" = 'run at a gallop' [33, p. 35].

morphological paradigm*
∈   *quasi-binary relation*
⇒   *first domain*:*
    word form
⇒   *second domain*:*
    lexeme

natural language
⇒ *decomposition*:*
    { •   *Part of Language*
        ⇒ *decomposition*:*
            { •   *taigen*
              •   *yogen*
            }
      •   *sign of syntax alphabet*
    }

The *morphological paradigm** is a quasi-binary relation, that connects a lexeme with its combinatory variants. The *lexeme* is a taigen or yogen of a certain natural language; being a sign, it has a combination of figures in the aspect of expression, and it has a pattern in the aspect of content; in synthetic languages it has a developed morphological paradigm and is the central unit of lexicographic description.

Signs of Syntax Alphabet* are auxiliary syntactic means (at the macrolevel – prepositions, postpositions, particles, conjunctions, etc., at the microlevel – flexions, prefixes, infixes, postfixes, etc.) that serve for connecting the components of language structures and the formation of morphological paradigms [33, p. 35].

taigen

⇒ *decomposition**:
   {• *expanded taigen*
      ⇒ *decomposition**:
        {• *composite taigen*
         • *complex taigen*
        }
    • *reduced taigen*
      ⇒ *decomposition**:
        {• *contracted taigen*
         • *constricted taigen*
        }
   }

constricted taigen
⇒ *decomposition**:
   {• *informational taigen*
    • *physical taigen*
      ⇒ *decomposition**:
        {• *constant taigen*
         • *variable taigen*
        }
      ⇒ *decomposition**:
        {• *quantitative taigen*
         • *qualitative taigen*
        }
      ⇒ *decomposition**:
        {• *single-place taigen*
         • *multi-place taigen*
            ⊃ *intensive taigen*
            ⊃ *extensive taigen*
        }
   }

A *taigen* is a Part of Language that denotes an individ.

An *informational taigen* denotes an individ in the informational fragment of the World Model, a *physical taigen* denotes an individ in the physical fragment of the World Model.

A *constant taigen* denotes a constant individ, a *variable taigen* denotes a variable individ [35, pp. 70–72], [40, pp. 12–13].

yogen
⇒ *decomposition**:
   {• *expanded yogen*
      ⇒ *decomposition**:

$$\{ \bullet \quad composite\ yogen$$
$$\quad \bullet \quad complex\ yogen$$
$$\}$$
$$\quad \bullet \quad reduced\ yogen$$
$$\quad \Rightarrow decomposition^*:$$
$$\quad \{ \bullet \quad contracted\ yogen$$
$$\quad \bullet \quad constricted\ yogen$$
$$\quad \}$$
$$\}$$

contracted yogen
⇒ *decomposition**:
$$\{ \bullet \quad informational\ yogen$$
$$\quad \bullet \quad physical\ yogen$$
$$\quad \Rightarrow decomposition^*:$$
$$\quad \{ \bullet \quad constant\ yogen$$
$$\quad \bullet \quad variable\ yogen$$
$$\quad \}$$
$$\quad \Rightarrow decomposition^*:$$
$$\quad \{ \bullet \quad quantitative\ yogen$$
$$\quad \bullet \quad qualitative\ yogen$$
$$\quad \}$$
$$\quad \Rightarrow decomposition^*:$$
$$\quad \{ \bullet \quad single\text{-}place\ yogen$$
$$\quad \bullet \quad multi\text{-}place\ yogen$$
$$\quad \}$$
$$\}$$

multi-place yogen
⇒ *decomposition**:
$$\{ \bullet \quad intensive\ yogen$$
$$\quad \bullet \quad extensive\ yogen$$
$$\}$$

A *yogen* is a Part of Language that denotes an attribute of an individ.

An *informational yogen* denotes the attribute of an individ in the informational fragment of the World Model, a *physical yogen* denotes the attribute of an individ in the physical fragment of the World Model.

A *constant yogen* denotes a constant attribute of an individ, a *variable yogen* denotes a variable attribute of an individ [35, pp. 71–74], [40, p. 12–13].

The lexemes in the knowledge base are described in the form shown in Fig. 2.

The construction, which is the result of lexical analysis, is shown in Fig. 3. This construction includes the decomposition of the source text into fragments as well as an indication of the belonging of these fragments to a particular lexeme, nominative unit, or sign of syntax alphabet.

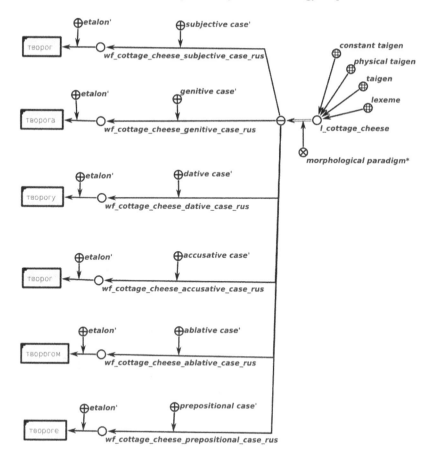

Fig. 2. The description of the lexeme in the knowledge base

5   Syntactic Analysis

The agent of the syntactic analysis performs the transition from the lexically marked text to its syntactic structure based on the rules described in the corresponding subject domain. A fragment of the subject domain ontology is represented below:

part of the sentence'
∈   *role relation*
⇒ *decomposition*:*
    { • *principal part of the sentence'*
      • *subordinate part of the sentence'*
    }

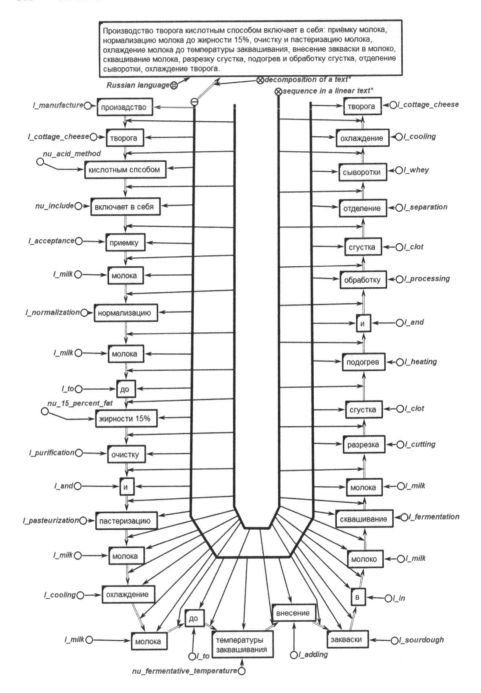

Fig. 3. The result of lexical text analysis

principal part of the sentence'
⇒ *decomposition**:
    { •   *grammatical subject'*
       •   *grammatical predicate'*
       •   *grammatical direct object'*
    }

subordinate part of the sentence'
⇒ *decomposition**:
    { •   *grammatical indirect object'*
       •   *grammatical attribute'*
       •   *grammatical circumstance'*
    }

A *Part of the Sentence'* is a relation that connects the decomposition of a text with a file, whose contents (Part of Language) play a certain syntactic role in the decomposed text [33, p. 35].

The *grammatical subject'* is one of the principal role relations that connects the decomposition of a text with the file, the contents of which denotes the starting point of the event description selected by the observer.

The *grammatical direct object'* is one of the principal role relations that connects the decomposition of a text with the file, the contents of which denotes the final point of the event description selected by the observer.

The *grammatical predicate'* is one of the principal role relations that connects the decomposition of the text with the file, the contents of which denotes the mapping by the observer of the starting point of the event description to the final point [44, p. 184].

A *grammatical circumstance'* is one of the subordinate role relations that connects the decomposition of a text with a file, the contents of which denote either a modification or localization of the grammatical predicate; the grammatical circumstance of degree and the grammatical circumstance of manner denote the modification of the grammatical predicate, the grammatical circumstance of place and the grammatical circumstance of time denote the spatial and, accordingly, the temporal localization of the grammatical predicate.

A *grammatical attribute'* is one of the subordinate role relations that connects the decomposition of a text with the file, the contents of which denote a modification of the grammatical subject, grammatical object, grammatical circumstance of place and time [36], [37, pp. 352–354, 357], [41, pp. 29–33].

grammatical circumstance'
⇒ *decomposition**:
    { •   *grammatical circumstance of manner'*
       •   *grammatical circumstance of place'*
          ⇒ *decomposition**:
              { •   *static grammatical circumstance of place'*
                 •   *dynamical grammatical circumstance of place'*

> }
> - *grammatical circumstance of degree'*
> - *grammatical circumstance of time'*
>   - ⇒ *decomposition*:*
>   - { • *static grammatical circumstance of time'*
>   - • *dynamical grammatical circumstance of time'*
>   - }
> }

A fragment of the ontology that is the result of this stage is represented in Figs. 4 and 5. The fragment shown in the figures includes part of the syntactic structure of this text.

6   Construction in Terms of TAPAZ-2

The agent of semantic analysis performs the transition from the processed text to its semantics formulated in terms of TAPAZ-2 on the basis of the rules described in the corresponding subject domain [28, 29, 39, 42, 44, 46, 48]. A fragment of the ontology of this subject domain is represented below:

participant of the influence'
:=   [participant of the event']
∈   *role relation*
⇒   *first domain*:*
     individ
⇒   *second domain*:*
     action
⇒ *decomposition*:*
     { • *subject'*
          ⇒ *decomposition*:*
              { • *inspirer'*
                - • *initiator'*
                - • *spreader'*
                - • *creator'*
              }

     - • *instrument'*
          ⇒ *decomposition*:*
              { • *suppressor'*
                - • *activator'*
                - • *converter'*
                - • *enhancer'*
              }

     - • *mediator'*
          ⇒ *decomposition*:*

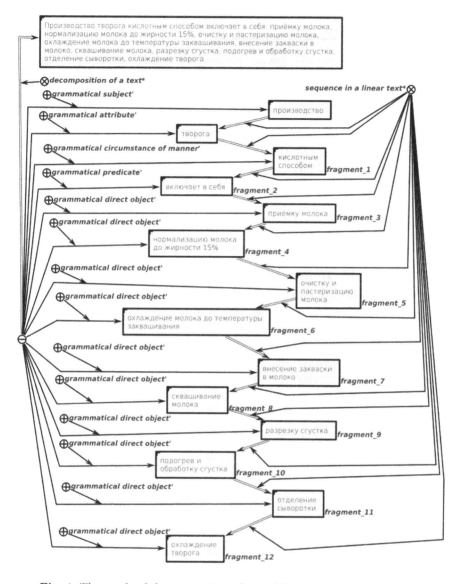

Fig. 4. The result of the syntactic analysis of the text, the first fragment

{ • *locus'*
  • *source'*
  • *landmark'*
  • *carrier'*
  • *acceptor'*
  • *adapter'*
  • *stock'*
  • *material'*

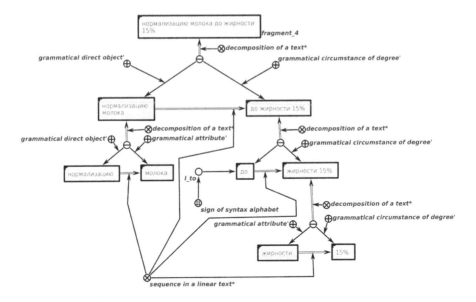

Fig. 5. The result of the syntactic analysis of the text, the second fragment

- - *regulator'*
  - *model'*
  - *chronotope'*
  - *retainer'*
  - *separator'*
  - *resource'*
  - *stimulus'*
  - *indicator'*
  }
- *object'*
  ⟹ *decomposition**:
  { • *hull'*
  - *coating'*
  - *kernel'*
  - *interlayer'*
  }
- *product'*
  ⟹ *decomposition**:
  { • *semi-product'*
  - *billet'*
  - *prototype'*
  - *end item'*
  }
}

An *individ* is a kind of the pattern as a separate entity in the selected fragment of the World Model [33, p. 34].

A *participant of the action** is a role relation, connecting the action with the individ that participates in it.

A *subject** is the originator of the action, varieties of the subject: *inspirer** – involves into the action, *initiator** – initiates the action, *spreader** – spreads the action, *creator** – completes the action by making a product from the object.

An *instrument** is the performer of the action, the closest individ to the subject, varieties of the instrument: *suppressor** – suppresses the resistance of the mediator, *activator** – directly affects the mediator, *converter** – converts the mediator into the instrument, *enhancer** – increases the effect on the mediator.

A *mediator** (mediator of the action) is the closest individ to the object; varieties of the mediator: *locus** is the closest environs of the object partially or completely surrounding the object that localizes the object in space and thereby containing (enclosing) it, *source** – provides instructions for the instrument, *landmark** – orientates the impact on the object, *carrier** – carries the object, *acceptor** – catches the object, *adapter** – adapts the instrument to affect the object, *stock** is the object collected for processing, *material** is the object used as a raw material for making a product, *regulator** – serves as an instruction in making a product from the object, *model** is the physical or informational original sample for making a product from the object, *chronotope** – localizes the object in time, *retainer** – turns a variable locus of the object into a constant one, *separator** – sorts the object, *resource** – feeds the instrument, *stimulus** – reveals the parameter of the object, *indicator** – displays a parameter of impact on the object or a parameter of the product as the result of subject's impact on the object.

An *object** is the recipient of the action, varieties of the object: *hull** is the individ's shell, *coating** is the outer insulation of the individ's shell, *kernel** is the core of the individ, *interlayer** is the inner insulation of the individ's shell.

A *product** is the result of the subject's impact (action) on the object (the individ adapted to a given role in a new action), varieties of the product: *semiproduct** is the product half-made from raw materials, *billet** is the object turned into a raw material, *prototype** is the prototype product, *end item** is the finished product [46, p. 10, 15–16].

TAPAZ distinguishes between physical and informational processes, since on the highest abstract semantic level the physical action was considered as an influence of one individ onto another through its shell, and the informational action – through its surroundings [26,27,30], [42, p. 12]. Below is the classification of semantic elements (macroprocesses) of TAPAZ written by means of the SC-code [42, p. 34], [44, p. 185].

influence

:= [action]*:

⇒ *subdividing**:

Typology by the kind of interaction of participants ˆ

= {•   *normalization group*
  •   *transformation group*
  •   *exploitation group*

- *activation group*
}

A *normalization group* represents an influence, during which the interaction is carried out between the object and the product. A *transformation group* represents an influence, during which the interaction is carried out between the object and the product. An *exploitation group* represents an influence, during which the interaction is carried out between the instrument and the mediator. An *activation group* represents an influence, during which the interaction is carried out between the subject and the instrument.

influence

⇒ *subdividing**:

Typology of influences by the type of interacting subsystems ˆ

= {• *shell-surroundings subgroup*
- *core-shell subgroup*
- *shell-core subgroup*
- *surroundings-shell subgroup*
}

⇒ *subdividing**:

Typology of influences by phases of influence increase ˆ

= {• *generation raw*
- *initiation raw*
- *accumulation raw*
- *amplification raw*
}

A *generation raw* is a raw, which is a transition in each subsystem from one level, for example, surroundings-shell one, to another, for example, shell-core one. An *initiation raw* is a raw, during which it starts in each subsystem. An *accumulation raw* is a raw, during which it accumulates in each subsystem. An *amplification raw* is a raw, during which it is amplified.

influence

⇒ *subdividing**:

Typology of influences by the type of the instrument ˆ

= {• *informational action*
- *physical action*
}

An *informational action* is an influence, in which the subject's surroundings acts as an instrument. A *physical action* is an influence, in which the subject's shell acts as an instrument.

Below is a formal specification of classes of influences used in the example.

Specified classes of influences

⊃ {• *mold*
⇐ *intersection**:
{• *transformation group*
- *surroundings-shell subgroup*

- • *generation raw*
  - • *physical action*
  }

- • *attract*
  ⇐ *intersection**:
    {• *activation group*
    - • *surroundings-shell subgroup*
    - • *initiation raw*
    - • *physical action*
    }

- • *eviscerate*
  ⇐ *intersection**:
    {• *transformation group*
    - • *core-shell subgroup*
    - • *generation raw*
    - • *physical action*
    }

- • *annihilate*
  ⇐ *intersection**:
    {• *transformation group*
    - • *shell-surroundings subgroup*
    - • *generation raw*
    - • *physical action*
    }

- • *insert*
  ⇐ *intersection**:
    {• *exploitation group*
    - • *shell-core subgroup*
    - • *initiation raw*
    - • *physical action*
    }

- • *disband*
  ⇐ *intersection**:
    {• *transformation group*
    - • *shell-surroundings subgroup*
    - • *amplification raw*
    - • *physical action*
    }

- • *unclamp*
  ⇐ *intersection**:

{• *transformation group*
 • *core-shell subgroup*
 • *amplification raw*
 • *physical action*
}

• *disconnect*
  ⇐ *intersection**:
     {• *exploitation group*
      • *core-shell subgroup*
      • *generation raw*
      • *physical action*
     }
}

The complete list of classes of influences is represented in the table in Fig. 6.

The transition can be carried out in 2 stages:

– the transition from the initial version of the text to the reconstructed one;
– the transition from the reconstructed text to semantics.

The reconstruction of the text occurs through the reconstruction of the missing parts of the sentence based on the World Model or the Linguistic Image of the World and then through normalization of its syntactic structure by rewriting the Parts of the Sentence.

During the work, the following rules for the reconstruction of the text were formulated:

– the grammatical attribute of the initial text is mapped to the grammatical direct object of the reconstructed text (for example, the grammatical attribute *творога* = *cottage cheese's* of the initial text is mapped to the grammatical direct object of the reconstructed text *творог* = *cottage cheese*);
– the grammatical direct object of the initial text is displayed in the grammatical predicate of the reconstructed text (for example, the grammatical direct object *производство* = *a production* of the initial text is mapped to the grammatical predicate of the reconstructed text *производит* = *produces*).

The result of reconstructing the initial text under consideration: «Некто принимает молоко, затем окисляет молоко, а именно: нормализует молоко до 15-процентной жирности, затем очищает молоко, затем пастеризует молоко, затем охлаждает молоко до определённой температуры, затем вносит закваску в молоко, затем сквашивает молоко, затем режет сгусток, затем подогревает сгусток, затем обрабаты- вает сгусток, затем отделяет сыворотку, затем охлаждает сгусток и, в итоге, производит творог»[2].

---

[2] "Someone accepts milk, then acidifies milk, namely: normalizes milk to 15% fat, then purifies milk, then pasteurizes milk, then cools milk to a certain temperature, then adds sourdough to milk, then ferments milk, then cuts the clot, then heats the clot, then processes the clot, then separates whey, then cools the clot, and, as a result, produces cottage cheese".

		I		II		III		IV	
A	a	1	perceive	2	reflect	3	comprehend	4	understand
		attract	57	cumulate	58	constrict	59	attain	60
	b	5	adopt	6	memorize	7	contemplate	8	learn
		absorb	61	accumulate	62	center	63	assimilate	64
	c	9	feel	10	behold	11	feel profoundly	12	experience
		over absorb	65	concentrate	66	centrifuge	67	dissimilate	68
	d	13	reject	14	erase	15	rethink	16	overcome
		expel	69	decompress	70	force off	71	disassociate	72
B	a	17	notify	18	advertise	19	instill	20	state
		approach	73	joint	74	press down	75	connect	76
	b	21	explain	22	propagandize	23	prove	24	certify
		insert	77	pump	78	press in	79	link	80
	c	25	reveal	26	prophesize	27	enlighten	28	divine
		conduct	81	spread	82	squeeze out	83	disconnect	84
	d	29	darken	30	encode	31	discredit	32	disavow
		take out	85	pull up	86	push out	87	unlink	88
C	a	33	inform	34	interest	35	assure	36	predispose
		touch on	89	envelope	90	clamp	91	mold	92
	b	37	admonish	38	teach	39	convince	40	nurture
		rip up	93	fill up	94	press	95	form	96
	c	41	pierce	42	intend	43	transfigure	44	reincarnate
		penetrate	97	overflow	98	unclamp	99	eviscerate	100
	d	45	pester	46	mesmerize	47	lose conscious	48	go mad
		punch	101	uplift	102	disband	103	annihilate	104
D	a	49	recollect	50	recreate	51	restart	52	render
		recrystallize	105	reintegrate	106	regenerate	107	restore	108
	b	53	reproduce	54	reclaim	55	renew	56	revive
		recuperate	109	rehabilitate	110	reactivate	111	reanimate	112

Fig. 6. The Semantic Classifier or Paradigm of Actions (Macroprocesses) where: I – initiation raw, II – accumulation raw, III – amplification raw, IV – generation raw; A – activation group, B – exploitation group, C – transformation group, D – normalization group; a – surroundings-shell subgroup, b – shell-core subgroup, c – core-shell subgroup, d – shell-surroundings subgroup.

During the work, the following rules for the transition to semantics were also formulated:

- the grammatical direct object of the reconstructed text is mapped to the grammatical object (for example, the grammatical direct object *творог = cottage cheese*);
- the grammatical predicate of the reconstructed text is mapped to the action (for example, the grammatical predicate *производит = produces*).

When combining the transition rules from the initial version of the text to the reconstructed one with the rules for the transition to semantics, it is possible to obtain the following rules that provide a one-step transition:

- the grammatical attribute of the initial text is mapped to the object;
- the grammatical direct object of the initial text is mapped to the action.

The final result is shown in Fig. 7. The fragment of the knowledge base represented in it contains a decomposition of the influence on the sub-influences, an indication of the attachment of the decomposable influence and ones obtained as a result of this process to a certain class of them from the above classification as well as an identification of the action participants.

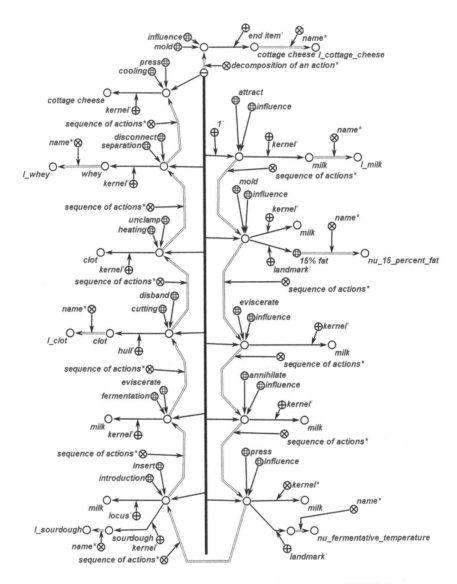

Fig. 7. The result of the transition to the terms of TAPAZ-2

7   Integration into the Knowledge Base

The agent of merging structures in the knowledge base integrates the structure obtained as a result of text analysis into the knowledge base. The process involves searching for and resolving contradictions.

As an example, we can present a situation when there is a fragment in the knowledge base that describes an influence that is of the same type as shown in Fig. 8.

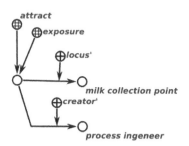

Fig. 8. The construction that was present in the knowledge base before merging

In this case, the models are merged. The resulting construction is shown in Fig. 9.

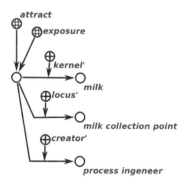

Fig. 9. The result of merging constructions

8   Conclusion

TAPAZ–2 is the second version and updated edition of the Theory for Automatic Generation of Knowledge Architecture for Computer Modeling of Human Intellectual Activity (Artificial Intelligence), including Inventive Problem Solving. TAPAZ–2 has never been positioned as a "sematic language" and is not such, in any case, as some researchers can understand it, i.e., "the semantic language for text representation", just as Marvin Minsky's frameworks for representing and transformation knowledge are not a semantic language. The formal apparatus TAPAZ–2, being the finalization of V. V. Martynov's Universal Semantic Code (USC), is intended for algebraic coding of semantics, i.e., the meaning of signs (and not only linguistic ones), the sense of sentences and the content of patterns in the World Model, and for the construction of knowledge architecture, i.e., for the calculation of subject domains and semantics of subject domains as well as automatic semantic markup of structured and unstructured natural language content.

The main difference of the TAPAZ–2 Semantic Code from the "semantic languages" is that in it the semantic counterpart is not attributed to algebraic expressions but is derived from their algebraic structure on the basis of special rules of interpretation [39], i.e., the TAPAZ–2 Semantic Code is unconventional and in this part has no world analogues.

We emphasize that 'subject', 'instrument', 'mediator', 'object' or 'product', and their varieties in TAPAZ are role relations, i.e., the roles of individs participating in the event [44, p. 182], regardless of how the observer perceives this event or describes it with the help of sentences of any natural language: the basis of the TAPAZ meta-apparatus (terminological system) is based on semantic categories independent of the observer's point of view [39,42]. The roles of individuals in TAPAZ constitute a closed vector list, they are calculated by TAPAZ-algebra, therefore each role has its own algebraic formula, from the structure of which this role is derived using strict rules for interpreting typical combinations of individs and reading algebraic formulas [39, p. 57–58], [42, p. 27–28], i.e., role semantics are not ascribed to formulas but derived from them. Moreover, the closed list of TAPAZ individs' roles indicates the order of the roles as well as the order of transforming one role into another. Such an opportunity is provided by the TAPAZ Semantic Code, which similarly encodes and decodes all macroprocesses and processes of specialized subject domains, simultaneously calculating them. The TAPAZ Semantic Code combines an algebraic formula with a semantic counterpart derived from its structure [72]. It is through decoding the patterns of the World Model and not through decoding the categories of the Linguistic Image of the World [59, p. 5] the TAPAZ Semantic Code decodes the meanings of words and word combinations or the sense of sentences and texts in natural language, i.e., natural language semantics. The closed list of TAPAZ roles of individs constitutes the TAPAZ Role List, but this is only a small fragment of the system, all the power of which is contained in the TAPAZ Knowledge Graph[3].

There is no possibility to reproduce in one article everything that has been published since the 90s of the last century in leading domestic and foreign scientific journals and collection of scientific papers in Russian and English on the algebraic apparatus of TAPAZ, namely, the properties of operations and individ variables, rules for constructing, limiting, reducing, and transforming formulas, rules for interpreting typical combinations of individs, vectors of macroprocesses in the basis of the Semantic Classifier (Fig. 6 and 10), mathematical properties of the Knowledge Graph, and the Role List of Individs, and so on, detailed bibliographic links and URL to previous publications were given, first of all, http:// tapaz.by, where these publications are posted, you are welcome to visit the site.

The semantic code of TAPAZ–2 has a variety of applications, it can be used in the interface, universal problem solver, search engines, machine learning, and, of course, for automatic semantic markup of content in Russian and English languages.

Why the TAPAZ–2 Semantic Classifier, Knowledge Graph, and Role List of Individs can be used as a top-level ontology in the Semantic Web? Based on the Semantic Classifier and supplemented by the Role List of Individs, the TAPAZ–2 Knowledge Graph is a top-level ontology, because, firstly, it operates with algebraic formulas for unconventional coding and decoding of the meaning of signs and the sense of sentences in the Linguistic Image of the World as well as the content of patterns in the World Model; secondly, it calculates both the subject domains themselves and the semantics of each individual subject domain; thirdly, it has the factorial power of semantic calculation, and so high that it is necessary to use special methods of reducing, dividing, or limiting the depth of

---

[3] The progress of deciphering the algebraic formulas of the TAPAZ Role List and the degree of the research novelty carried out can be seen by comparing the first list with nine deciphered formulas for the roles of individs [28, p. 39] with the current one, in which all 32nd formulas are deciphered [46, p. 15–20], while, we repeat, the closest foreign analogue of TAPAZ – the Active Vocabulary technology, predominantly based on the theory of semantic cases by Ch. Fillmore [10,14,19,21] and R. Jackendoff's early works [51,52], which was standardized and approved in 2017 by the W3C Consortium within the framework of Semantic Web project and then Schema.org project – only 6 roles were empirically identified, i.e., manually without relying on any algebra [1,65,66], therefore it is impossible to verify their non-contradictivity, independence, and completeness, thereby avoiding Russell's paradox, which inevitably arises when the theory and metatheory, language and metalanguage, semantics and metasemantics are mixed. It is because of this the developers of Semantic Web, despite titanic efforts to standardize the technology, have so far failed to reduce various subject ontologies to the top-level ontology. As you can see, the power of the TAPAZ semantic markup, only in terms of the typical roles of individs, not to mention the TAPAZ-algebra and generated by it the Paradigm of Actions and the Knowledge Graph, is 5 times greater than the power of semantic cases by Ch. Fillmore or the Active Vocabulary technology of W3C Consortium.

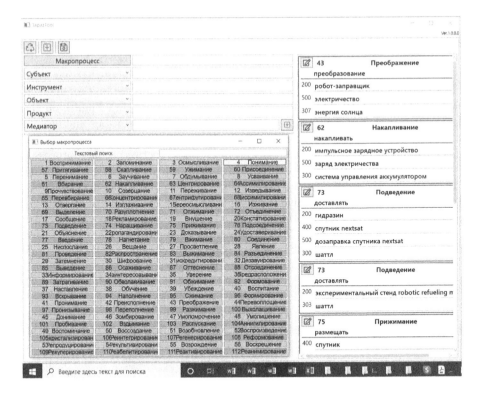

Fig. 10. The working window of the software tool with an expanded tab

Graph to make it suitable for generation, processing, and storage using modern computing facilities [48]. The number of semantic code formulas generated by the TAPAZ–2 Knowledge Graph is 8.2×10^{245}, while The Dictionary of the modern Russian literary language in 17 volumes contains 120,480 words, the declared volume of the Big Academic Dictionary of the Russian Language is 150,000 words, and the available electronic resources of the Institute of Linguistic Studies of the Russian Academy of Sciences include 1.4 billion of word usage for about 5 million Russian words of the 18th–21st centuries. We are not aware of any examples of other top-level ontologies with similar properties.

The article proposes a new approach to the machine understanding of texts in natural language (Natural Language Understanding, NLU), based on the formalization of the World Model using algorithms of the Theory for Automatic Generation of Knowledge Architecture (TAPAZ-2) and the immersion of the obtained semantic formalisms into the software environment using Open Semantic Technology for Intelligent Systems (OSTIS) that operates with original dynamic graph models – semantic networks in the form of specially oriented taxonomies and ontologies represented in the SC-code (Semantic Computer Code). The resulting taxonomic and ontological set is universal and can be used for machine understanding of collections of texts of various subject domains in various natural languages. The advantages of the approach are:

- decoding the meaning of signs and sense of sentences through decoding the patterns of the World Model, which provides the ability to support analytical activities and solve inventive problems not only by analogy [42, p. 39], [44, p. 192], [46, p. 16];
- a unified top-level algebraic ontology adapted to the semantization of the Internet;
- standard dynamic graph representation of any type of knowledge within a single knowledge base, regardless of the platform or system [7,8,67];
- Semantic Classifier, Role List of Individuals, and Knowledge Graph, significantly superior to their analogues in terms of the capacity of semantic calculus [1,3,4,10–20,51,52,65,66,68];
- semantic, mathematical, and software algorithms that can significantly increase the accuracy and speed of search engine operation;
- machine-friendly parsing that provides a straightforward transition to automatic semantic markup of content;
- compatibility with statistical methods and any types of machine learning that scale the obtained results and reduce the complexity and labor intensity of the knowledge base development.

Acknowledgment. The authors thank the Department of Intelligent Information Technologies of the Belarusian State University of Informatics and Radioelectronics, the Department of Theory and Practice of the Chinese Language of the Minsk State Linguistic University for the help and valuable comments.

References

1. Activity Vocabulary. W3C Recommendation. https://www.w3.org/TR/activitystreamsvocabulary/#dfn-activity. Accessed 29 Oct 2021
2. Ashtadhyayi or Sutrapath of Panini. https://sanskritdocuments.org/doc_z_misc_major_works/aShTAdhyAyI.pdf. Accessed 29 Oct 2021
3. Berners-Lee, T., Hendler, J., Lassila, O.: The semantic web: a new form of web content that is meaningful to computers will unleash a revolution of new possibilities. Sci. Am. **284**(5), 34–43 (2001)
4. Berners-Lee, T., Shedbolt, N., Hall, W.: Semantic web revisited. IEEE Intell. Syst. **21**(3), 96–101 (2006)
5. Bobrow, D.G., Winograd, T.: An overview of KRL, a knowledge representation language. Cogn. Sci. **1**(1), 3–46 (1977)
6. Chernigovskaya, T.V.: How the Internet has changed our brain. https://golbis.com/pin/neyrolingvist-tatyana-chernigovskaya-kakinternet-vliyaet-na-nash-mozg-8. Accessed 29 Oct 2021
7. Davydenko, I.: Ontology-based knowledge base design. In: Golenkov, V. (ed.) Open Semantic Technologies for Intelligent Systems, pp. 57–72. Belarusian State Univ. of Informatics and Radioelectronics Publ., Minsk (2017)

8. Davydenko, I.: Semantic models, method and tools of knowledge bases coordinated development based on reusable components. In: Golenkov, V. (ed.) Open Semantic Technologies for Intelligent Systems, pp. 99–118. Belarusian State Univ. of Informatics and Radioelectronics Publ., Minsk (2018)

9. Domnina, T.N., Khachko, O.A.: Scientific journals: quantity, growth rates. http://www.benran.ru/SEM/Sb_15/sbornik/83.pdf. Accessed 29 Oct 2021

10. Fillmore, C.J.: The case for case. In: Bach, E., Harms, R. (eds.) Universals in Linguistic Theory, pp. 1–88. Harper and Row, NewYork (1968)

11. Fillmore, C.J.: Types of lexical information. In: Studies in Syntax and Semantics, pp. 109–137. Reidel, Dordrecht (1969)

12. Fillmore, C.J.: Verbs of judging: an exercise in semantic description. In: Studies in Linguistic Semantics, pp. 272–289. Holt, Rinehart and Winston, New York (1971)

13. Fillmore, C.J.: The case for case reopened. Syntax Semant. **8**, 59–81 (1977)

14. Fillmore, C.J.: Frame semantics. Papers Prepared for the 1981 Seoul International Conference on Linguistics, pp. 111–137. Hanshin Publishing Co., Seoul (1982)

15. Fillmore, C.J.: Frames and the semantics of understanding. Quaderni di Semantica **6**(2), 222–254 (1985)

16. Fillmore, C.J.: Corpus linguistics vs. computer-aided armchair linguistics. In: Proceedings from a 1991 Nobel Symposium on Corpus Linguistics, pp. 35–66. Mouton de Gruyter, Stockholm (1992)

17. Fillmore, C.J.: Encounters with language. Comput. Linguist. **38**(4), 701–718 (2012)

18. Fillmore, C.J., Atkins, B.T.S.: Towards a frame-based lexicon: the semantics of RISK and its neighbors. In: Frames, Fields and Contrasts, Hillsdale, NJ, pp. 75–102. Lawrence Erlbaum Associates (1992)

19. Fillmore, C.J., Atkins, B.T.S.: Starting where the dictionaries stop: the challenge for computational lexicography. In: Computational Approaches to the Lexicon, pp. 349–393. Oxford University Press, Oxford (1994)

20. Fillmore, C.J., Atkins, B.T.S.: Polysemy: Theoretical and Computational Approaches. Oxford University Press, Oxford (2000)

21. Fillmore, C.J.: Frame semantics and the nature of language. In: Annals of the New York Academy of Sciences: Conference on the Origin and Development of Language and Speech, vol. 280, no. 1, pp. 20–32 (1976)

22. Golenkov, V., Guliakina, N., Davydenko, I., Eremeev, A.: Methods and tools for ensuring compatibility of computer systems. In: Golenkov, V. (ed.) Open Semantic Technologies for Intelligent Systems (OSTIS), vol. 3, pp. 25–52. Belarusian State Univ. of Informatics and Radioelectronics Publ., Minsk (2019)

23. Golenkov, V., et al.: From training intelligent systems to training their development tools. In: Golenkov, V. (ed.) Open Semantic Technologies for Intelligent Systems (OSTIS), vol. 2, pp. 81–98. Belarusian State Univ. of Informatics and Radioelectronics Publ., Minsk (2018)

24. Golenkov, V.V., Gulyakina, N.A.: A project of an open semantic technology for the component design of intelligent systems. In: Ontology of Design, vol. 1, no. 1, pp. 42–64. Samara National Research Univ. Publ., Samara (2014)

25. Golenkov, V.V., Gulyakina, N.A.: A project of an open semantic technology for the component design of intelligent systems. In: Ontology of Design, vol. 4, no. 2, pp. 34–53. Samara National Research Univ. Publ., Samara (2014)

26. Hardzei, A.: Procedural semantics and calculus of subject domains. In: Leschenko, M. (ed.) Conference 1994, Language: Semantics, Syntactics, Pragmatics, vol. 1, pp. 16–17. Minsk State Linguistic Univ. Publ., Minsk (1994)

27. Hardzei, A.: Cognitive approach to teaching of signs. In: Gabis, A.A., Detskina, R.V., Zubov, A.V., Karpilivich, T.P., Mihnevich, A.E., Piotrovsky, R.G. (eds.) Conference 1995, Computer Programs in Teaching Byelorussian and Foreign Languages, pp. 18–20. Minsk State Linguistic Univ. Publ., Minsk (1995)
28. Hardzei, A.: The Deductive Theory of Language. Belarus Science Publisher, Minsk (1998)
29. Hardzei, A.: The Principles of Evaluating the Semantics of Subject Domains. Belarusian State University Publisher, Minsk (1998)
30. Hardzei, A.: The architecture of linguistic representatives of macroprocesses. In: Language in the Light of the Classical Heritage and Modern Paradigms, pp. 24–25. Grodno State Univ. Publ., Grodno (2000)
31. Hardzei, A.: Parts of language instead of parts of speech. In: Language Verb Sentence, pp. 258–271. Smolensk Pedagogical State Univ. Publ., Smolensk (2000)
32. Hardzei, A.: The paradigm of parts of language. In: Emelyanova, S., Rychkova, L., Nikitevich, A. (eds.) Conference 2003, Word Formation and Nominative Derivation in Slavic Languages, pp. 173–179. Grodno State Univ. Publ., Grodno (2003)
33. Hardzei, A.: The foundations of combinatory semantics. In: Rychkova, L.V., Voronovich, V.L., Emelyanova, S.A. (eds.) Word and Vocabulary = Vocabulum et vocabularium, pp. 32–35. Grodno State Univ. Publ., Grodno (2005)
34. Hardzei, A.: Linguistic propaedeutics. In: Proceedings of IV Republican Research Conference "Belarus in the Modern World", pp. 226–229. The Republican Institute of Higher School Publ., Minsk (2005)
35. Hardzei, A.: Parts of language and the procedures of its delineation. In: Hardzei, A., Hongbin, W. (eds.) The Paths of the Middle Kingdom, vol. 1, pp. 69–75. Belarusian State Univ. Publ., Minsk (2006)
36. Hardzei, A.: Theoretical grammar of oriental languages: lecture course. Electronic Data, 1 electronic optical disc (CD-ROM), Minsk (2007)
37. Hardzei, A.: Virtual string as a syntactical code of a sentence (by the examples of the Chinese language). In: Proceedings of International Research Conference "Language, Society and Problems of Intercultural Communication", pp. 349–358. Grodno State Univ. Publ., Grodno (2007)
38. Hardzei, A.: The meaning of logical and semantic paradoxes for language theory. In: Readings from V. A. Karpov, pt. 1, pp. 9–18. Belarusian State Univ. Publ., Minsk (2011)
39. Hardzei, A.: Theory for automatic generation of knowledge architecture (TAPAZ-2) and further minimization of semantic calculus. In: Proceedings of IV International Scientific and Technical Conference "Open Semantic Technologies for Intelligent Systems (OSTIS-2014)", pp. 49–64. Belarusian State Univ. of Informatics and Radioelectronics Publ., Minsk (2014)
40. Hardzei, A.: About the combinatorics of numerical signs in the Chinese language. In: Scientific Readings Dedicated to Viktor Vladimirovich Martynov, vol. 2, pp. 12–14. The Republican Institute of Higher School Publ., Minsk (2015)
41. Hardzei, A.: Dynamic syntax: a semantic view. Foreign Lang. High. Sch. **43**(4), 26–34 (2017)
42. Hardzei, A.: Theory for automatic generation of knowledge architecture: TAPAZ-2. The Republican Institute of Higher School Publ., Minsk (2017). http://tapaz. by. Accessed 29 Oct 2021
43. Hardzei, A.: Attributive-predicative syntagm as a language universal. Foreign Lang. High. Sch. **51**(4), 7–19 (2019)

44. Hardzei, A.: Plagiarism problem solving based on combinatory semantics. In: Golenkov, V., Krasnoproshin, V., Golovko, V., Azarov, E. (eds.) OSTIS 2020. CCIS, vol. 1282, pp. 176–197. Springer, Cham (2020). https://doi.org/10.1007/978-3-030-60447-9_11

45. Hardzei, A.: About declarative and procedural knowledge representation. Foreign Lang. High. Sch. **58**(3), 5–12 (2021)

46. Hardzei, A.: Semantic markup of the event and its display by means of the Chinese and Russian languages. Foreign Lang. High. Sch. **57**(2), 5–26 (2021)

47. Hardzei, A., Kewen, S.: Typological aspects of word formation. In: The Paths of the Middle Kingdom, vol. 2, pp. 40–53. The Republican Institute of Higher School Publ., Minsk (2011)

48. Hardzei, A., Udovichenko, A.: Graph of TAPAZ–2 semantic classifier. In: Golenkov, V. (ed.) Open Semantic Technologies for Intelligent Systems (OSTIS), vol. 3, pp. 281–284. Belarusian State Univ. of Informatics and Radioelectronics Publ., Minsk (2019)

49. Harris, Z.S.: Co-occurrence and transformation in linguistic structure. Language **33**(3), 283–340 (1957)

50. Ivanov, S.: The number of scientific publications in the world is increasing every year, with the bulk of the growth accounted for by developing countries. https://hightech.fm/2018/12/24/science-2. Accessed 29 Oct 2021

51. Jackendoff, R.: X-Bar Syntax: A Study of Phrase Structure. MIT Press, Cambridge (1977)

52. Jackendoff, R.: Semantic Interpretation in Generative Grammar. MIT Press, Cambridge (1972)

53. Knorozov, Y.V.: On the classification of signaling. In: Basic Problems of African Studies, pp. 324–334. Science Publ., Moscow (1973)

54. Martynov, V.V.: Semeiological Foundations of Computer Science. Science and Technics Publishing, Minsk (1974)

55. Martynov, V.V.: Universal Semantic Code. Grammar. Dictionary, Texts. Science and Technics Publishing, Minsk (1977)

56. Martynov, V.V.: Universal Semantic Code: USC'3. Science and Technics Publishing, Minsk (1984)

57. Martynov, V.V.: Universal semantic code: USC'4. In: Preprint of Institute of Linguistics of Academy of Science of BSSR, no. 2, pp. 19–24. Science and Technics Publishing, Minsk (1988)

58. Martynov, V.V.: Universal semantic code: USC'5. In: Preprint of Minsk State Linguistic University, no. 4, pp. 5–16. Minsk State Linguistic Univ. Publ., Minsk (1995)

59. Martynov, V.V.: About A. Hardzei's book "the deductive theory of language". In: Hardzei, A. (ed.) The Deductive Theory of Language, pp. 57–58. Belarus Science, Minsk (1998)

60. Martynov, V.V.: Foundations of Semantic Coding. Experience of Knowledge Representation and Transformation. European Humanitarian Univ. Publ., Minsk (2001)

61. Martynov, V.V.: In the Center of Human Conscious. Belarusian State Univ. Publ., Minsk (2009). https://dokumen.tips/documents/-55cf9b12550346d033a49d65.html. Accessed 29 Oct 2021

62. Minsky, M.: A framework for representing knowledge, June 1974. https://dspace.mit.edu/bitstream/handle/1721.1/6089/AIM306.pdf?sequence-2. Accessed 29 Oct 2021

63. Rippa, S.P., Lyashenko, O.M.: Semantic platforms of knowledge bases software in informatics. In: Proceedings of Odessa Polytechnic University, vol. 1, no. 40, pp. 91–96. Odessa Polytechnic Univ. Publ., Odessa (2013)

64. Romanovskaya, E.V.: The theory of fascination in the context of the problems of literary translation (on the example of translations of the Chinese classical poetry "Shi"). Proc. Gomel State Univ. named after Francisk Skorina 1(122), 125–131 (2019)

65. Schema.org Vocabulary, version 8.0. https://schema.org. Accessed 29 Oct 2021

66. Semantic Web. https://www.w3.org/standards/semanticweb. Accessed 29 Oct 2021

67. Shunkevich, D.: Agent-oriented models, method and tools of compatible problem solvers development for intelligent systems. In: Golenkov, V. (ed.) Open Semantic Technologies for Intelligent Systems, vol. 2, pp. 119–132. Belarusian State Univ. of Informatics and Radioelectronics Publ., Minsk (2018)

68. Stowell, T.A.: Origins of phrase structure (1981). http://www.ai.mit.edu/projects/dm/theses/stowell81.pdf. Accessed 29 Oct 2021

69. Toporov, V.N.: On some analogies to the problems and methods of modern linguistics in the works of ancient Indian grammarians. Briefs Inst. Peoples Asia 57, 123–133 (1961)

70. Voloshina, O.A.: On the structure and linguistic terminology of Panini's grammar and its influence on European linguistics. Bull. Russ. State Univ. Humanit. Ser. Hist. Philol. Culturology Orient. Stud. 52, 161–172 (2010)

71. Wierzbicka, A.: Semantic Primitives. Athenäum-Verl., Frankfurt (1972)

72. Wolniewicz, B.: A formal ontology of situations. Stud. Logica. 41(4), 381–413 (1982). https://doi.org/10.1007/BF00403338

Ontology-Based Natural Language Texts Generation from Knowledge Base

Longwei Qian$^{(\boxtimes)}$ and Wenzu Li

Department of Intelligent Information Technology, Belarusian State University of Informatics and Radioelectronics, Minsk, Republic of Belarus
qianlw1226@gmail.com

Abstract. In the knowledge-based intelligent system, the natural language interface is responsible for implementing communication between end-users and intelligent system using natural language. However the internal information of intelligent system is represented in a certain kind of specific format (knowledge base). When intelligent system need to exchange information with the end-users, it is necessary for natural language interface to obtain the ability to convert fragment of the knowledge base into natural language text. Due to the diversity and complexity of natural language, generating fluent, appropriate natural language text is still a significant challenge. By comparing other methods converting structured data into natural language text, this article describes the characteristics of fragment of knowledge base and the difficulties in natural language generation. The article proposed a unified semantic model to development of natural language generation component of natural language interface. The development of natural language generation component requires a combination of various types of knowledge about linguistics and various problem solving models oriented on natural language generation. In this article the main novelty is that in the unified semantic model the various approaches and linguistic knowledge about natural language generation can be integrated to generate natural language text from the fragment of knowledge base represented in graphical form.

Keywords: natural language generation · Ontology · Knowledge base · Natural language interface · Knowledge-based system

1 Introduction

The article is based on the paper [16] that describes an approach for converting fragment of knowledge base into natural language text and the processing of the natural language generation. The main point is to create natural language generation component of natural language interface within the framework of the Open Semantic Technology for Intelligent Systems (OSTIS) project [10]. The process of development for natural language generation component and implementation details can be found in the original article.

© The Author(s), under exclusive license to Springer Nature Switzerland AG 2022
V. Golenkov et al. (Eds.): OSTIS 2021, CCIS 1625, pp. 222–241, 2022.
https://doi.org/10.1007/978-3-031-15882-7_12

The natural language interface is a significant part of user interface of intelligent systems. Its main task is to message exchange between end-users and intelligent systems using natural language. From the perspective of intelligent systems, the message that entered or obtained by user generally is represented in a external form. Natural language is one of the most common external form. Therefore, the natural language interface needs the ability to process the natural language text.

From the view of artificial intelligent natural language processing mainly realizes the computer's cognition about the real world of human-being. The most of research works are focus on the solution of natural language analysis, in contrast, there are relatively fewer researches on problems of natural language generation. Though in the filed of natural language generation there are fewer works, the research directions in natural language generation are diverse due to the difficulty to precisely define natural language generation. Currently in these research of natural language generation there is agreement that the output of natural language generation system is natural language text, however the exact form of the input is substantially difficult to be defined. Generally speaking, in the field of natural language generation there are following forms of the input: structured forms (e.g., tabular data, knowledge base), semi-structured textual forms, unstructured textual forms.

From the view of natural language generation, data-text generation, the machine translation, text generation from visual data such as image or video entirely are instances of natural language generation. Therefore there are usually the following main difficulties in terms of natural language generation:

- Analysis and processing of the input data forms;
- Analysis of characteristics of the target text generated by intelligent system.

Nowadays the intelligent system is widely applied in various fields. In the development of intelligent system the knowledge-based system is considered as one of the most cutting-edge directions, in particular after the concept of knowledge graph was proposed by Google [3]. In order to achievement of more conveniently interaction between this kind of intelligent system and users, it's necessary to develop the component of natural language interface, which has the capacity to process the fragment of knowledge base and generate fluent natural language text to the users that satisfies the grammar of the natural language. This kind of natural language generation system had widely developed as part of natural language interface with the increase of computing power and the proposal of the novel models. However, due to the various input data forms in graphical structures and the optional multi-language for the output, the task of natural language generation is still an open challenge.

The rest of this article is organized as follows: Sect. 2 reviews the related works, analyses existing methods and unsolved problems. Section 3 introduces proposed semantic model to development of natural language generation component of natural language interface, involved in knowledge base of linguistics and problem solvers oriented on natural language generation. Section 4 describes an example of implementation: Chinese language generation using constructed semantic model. Finally, we conclude our work in Sect. 5.

2   Analysis of Related Works for Natural Language Generation

The article is dedicated to development of natural language generation component of natural language interface. However, in the classical approaches (for example, model-oriented approach) to create user interface, flexibility of user interface modification and its effective implementation remain unresolved [19]. Moreover, due to absence of unified principle for user interface design, it's impossible to develop the natural language generation system as separated component that can be reused in development of other user interface.

The task of the natural language generation component in this article is to generate natural language text from structured form, in particular, from fragment of knowledge base. At the early stage, the successful natural language generation systems are widely applied in the weather reporting, "robo-journalist" and so on, which generate fluent natural language text from the tabular data or data of information box by filling placeholders in a predefined template [15]. From the users point of view, the generated text using these predefined templates is relatively simple and inflexible. With the development of technology, the rule-based approaches could generate more complex and flexible text on the basis of a serious of grammar and heuristic rules. In these rule-based approaches the linguistic rules usually are the main influencing factors for generation of natural language text. In the research of linguistics, linguists proposed many linguistic theories that focus on analysing natural language text, for example, the dependency grammar is used to analyse the syntactic structure of sentence. However these approaches lack supporting of unified basis for representing various linguistic knowledge. Moreover, traditional rule-based approaches focus not on the semantic of natural language text, but rather on the syntax.

In most natural language generation systems the classic pipeline architecture [18] has been often applied. From the point of view of this pipeline, there are generally the six tasks in natural language generation systems (Fig. 1). In fact, the classic pipeline architecture can be considered as the modular approach to solve the natural language generation problem. The different subsets of the tasks in the pipeline can be considered as different modules. However, the biggest problem for the ordering of the modular approach is the generation gap [13] that refers to the mistakes of early tasks in the pipeline passed further downstream. In addition, for problems of each module in natural language generation system, the combination and modification of problem solving models to solve the problems of each module is lack of any single basis. Therefore development of such system leads to significant overhead costs.

In the subtask of SemEval AMR-to-English generation, the abstract AMRs to be converted into syntactic structures by a symbolic generator, then the syntactic structures are linearized with an off-the-shelf tools (e.g. statistical linearizers) [21].

Currently the neural network model is widely applied for natural language generation task, the most influential deep learning architecture for natural language generation is the Encoder-Decoder [22]. The encoder encodes various kinds of input (e.g., natural language text, structured data, image and even knowledge base) into a low dimension vector representing the semantic of the input. The decoder generates natural language text from the vector embedding. In most applications, RDF and others the knowledge representation forms are widely used as a kind of input of modern neural generator in the user interface of knowledge-based system constructed by the W3C standards. The WebNLG [8] is a project oriented on developing technologies that give humans easy access to machine-readable data of Web, which is in form of RDF. The WebNLG project focus on developing neural generator based on neural network models. Therefore in WebNLG project the related datasets for neural network models are constructed in the form of Data/Text pairs where the data is a set of triples extracted from DBpedia [2] and the text is a verbalization of these triples. However the neural generators developed on the basis of these datasets usually ignore the distinction between text planning and realization that causes difficulties in controlling over the generated text structure [5]. Moreover dataset acquiring is another issue for neural generator, neural network model is a data-driven approach for natural language generation. In the development of neural generator the high quality aligned training data is the core. For Chinese language generation, there are high quality Chinese knowledge bases, such as CN-DBpedia [24], zhishi.me [4] where data is in form of RDF, but the aligned Data/Text pairs datasets are difficult to construct.

Nowadays the most research works focus on applying the neural network model to resolve the natural language generation task, the rarer works are in the research of the ruled-based methods for natural language generation. The system NaturalOWL [6] proposed to construct generation resource to verbalize OWL. The system in fact is a symbolic generator; manually constructed templates and rules in this system are used to determine the quality of the generated text. The single model cannot solve the efficiency and quality of generated texts simultaneously, for example, when the high quality dataset is absent for certain languages, performance of natural language generation system will be greatly reduced. The efficiency of integration and the execution of various models are the main problems for current natural language generation systems.

From the above analysis, it can be seen that the mentioned approaches can solve partial problems for development of natural language generation component of natural language interface. It is still an unsolved problem to effectively integrate different approaches in a unified model for development of natural language generation component. Based on the analysis of related works, for developing natural language generation component of natural language interface, the integrated approaches within a unified basis will be considered to solve the various problems of natural language generation.

3 Proposed Approach

We propose to develop a unified semantic model for construction of natural language generation component underlying the principle of ontology-based user interface design. The compatibility of constructed various components of the

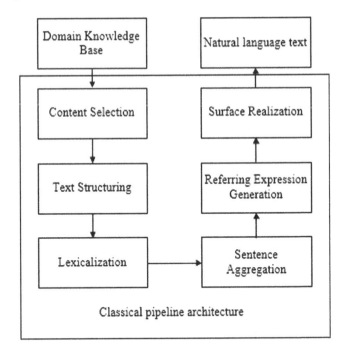

Fig. 1. Classic pipeline of natural language generation

computer systems were solved within the framework of OSTIS Technology. The development of natural language generation component using ontological approach is the construction of the ontological model (semantic model) of natural language generation component.

The natural language interface is developed as subset of user interface of the ostis-system. The systems developed by the OSTIS Technology are called ostis-system. A semantic model (sc-model) of the ostis-system is described using the SC-code. The SC-code is a semantic network language with set-theoretic interpretation. For visualization of SC-code [10] the SCg-code, SCn-code, and SCs-code are the universal variants.

Each ostis-system consists of sc-model of knowledge base, sc-model of problem solver and sc-model of user interface. The sc-model of knowledge base is based on several basic principles that provides the ability to represent knowledge of various types in the knowledge base [9]. The sc-model of problem solver is interpreted as a hierarchical system of agents react to situation and events in sc-memory and interact with each other in the sc-memory [20]. The sc-model of user interface is based on some principles to resolve specific interface tasks [19].

The basis of the knowledge base of any ostis-system is a hierarchy of subject domains and the corresponding ontologies. The structure of knowledge base is an interconnection of various subject domains that allow to consider objects of research on different levels in detail. Each ontology is interpreted as a specification of a system of concepts used in this subject domain. The each subject domain is represented by the distinguished ontologies, which reflect various types of the concept features in corresponding subject domain, for example, *terminological ontology, set-theoretical ontology, logical ontology* and so on.

Generally speaking, each class of problems which are able to be solved by intelligent system corresponds to some *problem-solving model* [20]. With the development of artificial intelligence technology, a number of such models have been developed, such as classical algorithms, procedural programs, logical models, neural network models and so on. Within the framework of OSTIS Technology, the problem solver is implemented using multi-agent approach, within problem solver several different problem-solving models can be used. It is assumed that each problem-solving model corresponds to some sc-agents. The sc-model of problem solver provides possibilities to integrate various types of problem-solving models when solving the same complex problem.

3.1   The System Architecture for Natural Language Generation Component

The natural language generation is just considered as a component of natural language interface of ostis-system. Based on the design principle of user interface of ostis-system, natural language interface is a specialized ostis-system oriented on the natural language processing task solution, which consists of the knowledge base about linguistics and problem solvers for natural language processing. The natural language generation component generating natural language text from knowledge base of specific ostis-system is developed on the basis of the principles of designing natural language interface. The general architecture for natural language generation component is shown in Fig. 2.

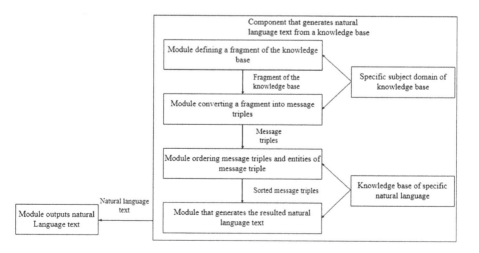

Fig. 2. The architecture of development of natural language generation component

The modules of architecture mainly correspond to classical pipeline of natural language generation. The knowledge base of natural language interface provide the necessary linguistic knowledge for generating natural language text. In the knowledge base of specific natural language linguistic knowledge about various levels of natural language text is described, such as knowledge base about basic word, syntactic and semantic structure. In the term of certain specific natural language some specific words that can serve as predicates have predicate-argument structures. These predicate-argument structures provide the specific linguistic knowledge for rule construction for natural language generation and can be encoded into knowledge base of specific natural language through SC-code.

From the perspective of ostis-system, any text is a file (i.e., an sc-node with content or sc-link). An example of such a sc-node will be shown in discussion of construction of knowledge base. In the SC-code the sc-link is usually used to represent any text. For natural language generation, each sc-link can be appropriately filled with corresponding words to generate resulted text, which satisfies syntax of certain language. Within the situation of limited computing resources and inflexible given sc-structures the template-based method is the best choice.

According to the above mentioned architecture for natural language generation component problem solver of natural language generation need to be developed. In the framework of Technology OSTIS the development of problem solver is considered as the development of a group of sc-agents that achieves the function of each module. The advantage of ontology-based problem solver design is the realization of the function of each module can adopt various suitable approaches (such as, neural network, logical and so on). Therefore, it's easy to supplement developed module with new components or make changes in already existing components. For the developed natural language generation component of ostis-system, each sc-element of sc-structure has implicit semantics that is not easy to be processed directly. In the proposed approach sc-structure will be converted into corresponding message triples based on a series of prepossessing, which are easier to express as natural language text.

3.2 The Structure of the Knowledge Base of the Natural Language Interface

The knowledge base of the natural language interface includes two part: knowledge base of specific natural language and knowledge base about specific subject domain (Fig. 3).

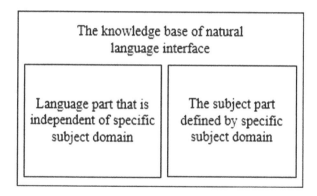

Fig. 3. The knowledge base of natural language interface

Moreover, the natural language generation component has own problem solvers oriented on natural language generation from the fragment of knowledge base about specific subject domain based on linguistic ontologies. The language part is the ontological model of knowledge base of specific natural language (e.g., sc-model of knowledge base about Chinese language processing). The subject part is sc-model of knowledge base about specific subject domain (e.g., Discrete Mathematics, History). Among them, the language part can be generally used with other specific domain to develop the natural language interface.

The upper level of fragment of knowledge base directly related with natural language interface is shown below. The fragment of knowledge base provides a kind of formal representation for the various kinds of linguistic knowledge about natural language processing. The *Knowledge base of Linguistics* generally consists of the following sections:

- **Section. Subject domain about processing of Chinese language texts**;
- **Section. Subject domain about processing of English language texts**;
- **Section. Subject domain about processing of Russian language texts**.

In order to implement translation mechanism to generate natural language text from the internal fragment of knowledge base, the lexical analysis, syntactic analysis and even semantic analysis of natural language text is the significant need. Look at a general structure of *Section. Subject domain about processing of Chinese language texts* represented in SCn. The lexical information, syntax and semantics of Chinese language texts become the main object of research in *Section. Subject domain about processing of Chinese language texts*. From the view of knowledge base, *Section. Subject domain about processing of Chinese language texts*, in turn, generally consists of the following sections:

- **Section. Subject domain of lexical analysis**;
- **Section. Subject domain of syntactic analysis**;
- **Section. Subject domain of semantic analysis**.

The *Section. Subject domain of lexical analysis*, the *Section. Subject domain of syntactic analysis* and the *Section. Subject domain of semantic analysis* describe specification of a system of concepts, logical rules and even other knowledge from the lexical aspect, syntactic aspect and semantic aspect of the Chinese language, respectively.

In the Fig. 4, a logical statement in the logical ontology represented in SCg indicates a simple heuristic rule constructed in *Section. Subject domain of Chinese language texts*. The heuristic rule can be used to generate a simple declarative sentence based on template. When the role relation (i.e., semantic subject, semantic predicate, etc.) of each element of a message triple is determined, the identifier of specific sc-node can be served as the subject, predicate and object of generated sentence, respectively.

The *Section. Subject domain of specific domain* represents the knowledge about specific subject domain. For example, in the knowledge base of OSTIS intelligent tutoring system for Discrete Mathematics, the subject part contains concepts, relation and other various types of knowledge about the subject domain Discrete mathematics, such as the type of theorem, inclusion relation of graph theory and so on.

In the knowledge base of ostis-system, any natural language text is defined as a file represented in sc-link, name of each sc-element is an arbitrary unique string stored in the sc-link. In the SC-code the system identifier commonly used as the name for sc-elements. The system identifier is unique for a sc-element within the entire knowledge base of a given ostis-system. An example of sc-link is shown in Fig. 5. The Fig. 5 indicates the fact that the system identifier of sc-node is described in English language text.

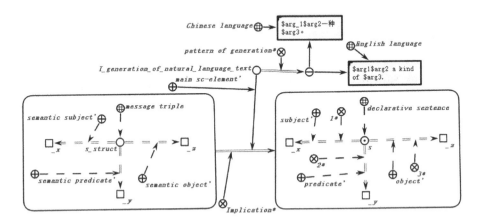

Fig. 4. Logical statement used for generating natural language text

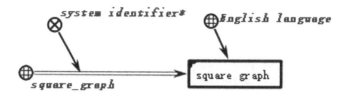

Fig. 5. Representation of natural language text in the knowledge base

Due to the lack of morphological characteristic of Chinese language texts, the expression of word is defined as lexical unit (segment unit) [17]. However, considered into other natural language text with inflectional forms, the lexical units in the knowledge base are not directly described in the form sc-link. An example of description of lexical unit is shown in Fig. 6. In order to utilize traditional syntactical logical rules to generate natural language texts, in the *Section. Subject domain of lexical analysis* we construct corresponding ontologies for markup of lexical units. Generally in the specific subject domain of knowledge base, there are obvious distinguish between the system identifier and the name of the sc-elements used in lexical units. For generating suitable resulted text, the lexical units for corresponding sc-elements have to be provided in the specific subject domain of knowledge base.

In Fig. 6, The sc-structure specifies that a sc-node whose system identifier is "I_ch_live", as well as this sc-node represents a lexical unit, which is a intransitive verb. i.e., the part-of-speech of the lexical unit and other knowledge also can be described in the knowledge base. These information helps to determinate syntactic structure, as well as select the most appropriate words in the resulted generated texts. The sc-structure indicates the standard representation of lexical unit in Chinese language.

The syntactic information of Chinese language text is described in the *Section. Subject domain of syntactic analysis*. The various role relations as which lexical units serve in natural language text, and the classifications of sentence are the main objects of research. With the help of the constructed ontologies in this *Section. Subject domain of syntactic analysis*, we can determinate the composition of the resulted generated texts.

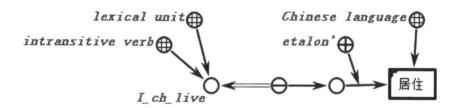

Fig. 6. Description of the lexical unit in the knowledge base

Furthermore, the information about semantic level of lexical units is essential for constructing syntactic structure. In the *Section. Subject domain of semantic analysis*, the knowledge about semantic level has to be provided. Among them, the most important core part is the semantic role frame of lexical units that served as predicate. For construction of ontologies of lexical units, some general-purpose lexical unit would be to exploit, such as Chinese WordNet [23], Chinese part of ConceptNet [1] and so on.

In the *Section. Subject domain of semantic analysis*, with the help of the CPB, Mandarin VerbNet [12], and other linguistic resource, we will consider the concepts, such as semantic frame of predicate, semantic role and so on. The *Section. Subject domain of semantic analysis* provides the semantic information for certain lexical units and semantic role relation of lexical units in natural language text. The general-purpose lexical units, however, often do not cover the highly technical concepts of specific subject domain. Sometimes it is necessary to tailor or select lexical units from general-purpose lexical units that are suitable for development of a specific subject domain knowledge base. The knowledge about semantic level is shown in Fig. 7.

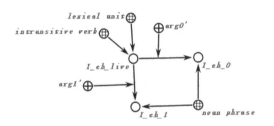

Fig. 7. Description of semantic information of the lexical unit

In Fig. 7, the sc-structure indicates predicate-argument relation using role relations "arg0" and "arg1" in the linguistic theory FrameNet. The role relation "arg0" and "arg1" indicate the lexical units "I_ch_0" and "I_ch_1" can be served as the subject and object of generated text, respectively. The corresponding lexical units have to be a kind of noun phrase.

3.3   The Structure of the Problem Solver of the Natural Language Interface

Within the OSTIS Technology, the development of problem solvers is based on the agent oriented principle. The multi-agent approach to the construction of problem solvers provides the flexibility and modularity, as well as provides the ability to integrate various problem-solving models to complex problem solutions. For design of natural language generation component, a hierarchical system of agents (sc-agents) oriented on solving natural language generation problem need to be developed.

It is worth noting that the development of agents usually should be based on certain principles of a particular natural language. Due to the diversity of natural language, when developing problem solvers for solving the problem of texts generation of a particular natural language, it is required to take into account the features and characteristics of a particular natural language, including aspects of lexical analysis, parsing, semantic analysis and also other text processing. In order to implement a specific natural language interface of the ostis-system that could generate texts of a specific natural language, it may be necessary to develop additional sc-agents depending on the features of a particular natural language. For example, for Chinese language texts, in contrast to European languages, there are potential boundaries between Chinese characters in the written form of the Chinese language, but which are not indicated in the writing (lack of natural space as the written form of European languages). Thus, when developing a Chinese language interface of ostis-system, it is necessary to supplement the sc-agents, that divide the Chinese language text into segmentation units (a term in the standard of Chinese language processing) and other agents that depend on the characteristics of the Chinese language.

Underlying the principle of problem solvers design within the OSTIS Technology, noticed that copies of the same sc-agent or functionally equivalent sc-agents may work in different ostis-system, being physically different sc-agents, it is rational to not just consider properties and typology of sc-agents but the classes of functionally equivalent sc-agents. The abstract sc-agent is a certain class of functionally equivalent sc-agents. In order to achieve the functions of natural language interface, it is necessary to develop a series of sc-agents, which are included in the problem solver of natural language interface.

- Abstract sc-agent translating natural language texts into the fragments of knowledge base;
- Abstract sc-agent generating natural language texts from the fragments of knowledge base;
- Abstract sc-agent verifying the knowledge base.

Abstract sc-agent generating natural language texts from the fragments of knowledge base is a group of sc-agents that implement the mechanisms of natural language generation from the fragment of knowledge base, i.e. given a sc-structure containing a set of basic sc-constructions, sc-agents generate a corresponded fluent natural language text for it. The development of *Abstract sc-agent generating natural language texts from the fragments of knowledge base* corresponds to each module of the architecture of development of natural language generation component. In the technology framework of OSTIS, the implementation of an abstract sc-agent could be decomposed into constructing a collection of simpler abstract sc-agents. The *Abstract sc-agent generating natural language texts from the fragments of knowledge base* generally consists of following sc-agents:

- Abstract sc-agent determining certain fragment of knowledge base;
- Abstract sc-agent forming structure of generated text;

- Abstract sc-agent for micro-planning;
- Abstract sc-agent for realization of resulted text.

The implementation of module defining a fragment of the knowledge base in the knowledge base of ostis-system can be considered to develop a group of abstract sc-agents. The general structure of the **Abstract sc-agent determining certain fragment of knowledge base** can be considered:

- Abstract sc-agent determining sc-structure;
- Abstract sc-agent dividing determined sc-structure into basic sc-constructions;
- Abstract sc-agent determining the candidate sc-constructions;
- Abstract sc-agent converting candidate sc-constructions into message triples.

Abstract sc-agent for determining sc-structure - the groups of agents that provide the solution that retrieval sc-structure from the specific subject domain of knowledge base. The sc-structure will be transformed to natural language texts. This stage is to determine what we want to talk.

Abstract sc-agent dividing determined sc-structures into basic sc-constructions - the agents that implement the mechanisms of decomposition of retrieved sc-structure into basic sc-constructions, which can be transferred into message triples. Sometime several message triples transformed from sc-constructions are redundancy, so the system finally selects among the basic sc-constructions the ones to be transferred.

Abstract sc-agent determining the candidate sc-constructions - the agents that implement the mechanism of determination of appropriate candidate sc-constructions that satisfy specific end-users.

Abstract sc-agent converting candidate sc-constructions into message triples - the agents that implement the mechanism of conversion of candidate sc-constructions to message triples.

Abstract sc-agent forming structure of generated text - the agents that solve two classes of problems which affects the resulted text: the sequence of transformed message triples; the sequence of entities of each message triple. The following structure of this abstract sc-agent is considered:

- Abstract sc-agent ordering message triples;
- Abstract sc-agent ordering entities of every message triple.

Abstract sc-agent for micro-planning - the agents that implement the mechanism of transferring message triples to abstract sentence specifications that are varied according to natural language generation system, for example, the simple text templates with slots, syntactic structures and so on. The general structure of **Abstract sc-agent for micro-planning** can be considered:

- Abstract sc-agent constructing abstract sentence specifications;
- Abstract sc-agent for sentence aggregation;
- Abstract sc-agent generating the referring expression.

Abstract sc-agent for realization of resulted text - the group sc-agents that implement the mechanisms of filling the sc-links into abstract sentence specifications to generate natural language text, i.e. retrieving resulting forms of lexical units according to rules, as well as filling and concatenating the sc-links.

The main task of natural language generation component is to convert given sc-structure to natural language text. Within the framework of OSTIS Technology, the problem solvers are developed to solve such complex problem. In addition, in the term of implementation, sc-agent programs can implement logical reasoning based on a hierarchy of statements comprised in the logical ontology, as well as the data-driven learning algorithms using various programming language. Therefore, it becomes possible to combine various approaches and linguistic knowledge to generate natural language text.

4   Implementation of the Proposed Approach

On the basis of above constructed linguistic ontologies and problem solvers in the ostis-system, as a example, processing stages for generating Chinese language text from the fragment of knowledge base will be considered.

Several constraints are defined:

- The input is sc-structure, which is completed and has sense;
- The input given sc-structure formally represented in the specific subject domain of knowledge base (Discrete Mathematics);
- The output is a simple narrative Chinese sentence;
- The knowledge base includes entity signs with Chinese identifier, which will be used in the resulted sentence.

The realization of natural language generation is roughly divided into two steps: rule-based symbolic generator converting sc-structure of knowledge base to message triples; template-based, rule-based or statistical generator (when high quality aligned dataset is accessible) translating message triples to natural language text. Each step is responsible by a group of sc-agents with help of linguistic ontologies. Currently, for our task the construction of the high quality aligned dataset is time-consuming and lengthy process. In this article, we just use template-based and rule-based approach to illustrate the process to generate a simple narrative Chinese sentence.

Step 1. A retrieved sc-structure formally represented in SCg is given (Fig. 8).

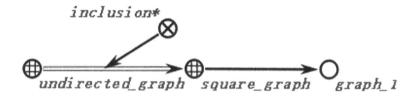

Fig. 8. Sc-structure of subject domain "Discrete Mathematics" of knowledge base

Step 2. The given sc-structure is transferred into basic sc-constructions (Fig. 9). The basic sc-construction generally consists of sc-nodes and sc-connectors. According to the principles of OSTIS Technology, the sc-connectors all represent certain relationships which either implicitly have a clear semantic interpretation (e.g.. membership) or explicitly to be expressed through specific sc-node. In the Fig. 9, the first basic sc-construction indicates a membership connection between two sc-nodes (sc-class and sc-node), and the second basic sc-construction indicates **inclusion*** relationship between two sc-nodes (two sc-classes).

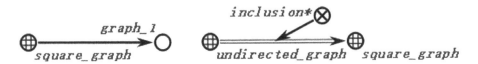

Fig. 9. Two converted basic sc-structures

Step 3. These basic sc-constructions are considered as candidate sc-constructions which will be converted to message triples. In some cases, the candidate sc-constructions may need to be selected from all the converted basic sc-constructions. The membership connection and **inclusion*** relationship are transferred into corresponding properties of message triples "instanceOf" and "inclusion", respectively. In the Fig. 10, we just show the conversion of the first basic sc-construction, the same for second one.

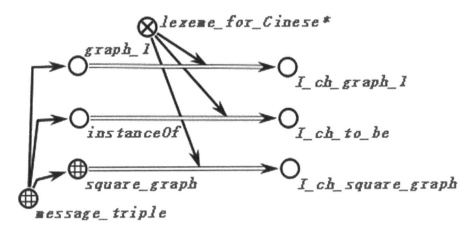

Fig. 10. Message triple transferred from first basic sc-construction

Step 4. For each property of message triples, a suitable predicate-argument structure from the linguistic ontologies is matched. In this example, for first message triple (the order is sorted result) the specific template shown in the Fig. 1 will be used, for second message triple a predicate-argument structure will be matched in the corresponding subject domain mentioned above.

Step 5. The agent fills the sc-links of corresponded sc-nodes of message triples, i.e. a certain sc-link needs to be filled with the result of a certain inflection form of a lexical unit. The **referring expression*** indicates that the content of sc-link will be used in the resulted text. In the knowledge base the identifier of each sc-node of message triples corresponds to a certain lexical unit of specific language. The description of knowledge about lexical units is stored in the linguistic knowledge base. According the characteristic of Chinese language, there is not a certain inflection form for lexical units, e.g., the result of a lexical unit "square graph" in Chinese (Fig. 11). Therefore, the processing of this step is relative simpler.

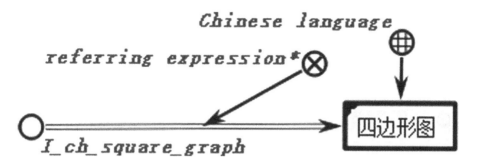

Fig. 11. The sc-link filled by the Chinese lexical unit "square graph"

Step 6. Previous sc-links are concatenated to generate the resulted Chinese sentence according to valid ordering (Fig. 12). In the Fig. 12, the relationships between each sc-node and sc-link, which are not shown, are the **referring expression***. 为了节省空间。

For first sc-structure, based on the template expression referring to the lexical unit "graph 1" is served as the subject. The lexical unit "square graph" is served as object in Chinese language. The template is predefined with fixed phrase, in the Fig. 12, the sc-link without corresponding lexical unit is the fixed part. For second sc-structure, according to the matched structure the lexical unit "undirected graph" and "square graph" are served as subject and object of Chinese language sentence.

As a result of implementation of these steps, a fragment (formally represented in sc-structure) of subject domain (Discrete Mathematics) of knowledge base is transferred into Chinese language sentence "图1(graph1)是(is)一种(a kind of)四边形图(square graph), 无向图(undirected graph)包括(includes)四边形图(square graph)" to ordinary end-users.

Nowadays automatic metrics and manual evaluation are two main types of methods for evaluating generated natural language text. The BLEU [14] and ROUGE [11] and METEOR [7] score are widely used as the automatic metrics. We begin by comparing the natural language text, which is generated by the system, with the natural language text described by human using the common automatic metrics BLEU. Notice that we couldn't compare the performance of system with other state-of-the-art system due to the absence of the system for processing complex semantic structure in knowledge base.

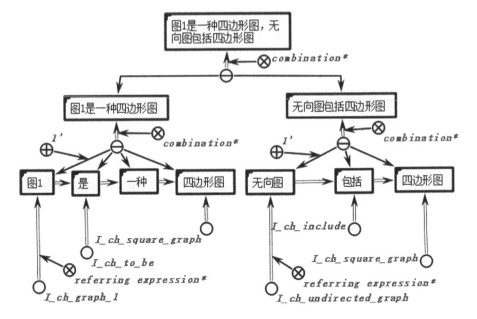

Fig. 12. Generation of Chinese sentence corresponding to sc-structure

As a rule, the cumulative score from BLEU-1 to BLEU-4 is usually reported for the performance of a text generation system. Table 1 shows that performance of different approaches for generating text. The templates are usually predefined by human, therefore, the text generated according to templates can get high scores. The BLEU-4 score "0.00" indicates the predefined templates is not flexible. However, for multiple sc-sentences, these approaches couldn't obtain satisfactory scores. The system still has certain deficiencies when generating longer natural language text.

Table 1. Evaluation of Approaches for Text Generation

	Template-based for one basic sc-sentence	Rule-based for one basic sc-sentence	Template-based/rule-based multiple basic sc-sentences
BLEU-1	1.00	0.76	0.62
BLEU-2	1.00	0.63	0.51
BLEU-3	1.00	0.51	0.38
BLEU-4	0.00	0.33	0.19

5   Conclusion

This article proposes a unified semantic model for natural language generation from knowledge base. In order to appropriately solve the complex problem, the various types of linguistic knowledge base and various problem solving models oriented on natural language generation are constructed. We conducted an example implementation for Chinese language generation and quality evaluation of generated text and analysed some drawback of system.

The proposed approach has the following advantages:

- The semantic model is possible to generate fluent, coherent, and multi-sentence natural language texts appropriating for end-users;
- The semantic structure that processed by this model is more complex than simple tabular or triples structure;
- as a part of the model, the Chinese linguistic knowledge base is designed to generate grammatically similarity texts. The knowledge base make the model more explanatory than statistical model.

We are currently working towards implementing the model for Chinese language generation in restricted conditions. The generalization ability of model is still worth to research. In the future, if the aligned training dataset are constructed or possible to access, the more intelligent problem solving models (e.g.. neural network models) will be combined into system, the performance of system will be further improved.

References

1. Chinese part of ConceptNet. https://conceptnet.io/c/en/chinese. Accessed 04 Oct 2021
2. DBpedia. https://www.dbpedia.org/. Accessed 04 Oct 2021
3. Introducing the Knowledge Graph: Things, Not Strings. https://blog.google/products/search/introducing-knowledge-graph-things-not/. Accessed 04 Oct 2021
4. Zhishi.me. https://zhishi.me/. Accessed 08 Oct 2021
5. Amit, M., Yoav, G., Ido, D.: Step-by-step: separating planning from realization in neural data-to-text generation. In: Proceedings of the 2019 Conference of the North American Chapter of the Association for Computational Linguistics: Human Language Technologies, Volume 1 (Long and Short Papers), USA, Minneapolis, pp. 2267–2277 (2019)
6. Androutsopoulos, I., Lampouras, G., Galanis, D.: Generating natural language descriptions from OWL ontologies: the NaturalOWL system. J. Artif. Intell. Res. **48**(01), 671–715 (2013)
7. Banerjee, S., Lavie, A.: METEOR: an automatic metric for MT evaluation with improved correlation with human judgments. In: Proceedings of the ACL Workshop on Intrinsic and Extrinsic Evaluation Measures for Machine Translation and/or Summarization, Ann Arbor, Michigan, pp. 65–72. Association for Computational Linguistics, June 2005

8. Claire, G., Anastasia, S., Shashi, N., Perez-Beltrachini, L.: The WebNLG challenge: generating text from RDF data. In: Proceedings of the 10th International Conference on Natural Language Generation, Spain Santiago de Compostela, pp. 124–133 (2017)

9. Davydenko, I.: Semantic models, method and tools of knowledge bases coordinated development based on reusable components. In: 8th International Scientific and Technical Conference "Open Semantic Technologies for Intelligent Systems", Minsk, Belarus, pp. 99–118 (2018)

10. Golenkov, V., Gulyakina, N.: Project of open semantic technology of component designing of intelligent systems. Part 1 principles of creation. Ontol. Des. **1**(11), 42–64 (2014)

11. Lin, C.Y.: ROUGE: a package for automatic evaluation of summaries. In: Text Summarization Branches Out, Barcelona, Spain, pp. 74–81. Association for Computational Linguistics, July 2004

12. Liu, M.J., Wang, M.Y.: Chinese verbs and their categorization: construction and application of the semantic network of Chinese verbs. Lexicographical Stud. **2019**(02), 42–60 (2019)

13. Meteer, M.W.: Bridging the generation gap between text planning and linguistic realization. Comput. Intell. **07**(04), 296–304 (1991)

14. Papineni, K., Roukos, S., Ward, T., Zhu, W.: BLEU: a method for automatic evaluation of machine translation. In: Proceedings of the 40th Annual Meeting on Association for Computational Linguistics (ACL), USA, Philadelphia, Pennsylvania, pp. 311–318 (2002)

15. Plachouras, V., et al.: Interacting with financial data using natural language. In: SIGIR 2016, Italy, Pisa, pp. 1121–1124 (2016)

16. Qian, L., Li, W.: Ontological approach for generating natural language texts from knowledge base. In: 11th International Scientific and Technical Conference "Open Semantic Technologies for Intelligent Systems", Minsk, Belarus, pp. 159–168 (2021)

17. Qian, L., Sadouski, M., Li, W.: Ontological approach for Chinese language interface design. In: Golenkov, V., Krasnoproshin, V., Golovko, V., Azarov, E. (eds.) OSTIS 2020. CCIS, vol. 1282, pp. 146–160. Springer, Cham (2020). https://doi.org/10.1007/978-3-030-60447-9_9

18. Reiter, E.: Pipelines and size constraints. Comput. Linguist. **26**(02), 251–259 (2000)

19. Sadouski, M.: Ontological approach to the building of semantic models of user interfaces. In: 12th International Scientific and Technical Conference "Open Semantic Technologies for Intelligent Systems", Minsk, Belarus, pp. 105–116 (2022)

20. Shunkevich, D.V.: Ontological approach to the development of hybrid problem solvers for intelligent systems. In: 11th International Scientific and Technical Conference "Open Semantic Technologies for Intelligent Systems", Minsk, Belarus, pp. 63–74 (2021)

21. Simon, M., Roberto, C., Alicia, B., Leo, W.: FORGe at SemEval-2017 Task 9: deep sentence generation based on a sequence of graph transducers. In: Proceedings of the 11th International Workshop on Semantic Evaluation (SemEval-2017), Vancouver, Canada, pp. 920–923 (2017)

22. Sutskever, I., Vinyals, O., Le, Q.V.: Sequence to sequence learning with neural networks. In: NIPS 2014, Montreal, Canada, pp. 3104–3112 (2014)

23. Wang, S., Bond, F.: Building the Chinese open wordnet (COW): starting from core Synsets. In: Proceedings of the 11th Workshop on Asian Language Resources, Nagoya, Japan, pp. 10–18 (2013)
24. Xu, B., et al.: CN-DBpedia: a never-ending Chinese knowledge extraction system. In: Benferhat, S., Tabia, K., Ali, M. (eds.) IEA/AIE 2017. LNCS (LNAI), vol. 10351, pp. 428–438. Springer, Cham (2017). https://doi.org/10.1007/978-3-319-60045-1_44

Semantic Approach to User Answer Verification in Intelligent Tutoring Systems

Wenzu Li[✉] and Longwei Qian

Belarusian State University of Informatics and Radioelectronics, Minsk, Belarus
lwzzggml@gmail.com
https://www.bsuir.by/ru/kaf-iit/sostav-kafedry

Abstract. A semantic approach to develop a problem solver for automatic verification of user answers in intelligent tutoring systems built on OSTIS Technology is proposed in this article. In the framework of OSTIS Technology, the problem solvers are developed based on multi-agent technology. The developed problem solver allows to automatically verify the completeness and correctness of user answers based on semantics by calling the corresponding sc-agent according to the type of test questions (judgement questions, multiple-choice questions, questions of definition interpretation, etc.). For some questions of definition interpretation with multiple standard answers, the problem solver allows to pre-screen a semantic fragment of the standard answer that best matches the user answer according to the semantic fragment of the user answer, and then verify the completeness and correctness between them. At the same time, since the standard answers and user answers to some questions do not match on the surface, but the logical formulas used to formalize them satisfy logical equivalence, the developed problem solver can also determine whether the standard answer and user answer satisfy logical equivalence.

Keywords: Ontology · Logical formulas · OSTIS Technology · Problem solver · Knowledge base · Intelligent tutoring systems · Answer verification

1 Introduction

As an important branch of computer technology, artificial intelligence technology is being widely used in the field of education. The combination of artificial intelligence technology and education can not only provide new teaching platforms and teaching methods, but also greatly improve the learning efficiency and knowledge retrieval efficiency of learners. Especially since the outbreak of COVID-19, the importance of intelligent tutoring systems (ITS) in education has become more prominent, and it can also ensure the fairness of education as much as possible [9,18].

With the continuous maturity of ITS development technology and the continuous improvement of development standards, domain experts and developers generally believe that ITS should at least contain the following basic functions:

© The Author(s), under exclusive license to Springer Nature Switzerland AG 2022
V. Golenkov et al. (Eds.): OSTIS 2021, CCIS 1625, pp. 242–266, 2022.
https://doi.org/10.1007/978-3-031-15882-7_13

- automatic verification of user answers, if there is an error, the reason for the error and corrective actions need to be given;
- automatic adjustment of the learning progress and content depending on the learner's learning situation and learning level;
- automatic generation of various test questions and exercises;
- having the ability to understand and generate natural language, and realize relatively free Human-Machine dialogue;
- ability to interpret the teaching content;
- automatic problem solving based on understanding of the learning content.

The most important function of ITS is the automatic verification of user answers, which allows quickly and efficiently check of the user's mastery of new knowledge, enabling users to acquire as much knowledge as possible within a limited time. Typically user answer verification needs to address the following basic tasks:

1. objective question user answer verification and subjective question user answer verification;
2. analysis of completeness and correctness of user answers;
3. verification a class of test question with multiple standard answers that do not satisfy logical equivalence (e.g., the definition of a square);
4. whether the logical formula of standard answer and user answer meets the equivalence (In OSTIS Technology, the logic formula is a powerful tool for the formal representation of knowledge, which is extended based on the first-order predicate logic expression. The logical formula inherits all the operational properties of the first-order predicate expression);
5. analysis of the logical rationality of user answers and the correctness of transitions between solution stages.

According to the type of test questions user answer verification is divided into: 1. subjective question user answer verification; 2. objective question user answer verification. Objective questions refer to a type of question that has a unique standard answer. In this article, objective questions include: judgment questions, fill in the blank questions and multiple-choice questions. Subjective questions have more than one potential correct answer and sometimes have room for a justified opinion. Subjective questions in this article include: proof questions, definition explanation questions and theorem interpretation questions. Since objective questions have fixed standard answers, their user answer verification is relatively simple, but subjective question answer verification requires knowledge of linguistics, natural language processing (NLP) and etc., so currently only some ITS have the function of subjective question user answer verification [8,10].

With the development of deep learning, semantic web and NLP technology, subjective question answer verification has become a very important area of research. Therefore, we have introduced in detail the existing subjective question answer verification approaches and their disadvantages and advantages in the literature [8], and on the basis of these approaches, we propose an semantic-based answer verification approaches (objective question answer verification and subjective question answer verification). The basic principle of this approach is to first decompose the semantic graph of the standard answer and the semantic graph of the user answer into substructures according to the knowledge description rules in the OSTIS technical framework (Open Semantic Technology for Intelligent Systems), and then calculate the similarity between the semantic graphs based on the matching relationship between the decomposed substructures, finally, the completeness and correctness of the user's answer are judged according to the calculated similarity [1,4,6]. A semantic graph is a network that represents semantic relationships between concepts in the physical world. In the OSTIS technical framework, the semantic graph is constructed and described using SC-code (as a basis for knowledge representation within the OSTIS Technology, a unified coding language for information of any kind based on semantic networks is used, named SC-code). The user answer in natural languages is converted to SC-code using the natural language interface [12].

In the literature [8], the basic principle of verifying user answers based on semantics is only introduced from the theoretical aspect, and the feasibility of the proposed approach is analyzed, but the algorithm implementation process of the proposed approach is not specifically introduced in the article. Therefore, in this article, a problem solver for answer verification in the ostis-systems (computer system built using OSTIS Technology) is developed based on the answer verification approach proposed in [8]. One of the key components of each intelligent system is the problem solver, which provides the ability to solve various problems. The developed problem solver mainly solves the tasks (1), (2), (3) and (4) listed above, and solutions for the remaining tasks will be described in subsequent articles. The discrete mathematics tutoring system developed based on OSTIS Technology was selected as a demonstration system for problem solver.

2   Existing Approaches and Problems

2.1   Ontology Mapping

According to the type of knowledge in the knowledge base of the ITS, answer verification can be divided into:

- factual knowledge answer verification;
- logical knowledge answer verification.

Factual knowledge refers to knowledge that does not contain variable types, and this type of knowledge expresses facts. In the knowledge base of ostis-systems, objective questions and their answers are usually described based on factual knowledge. The user answers to objective questions in natural language are already aligned (entity alignment) with the existing knowledge in the knowledge base when they are converted to SC-code using the natural language interface. Therefore, it is not necessary to consider the similarity between relations or concepts from the perspective of natural language when calculating the similarity between semantic graphs of answers to objective questions. That is, sc-nodes that represent the same relation or concept in the knowledge base have a unique main identifier.

Logical knowledge usually contains variables, and there are logical relations between knowledge. In the ostis-systems SCL-code (a special sub-language of the SC language intended for formalizing logical formulas) is used to represent logical knowledge. The answers to subjective questions in the knowledge base are described according to logical formula using logical knowledge. Because, the semantic graph used to represent the answer to subjective question in the ostis-systems contains variables (equivalent to the bound variable in the predicate logic formula), and there is a strict logical order between sc-nodes in the semantic graph. Therefore, when using the problem solver to calculate the similarity between the semantic graph of standard answer and the semantic graph of user answer, it is necessary to establish the mapping relationship between the potential equivalent variables between the two semantic graphs according to the semantic structure and the position of the variables in the semantic graph. Establishing the mapping relationship of potential equivalent variables between semantic graphs is the most critical step in subjective question answer verification. In this article, the semantic graph representing the answer can be regarded as a partial fragment of the ontology (ontology is a type of knowledge, each of which is a specification of the corresponding subject domain, focused on describing the properties and relations of concepts that are part of the specified subject domain) [1,5,8]. Therefore, the mapping relationship between semantic graphs can be established by referring to the approach to establishing the mapping relationship between ontologies. Currently, many tools and algorithms have been developed for establishing mapping relationships between ontologies, which will be discussed in detail below.

With the rapid development of the new generation of semantic web, ontology as the basis of semantic web has become a research hot-spot, and many ontology libraries with rich semantic information and practical value have emerged. These ontology libraries have huge differences due to different application purposes, developers and application fields, and cannot effectively communicate and inter-operate with each other. The ontology mapping is a key step to solve the heterogeneity of ontology and realize knowledge sharing and ontology inter-operation. The basic principle of ontology mapping is to calculate the similarity between elements (attributes, instances and concepts) in different ontology, and then establish the mapping relationship between elements based on the mapping strategy and the calculated similarity [9].

Due to the rapid development of ontology mapping related technologies, many terms with different names but similar semantics have emerged, such as **Ontology Fusion, Ontology Matching, Ontology Alignment, Ontology Merging, Ontology Mapping** and **Ontology Integration**. It is generally believed that ontology alignment, ontology mapping and ontology matching are terms with the same semantics. Ontology merging, ontology fusion, and ontology integration generally produce new ontology, and ontology mapping is their foundation [11,16]. Ontology mapping involves multiple implementation steps, such as ontology preprocessing, since the focus of this article is on the establishment of element mapping relationships between ontologies, other implementation steps will not be described in detail.

There are already many mature ontology mapping algorithms and mapping systems:

- a comprehensive similarity calculation algorithm that establishes semantic mapping relationships between elements (attributes, instances and concepts) between RDFS ontology is introduced in literature [19]. Taking concepts between ontology as an example, the algorithm first uses Edit Distance (Levenshtein Distance) to calculate the similarity of names between concepts, and then calculates the similarity of the instances of the concept according to the ratio of the number of instances matched between the concepts and the number of all instances, and finally, the structural similarity of the concepts is calculated according to the relationship between the number of the same father and child concepts and the number of all adjacent concepts between the concepts. By setting different weights, the above three types of similarity are combined to calculate the final similarity between concepts. Finally based on the mapping strategy and the comprehensive similarity between concepts, the mapping relationship of equivalent concepts between different ontology is established;
- with the rapid development of machine learning technology, many ontology mapping approaches based on machine learning algorithms have emerged. An approach to alignment of entities between knowledge graphs based on machine learning algorithm is introduced in the literature [20]. Knowledge graphs are used to formally describe the interrelationships between things in the objective world. The approach consists of two parts: 1. knowledge representation learning; 2. learning of mapping relationships between entities. Knowledge representation learning refers to the use of machine learning algorithms to learn the semantic representation of entities and relationships in the knowledge graph. The learning of the mapping relationship between entities refers to learning the mapping relationship of entity pairs between knowledge graphs according to the manually labeled data sets [14];
- with the rapid development of semantic web and knowledge graph, many ontology mapping systems with practical value have been developed, such as RiMOM and ASMOW. RiMOM is an ontology mapping system developed based on Bayesian decision theory. RiMOM allows the use of similarity propagation theory and multiple heuristic rules to establish the mapping relationship between concepts. ASMOV is an automated ontology mapping tool developed by Jean-Mary et al. Its goal is to promote the integration of heterogeneous ontology. ASMOV uses an iterative calculation method to analyze multiple characteristics of elements to calculate the similarity of element pairs between ontology, and to establish mapping relationships between attributes, instances and concepts in turn [9,17,21].

Although the ontology mapping approaches introduced above have many advantages, they also have many problems:

- the traditional ontology mapping algorithm requires iterative calculation of the similarity between the current element in the source ontology and each element in the target ontology. Therefore, when the amount of knowledge contained in the ontology is very large, it may take several minutes or more to establish the mapping relationship between the ontology, and real-time mapping cannot be performed;
- the ontology mapping algorithm based on machine learning improves the efficiency and accuracy of ontology mapping to a certain extent, but this approach requires significant labor costs to label the training data;
- the establishment of ontology mapping relationship is a very complicated process, and no method is perfect. At the same time, the rapid development of big data has led to the generation of big ontology, the existing approaches have been unable to establish the mapping relationship between ontologies in the big data environment.

Establishing the mapping relationship of potential equivalent variable sc-node pairs between the semantic graphs of the answers to subjective question is a key step in verifying answers to subjective questions. The part of the process of establishing the mapping relationship between potential equivalent variable sc-node pairs is similar to the establishment of the mapping relationship between the equivalent element pairs of the ontology. However, in the ostis-systems, the knowledge base is constructed using SC-code, and the knowledge in the knowledge base has a specific knowledge representation approach and knowledge structure, so the existing ontology mapping algorithms cannot be used directly. Therefore, based on the existing ontology mapping approach and OSTIS Technology, an approach to establish the mapping relationship of the potential equivalent variable sc-node pairs between the semantic graphs of the answers to subjective questions based on the semantic structure is proposed in this article.

2.2   Converting Logical Formula to Prenex Normal Form (PNF)

In predicate logic, usually a predicate logic formula has multiple equivalent predicate logic formulas. Since the logical formulas in the ostis-systems are extended based on the first-order predicate logical formula, the logical formulas used to formalize knowledge in the knowledge base sometimes also have equivalent logical formulas [11]. Therefore, when verifying the answer to the subjective question, if the semantic graph of the standard answer and the semantic graph of the user answer do not completely match, it is necessary to judge whether they satisfy the logical equivalence. It is very difficult to use algorithms in predicate logic to directly judge whether two predicate logical formulas are equivalent, but according to the theorem of predicate logic formulas: any predicate logical formula is equivalent to a prenex normal form (PNF), so we can consider converting different predicate logic formulas into PNF, and then judge whether they meet the equivalence [3,13]. When converting the predicate logic formula to the PNF, if different conversion rules or different quantifier extraction orders are used, the

PNF will not be unique. However, as long as the conversion rules are strictly restricted during the conversion process, this situation can be avoided. Therefore, when verifying the answer to a subjective question, we can also use some strict constraints to convert the semantic graph representing the answer into PNF representation in a similar way.

Definition 1: a well-formed formula of the predicate calculus is in prenex normal form if all the quantifiers stand at the front, and any other logical constant stands within the scope of all the quantifiers.

PNF can be expressed as the following form:

$Q_1 x_1 Q_2 x_2 ... Q_n x_n A$ where $Q_i (i = 1, ...n)$ is $\forall$ or $\exists$, $x_i (i = 1, ...n)$ is an object variable, and A is a predicate logical formula without quantifiers [7,11].

Converting the predicate logic formula to the PNF is the most basic step in formal deductive reasoning and resolution deductive reasoning. At present, researchers have developed very classic algorithm. The conversion of predicate logic into PNF mainly includes the following steps:

1. eliminating the implication connective ($\rightarrow$) and equivalent connective ($\leftrightarrow$) in the predicate logic formula;
2. moving all negative connectives ($\neg$) to the front of the atomic predicate formulas;
3. standardize the variables apart (using renaming or substitution rules to make all variables different);
4. using the scope contraction and expansion formula to move all the quantifiers to the front of the formula.

Although the algorithm described above can convert any predicate logic formula to the PNF, the PNF obtained by the above algorithm is not unique, and in order to increase the logical knowledge representation and processing ability in the ostis-systems, the logical formula compared with predicate logic formula, some unique knowledge formalization approaches and rules are added, so the existing algorithm cannot be used directly. Therefore, based on the existing algorithm and OSTIS Technology, this article proposes an approach to convert the semantic graph based on the logical formula description into the PNF representation under restricted conditions in order to further verify the answer to the subjective question [3,4].

3   Proposed Approach

Based on the OSTIS Technology for the design and development of semantic intelligence systems, and the accompanying standards, approaches, development platforms and knowledge editing tools, an approach to development of a problem solver for automatic answer verification in ostis-systems is proposed in this article.

Every ostis-system includes the following components: 1. a platform for interpretation semantic models of ostis-systems; 2. a semantic model of ostis-systems using SC-code (sc-model of ostis-systems). Among them, the sc-model of the ostis-systems includes: 1. sc-model of the interface; 2. sc-model of the problem solver; 3. sc-model of the knowledge base. The details of designing and constructing problem solvers and knowledge bases using OSTIS Technology are described in [4].

Using the knowledge representation model, knowledge editing tools and development standards provided by OSTIS Technology in this work will provide the following advantages:

- the developed problem solver can be easily transplanted to each other between ostis-systems;
- checking the completeness and correctness of user answers from a semantic point of view;
- storing the user's results of each test in the knowledge base;
- analysis of user testing results in accordance with the most basic semantic structures and provision of relevant reference opinions;
- the process of verifying answers does not depend on natural languages (such as Russian, English, Chinese, etc.).

Next, the development and implementation process of the problem solver for automatic answer verification will be described in detail. To illustrate how the problem solver works, the illustrations and knowledge base fragments selected in this article are in English, but essentially the developed solver does not rely on any natural language.

4   Development of Problem Solver

In the ostis-systems, the problem solvers are constructed based on a multi-agent approach. According to this approach, the problem solver is implemented as a set of agents called sc-agents. All sc-agents interact through common memory, passing data to each other as semantic network structures (sc-texts) [4,5].

The developed problem solver for answer verification in this article needs to have the following abilities:

- the problem solver not only allows verification of answers to objective questions with one correct answer option, but also allows verification of answers to objective questions with multiple correct answer options (such as, partially fill in the blank questions and multiple-choice questions with multiple options);
- the correctness and completeness of user answers to subjective questions need to be verified (such as, the answer is partially correct, or the answer is correct but incomplete, etc.). If the subjective question has multiple logically in-equivalent standard answers (for example, the definition of triangle), the problem solver allows to automatically select an appropriate standard answer based on the user answer and then calculate the similarity between them. For subjective questions, although the standard answer and user answer do not exactly match, the logical formulas used to formalize them may be equivalent. Therefore, the problem solver also needs to convert the semantic graphs

used to represent the answers into the PNF representation, and then verify the answer again. Finally, if the user answer is not completely correct, the problem solver can also automatically find out the part of the user answer that is wrong and display the correct standard answer to the user.

In the framework of OSTIS technology, problem solvers are all hierarchical systems of knowledge processing agents in semantic memory. To solve the tasks listed above, some sc-agents are developed in this article. The hierarchy of the knowledge processing agents in the problem solver for automatic answer verification is shown as follows.

Problem Solver For Automatic Answer Verification

- *sc-agent for computing semantic similarity of factual knowledge;*
- *sc-agent for processing semantic similarity calculation results of factual knowledge;*
- *sc-agent for computing semantic similarity of logical knowledge;*
- *sc-agent for converting logical formula into PNF.*

The basic principle of automatic answer verification in this article is to calculate the similarity between the semantic graph of the user answer and the semantic graph of the standard answer. In the knowledge base, answers to subjective questions and answers to objective questions are described using logical knowledge and factual knowledge, respectively [8]. Therefore, when using the developed problem solver to verify answers, different sc-agent is automatically initiated to implement answer verification based on the type of test question. It should be emphasized that answer verification is only a primary function of the developed problem solver. It also allows starting different sc-agents to compute the similarity between any two semantic fragments in the knowledge base.

When verifying the answers to objective questions, the startup sequence of sc-agents is as follows:

1. if the problem solver believes that the current question is an objective question, the sc-agent for computing semantic similarity of factual knowledge is initiated and starts calculating the similarity between the semantic graph of user answer and the semantic graph of standard answer;
2. when the first step is completed, the sc-agent for processing semantic similarity calculation results of factual knowledge is initiated. The final verification result is given by this sc-agent based on the type and characteristics (for example, multiple-choice questions with multiple correct options) of the test questions and similarity between answers.

When verifying the answer to the subjective question, the startup sequence of sc-agents is as follows:

1. if the problem solver believes that the current question is a subjective question, the sc-agent for computing semantic similarity of logical knowledge is initiated;

2. if the similarity between the answers calculated in the first step is not equal to 1, it is considered that logical equivalence may be satisfied between them. Therefore, the problem solver automatically calls the sc-agent for converting logical formula into PNF. This sc-agent converts the semantic graph of the standard answer and the semantic graph of the user answer into PNF representation;
3. the problem solver once again initiates the sc-agent for computing semantic similarity of logical knowledge, and starts to calculate the similarity between the standard answer in the PNF representation and the user answer. If the similarity between them is still not equal to 1, the problem solver uses the result obtained in the first step as the final answer verification result.

Next, the development process and working algorithm of each sc-agent will be introduced in detail.

4.1 SC-Agent for Computing Semantic Similarity of Factual Knowledge

The main task of the sc-agent for computing semantic similarity of factual knowledge is to calculate the similarity between semantic graphs described based on factual knowledge. Since the answers to objective questions are described using factual knowledge, this sc-agent allows to calculate the similarity between answers to objective questions. The similarity between answers is the basis for the objective question answer verification. Since user answers in natural language are already aligned with the existing knowledge in the knowledge base when they are converted into SC-code, therefore, the similarity between semantic graphs is calculated based on various knowledge representation structures and semantic [2,8].

The sc-agent for computing semantic similarity of factual knowledge needs to complete the following tasks:

1. based on the semantic structure describing factual knowledge within the framework of OSTIS Technology, the semantic graph of user answers and the semantic graph of standard answers are decomposed into substructures;
2. using formulas (1), (2), and (3) to calculate the precision P_{sc}, recall R_{sc} and similarity F_{sc} between semantic graphs.

$$P_{sc}(s, u) = \frac{|T_{sc}(s) \otimes T_{sc}(u)|}{|T_{sc}(u)|} \tag{1}$$

$$R_{sc}(s, u) = \frac{|T_{sc}(s) \otimes T_{sc}(u)|}{|T_{sc}(s)|} \tag{2}$$

$$F_{sc}(s, u) = \frac{2 \cdot R_{sc}(s, u) \cdot P_{sc}(s, u)}{R_{sc}(s, u) + P_{sc}(s, u)} \tag{3}$$

The meanings of the parameters in the formulas are as follows:

– $T_{sc}(u)$ - all substructures after user answer decomposition u;
– $T_{sc}(s)$ - all substructures after standard answer decomposition s;
– $\otimes$ - binary matching operator that represents the number of substructures matched between the substructure of the standard answer and the substructure of the user answer.

Next, the working algorithm of this sc-agent will be introduced in detail:

Algorithm 1—The working algorithm of sc-agent for computing semantic similarity of factual knowledge

Input: Semantic model of objective question and the corresponding semantic graph of user answer and semantic graph of standard answer.

Output: The calculated precision, recall, and similarity between the answers, as well as some semantic structures for recording the sc-agent execution results.

1. checking whether the semantic graph of the standard answer and the semantic graph of the user answer exist simultaneously, if so, go to step 2), otherwise go to step 10);
2. decomposition of the semantic graph of standard answer and semantic graph of user answer into substructures based on the rules for describing factual knowledge [8];
3. iterative traversal of each substructure of standard answer and user answer, classifying them according to the type of substructure (three element sc-construction, five element sc-construction, etc.) and counting the number of all substructures;
4. random selection of one type of substructure from the set of recorded standard answer substructure types;
5. based on the standard answer substructure type selected in step 4), selecting the appropriate substructure type from the set of recorded user answer substructure types;
6. iterative comparison of each substructure with the same substructure type between the standard answer and the user answer and recording the number of matched substructures. The criterion for judging the matching of the same type of substructures is that the sc-nodes at the corresponding positions between the two substructures have the same main identifier. If the substructure contains sc-links, the contents of the sc-links at the corresponding positions must be also the same;
7. repeat step 4—step 6 until all types of substructures have been traversed;
8. calculation of precision, recall and similarity using formulas (1), (2) and (3) and generation of semantic fragments to record the running results of the sc-agent;
9. removing all temporarily created sc-elements;
10. exit the program.

4.2   SC-Agent for Processing Semantic Similarity Calculation Results of Factual Knowledge

The sc-agent for computing semantic similarity of factual knowledge only calculates the precision, recall and similarity between the standard answer and the user answer to the objective questions. However, because some objective questions have multiple correct options, it is necessary to comprehensively consider the precision, recall and similarity to fully judge the correctness of a question. Therefore, the sc-agent for processing semantic similarity calculation results of factual knowledge is developed in this article, its main task is to judge the completeness and correctness of the current objective question according to the evaluation strategies of objective questions and the three information measurement parameters calculated in the previous step [8,9].

The evaluation strategies for the completeness and correctness of objective questions are as follows:

- if the current test question has only one correct answer option (judgment questions, multiple-choice questions with a correct option and partially fill in the blank questions), then the question is considered correct only if there is an exact match between the standard answer and the user answer ($F_{sc} = 1$), otherwise the question is wrong;
- if the current test question has more than one correct answer option (such as, partially fill in the blank questions and multiple-choice question with multiple correct options), it is divided into the following situations:
  - as long as a wrong answer option is included in the user answer, the test question is considered wrong. At this point the similarity and precision are both less than 1 ($F_{sc} < 1$ and $P_{sc} < 1$);
  - all answer options contained in the user answer are correct, but the number of correct answer options is less than the number of correct answer options contained in the standard answer, then the test question is considered partially correct and incomplete. In this case, the precision is equal to 1, the similarity is less than 1, and the ratio of the number of all options in the user answer to the number of all options in the standard answer is the recall ($F_{sc} < 1$ and $P_{sc} = 1$);
  - if all options included in the standard answer exactly match the options included in the user answer, the test question is considered to be completely correct ($F_{sc} = 1$);

Next, the working algorithm of this sc-agent will be introduced in detail:

Algorithm 2—The working algorithm of sc-agent for processing semantic similarity calculation results of factual knowledge

Input: The semantic model of specific objective question, and calculated precision, recall, and similarity between answers.

Output: The final answer verification result, and some semantic fragments for displaying the answer verification result.

1. checking whether all input parameters used for sc-agent work meet the conditions, if so, go to step 2), otherwise, go to step 5);
2. based on the evaluation strategies of objective questions and the calculated precision, recall and similarity between the answers, checking the correctness and completeness of specific objective question;

3. generation of some semantic fragments for recording the results of the sc-agent execution;
4. removing all temporarily created sc-elements;
5. exit the program.

The completeness and correctness of any type of objective question can be verified by combining the sc-agent for computing semantic similarity of factual knowledge and sc-agent for processing semantic similarity calculation results of factual knowledge. Figure 1 shows an example of automatic verification of completeness and correctness of answers to multiple-choice questions in SCg-code (SCg-code is a graphical version for the external visual representation of SC-code) [1,4].

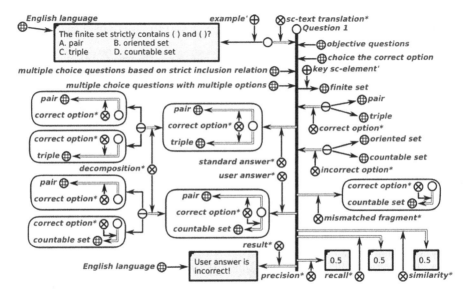

Fig. 1. An example of automatic verification of answers to the multiple-choice questions.

4.3 SC-Agent for Computing Semantic Similarity of Logical Knowledge

Calculating the similarity between semantic graphs described using logical knowledge is the main task of the sc-agent for computing semantic similarity of logical knowledge. Since the semantic graphs of answers to subjective question in the knowledge base of the ostis-systems are described based on logical formulas using logical knowledge (SCL-code), the similarity between the semantic graphs of the answers can be calculated by this sc-agent [4,8]. Because the answers to subjective questions are not unique, the similarity between answers becomes an important indicator for automatic verification of answers to subjective questions.

It is important to emphasize that user answers in natural language are converted into SCL-code using natural language interfaces. So the factual knowledge (such as, the constant sc-nodes used to represent relations or concepts) contained in the user answers to the subjective questions is already aligned with the knowledge in the knowledge base before the answers to the subjective question are verified [12]. Therefore, the similarity between semantic graphs described using logical knowledge is calculated in this article according to semantics and the representation rules of logical knowledge.

The sc-agent for computing semantic similarity of logical knowledge needs to complete the following tasks:

1. automatic selection of a potential equivalent standard answer from multiple standard answers;
2. decomposition of the semantic graph of user responses and the semantic graph of standard responses into substructures, based on various semantic structures describing logical knowledge within the framework of OSTIS Technology;
3. establishing the mapping relationship of potential equivalent variable sc-node pairs between the semantic graph of the user answer and the semantic graph of the standard answer;
4. calculating the precision P_{sc}, recall R_{sc} and similarity F_{sc} between semantic graphs described using logical knowledge using formulas (1), (2), and (3).

Automatic Selection of Potential Equivalent Standard Answer

For some subjective questions, there are usually multiple standard answers, and there is no logical equivalence between the logical formulas that formalize these answers. For example, the definition of equivalence relation: 1. equivalence relation is a binary relation that is reflexive, symmetric and transitive; 2. if a binary relationship is a tolerant relationship and a transitive relationship, then it is an equivalence relation. As can be seen from the above example, before calculating the similarity between answers to subjective questions, it is sometimes necessary to pre-screen a standard answer that best matches the user answer from multiple possible standard answers.

If a subjective question has multiple standard answers, and the logical formulas used to formalize them are not logically equivalent, the biggest difference between these answers is the predicates used to describe them (i.e. the constant sc-nodes used to represent relations, concepts and elements in the semantic graphs of answers to subjective questions are different) [11]. Therefore, an approach to filter out the standard answer that best matches the user answer based on the predicate similarity between the answers is proposed in this article.

The implementation process of the approach to filter out the standard answer that best matches the user answer based on the predicate similarity is as follows:

1. if this sc-agent believes that the current question has more than one standard answer, all non-repeating predicates in each answer will be found by it;
2. iterative calculation of similarity between all the predicates in the user answer and all the predicates in each standard answer using formulas (1), (2), and (3). The new meanings of some parameters in the formula are as follows:

- $T_{sc}(u)$ - all non-repeated predicates in the user answer u;
- $T_{sc}(s)$ - all non-repeated predicates in the standard answer s;
- $\otimes$ - binary matching operator, which indicates the number of matches between all predicates in the standard answer and all predicates in the user answer.

3. selecting the standard answer with the greatest similarity to the user answer as the final standard answer.

Figure 2 shows an example of filtering a standard answer in advance that best matches the user answer based on the predicate similarity between answers in SCg-code.

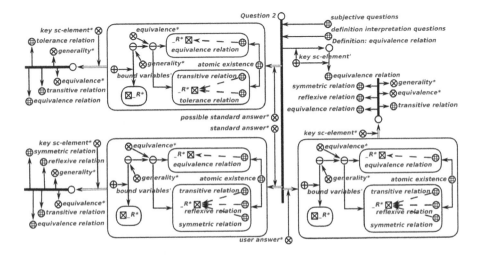

Fig. 2. An example of filtering a standard answer that best matches the user answer.

The Establishment of Mapping Relationship of the Potential Equivalent Variable SC-Node Pairs Between Answers

Since the variables sc-nodes are included in the semantic graphs of the answers to subjective questions, when calculating the similarity between answers to subjective questions, the most important step is to establish the mapping relationship (injection) of potential equivalent variable sc-node pairs between answers [15,16]. Therefore, based on the existing ontology mapping tools and methods, an approach to establish the mapping relationship of potential equivalent variable sc-node pairs the based on various semantic structures (various sc-constructions) is proposed in this article. In order to establish the mapping relationship of potential equivalent variable sc-node pairs, the following problems need to be solved:

1. determining the position of each variable sc-node in the semantic graph;
2. determining the semantic connotation expressed by the variable sc-nodes in the semantic graph.

Usually any predicate logic formula can be seen as consisting of two parts: 1. connective (such as implication ($\rightarrow$) and negation ($\neg$), etc.) used to describe properties and logical relations, and quantifiers (existential quantifier ($\exists$) and universal quantifier ($\forall$)) used to carve the existence and arbitrariness of bound variables; 2. atomic predicate formula that uses predicates to describe variable attributes or relationships between variables. Since the logic formulas in this article are mainly used to formally represent the definitions of some relations and theorems in the ostis-system, only bound variables are included in the logic formulas involved in this article [8,11]. The semantic graph used to describe the answers to subjective questions in the knowledge base of ostis-systems is constructed based on the logical formula, so this type of semantic graph can also be seen as composed of these two parts.

In ostis-systems, this type of sc-construction composed of relation sc-node, sc-tuple, sc-connector and role relation sc-node is used to describe quantifiers and logical connectives, atomic predicate formula or multiple atomic predicate formulas connected using the same conjunctive connective are contained in the sc-structure (this type of sc-structure is seen as an atomic existence in the semantic graph) and connected with the corresponding sc-tuple, and these sc-elements together constitute the semantic graph used to represent the answer. The atomic predicate formula is described using various sc-constructions. All sc-tuples and sc-connectors in the semantic graph form a tree, which completely describes the logical order between quantifiers and connectives and their positions in the logical formula. Because the sc-structure containing the atomic predicate formula is connected to the corresponding sc-tuple, as long as the position of each sc-tuple and sc-structure in the semantic graph is determined, the position of each variable sc-node in the semantic graph can be determined. In order to determine the position of each variable sc-node in the semantic graph, an approach to numbering each sc-tuple and sc-structure in the semantic graph based on the depth-first search strategy (DFS) is proposed in this article. The numbering process is as follows:

1. starting from the root of the tree structure composed of sc-tuples, each sc-tuple node in the tree is numbered in turn according to the DFS strategy (the numbering sequence starts from 0). If some nodes in the tree have multiple child nodes, these child nodes are numbered in the order of node priority specified below:
   - if the parent node and child nodes form a semantic structure that expresses the implication connective, then the priority of the conditional node (this node is connected with the parent node using a role relation "if'") is greater than the priority of the conclusion node. That is, the sc-tuple indicating the conditional node will be numbered preferentially;
   - if a node has multiple child nodes, and there is only one node representing negative connective in the child nodes, then the priority of this node is higher than other nodes. If there are multiple nodes representing negative connective in the child nodes, their priority is related to their height in

the tree, the higher the corresponding height of the node, the higher the priority;
- in the current version, for other cases, a node is randomly selected to be numbered according to the DFS strategy.
2. based on the numbering sequence of the sc-tuple, each sc-tuple in the tree is traversed in turn, and the sc-structures connected to the current sc-tuple are numbered at the same time (the numbering sequence starts from 1). If an sc-tuple connects multiple sc-structures, these sc-structures will be numbered according to the priority specified below:
    - if there are multiple sc-structures connected to the sc-tuple representing a universal quantifier or an existential quantifier, the sc-structure containing only the variable sc-nodes is numbered preferentially;
    - if there are multiple sc-structures connected to the sc-tuple representing the implication connective, the sc-structure representing the condition is numbered preferentially;
    - in the current version, for other cases, the numbering is based on the number of elements contained in the sc-structure. The smaller the number of elements contained in the sc structure, the priority will be given to numbering it.

Since the atomic predicate formulas are contained in the corresponding sc-structures, once the position of each sc-structure in the semantic graph is determined, the position of each atomic predicate formula in the semantic graph can be determined indirectly. When verifying the answers to objective questions, if the standard answer and the user answer exactly match, the atomic predicate formulas with the same semantics between the answers have the same position in the semantic graph (that is, the numbering of sc-structure is the same). Because the semantics of atomic predicate formulas are expressed by various sc-constructions, the mapping relationship of potential equivalent variable sc-node pairs between the answers will be established based on the matching relationship of the sc-constructions in the same position between the answers [2,8,9]. The process of establishing the mapping relationship of the potential equivalent variable sc-node pairs is as follows:

1. each time a sc-structure pair with the same number is retrieved from the semantic graph of standard answer and the semantic graph of user answer based on the numbering order of the sc-structures;
2. based on the priority of various types of sc-constructions (from high to low), it is judged in turn whether this type of sc-construction is included in the current sc-structure pair at the same time. If so, then, based on the matching relationship of each sc-element between the current type sc-construction, the mapping relationship of the potential equivalent variable sc-node pairs between the current sc-construction pair is established. The priority of various types of sc-constructions, and the judgment criteria for complete matching of the same type of sc-construction are as follows:
    - since there may be multiple sc-constructions contained in the same sc-structure, in order to ensure the accuracy and uniqueness of the mapping

relationship of the potential equivalent variables sc-node pairs between sc-constructions. Therefore, the mapping relationship between variables sc-nodes will be established based on the priority of various types of sc-constructions. The current version has 14 types of sc-constructions, and their priority is related to the number of sc-nodes contained within them. The greater the number of sc-nodes included in the sc-construction, the higher its priority. If the number of sc-nodes is the same, the greater the number of variables sc-nodes included in the sc-construction, the higher its priority;

– the criteria for judging the matching of the same type of sc-constructions include: 1. the constant sc-nodes at the corresponding positions have the same main identifiers or they have the same numbers in the semantic graph; 2. there is a mapping relationship between the variable sc-nodes of the corresponding position, or there is no mapping relationship between the corresponding position variable sc-nodes and there is no mapping relationship between them and other variables sc-nodes. If any pair of sc-constructions satisfies the above two conditions at the same time, the mapping relationship between the corresponding position variables sc-nodes between the sc-constructions will be established.

3. repeat step 1—step 2 until the mapping relationships of all potential equivalent variable sc-node pairs between semantic graphs are established.

Figure 3 shows an example of establishing the mapping relationship of potential equivalent variable sc-node pairs between semantic graphs based on the numbering of sc-structures in SCg-code.

In Fig. 3, the definition of the inclusion relation is described in the form of a semantic graph $(\forall A \forall B (A \subseteq B) \leftrightarrow \forall a (a \in A \rightarrow a \in B))$.

After the mapping relationships between the potential equivalent variable sc-node pairs between the semantic graphs are established, the similarity between the answers can be calculated using formulas (1), (2), and (3). The criteria for judging the matching of substructures are: 1. the constant sc-nodes in the corresponding position between substructures have the same main identifier or the same numbering in the semantic graphs (sc-tuple and sc-structure); 2. there is a mapping relationship between the variable sc-nodes at the corresponding position between the substructures.

Next, the working algorithm of this sc-agent will be introduced in detail:

Algorithm 3—The working algorithm of sc-agent for computing semantic similarity of logical knowledge

Input: The semantic model of specific subjective question and the corresponding semantic graph of user answer and the semantic graph of standard answer.

Output: The calculated precision, recall, and similarity between the answers, as well as some semantic structures for recording the sc-agent execution results.

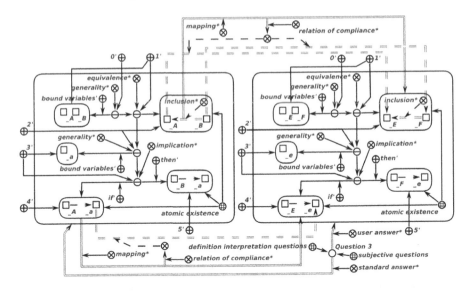

Fig. 3. An example of establishing the mapping relationship of potential equivalent variable sc-node pairs.

1. checking whether the semantic graph of the user answer and the semantic graph of the standard answer exist simultaneously, if so, go to step 2), otherwise, go to step 12);
2. checking if there are multiple standard answers for the current test question, if so, based on the approach introduced earlier, a standard answer that best matches the user answer is automatically selected;
3. decomposition of the semantic graph of standard answer and the semantic graph of user answer into substructures based on the rules for describing logical knowledge;
4. numbering of sc-tuples and sc-structures in the semantic graph of standard answer and the semantic graph of user answer, respectively, and establishing the mapping relationship of potential equivalent variable sc-node pairs between answers;
5. iterative traversal of each substructure of standard answer and user answer, classifying them according to the type of substructure and counting the number of all substructures;
6. random selection of one type of substructure from the set of recorded standard answer substructure types;
7. based on the standard answer substructure type selected in step 6), selecting the appropriate substructure type from the set of recorded user answer substructure types;
8. iterative comparison of each substructure with the same substructure type between the standard answer and the user answer and recording the number of matched substructures;
9. repeat step 6—step 8 until all types of substructures have been traversed;

10. calculation of precision, recall and similarity using formulas (1), (2) and (3) and generation of semantic fragments to record the running results of the sc-agent;
11. removing all temporarily created sc-elements;
12. exit the program.

After calculating the precision, recall and similarity between the answers to the subjective questions, the correctness and completeness of the user answer can be judged. Based on the calculated similarity, the completeness and correctness of the user answers are classified into the following situations:

- if the similarity is equal to 1, the user answer is completely correct ($F_{sc} = 1$);
- if the similarity is less than 1 ($F_{sc} < 1$), it can be subdivided into the following situations:
  - for the current question, if the sc-agent for computing semantic similarity of logical knowledge is executed twice, the user answer is partially correct and incomplete, and the result obtained when this sc-agent is executed for the first time is the final answer verification result;
  - if the sc-agent for computing semantic similarity of logical knowledge is executed only once, then the standard answer and the user's answer may satisfy the logical equivalence, so further judgments need to be made according to the calling sequence of the sc-agent described earlier.

4.4   SC-Agent for Converting Logical Formula into PNF

As we have introduced before, when verifying the answers to subjective questions, if the similarity between the standard answer and the user answer is not equal to 1, it is necessary to further determine whether they meet logical equivalence. The key step in judging whether the answers satisfy logical equivalence is to convert them into a unified normative form. Therefore, the basic function of the sc-agent for converting logical formula into PNF is to convert semantic graph described based on logical formulas into PNF representation. In OSTIS Technology, since the logic formula inherits all the logical operation properties of the predicate logic formula, when the logic formula is converted to the PNF according to the conversion rules in the predicate logic, the PNF obtained is not unique [3,11].

The main reasons why PNF is not unique in predicate logic include the following:

1. due to the use of different conversion rules (equivalence rule and renaming rule). For example, convert $(\forall x F(x) \wedge \neg \exists x G(x))$ into PNF:
   - $\forall x F(x) \wedge \neg \exists x G(x)$
     $\Leftrightarrow \forall x F(x) \wedge \forall x \neg G(x)$
     $\Leftrightarrow \forall x (F(x) \wedge \neg G(x))$, (equivalence rule)
   - $\forall x F(x) \wedge \neg \exists x G(x)$
     $\Leftrightarrow \forall x F(x) \wedge \forall y \neg G(y)$, (renaming rule)
     $\Leftrightarrow \forall x \forall y (F(x) \wedge \neg G(y))$, (rule of expansion of quantifier scope)

2. the order of quantifiers in PNF. For example, convert $(\forall x F(x) \wedge \exists y G(y))$ into PNF:
 - $\forall x F(x) \wedge \exists y G(y)$
   $\Leftrightarrow \forall x \exists y (F(x) \wedge G(y))$, (rule of expansion of quantifier scope)
 - $\forall x F(x) \wedge \exists y G(y)$
   $\Leftrightarrow \exists y \forall x (F(x) \wedge G(y))$, (rule of expansion of quantifier scope)

As can be seen from the above example, usually the PNF of the predicate logic formula is not unique. However, in order to ensure the accuracy of automatic answer verification in the ostis-systems, only by converting the semantic graph representing the answer into a unique PNF representation, can the equivalence judgment between the answers be continued. Therefore, in order to convert the logical formula into a unique PNF, based on the rules of converting the predicate logic formula into the PNF and the processing rules of logical knowledge in OSTIS Technology, this article proposes a rule of converting the logical formula into a unique PNF under restricted conditions [4,7]. The conversion rules mainly include the following:

 - in order to solve the problem that PNF is not unique due to the use of different conversion rules, we stipulate that the renaming rule should be preferentially used when converting logical formulas into PNF. It should be emphasized that if this form of logical formula $(\forall x (F(x) \wedge \neg G(x)))$ appears in the answer, it will be converted into PNF according to the following rules. $\forall x (F(x) \wedge \neg G(x))$ $\Leftrightarrow \forall x F(x) \wedge \forall x \neg G(x)) \Leftrightarrow \forall x \forall y (F(x) \wedge \neg G(y))$;
 - in order to make the order of the quantifiers in PNF unique, this article proposes an approach to move all the quantifiers in the logic formula to the front of the formula strictly according to the priority of the quantifiers (when using the quantifier scope extension rule). The approach includes the following situations:
   • if there is no quantifier at the front of the logical formula, first move all existential quantifiers in the formula to the front of the formula, and then move universal quantifiers to the front of the formula;
   • if the last quantifier at the front of the logical formula is a universal quantifier, first move all universal quantifiers in the formula to the front of the formula, and then move the existential quantifiers to the front of the formula;
   • if the last quantifier at the front of the logical formula is a existential quantifier, first move all existential quantifiers in the formula to the front of the formula, and then move the universal quantifiers to the front of the formula.
 - in order to simplify the knowledge processing in the ostis-systems, when converting the logical formula into PNF, it is only necessary to eliminate the implication connective. The two sub-formulas connected by equivalent connective are regarded as two independent logical formulas, and they are converted into PNF respectively;

– when converting logical formulas into PNF, it is usually necessary to merge multiple atomic predicate formulas connected by conjunctive connective into a whole first (that is, multiple sc-structures connected by conjunctive relation in the semantic graph are merged into one sc-structure).

Next, the working algorithm of this sc-agent will be introduced in detail:

Algorithm 4—The working algorithm of sc-agent for converting logical formula into PNF

Input: The semantic model of specific subjective question and the corresponding semantic graph of user answer and the semantic graph of standard answer.

Output: Semantic graph of user answer and semantic graph of standard answer in PNF form.

1. checking whether all input parameters used for sc-agent work meet the conditions, if so, go to step 2), otherwise,go to step 9);
2. if there are multiple sc-structures connected by the same conjunctive relation in the current semantic graph, all sc-constructions in them will be merged into one sc-structure;
3. eliminating all implication connectives in the semantic graph;
4. moving all negative connectives in the semantic graph to the front of the corresponding sc-structure;
5. using renaming rule to make all bound variables different in the semantic graph;
6. according to the quantifier arrangement rule introduced above, move all the quantifiers in the semantic graph to the front of the logical formula;
7. checking again whether there are sc-structures that can be merged in the semantic graph, and if they exist, merge all sc-constructions contained in them into one sc-structure;
8. removing all temporarily created sc-elements;
9. exit the program.

The use of sc-agent for converting logical formula into PNF can convert the semantic graph representing the answers into an equivalent and unique PNF representation. Combining sc-agent for computing semantic similarity of logical knowledge and sc-agent for converting logical formula into PNF can verify whether the standard answer and the user answer satisfy logical equivalence. Figure 4 shows an example of converting Fig. 3 into PNF representation in SCg-code. $(\forall A \forall B(A \subseteq B) \leftrightarrow \forall a(a \in A \rightarrow a \in B)) \Leftrightarrow (\forall A \forall B(A \subseteq B) \leftrightarrow \forall a(\neg(a \in A) \lor a \in B))$.

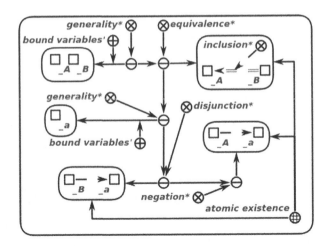

Fig. 4. An example of converting the semantic graph representing the answer into the PNF representation.

5   Conclusion and Further Work

Automatic verification of answers to test questions is an indispensable function of ITS. It can not only quickly and efficiently check the knowledge level of users, but also help educators save a lot of time, thereby greatly improving their learning and work efficiency. Therefore, based on the above reasons, a semantic approach to developing a problem solver for automatic answer verification in the ITS developed using OSTIS Technology is proposed in this article, and then based on the proposed semantic approach, the development process and working algorithm of the problem solver are introduced in detail. Among them, one of the most important features of the developed problem solver is that it can verify the correctness and completeness of the answers to the test questions. Since the problem solver is developed based on multi-agent technology, a set of sc-agents for solving different tasks is developed in order to solve the task requirements listed in the article. The developed problem solver allows to initiate different sc-agent based on the type of test question to achieve automatic answer verification.

The developed problem solver has the following advantages:

- verifying the correctness and completeness of user answers based on semantics;
- for subjective questions, it is possible to judge whether there is a logical equivalence between any two logic formulas used to formalize them;
- using the developed problem solver it is also possible to calculate the similarity between any two semantic fragments in the knowledge base;
- because all sc-agents in the problem solver exchange information through sc-memory, sc-agents for implementing new functions can be easily added to the system;

– since ostis-systems have the same knowledge processing model and knowledge representation structure, the developed problem solver can be easily transplanted to other ostis-systems.

In future work, a sc-agent for simple dialogue with users will be developed, it is mainly used to process the user question request and provides some constructive comments to the user by analyzing the verification result of the user answer.

References

1. IMS.ostis Metasystem. https://ims.ostis.net. Accessed 6 Oct 2021
2. Anderson, P., Fernando, B., Johnson, M., Gould, S.: SPICE: semantic propositional image caption evaluation. In: Leibe, B., Matas, J., Sebe, N., Welling, M. (eds.) ECCV 2016. LNCS, vol. 9909, pp. 382–398. Springer, Cham (2016). https://doi.org/10.1007/978-3-319-46454-1_24
3. Fujiwara, M., Kurahashi, T.: Prenex normal form theorems in semi-classical arithmetic. J. Symb. Logic **86**, 1–31 (2020)
4. Golenkov, V.V., Gulyakina, N.A.: Project of open semantic technology for component design of intelligent systems. Ontol. Des. **1**(11), 42–64 (2014)
5. Golenkov, V.V., Gulyakina, N.A., Davydenko, I.T., Eremeev, A.P.: Methods and tools for ensuring compatibility of computer systems. In: 9th International Scientific and Technical Conference "Open Semantic Technologies for Intelligent Systems", pp. 25–52. Belarus Minsk (2019)
6. Golovko, V.A., et al.: Integration of artificial neural networks and knowledge bases. Ontol. Des. **29**, 366–386 (2018)
7. Kowalski, R.: Predicate logic as programming language. In: IFIP Congress, vol. 74, pp. 569–544 (1974)
8. Li, W., Grakova, N., Qian, L.: Ontological approach for question generation and knowledge control. In: Golenkov, V., Krasnoproshin, V., Golovko, V., Azarov, E. (eds.) OSTIS 2020. CCIS, vol. 1282, pp. 161–175. Springer, Cham (2020). https://doi.org/10.1007/978-3-030-60447-9_10
9. Li, W., Qian, L.: Development of a problem solver for automatic answer verification in the intelligent tutoring systems. In: 11th International Scientific and Technical Conference "Open Semantic Technologies for Intelligent Systems", pp. 169–178. Belarus Minsk (2021)
10. Li, X.: Realization of automatic scoring algorithm for subjective questions based on artificial intelligence. J. Jiangnan Univ. (Nat. Sci. Ed.) **8**(3), 292–295 (2009)
11. Pan, M., Ding, Z.: A simple method for solving pyrenex disjunction (conjunction) normal forms. Comput. Eng. Sci. **30**(10), 82–84 (2008)
12. Qian, L., Sadouski, M., Li, W.: Ontological approach for Chinese language interface design. In: Golenkov, V., Krasnoproshin, V., Golovko, V., Azarov, E. (eds.) OSTIS 2020. CCIS, vol. 1282, pp. 146–160. Springer, Cham (2020). https://doi.org/10.1007/978-3-030-60447-9_9
13. Qiu, D.: Automatic logic reasoning in artificial intelligence. Artif. Intell. Robot. Res. **08**(01), 7–16 (2019)
14. Socher, R., Chen, D., Manning, C.D., Ng, A.: Reasoning with neural tensor networks for knowledge base completion. In: Advances in Neural Information Processing Systems, pp. 926–934. MIT (2013)

15. Su, j., Wang, Y., Jin, X., Li, M., Cheng, X.: Knowledge graph entity alignment with semantic and structural information. J. Shanxi Univ. (Nat. Sci. Ed.) **42**(01), 23–30 (2019)
16. Wang, H., Zhang, Y.: A survey on research progress of text similarity calculation. J. Beijing Inf. Sci. (Technol. Univ.) **34**(01), 68–74 (2019)
17. Wang, X., Hu, Z., Bai, R., Li, Y.: Review on concepts, processes, tools and methods of ontology integration. Libr. Inf. Service **55**(16), 119–125 (2011)
18. Xu, G., Zeng, W., Cuilan, H.: Research on intelligent tutoring system. Appl. Res. Comput. **26**(11), 4019–4022 (2009)
19. Zhang, Z.P., Zhao, H.L.: Ontology integration method based on RDFS. Comput. Eng. Appl. **44**(15), 131–135 (2008)
20. Zhu, J., Qiao, J., Lin, S.: Entity alignment algorithm for knowledge graph of representation learning. J. Northeastern Univ. (Nat. Sci.) **39**(11), 1535–1539 (2018)
21. Zhuang, Y., Li, G., Feng, J.: A survey on entity alignment of knowledge base. J. Comput. Res. Dev. **53**(01), 165–192 (2016)

Subsystem for Intelligent Systems' Users Training

Natalia Grakova[1]([✉]) [ID], Maria Koroleva[2] [ID], Daniil Shunkevich[1] [ID], and Georgiy Bobrov[2] [ID]

[1] Belarusian State University of Informatics and Radioelectronics, Minsk, Belarus
{grakova,shunkevich}@bsuir.by
[2] Bauman Moscow State Technical University, Moscow, Russian Federation

Abstract. The article proposes a method for addressing the issue of training both end users and developers of intelligent systems. Each intelligent system would be supplemented with a module that serves as an intelligent training subsystem, with the aim of instructing both end users and developers of the main system in the fundamentals of using, operating, and developing the system. As a foundation for the implementation of this approach, it is proposed to use an Open Semantic Technology for Intelligent Systems (OSTIS Technology).

Keywords: OSTIS · intelligent system · intelligent learning system · ontological approach

1 Introduction

This work is a continuation and development of the work [9], in particular, the ideas proposed in this work are proposed to be developed in the direction of integrating semantic and pragmatic technologies in the context of building learning systems. The report also includes brand-new findings about the description of an intelligent system's internal knowledge base, which includes its structure and operating principles.

Artificial intelligence technologies are currently being quickly developed and employed in many different areas of human endeavor. Unfortunately, rather than intelligent systems, which have significantly higher requirements, the topic is more frequently asked regarding systems that incorporate elements of artificial intelligence. The most important of these requirements is the *learnability* of the system, that is, its ability to acquire new knowledge and skills, and, in particular, *unlimited learnability*, that is, such a degree of learnability, when no constraints are imposed on the typology of this knowledge and skills. In other words, a system with *unlimited learnability* can, if necessary, acquire any knowledge and the ability to solve any problem over time. Let's be clear that this does not imply that any given system will be able to handle any problem; rather, it indicates that the system can learn to solve the necessary problem while there are no underlying limitations on the type of problems that can be solved [6].

V. Golenkov et al. (Eds.): OSTIS 2021, CCIS 1625, pp. 267–281, 2022.
https://doi.org/10.1007/978-3-031-15882-7_14

The existence of a sizable number of works on this subject since the mid-1980s confirms the relevance of the development of training systems intended to hasten the user's familiarization process with a complicated technical system and boost the efficiency of its use [11,20].

At the same time, intelligent computer systems are complex technical systems, the development and even usage of which often require high professional qualities. In particular, the following problems are relevant:

– the lack of efficiency of using modern intelligent systems, the complexity of their implementation and maintenance, which are largely determined by the high threshold of entry of end-users into intelligent systems;
– the user often does not use a significant part of the functions of even traditional computer systems simply for the reason that they do not know about their availability and do not have a simple mechanism to find out about them. For intelligent systems, this problem is even more pressing;
– there are high costs for training developers of intelligent systems, their adaptation to the features of the organization of a particular intelligent system.

These difficulties are connected not only with the inherent complexity of intelligent computer systems compared to traditional computer systems but also with the low level of documentation for such systems, the inconvenience of using such documentation, the complexity of localization of tools and the scope of solving a particular problem both for the end-user and for the developer.

2   Proposed Approach

An approach to resolving these issues is suggested within the context of this article. It entails the addition to each intelligent system of a module that serves as an intelligent training subsystem, with the aim of instructing both the end-user and the main system's developer in the fundamentals of using, operating, and developing the system.

In other words, even if an intelligent system is not initially intended to be a training system, it must have some of the functions of a training system. This is an example of the core notion of the proposed approach. Therefore, the end user should be able to study both the fundamentals of using an intelligent system and learn new information about the field for which it is being developed. To study the principles of the system's internal organization, its operation, and the functions of particular system components, as well as to localize the system's component on which they need to gain knowledge in order to modify the functionality of the system, is necessary for the developer of intelligent systems.

To implement this idea, an intelligent system must contain not only knowledge about the subject domain, for which it is designed, but also

– knowledge about the user, their experience, skills, preferences, interests;
– knowledge about itself, its architecture, components, functions, operating principles, etc.;

- knowledge about current problems in the development of the system and its maintenance.
- knowledge about the problems that the system solves independently at the moment and the problems that are planned to be solved in the future;

A common formal foundation for the representation of knowledge of diverse forms as well as a common foundation for various types of means of processing this knowledge are required for the representation and processing of all of the aforementioned.

As such a foundation, it is proposed to use an Open semantic technology for intelligent systems (*OSTIS Technology*) [7], which allows integrating any type of knowledge and any problem-solving model. The systems being developed on the basis of this technology are called *ostis-systems*.

The usage of the OSTIS Technology gives the following advantages for solving the specified problem:

- The technology is based on the *SC-code* – a universal and unified language for encoding information in the dynamic graph memory of computer systems. The SC-code allows representing <u>any</u> information in a <u>unified</u> (similar) form, which will make the proposed approach universal and suitable for any class of intelligent systems;
- The OSTIS Technology and, in particular, the SC-code, can be easily integrated with any modern technology, which will allow applying the proposed approach to a large number of already developed intelligent systems;
- The SC-code allows storing and describing in the ostis-system knowledge base any external (heterogeneous) information in relation to the SC-code in the form of internal files of ostis-systems [1]. Thus, the knowledge base of the training subsystem can explicitly contain fragments of existing documentation for the system, represented in any form;
- Within the framework of the OSTIS Technology, models of the ostis-system knowledge bases [4], ostis-system problem solvers [13] and ostis-system user interfaces [3] have already been developed, asserting their full description in the system knowledge base. Thus, for ostis-systems, the proposed approach is implemented much easier and provides additional advantages, which are discussed in more detail in this article [5];
- One of the main principles of the OSTIS Technology is to ensure the flexibility (modifiability) of systems developed on its basis. Thus, the usage of the OSTIS Technology will provide an opportunity for the evolution of the intelligent learning subsystem itself.
- The use of OSTIS Technology as the basis for the implementation of the proposed approach allows for the convergence of both different approaches and teaching methods, as well as different approaches to solving problems, which ultimately will help achieve a synergistic effect and significantly increase the efficiency of both learning processes and in general processes of functioning of the intellectual system itself [19].

It is important to note that the approach proposed in this paper can be the basis for integration in the context of the development of intelligent learning systems of semantic technologies and pragmatic technologies [2, 15], which are currently being actively developed and implemented in the educational sphere [18], in particular, in the methods and systems of teaching foreign languages [16, 17].

In addition, a description of the structure and principles of operation of an intelligent system within this system itself using the ontological approach will not only improve the efficiency of training users of an intelligent system, but also increase the efficiency of the processes of development and maintenance of an intelligent system, as shown in a number of works [10].

Further, let us consider in more detail the possibilities of using the OSTIS Technology for the development of intelligent learning systems.

3   Intelligent Learning Systems

Intelligent learning systems (ILS) are an important class of intelligent systems. Such systems, in comparison with traditional e-learning systems (for example, electronic textbooks), have a number of significant advantages [8]. At the same time, the issue of intellectualization of the learning process remains relevant [21–23] including with the usage of semantic technologies [12]. At the same time, as can be seen from the above papers, the relevance of this issue is realized by specialists in the field of education and not only by specialists in the field of intelligent system development.

In the case of the implementation of ILS based on the OSTIS Technology, additional features appear, which include the following:

- The user is explicitly shown the semantic structure of the educational content being studied and the subject domain being researched. Visualization of any level of the chosen semantic structure is possible concurrently;
- The knowledge base's explicit placement of all subject conformities and idea relationships allows the user to acquire information that is sufficiently comprehensive about the researched subject domain. As a result, all of its facets are reflected;
- It is possible to browse the semantic space of the subject domain in addition to reading the textbook's contents and illustrative resources;
- The user is free to ask any questions and problems on the area of study that they want. This is accomplished by integrating a problem solver into the ILS that can address issues based on their formulations, including those provided by the user. At the same time, even if the solution method (for instance, an algorithm) is unknown to the stated problem solver, it can nevertheless figure out how to solve the problem;
- Under the guidance of the system, the user is given the chance to practice (get practical skills) resolving a range of issues in the studied topic domain. Additionally, the system
  - performs a semantic examination of the correctness of solutions according to the solution protocols and freely created replies (results);
  - locates the user's faults in problem-solving, ascertains their root cause, and provides the user with the necessary advice.

- The ILS features an intelligent user interface with computer (virtual) models of various objects from the research domain, enabling the system to "understand" (analyze the semantics) human actions on the transformation of these objects. The interactive virtual laboratory atmosphere of the electronic textbook is elevated greatly as a result of all of this;
- The user is able to choose any of the numerous synonymous terms (identifiers) stored in the system knowledge base when interacting with it. Additionally, these terms could come from several natural languages;
- The implementation of a user interface that speaks to them in natural language is a real possibility (thanks to the wide possibilities of semantic analysis of user messages and the possibilities of synthesis of messages addressed to users at the semantic level);
- Reorienting the ILS to serve users in a new natural language is relatively simple (since the major part of the ILS knowledge base, which directly describes the semantics of the corresponding subject domain, is independent of the external language including the natural one);
- The user can select the order in which to study the educational content (route-based navigation through the educational content), although pertinent suggestions are provided;
- In the book of problems and laboratory-based works, the user can select the problems being solved, but the suitable suggestions are offered. These suggestions are meant to reduce the amount of problems that need to be solved in order to ensure that the necessary practical skills are acquired;
- The system lacks a unique mode for controlling (verifying, testing) knowledge. By observing and scrutinizing user behavior as they approach various issues in the subject domain under study, such control is carried out for the user in an effortless manner. To do this, the ILS knowledge base provides details on the kinds of problems and laboratory-based assignments that the user should complete for adequate, good, and exceptional assimilation of the instructional material, respectively;
- Multiple independent ILS from related disciplines can easily be combined into a single textbook, which gives students the chance to pose questions and solve issues at the nexus of various fields;
- The ILS user operates under the direction and guidance of an intelligent assistant, which enables the user to rapidly and efficiently become familiar with the system's capabilities. In actuality, this is really an ILS user's manual intended to serve as a semantic electronic textbook;
- There is a rare opportunity to verify the semantic correctness of the information resource being created when constructing the ILS knowledge base:
  - correctness of definitions and statements;
  - correctness of the usage of various concepts;
  - correctness of algorithms;
  - correctness of proofs of theorems;
  - etc.

The structure of the subsystem for educating users of an intelligent system can be used to implement some of these opportunities (or, in the worst case scenario, all of them). Let's go on to a closer look at the suggested subsystem's architecture.

4 Architecture of the Subsystem for Training Users of Intelligent Systems

Figure 1 shows the architecture of the proposed *subsystem for training users of intelligent systems*. To implement the interaction of the *subsystem for training users of intelligent systems*, implemented on the basis of the OSTIS Technology, with the main intelligent system, it is planned to develop an interface component, which is also part of the subsystem. It is important to note that for different intelligent systems, such components will be largely overlapping, which is due to the features of the OSTIS Technology itself, which, in turn, will reduce the cost of integrating the training subsystem and the main intelligent system.

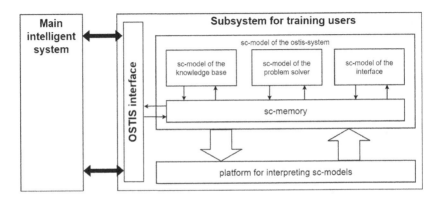

Fig. 1. The architecture of the subsystem for training users of intelligent systems

If the intelligent system under consideration is an ostis-system, its integration with the *subsystem for training users of intelligent systems* is carried out more deeply, and the architecture of the resulting integrated system can be represented as follows (Fig. 2). As can be seen from the figure, the components of the *subsystem for training users of intelligent systems* solely complement the already existing in the main ostis-system components, which allows minimizing the cost of integrating the *subsystem for training users of intelligent systems* and the main ostis-system.

5 Examples of the Representation of Various Types of Knowledge Within the Framework of the Subsystem for Training Users of Intelligent Systems

As we describe various types of knowledge in the subsystem for training users of intelligent systems, let's look at a few instances that demonstrate the potential of the method suggested within the framework of the OSTIS Technology to

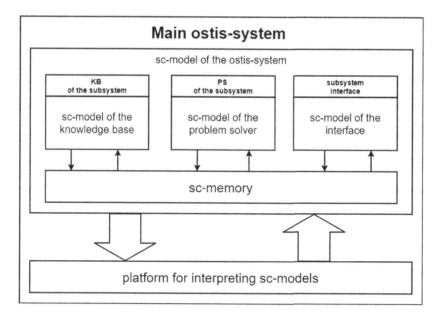

Fig. 2. The architecture of the subsystem for training users of intelligent systems as part of another ostis-system

the building of knowledge bases. The SCg- and SCn-codes, which are the languages for the external representation of SC-code constructs, will be used for the illustrations, according to [1].

5.1 Specification of Users Within the Knowledge Base of the Intelligent Learning Subsystem

Figure 3 in the SCg-code shows various information about a particular user of the intelligent system. This example shows how using the knowledge base structuring tools developed within the framework of the OSTIS Technology [4], it is possible to describe various types of information about the same entity in the knowledge base, in particular, the current employment and professional skills of the user. Any other information about the user can be described in the same way.

Figure 4 in the SCg-code shows an example of describing information about the performers of a certain project who take on various roles in it. From the point of view of the knowledge base structure, this information is part of the *structure and organization of the computer system project* section.

Figure 5 in the SCg-code shows an example of a description of project tasks and their performers, taking into account the qualifications of each performer. From the point of view of the knowledge base structure, this information is part of the *current processes of computer system development* section.

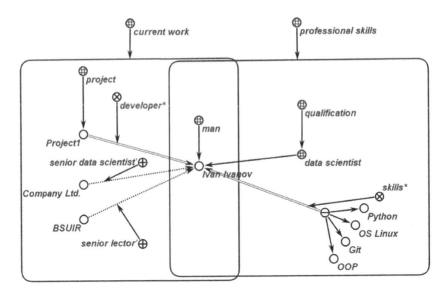

Fig. 3. The description of the user of the intelligent system

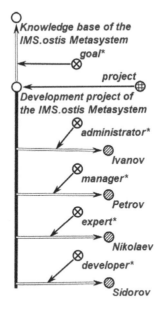

Fig. 4. The description of the performers of the project for the development of some intelligent system

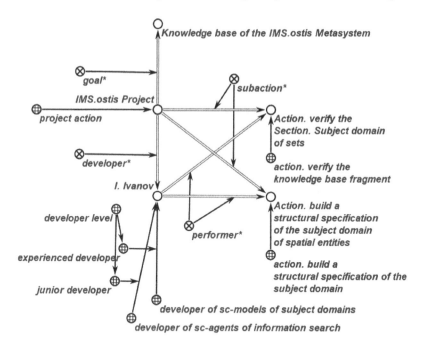

Fig. 5. The description of the project tasks

5.2 Specification of the System Structure and Principles of Its Operation Within the Knowledge Base

As examples of the specification of the system structure and principles of its operation within the knowledge base, consider the description of two key components of the ostis-system – a platform for semantic models interpreting and an intelligent problem solver.

Currently, a software version of the implementation of the platform for semantic models of ostis-systems interpreting is actively used [14]. Below is a description of the general structure of the software platform implementation in the SCn language.

Software version of the implementation of the platform for interpreting sc-models of computer systems
⇒   *decomposition of the software system*:*
     {•   *Implementation of the interpreter of sc-models of user interfaces*
     •   *Software model of sc-memory*
     }

Software model of sc-memory
:=   [A software model of semantic memory implemented on the basis of tradi-
        tional linear memory and that include storage facilities for sc-constructs
        and basic tools for processing these constructs, including ones for the
        remote access to them via appropriate network protocols]
∈   *software model of sc-memory based on linear memory*
⇐   *software model*:*
        sc-memory
⇒   *component of the software system*:*
        •   *Implementation of the sc-storage and means of access to it*
        •   *Implementation of the subsystem of interaction with the
                environment using network protocols*
        •   *Implementation of a basic set of platform-dependent sc-agents
                and their common components*
        •   *Implementation of the scp-interpreter*
        •   *Implementation of auxiliary tools for working with sc-memory*

Implementation of the sc-storage and means of access to it
⇒   *component of the software system*:*
        •   *Implementation of the sc-storage*
                ∈   *implementation of the sc-storage based on linear memory*
                ⇒   *class of software system objects*:*
                        segment of the sc-storage
                        :=   [a page of the sc-storage]
                        ⇒   *generalized part*:*
                                element of the sc-storage
        •   *Implementation of file memory of the ostis-system*

The knowledge base can describe the key ideas and interactions between
them necessary to comprehend the system's principles in addition to the system's structure. Here are some SCn language samples of descriptions of these
knowledge base fragments.

sc-address
:=   [an address of the element of the sc-storage that corresponds to the spec-
        ified sc-element, within the current state of the Implementation of the
        sc-storage as part of the software model of sc-memory]
⇒   *family of relations that precisely define the structure of a given entity*:*
        {•   *segment number of the sc-storage**
         •   *number of the element of the sc-storage within the segment**
        }

element of the sc-storage
:=   [an element of the sc-storage that corresponds to the sc-element]

:= [a data structure, each instance of which corresponds to one sc-element
within the sc-storage]
:= [a cell of the sc-storage]
:= [an image of the sc-element within the sc-storage]
⇒ *subdividing*:*
{• *element of the sc-storage that corresponds to the sc-node*
• *element of the sc-storage that corresponds to the sc-arc*
}

element of the sc-storage that corresponds to the sc-node
⇒ *family of relations that uniquely define the structure of a given entity*:*
{• *label of the syntactic type of the sc-element**
• *label of the access level of the sc-element**
• *sc-address of the first sc-arc that goes out of this sc-element**
• *sc-address of the first sc-arc that comes in this sc-element**
• *contents of the element of the sc-storage**
⇒ *second domain*:*
contents of the element of the sc-storage
:= [the contents of the element of the sc-storage that
corresponds to the internal file of the ostis-system]
}

element of the sc-storage that corresponds to the sc-arc
⇒ *family of relations that uniquely define the structure of a given entity*:*
{• *label of the syntactic type of the sc-element**
• *label of the access level of the sc-element**
• *sc-address of the first sc-arc that goes out of this sc-element**
• *sc-address of the first sc-arc that comes in this sc-element**
• *specification of the sc-arc within the sc-storage**
⇒ *second domain*:*
specification of the sc-arc within the sc-storage
}

specification of the sc-arc within the sc-storage
⇒ *family of relations that uniquely define the structure of a given entity*:*
{• *sc-address of the initial sc-element of the sc-arc**
• *sc-address of the final sc-element of the sc-arc**
• *sc-address of the next sc-arc that goes out of the same
sc-element**
• *sc-address of the next sc-arc that comes in the same sc-element**
• *sc-address of the previous sc-arc that goes out of the same
sc-element**
• *sc-address of the previous sc-arc that comes in the same
sc-element**
}

Similar terms can be used to describe the structure of the ostis-system's problem solver. According to the method for creating problem solvers suggested within the OSTIS Technology framework, the foundation of the solver is a hierarchical system of agents over semantic memory (sc-agents) [13]. The ostis-system knowledge base also contains a description of the solver's structure. The framework of the labeling quality control system for the formulation enterprise is thus described in the SCn-code.:

Problem solver of the labeling quality control system
⇒   *decomposition of an abstract sc-agent*:*
    {•   *Atomic abstract sc-agent of labeling recognition based on a neural network*
    •   *Non-atomic abstract sc-agent of decision-making*
        ⇒   *decomposition of an abstract sc-agent*:*
            {•   *Non-atomic abstract sc-agent of certain inference*
            •   *Non-atomic abstract sc-agent of reliable inference*
            •   *Atomic abstract sc-agent that implements the concept of a software package*
        }
    •   *Non-atomic abstract sc-agent of content-addressable retrieval*
    •   *Non-atomic abstract sc-agent of interpretation of control programs for a robotic installation*
        ⇒   *decomposition of an abstract sc-agent*:*
            {•   *Atomic abstract sc-agent of interpretation of the movement action*
            •   *Atomic abstract sc-agent of interpretation of the acquisition action*
        }
    }

Non-atomic abstract sc-agent of certain inference
⇒   *decomposition of an abstract sc-agent*:*
    {•   *Atomic abstract sc-agent that implements a certain inference strategy*
    •   *Non-atomic abstract sc-agent of logical rules interpretation*
    }

Non-atomic abstract sc-agent of reliable inference
⇒   *decomposition of an abstract sc-agent*:*
    {•   *Atomic abstract sc-agent that implements a reliable inference strategy*
    •   *Non-atomic abstract sc-agent of logical rules interpretation*
    }

Non-atomic abstract sc-agent of logical rules interpretation
⇒   *decomposition of an abstract sc-agent*:*
   {•   *Atomic abstract sc-agent of applying implicative rules*
     •   *Atomic abstract sc-agent of applying equivalence rules*
   }

Thus, the above examples show that within the framework of the knowledge base of the ostis system, various components of this system can be described with the necessary degree of detail, as well as any other information, including didactic information, necessary for teaching the user how to work with the ostis system and principles of the system itself.

6   Conclusion

An appropriate set of ontologies that describe knowledge about the intelligent system itself, its users, and tasks for its development, models of the subsystem for training users of intelligent systems, and a corresponding set of software agents that implement the functionality of the subsystem will be developed as part of the further development of the proposed idea.

The implementation of the proposed idea will allow:

– reducing the threshold of entry of end-users into intelligent systems as well as significantly improving the efficiency of using such systems;
– reducing the period of time needed for intelligent system developers to be trained, adapt to a certain intelligent system's features, and develop and improve the intelligent system. All of the aforementioned measures will also address the issue of staff churn at companies working on complicated intelligent systems, as well as lower the price of creating and maintaining intelligent systems and, as a result, increase their accessibility to end users.

Acknowledgment. The authors would like to thank the Department of Intelligent Information Technologies of the Belarusian State University of Informatics and Radioelectronics for the help and valuable comments.

The work was carried out with the partial financial support of the BRFFR and RFFR, project numbers F21PM-139 and 20-57-04002.

References

1. IMS.ostis Metasystem, June 2021. https://ims.ostis.net
2. Božek, P., Lozhkin, A., Galajdová, A., Arkhipov, I., Maiorov, K.: Information technology and pragmatic analysis. Comput. Inform. **37**, 1011–1036 (2018). https://doi.org/10.4149/cai.2018-4.1011
3. Boriskin, A., Koronchik, D., Zhukau, I., Sadouski, M., Khusainov, A.: Ontology-based design of intelligent systems user interface. In: Golenkov, V. (ed.) Otkrytye semanticheskie tehnologii proektirovanija intellektual'nyh sistem [Open Semantic Technologies for Intelligent Systems], pp. 95–106. BSUIR, Minsk (2017)

4. Davydenko, I.: Semantic models, method and tools of knowledge bases coordinated development based on reusable components. In: Golenkov, V. (ed.) Otkrytye semanticheskie tehnologii proektirovanija intellektual'nyh sistem [Open Semantic Technologies for Intelligent Systems], pp. 99–118. BSUIR, Minsk (2018)
5. Golenkov, V., Guliakina, N., Davydenko, I., Eremeev, A.: Methods and tools for ensuring compatibility of computer systems. In: Golenkov, V. (ed.) Otkrytye semanticheskie tekhnologii proektirovaniya intellektual'nykh system [Open Semantic Technologies for Intelligent Systems], pp. 25–52. BSUIR, Minsk (2019)
6. Golenkov, V., et al.: From training intelligent systems to training their development tools. Otkrytye semanticheskie tehnologii proektirovanija intellektual'nyh sistem [Open Semantic Technologies for Intelligent Systems], pp. 81–98 (2018)
7. Golenkov, V., Gulyakina, N., Davydenko, I., Shunkevich, D.: Semanticheskie tekhnologii proektirovaniya intellektual'nyh sistem i semanticheskie associativnye komp'yutery [Semantic technologies of intelligent systems design and semantic associative computers]. Otkrytye semanticheskie tehnologii proektirovanija intellektual'nyh sistem [Open Semantic Technologies for Intelligent Systems], pp. 42–50 (2019). (in Russian)
8. Golenkov, V., Tarasov, V., Eliseeva, O.: Intellektual'nye obuchayushchie sistemy i virtual'nye uchebnye organizatsii [Intelligent Learning Systems and Virtual Learning Organizations]. BSUIR, Minsk (2001)
9. Grakova, N., Koroleva, M., Bobrov, G.: Implementation principles of the training subsystem for end-users and developers of intelligent systems. In: Golenkov, V. (ed.) Open Semantic Technologies for Intelligent Systems, pp. 187–192. BSUIR, Minsk (2021)
10. Haav, H.M.: A comparative study of approaches of ontology driven software development. Informatica **29**, 439–466 (2018). https://doi.org/10.15388/Informatica.2018.175
11. Salas, E., Wilson, K.A., Priest, H.A., Guthrie, J.W.: Design, delivery, and evaluation of training systems. In: Handbook of Human Factors and Ergonomics, pp. 472–512. Wiley (2006). https://doi.org/10.1002/0470048204.ch18
12. Shikhnabieva, T.S.: Adaptivnye semanticheskie modeli avtomatizirovannogo kontrolya znanii [Adaptive Semantic Model of Automatic Knowledge Control]. In: Pedagogicheskoe obrazovanie v Rossii [Pedagogical Education in Russia], no. 7, pp. 14–20 (2016). (in Russian)
13. Shunkevich, D.: Agentno-orientirovannye reshateli zadach intellektual'nyh sistem [Agent-oriented models, method and tools of compatible problem solvers development for intelligent systems]. In: Golenkov, V. (ed.) Otkrytye semanticheskie tekhnologii proektirovaniya intellektual'nykh system [Open Semantic Technologies for Intelligent Systems], pp. 119–132. BSUIR, Minsk (2018). (in Russian)
14. Shunkevich, D., Koronchik, D.: Ontological approach to the development of a software model of a semantic computer based on the traditional computer architecture. In: Golenkov, V. (ed.) Otkrytye semanticheskie tekhnologii proektirovaniya intellektual'nykh system [Open Semantic Technologies for Intelligent Systems], pp. 75–92. BSUIR, Minsk (2021)
15. Svyatkina, M.N., Tarasov, V.B.: Logiko-algebraicheskie metody postroeniya kognitivnykh sensorov [Logic-algebraic methods for building cognitive sensors]. In: Golenkov, V. (ed.) Otkrytye semanticheskie tehnologii proektirovanija intellektual'nyh sistem [Open Semantic Technologies for Intelligent Systems], pp. 331–348. BSUIR, Minsk, BSUIR (2016). (in Russian)
16. Sykes, J.M.: Technologies for teaching and learning intercultural competence and interlanguage pragmatics, June 2017. https://doi.org/10.1002/9781118914069.ch9

17. Sysoyev, P.V., Zolotov, P.Y.: Formirovanie pragmaticheskoi kompetentsii studentov na osnove korpusnykh tekhnologii [formation of pragmatic competence of students on the basis of corpus technologies]. Yazyk i kul'tura [Language and Culture] (51), 229–246 (2020). https://cyberleninka.ru/article/n/formirovanie-pragmaticheskoy-kompetentsii-studentov-na-osnove-korpusnyh-tehnologiy. (in Russian)
18. Taguchi, N., Sykes, J.M. (eds.): Technology in Interlanguage Pragmatics Research and Teaching. John Benjamins, Amsterdam (2013)
19. Tarasov, V., Golenkov, V.: Sinergeticheskie uchebnye organizatsii v sfere vysshego obrazovaniya [Synergistic organizations in the field of higher education]. In: Golenkov, V. (ed.) Otkrytye semanticheskie tehnologii proektirovanija intellektual'nyh sistem [Open Semantic Technologies for Intelligent Systems], pp. 221–228. BSUIR, Minsk, BSUIR (2017). (in Russian)
20. Tracey, W.R.: Designing training and development systems. American Management Associations (1984)
21. Trembatch, V.M.: Elektronnye obuchayushchie sistemy s ispol'zovaniem intellektual'nykh tekhnologii [E-learning systems using intellectual techniques]. In: Otkrytoe obrazovanie [Open Education], no. 4, pp. 52–62 (2013). (in Russian)
22. Vagramenko, Y.A., Yalamov, G.Y.: Analiz napravlenii intellektualizatsii sovremennykh informatsionnykh sistem uchebnogo naznacheniya [Analysis of the directions of intellectualization of modern information systems of educational appointment]. In: Upravlenie obrazovaniem: teoriya i praktika [Education Management: Theory and Practice], no. 4(24), pp. 44–57 (2016). (in Russian)
23. Yalamov, G.Y., Shikhnabieva, T.S.: Adaptivnye obrazovatel'nye informatsionnye sistemy: podkhody k intellektualizatsii [Adaptive educational information systems: approaches to intellectualization]. In: Chelovek i obrazovanie [Human and Education], no. 4 (57), pp. 84–90 (2018). (in Russian)

A Neural-Symbolic Approach to Computer Vision

Aliaksandr Kroshchanka[1]([✉])[iD], Vladimir Golovko[1,2][iD], Egor Mikhno[1][iD],
Mikhail Kovalev[3][iD], Vadim Zahariev[3][iD], and Aleksandr Zagorskij[3][iD]

[1] Brest State Technical University, Brest, Belarus
kroschenko@gmail.com
[2] Pope John Paul II State School of Higher Vocational Education in Biala Podlaska,
Biała Podlaska, Poland
[3] Belarusian State University of Informatics and Radioelectronics, Minsk, Belarus

Abstract. The paper presents a general computer vision model based on neural-symbolic artificial intelligence capable of performing semantic analysis of a video stream. The proposed approach integrates artificial neural networks (ANN) with the knowledge base on the basis of an ontological approach. In this case, the knowledge base interacts with the neural networks as with agents and the results of their functioning are used for further semantic analysis. The problems of object detection and recognition of images, as well as emotions, are considered as tasks of computer vision. The features, advantages and prospects of using this model are described. Its implementation is considered on the example of an intelligent module that includes the FaceNet and eXnet neural network models for face identification and emotion recognition in the conversational modeling system.

Keywords: Neurosymbolic AI · Computer vision · Artificial neural network · Knowledge base · Logical inference

1 Introduction

In the last decade, there has been a steady tendency to widely use methods of machine learning and computer vision in various areas of human activities, primarily due to the successes of the artificial neural networks training theory [16] and increasing of hardware capabilities.

The development of applied methods in the field of computer vision leads to new original practical solutions.

The number of processes, which are being automated using new approaches in computer vision and which often could not be automated with acceptable quality earlier, is growing rapidly. In industries, it has become possible to reduce human participation in the process of product development and quality control

V. Golenkov et al. (Eds.): OSTIS 2021, CCIS 1625, pp. 282–309, 2022.
https://doi.org/10.1007/978-3-031-15882-7_15

[14, 15]; in medicine, computer vision is used to analyze medical images; in the transport industry, it helps to carry out visual control of maintaining traffic regulations and operate autonomous vehicles, in the energy sector, it is used to collect statistics, for example, on the use of solar panels.

Developments that are able not only to support basic functionality (even intelligent one) but also to conduct complex semantic analysis that produces new knowledge that can be used to improve the quality of the system as a whole are of incontestable value.

This combination involves the joint usage of ideas and methods from the fields of artificial neural and semantic models (and in the limit – connectionist and symbolic approaches in AI).

The advantage of artificial neural networks is that they can work with unstructured data. The main disadvantage of ANN is the lack of human-understandable feedback, which could be called a reasoning chain, i.e., it can be said that ANN work as a "black box" [5].

Symbolic AI is based on symbolic (logical) reasoning. Such AI allows solving problems that can be formalized and plays an important role in human knowledge [25, 39]. However, it is not designed to work with unstructured data. Thus, a proper combination of these approaches will allow transforming unstructured data into knowledge.

Work on improving the efficiency of hybrid computer vision systems can be carried out in two directions:

- improving the quality of recognition of objects;
- improving the semantic analysis of recognized objects.

For the simultaneous development of both directions, it is proposed to use the ideas of the neuro-symbolic approach [4, 10, 11, 17] implemented through interaction with ANN as with an agent. Thus, the knowledge base (KB) gets the opportunity to interact with ANN as with an intermediate analyzer, the results of operation of which are used for the subsequent semantic analysis. This will allow drawing additional conclusions, making management decisions and explaining the results obtained to a human.

In this paper, a model of a neuro-symbolic AI system is described, which is based on the integration [13] of various ANN models, which are engaged in solving problems of detection and recognition, with a knowledge base built on the basis of an ontological approach. An example of using the implementation of such a model as a subsystem in a conversational modeling system is given.

The article is structured as follows:

- in Sect. 2, the problem definition to develop a model of a computer vision system for the semantic analysis of a video stream based on a neuro-symbolic approach is presented;
- Section 3 is dedicated to the architecture of the developed model and the integration of its main components;

– Section 4 and 5 are concerned with the description of aspects of the implementation of a hybrid intelligent system for the semantic analysis of the emotional state of the user based on the proposed model;
– finally, in Sect. 6, the description of the hardware platform, on which the system described in Sects. 4 and 5 is launched, is given.

2   Problem Definition

In this section, we describe the formulation of the problem of developing a model of a computer vision system for semantic analysis of a video stream, based on a neurosymbolic approach.

In general, the problem solved by this system can be formulated as follows: there is a video stream that needs to be processed simultaneously by various recognition models; the results of recognition are subjected to semantic analysis for making various decisions in the future. An important aspect here is the support of an expandable list of existing models, which gives the system higher adaptability. Such a system can serve as a subsystem in a more general intelligent system and take on the role of a certain source of knowledge in it, which is used in its work.

The following requirements are imposed on the system that solves the assigned problem:

– joint use of various neural network models for the object detection and image recognition in the image;
– simplicity in adding new models;
– semantic analysis of the results of image recognition;
– availability of the usage of the results of semantic analysis;
– the possibility of explaining the results of this analysis to a human.

To meet the specified requirements, a model of neuro-symbolic AI is proposed, within the framework of which the interaction of ANN and KB is organized to solve the problems of image recognition and semantic analysis, respectively.

3   General Structure of the Model

In this section, we describe the structure of the proposed model and the approach used to integrate its main components.

The main components of the proposed system model are:

– an interface, which in the simplest case can be represented by a camera, the video stream from which is transmitted to the computer vision module;
– a computer vision module, in which the input video stream is split into separate frames, which are recognized by available neural network models, and the obtained recognition results are transmitted to the knowledge integrator;

– a knowledge integrator that forms the necessary constructs from the results of recognition and places the generated knowledge in the knowledge base;
– a knowledge base that connects the problems of object detection and image recognition being solved with neural network models that solve them, as well as the outputs of the activation of these models.
– a problem solver that performs semantic analysis of the results of recognition in the knowledge base.

Figure 1 shows the scheme of interaction of the above components. This scheme displays the upper layer of abstraction of the system components, which in practice can be implemented more comprehensively. The interaction between the above components can be implemented in various ways, for example, based on a network protocol, direct access within a monolithic architecture, shared access to some data storage, etc.

Let us consider in more detail the issues of integration of the main components of the hybrid system model.

3.1 Integration of the Computer Vision Module with the Knowledge Base

The integration of the computer vision module with the knowledge base as well as the direct implementation of the knowledge base and its processing are based on the usage of the OSTIS Technology [12].

Description of the OSTIS Technology. The OSTIS Technology is a complex (family) of technologies that provide design, production, operation and reengineering of intelligent computer systems (ostis-systems) aimed to automate a variety of human activities and are based on the semantic representation and ontological systematization of knowledge as well as agent-oriented knowledge processing [37].

An ostis-system is an intelligent computer system that is built in accordance with the requirements and standards of the OSTIS Technology. The model of the neuro-symbolic AI system being considered in this article is an ostis-system.

Among the advantages of ostis-systems, it is possible to distinguish:

– the ability to perform semantic integration of knowledge in own memory;
– the ability to integrate different types of knowledge;
– the ability to integrate various problem-solving models.

The internal language used by ostis-systems is called an SC-code. Any knowledge can be represented in the form of an SC-code construct. A set of knowledge forms the ostis-system knowledge base. It is quite convenient to operate with knowledge in such a form: the technology supports the search and generation of necessary constructs both according to special templates and elementwise. You can read more about knowledge representation using the SC-code here [21].

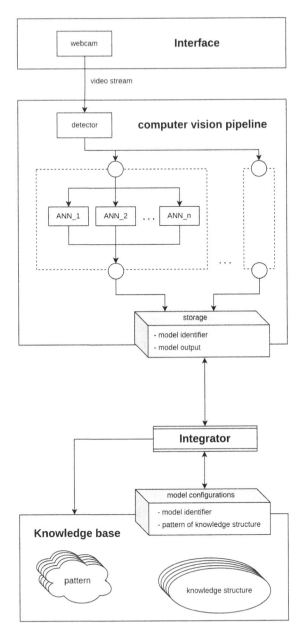

Fig. 1. The scheme of interaction of the main components of the system

Knowledge Integrator. To carry out a semantic analysis of the result of the functioning of the neural network model, it is necessary to place these results in the knowledge base, i.e., to transform information into knowledge. The problems of converting information into knowledge are the design of knowledge structures (defining the key nodes of the selected subject domain, their coordination with the formed knowledge base) and automation of the formation and placement of structures in the KB. Within the framework of the computer vision module, these problems are solved by the knowledge integrator, which places the results of the functioning of neural network models in the KB.

Neural network models solve the following problems:

- detection of objects (for example, faces);
- identification of detected objects of a certain class (for example, identification of a person by face);
- recognition of the class of all detected objects (for example, determination of additional human properties – gender, emotion, age group, etc.).

As a result of solving these problems, various knowledge is placed in the knowledge base:

- knowledge about the presence/absence of objects in the "field of vision";
- knowledge about the correspondence of the detected objects of a certain class to some entities available in the knowledge base (if there are no such entities, new ones are created);
- knowledge about the classes of detected objects and the periods, during which the objects corresponded to these classes.

Due to this unification of the problems that neural network models solve within the computer vision module, it is possible to achieve the independence of the operation of the integrator from particular neural network models. It would be adequate to formalize the specification of such models in the knowledge base, which includes:

- the type of problem being solved;
- input and output data (depending on the type of the problem);
- the work frequency (if necessary);
- the state (on/off);
- the identifier, by which the specification of the model in the knowledge base can be correlated with the model in the computer vision module.

The knowledge integrator receives the specifications of all neural network models presented in the computer vision module and performs the integration of knowledge in accordance with these specifications.

Figure 2 shows an example of formalization of the specification of a neural network model for recognizing emotions in the knowledge base.

This neural network model solves the problem of classifying emotions and outputs for each recognized class a degree of confidence that the recognized object belongs to this class. Further, in accordance with the period stated in the model specification, statistics of the operation of such a neural network model are accumulated.

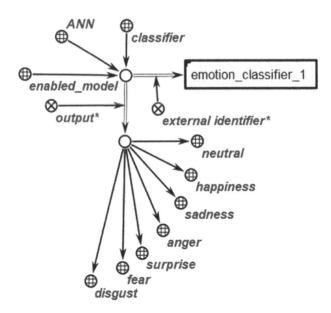

Fig. 2. An example of formalization of the specification of a neural network model for recognizing emotions in the knowledge base

Depending on the configuration of the neural network model, which indicates the need to place operation statistics, confidence percentage for the answers, active time, etc. into the knowledge base, the integrator chooses a template, according to which it will generate knowledge. Such templates are also presented in the knowledge base. Figure 3 shows an example of a template for generating the result of recognizing an object class over a certain period.

If it is necessary to use this template to place the results of functioning of some neural network model into the knowledge base, the knowledge integrator will substitute:

- the recognized class in place of the variable _class;
- the object that was being recognized in place of the variable _object;
- start time of statistics gathering in place of the variable _begin;
- completion time of statistics gathering in place of the variable _end.

After all the substitutions, the integrator generates the specified structure in the KB. An example of the knowledge structure that is formed based on the results obtained by the neural network model of emotion recognition of the computer vision module of the conversational modeling system is shown in Fig. 4.

The approach, when the integrator works with the specifications of neural network models in the knowledge base, allows:

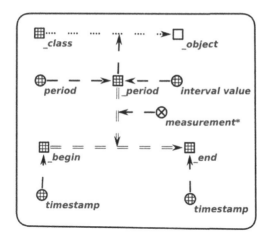

Fig. 3. A template for generating the result of recognizing an object class over a certain period

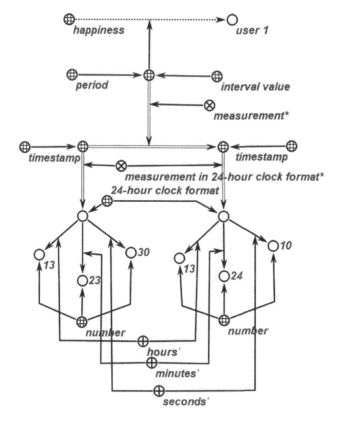

Fig. 4. An example of a representation of the user and their emotions for a certain period in the knowledge base

– avoiding overhead costs when integrating new neural network models, since it is enough only to describe the specification of the new model in the knowledge base;
– managing the computer vision module from the KB (for example, it is sufficient to add a neural network model to a set of switched-off models so that the computer vision module stops running this neural network model for a video stream).

4   The Computer Vision Module

In this section, we will describe the implementation of the computer vision module for hybrid intelligent system for assessing the user's emotional state based on the proposed model.

The logical development of the architectural ideas put up in the previous section is the stage of the implementation of a computer vision module.

The following requirements are imposed on the whole system project:

– The system should be able to identify the face of a person from the list of persons known to it;
– The system should be able to determine the fact of the appearance of an unknown person and add it to the list of persons known to it;
– The system should evaluate the emotional state of the person in the frame and respond accordingly;
– The system should accumulate statistical information about persons, who appeared in front of the camera, and their emotional state.

All the specified problems were solved within the framework of the developed computer vision module. Next, let us describe this module in detail.

4.1   Structure of the Computer Vision Module

The proposed model (Fig. 1) with independently connected neural network modules allows parallel calculations and thereby reducing the total time spent on processing input data. The usage of auxiliary modules and flexible configuration of connections by inputs and outputs allows avoiding repeated processing of input data for various neural network modules.

Based on the problem definition, we implemented the computer vision module of the conversational modeling system. Its structure is shown in Fig. 5. The scheme is greatly simplified from the point of view of interaction with the knowledge base and reflects only the sequence and connectivity of computer vision modules. Let us consider these modules in more detail.

The input module preprocesses frames. It performs image normalization and cropping for next stages of processing.

The face detection module solves the problem of detecting faces in the frame. As a detector the MTCNN model – Multitask Cascaded Convolutional Network [44] is used.

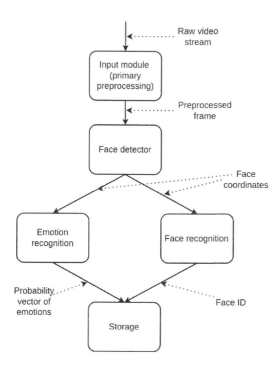

Fig. 5. The scheme of the computer vision module pipeline

The identification module is needed to recognize the face of the identified user. The processes that occur in the module are most fully represented in the flowchart in Fig. 6.

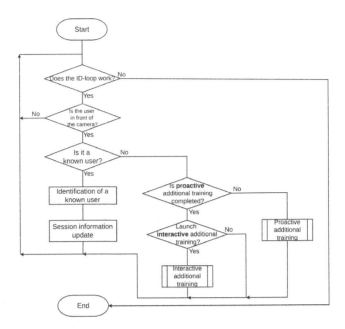

Fig. 6. The general flowchart of identification

In the considered implementation of the neuro-symbolic module of the conversational modeling system, the user identification function is one of the basic functions of the computer vision module, thanks to which purposeful interaction with the user is organized. To implement this function, the FaceNet [34] method is used. For this approach, classical models of deep convolutional neural networks with a triplet loss function are used. In our case, the ResNet [18] convolutional network was used. The general scheme of the model is shown in Fig. 7.

Fig. 7. The structure of FaceNet (original image from [34])

This model consists of successive layers of a deep convolutional neural network and L2-normalization using a triplet loss function at the training stage. At the output of the model, a 128-dimensional feature vector is formed, which can be used for the native comparison of faces.

The models from the dlib [23] library were used as the basic implementation. Let us consider a user identification algorithm that uses feature vectors.

1. For the each detected face, the feature vector is calculated using FaceNet;
2. After calculating the feature vector, it is compared with other feature vectors stored in the database. This comparison is performed with the preset threshold;
3. Based on the results obtained in item 2, an ID is assigned to the detected face.

Thus, a necessary condition for the functioning of the algorithm is the presence of pre-calculated feature vectors for known users. This approach allows identifying the user with acceptable speed and accuracy.

The advantage of the proposed approach is that the implementation of recognition does not require a large training dataset, since the used FaceNet model is pre-trained on a big dataset (it includes more than 3 million images) and can be used unchanged to identify people who were not included in this dataset.

So, for training we used only 49 photos (7 photos of each person). For testing, an independent test dataset of 14 photos and a set of video fragments were used to assess the quality of user recognition.

As a result of the evaluation of the proposed algorithm, the efficiency of face recognition was 95.84%. At the same time, the percentage of correctly recognized faces for the test dataset (due to its small size) was 100%.

The emotion recognition module is needed to determine the emotion of the detected face. This recognition is carried out in seven main classes: neutral, happiness, sadness, anger, fear, surprise, and disgust.

Recognition of user emotions is, in fact, a system-forming, main function in the proposed implementation of the neuro-symbolic module of the conversational modeling system. The main problem of the corresponding neural network model is to classify the emotions of a previously detected user.

The problem of classifying emotions by the image of the user's face is studied in many works (for example, [3, 35, 42], etc.). With the active development of deep neural network training technologies, special emphasis by solving this problem began to be placed on the CNN-architectures (Convolutional Neural Networks) of various configurations. So, state-of-the-art results of emotion recognition were obtained for the eXnet [32] architecture. This network is used as a basic model in the proposed system. Its structure is shown in Fig. 8.

In our work, a combined version of the training datasets from the well-known CK+ [28] dataset and datasets collected manually by the authors (the composition of the datasets is described in more detail below) is used. This approach allowed diversifying the training dataset, making it less synthetic, however, it did not solve all the problems with the quality of recognition.

When forming the final dataset, images of faces with expressions of emotions from three basic sources were used:

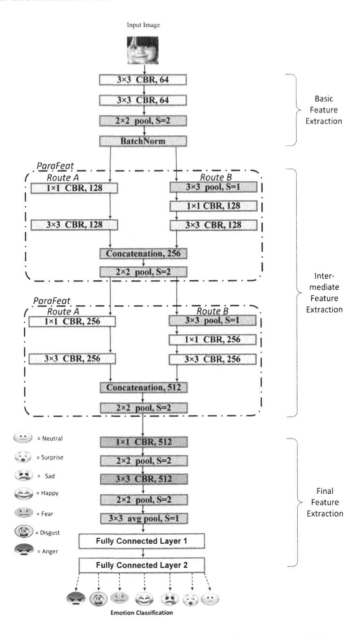

Fig. 8. The structure of eXnet (original image from [32])

1. The CK+ dataset. The training dataset consists of 4,615 images, the testing dataset consists of 554 images structured according to 7 basic recognizable classes of emotions. This dataset consists of video fragments in the format of 640 × 490 or 640 × 480 pixels. It should be noted, however, that the classes for this dataset differ from the abovementioned ones (for example, instead of a neutral emotion, there is contempt emotion). This was one of the reasons why there was a need to form a combined dataset;
2. The "Students and colleagues" dataset. This dataset was collected from data obtained by self-determined image collection and processing. It is a set of images of the faces of 38 people with the expression of basic emotions. The training part included 20,947 images, the testing part – 2,101;
3. Internet Emotions. This dataset was formed from images taken from the Internet and includes one-man photos of 295 people (268 images for training part and 27 images for testing part).

Thus, the total size of the training dataset was 25,830 images and the testing one – 2,682.

As a result of additional training of the eXnet model on the datasets described above, the results presented in Table 1 were obtained.

Table 1. Results of training the eXnet model

	avg. precision (with round)	avg. precision (without round)
CK+	0.877	0.859
Students and Colleagues	0.765	0.742
Internet	0.37	0.305

ck+, student_colleague and internet denote corresponding datasets.

Next, we will consider the additional training procedures for new unknown users.

4.2   Additional Training for New Unknown Users

In addition to identifying known users by the feature vectors that are present in the database, the system allows performing additional training for recognizing unknown users in real-time. Additional training here means calculating a set of feature vectors for new users and saving them for further usage in the identification process. This process is carried out within the framework of the so-called proactive and interactive additional training.

Proactive additional training (Fig. 9) is conducted without direct user participation while calculating feature vectors based on frames received from the video stream.

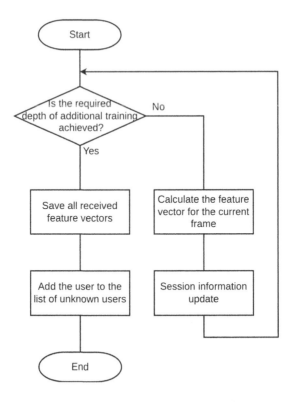

Fig. 9. The scheme of proactive additional training

Interactive additional training for new users (Fig. 10) conducted separately and with the direct participation of the user allows improving the results of proactive additional training and getting more representative feature vectors.

5 Semantic Analysis

The last and no less important aspect of the implementation of the neuro-symbolic module of the conversational modeling system is a semantic analyzer used to analyze the emotional state of the user and develop certain recommendations for conducting a conversation.

After solving the problem of recognition and placing the results of its solution in the knowledge base, we get a lot of opportunities for semantic analysis of what is recognized and usage of the results of this analysis to solve various problems.

If computer vision is the eyes of the system, then the knowledge base can be called its brain, in which there is a "comprehension" of what is seen, i.e., the generation of new knowledge and the initiation of any actions.

The described integration mechanism allows enriching the knowledge base with the results of recognition of various models used by the computer vision module (identification model and emotion recognition model). The processing of this

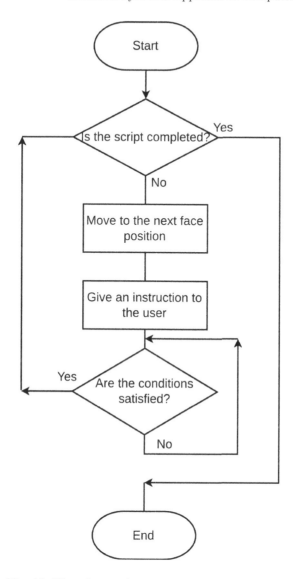

Fig. 10. The scheme of interactive additional training

knowledge will be no different from the processing of any other knowledge in the ostis-system, regardless of whether they got there from the computer vision module, any sensors, visual or natural language interface or in some other way. In this case, computer vision is another receptor of the system. Knowledge processing in the KB, i.e., semantic analysis, is performed by the problem solver. The problem solver is a set of agents that react to events in the knowledge base (for example, a problem definition), solve its problem (generating, transforming knowledge, accessing external systems) and put the result of the work in the same KB.

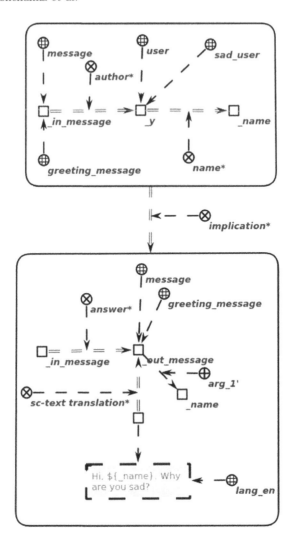

Fig. 11. An example of a logical rule that uses the result of recognizing a user's emotion

For example, one of the methods of knowledge processing can be the usage of logical inference [41], which generates new knowledge based on a set of rules. Logical rules, in the simplest case, can be represented by "if-then" bindings, where the "if" part describes the knowledge that must be in the knowledge base to make it possible for us to generate the knowledge described in the "then" part. The origin of such rules can be different: from adding them manually by knowledge base engineers to automatically generating them.

In the considered implementation of the neuro-symbolic module of the conversational modeling system, logical rules are used to generate some standard system responses to the interlocutor's messages. These rules use such knowledge as the identification of the interlocutor and their current emotion. Figure 11 shows a fragment of such a rule in a simplified form for clarity (in a real system, such rules have a more complex specification).

The meaning of the rule is as follows: if we received a greeting message from a user, whose emotion is recognized by the system as "sadness" and whose name the system knows, then we need to respond to this message with a greeting with a reference by name and ask the reason for sadness.

Integration of computer vision along with other sources of knowledge about the outside world with the knowledge base in the most audacious perspectives is seen as a way to build so-called strong artificial intelligence, when the system, in accordance with the methodology of the scientific method, will be able to:

- make observations about the outside world and put the knowledge obtained from these observations into the KB;
- based on this knowledge, using various methods (such as logical inference), assumptions (also knowledge) about the outside world will be generated;
- the assumptions will be tested in practice with the help of external manipulators;
- verified assumptions will turn into theorems (verified knowledge).

6   Hardware Architecture

In this section, we describe the hardware components of the system that we used to run it.

Taking into account the specifics as well as the capabilities of the current implementation of the platform, we have developed a hardware architecture framework to achieve the set research goal, the block diagram of which is shown in Fig. 12.

The main elements that build up the hardware of the system are:

- A single-board computer (SBC) that serves as a central device, on which the OSTIS virtual machine is run and, accordingly, the interpretation of intelligent agents and a list of peripheral devices that perform the functions of input and output of video and audio information as well as auxiliary devices that perform the functions of supporting neural network computing is carried out;
- To input video information, a camera (Video Camera Unit – VCU) is used designed to solve computer vision problems: detecting and tracking the user's face in the frame, identifying the user, recognizing the emotions of the subject in the frame based on frames from the video stream. According to the general scheme of the system model (Fig. 1), the camera transmits the video stream to the computer vision module (computer vision pipeline), and only then the information is sent to the internal part of the system for further processing. The peculiarity of the proposed solution, which gives it additional flexibility, is that the computer vision module can be deployed both on the single-board computer itself and on a separate machine (for example, a PC or a specialized device designed to solve problems of this type). Therefore, the camera can

be connected both to a single-board computer directly and to an external device that will transmit information through the abovementioned module to the central device where the OSTIS system core is run. The scheme of the hardware architecture considers the option when the camera is connected directly;

– To speed up the performance of operations on vectors and matrices when calculating neural networks on hardware with limited resources, which include single-board computers, it is proposed to use tensor coprocessors (Tensor Processing Unit – TPU) for neural network calculations.

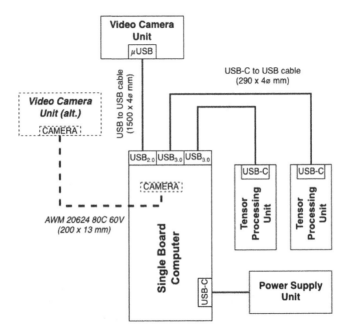

Fig. 12. The system hardware architecture

Let us focus on each of the hardware components of the system and consider them in more detail.

6.1   Single-Board Computer

A single-board computer (SBC) is a computer set up on a single printed circuit board, on which a microprocessor, RAM, I/O systems and other modules necessary for the operation of a computer are installed [22, 38].

As the basis of the hardware platform, it was proposed to use a single-board computer, since such a form factor, on the one hand, can provide the necessary and sufficient runtime environment for the OSTIS Technology in terms of performance and functionality and, on the other hand, preserve the minimum weight-and-dimensional and cost characteristics of computing tools, including for solving problems connected with the Internet of things and the usage of OSTIS within the framework of the "Edge Computing and AI" [26, 43] concept.

We have reviewed and compared the models of single-board computers on the local and international markets that are available for delivery to the territory of the Republic of Belarus. The model lines of computers from such manufacturers as Intel NUX, LattePanda, Rock Pi, UDOO, ODYSSEY [29] were considered. We have set the maximum cost of a single-board computer, so that it does not significantly exceed the cost of the option for the ARM architecture. The set cost was no more than $100, which significantly narrowed the search area.

Among the currently available models of single-board computers, the Rock Pi computer has become the most preferred option, namely the Rock PI X Model B model with the following characteristics [33]:

- Model: Rock Pi X B4E32
- CPU: X86 Intel(R) Atom(TM) x5-Z8350 Cherry Trail Quad-core processor 64bit 1.44 GHz/1.84 GHz (Turbo)
- RAM: 4 GB LPDDR3-1866 SDRAM
- Storage: internal – 32 GB eMMC module, external – micro-SD card (class 10 SDHC or SDXC type up to 128 GB)
- Networking: Wireless LAN 2.4/5.0 GHz IEEE 802.11b/g/n/ac, Bluetooth 5.0, Gigabit Ethernet LAN with Power over Ethernet (PoE) support
- Interfaces: 40-pin GPIO, 2 HDMI micro, 2-way MIPI DSI/CSI ports,
- Power: 5.1 V, 3 A power supply via USB-C or GPIO.
- Size: 85 mm × 54 mm (3.35″ × 2.13″)

The following sources provides more detailed features of the SBC central processor unit used in the project [19, 20], and the appearance of a single-board computer is shown in the Fig. 13:

Fig. 13. Rock Pi X B4E32 single-board computer

A distinctive feature of this single-board computer is the presence of ROM based on eMMC, which allows ensuring the functioning of the system and high-speed access to data on a solid-state drive without using an external SD drive. The maximum available capacity is 128 GB. The proposed architecture uses a version with 32 GB of memory, which is sufficient to contain the OS as well as the necessary software modules and OSTIS intelligent agents.

6.2   Video Camera

It is an element of the system, through which a video stream is received and transmitted to a single-board computer to solve subproblems connected with computer vision and recognition of visual images. It acts as the main channel of input information for the neural network modules of the system.

Within the current version of the hardware architecture, it is possible to connect various video cameras, depending on the type of video interface and the configuration of the device package, which will be directly determined by the type of problem being solved and the requirements for viewing angles, focal point, depth of field of the shown space, dimensions and scale of recognized objects in the image. The main difference between them is the design of the camera box itself as well as the type of interface that is used to connect them.

The camera is a separate device in its box, which can be set on a tripod and shoot at the level of the user's face. As such a removable camera, it is proposed to use the Sony PS3 Eye (Fig. 14) [30] device with the following characteristics [31]:

Fig. 14. The Sony PS3 Eye camera

– Manufacturer: Sony
– Camera chip: Sony SLEH-00448
– Type: Gaming webcam
– Generation: Seventh generation era

- Release date: October 2007
- Type: Color
- Video: 640 × 480 @ 60 fps, 320 × 240 @ 120 fps
- Field of view: 56° (close-up framing), 75° (long-shot framing)
- Image compression: uncompressed mode, JPEG compression
- Microphone: four-capsule microphone array
- Bitrate: 16-bit per sample at 48 kHz sampling rate
- Signal-to-noise ratio: 90 dB
- Interfaces: USB 2.0 (type-A)
- Platforms: PlayStation 3, Windows, Linux
- Dimensions: 80 × 55 × 65 mm
- Weight: 173 g

It should be noted that both cameras are used in a mode of obtaining images of relatively low resolution, i.e., 640 × 480 60 fps, 320 × 240 120 fps. This is done for two purposes: the first is to increase the performance of the video subsystem as well as to prevent the image obtaining process, which is resource-consuming for single-board computer processors, from becoming a "bottleneck" in the common processing pipeline; the second is that the image will be transformed into images with a lower resolution one way or another before processing by neural network models. Such a transformation is called "oversampling" or "resampling" that is usually performed in all machine vision systems to ensure a balance between performance and quality of work, since processing large-resolution images requires significantly large computing resources as well as time for training and performing neural network models. In the case of our proposed system, image resampling is carried out for user identification models in the format of 160 × 160 pixels as well as in the format of 48 × 48 pixels – for emotion recognition models. For this reason, for the development of the hardware architecture, we chose the Sony PS3 Eye camera, which is significantly inferior in characteristics to modern cameras but, on the other hand, has a minimum cost on the market relative to the quality of the optical system and the CCD-matrix installed in it, which allow solving the entire range of denoted machine vision problems.

6.3   Tensor Processing Unit

An important element of the hardware architecture is a tensor processing unit (TPU) for neural network computing to speed up the work of the neural network modules of the application [2].

   Since the processor of a single-board computer does not have an architecture that is optimally suitable for the parallel implementation of convolution and matrix multiplication operations, which form the computational basis of modern neural networks [24], it is highly advisable to have a specialized coprocessor in the system that allows implementing these operations.

   Tensor processing units are devices that are coprocessors controlled by a central processor and that operate with tensors – objects that describe transformations of elements of one linear space into another one and can be represented as multidimensional arrays of numbers [40], which are processed using such software libraries as, for example, "TensorFlow" and "TensorFlow Lite" [1,36]. They are usually equipped with own built-in RAM, operate with low-bit (8-bit) numbers and are highly specialized for performing such operations as matrix multiplication and convolution used for the operation of convolutional networks, which are the basis of many models of deep neural networks.

We have considered the model lines of tensor coprocessors of the main manufacturers of specialized purpose processors from Intel, NVidia and Google [6,27]. The most suitable option in terms of performance characteristics, cost, amount of documentation and open source projects is the "Coral USB Accelerator" processor, which was chosen as this component of the system [7].

This processor was developed by the Google corporation and is intended for usage with the TensorFlow machine learning library. This device, in comparison with GPUs, is designed to perform a large number of calculations with reduced accuracy (in integer arithmetic) with higher performance per watt. The device is implemented as a matrix multiplier controlled by the instructions of the central processor over the USB 3.0 bus. The peculiarities of computing architecture of the tensor processing unit are given in [7], and appearance of the entire device is shown in Fig. 15.

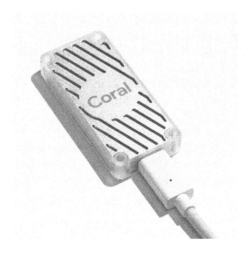

Fig. 15. The Coral USB Accelerator TPU device

The Coral USB Accelerator coprocessor can perform 4 trillion operations (teraflops) per second (TOPS), using 0.5 W for each TOPS (2 TOPS per watt). For example, it can perform tensor calculations for one of the most popular neural network architectures in technical vision problems, such as "MobileNet v2", with a performance close to 400 frames per second with a low energy consumption of about 1.5 W [9].

General view of the system hardware architecture is shown in Fig. 16.

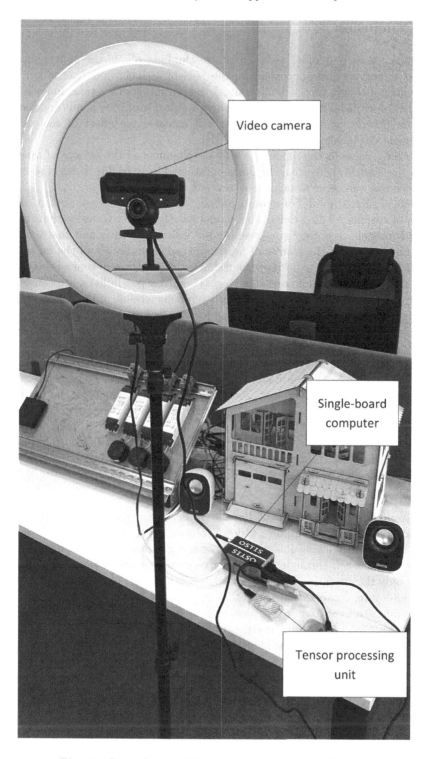

Fig. 16. General view of the system hardware architecture

7   Conclusion

Currently, more and more researchers are thinking about the convergence of various directions and approaches in the field of artificial intelligence [8]. This new and challenging turn will allow using the advantages of various independent branches of artificial intelligence in solving practical problems of any complexity, and the synergy achieved in this case will increase the effect of each of the components of technologies.

We have come to the moment in the development of the science of artificial intelligence, when there are no longer separate and isolated directions of research, and each one can serve to achieve a common goal.

The considered model of neuro-symbolic AI is an example of such a combination of various AI directions. This model has the ability to use various neural network models to solve various computer vision problems and to conduct a semantic analysis of the results of functioning of such models in the knowledge base. It is also possible to add new neural network models and control their operation mode through the knowledge base. The given possibilities are considered on the example of the implemented neuro-symbolic module of the conversational modeling system, which allows it to use for some of its answers the knowledge formed in the process of interaction with neural network models of user identification and recognition of their emotions.

In the article, a variant of a hardware platform for solving this problem based on "Rocks Pi X" single-board computer, "Sony PS3 Eye" video camera and the "Google Coral USB Accelerator" tensor processor is considered. The hardware and software architecture proposed by us allows providing the necessary level of performance not only of the semantic part oriented currently to general-purpose processors but also of the neural network part of the system due to the usage of a specialized tensor computing coprocessor as part of the system.

The described model creates the basis for further research in the field of developing:

- universal integration with the knowledge base of any neural network models that not only solve computer vision problems;
- an approach to deeper integration of neural network models with the knowledge base, when through the knowledge base it becomes possible to control not only the operating mode of neural network models but also their topology, architecture, combination with other models, etc.;
- an approach to automatic decision-making on the usage of a particular neural network model for solving system problems;
- an approach to usage of the knowledge base to improve the training of artificial neural networks;
- new hardware architectures that can support such systems.

References

1. Abadi, M., Barham, P., Chen, J., et al.: TensorFlow: a system for large-scale machine learning. In: 12th USENIX Symposium on Operating Systems Design and Implementation, pp. 265–283 (2016)
2. AI accelerator. https://en.wikipedia.org/wiki/AI_accelerator. Accessed June 2021
3. Benitez-Quiroz, C.F., Srinivasan, R., Martinez, A.M.: EmotioNet: an accurate, real-time algorithm for the automatic annotation of a million facial expressions in the wild, pp. 5562–5570 (2016)
4. Besold, T.R., et al.: Neural-symbolic learning and reasoning: a survey and interpretation, November 2017. https://arxiv.org/pdf/1711.03902.pdf. Accessed June 2021
5. Castelvecchi, D.: Can we open the black box of AI? Nat. News **538**(7623), 20–23 (2016)
6. Chen, Y., Xie, Y., Song, L., Chen, F., Tang, T.: A survey of accelerator architectures for deep neural networks. Engineering **6**(3), 264–274 (2020)
7. Coral USB accelerator datasheet. https://coral.ai/docs/accelerator/datasheet. Accessed June 2021
8. Domingos, P.: The Master Algorithm: How the Quest for the Ultimate Learning Machine Will Remake Our World. Basic Books (2015)
9. Edge TPU performance benchmark. https://coral.ai/docs/edgetpu/benchmarks. Accessed June 2021
10. d'Avila Garcez, A., et al.: Neural-symbolic learning and reasoning: contributions and challenges. In: Proceedings of the AAAI 2015 Propositional Rule Extraction Under Background Knowledge 11 Spring Symposium on Knowledge Representation and Reasoning: Integrating Symbolic and Neural Approaches. AAAI Press Technical report SS-15-03 (2015)
11. d'Avila Garcez, A., Lamb, L., Gabbay, D.: Neural-Symbolic Cognitive Reasoning. Cognitive Technologies, Springer, Heidelberg (2009). https://doi.org/10.1007/978-3-540-73246-4
12. Golenkov, V., Guliakina, N., Davydenko, I., Eremeev, A.: Methods and tools for ensuring compatibility of computer systems. In: Golenkov, V. (ed.) Open Semantic Technologies for Intelligent Systems, pp. 25–52. 2, BSUIR, Minsk (2019)
13. Golovko, V., et al.: Integration of artificial neural networks and knowledge bases. In: Open Semantic Technologies for Designing Intelligent Systems (OSTIS 2018): Materials of the International Science and Technology Conference, Minsk, 15–17 February 2018, pp. 133–145 (2018)
14. Golovko, V., Kroshchanka, A., Kovalev, M., Taberko, V., Ivaniuk, D.: Neuro-symbolic artificial intelligence: application for control the quality of product labeling. In: Golenkov, V., Krasnoproshin, V., Golovko, V., Azarov, E. (eds.) OSTIS 2020. CCIS, vol. 1282, pp. 81–101. Springer, Cham (2020). https://doi.org/10.1007/978-3-030-60447-9_6
15. Golovko, V., Kroshchanka, A., Mikhno, E.: Deep neural networks: selected aspects of learning and application. Pattern Recogn. Image Anal. **31**(1), 132–143 (2021). https://doi.org/10.1134/S1054661821010090
16. Golovko, V., Kroshchanka, A., Turchenko, V., Jankowski, S., Treadwell, D.: A new technique for restricted Boltzmann machine learning. In: 2015 IEEE 8th International Conference on Intelligent Data Acquisition and Advanced Computing Systems: Technology and Applications (IDAACS), Warsaw, vol. 1, pp. 182–186 (2015)

17. Hammer, B., Hitzler, P.: Perspectives of Neural-Symbolic Integration. Studies in Computational Intelligence, vol. 77. Springer, Heidelberg (2007). https://doi.org/10.1007/978-3-540-73954-8
18. He, K., Zhang, X., Ren, S., Sun, J.: Deep residual learning for image recognition, pp. 770–778 (2016)
19. Intel Atom Z8000 processor series, vol. 1. https://dl.radxa.com/rockpix/docs/hw/atom-z8000-datasheet-vol-1.pdf. Accessed June 2021
20. Intel Atom Z8000 processor series, vol. 2. https://dl.radxa.com/rockpix/docs/hw/atom-z8000-datasheet-vol-2.pdf. Accessed June 2021
21. Intelligent meta system (IMS). http://ims.ostis.net. Accessed June 2021
22. Isikdag, U.: Internet of Things: single-board computers. In: Isikdag, U. (ed.) Enhanced Building Information Models. SCS, pp. 43–53. Springer, Cham (2015). https://doi.org/10.1007/978-3-319-21825-0_4
23. King, D.E.: Dlib-ml: a machine learning toolkit. J. Mach. Learn. Res. **10**, 1755–1758 (2009)
24. LeCun, Y., Bengio, Y., Hinton, G.: Deep learning. Nature **521**(7553), 436–444 (2015)
25. Lehmann, F.: Semantic networks. Comput. Math. Appl. **23**(2–5), 1–50 (1992)
26. Li, P.: Arhitektura interneta veshhej. DMK Press (2018). in Russian
27. Li, W., Liewig, M.: A survey of AI accelerators for edge environment. In: Rocha, Á., Adeli, H., Reis, L.P., Costanzo, S., Orovic, I., Moreira, F. (eds.) WorldCIST 2020. AISC, vol. 1160, pp. 35–44. Springer, Cham (2020). https://doi.org/10.1007/978-3-030-45691-7_4
28. Lucey, P., Cohn, J.F., Kanade, T., Saragih, J., Ambadar, Z., Matthews, I.: The extended cohn-kanade dataset (CK+): a complete dataset for action unit and emotion-specified expression. In: IEEE Computer Society Conference on Computer Vision and Pattern Recognition, pp. 94–101 (2010)
29. Galkin, P., Golovkina, L., Klyuchnyk, I.: Analysis of single-board computers for IoT and IIoT solutions in embedded control systems. In: International Scientific-Practical Conference Problems of Infocommunications. Science and Technology (PIC S&T), pp. 297–302 (2018)
30. Play station eye. https://en.wikipedia.org/wiki/PlayStation_Eye. Accessed June 2021
31. PS3 eye camera technical specification. https://icecat.biz/en/p/sony/9473459/webcams-eye-camera-+ps3-1269549.html. Accessed June 2021
32. Riaz, M.N., Shen, Y., Sohail, M., Guo, M.: eXnet: an efficient approach for emotion recognition in the wild. Sensors **20**(4), 1087 (2020)
33. Rock Pi X hardware information. https://wiki.radxa.com/RockpiX/hardware. Accessed June 2021
34. Schroff, F., Kalenichenko, D., Philbin, J.: FaceNet: a unified embedding for face recognition and clustering, pp. 815–823 (2015)
35. Shojaeilangari, S., Yau, W., Nandakumar, K., Li, J., Teoh, E.K.: Robust representation and recognition of facial emotions using extreme sparse learning. IEEE Trans. Image Process. **24**(7), 2140–2152 (2015)
36. Shuangfeng, L.: TensorFlow lite: on-device machine learning framework. J. Comput. Res. Dev. **57**(9), 1839–1853 (2020)
37. Shunkevich, D.: Agent-oriented models, method and tools of compatible problem solvers development for intelligent systems. In: Golenkov, V. (ed.) Open Semantic Technologies for Intelligent Systems, pp. 119–132. 2, BSUIR, Minsk (2018)
38. Single-board computer. https://en.wikipedia.org/wiki/Single-board_computer. Accessed June 2021

39. Sowa, J.: Semantic networks. In: Encyclopedia of Artificial Intelligence. Expert Systems with Applications (1987)
40. Tensor processing unit. https://en.wikipedia.org/wiki/Tensor_Proces-sing_Unit. Accessed June 2021
41. Vagin, V., Zagoryanskaya, A., Fomina, M.: Dostovernii i pravdopodobnii vivod v intellektualnih sistemah, p. 704 p. (2008)
42. Wang, K., Peng, X., Yang, J., Meng, D., Qiao, Y.: Region attention networks for pose and occlusion robust facial expression recognition (2019). https://arxiv.org/abs/1905.04075. Accessed June 2021
43. Wang, X., Han, Y., Leung, V.C., Niyato, D., Yan, X., Chen, X.: Edge AI: Convergence of Edge Computing and Artificial Intelligence. Springer, Singapore (2020). https://doi.org/10.1007/978-981-15-6186-3
44. Zhang, K., Zhang, Z., Li, Z., Qiao, Y.: Joint face detection and alignment using multitask cascaded convolutional networks. IEEE Sig. Process. Lett. **23**(10), 1499–1503 (2016)

Ontological Model of Digital Twin in Manufacturing

Natalia Lutska[1], Oleksandr Pupena[1], Alona Shyshak[1],
Valery Taberko[2], Dzmitry Ivaniuk[2], Nikita Zotov[3](✉), Maksim Orlov[3],
and Lidiia Vlasenko[4]

[1] National University of Food Technologies, Kyiv, Ukraine
{pupena_san,al_sh_94}@ukr.net
[2] "Savushkin Product" JSC, Brest, Republic of Belarus
{tab,id}@pda.savushkin.by
[3] Belarusian State University of Informatics and Radioelectronics, Minsk,
Republic of Belarus
nikita.zotov.belarus@gmail.com
[4] Kyiv National University of Trade and Economics, Kyiv, Ukraine

Abstract. In this article, an approach to the continuous automation development of the processes of creation, evolvement, and usage of standards, based on ontological networks, is proposed. The existing international standards, reports, and guidelines in the field of Industry 4.0 and Industrial Internet of Things in the direction of digital twins (DT) are considered and analyzed.

The article is structured as follows: in the opening sections, the conceptions of standards involved in the creation of DT are represented; in the next sections, modern systematized (standardized) and applied functions of semantic and ontological networks in industry are considered; in the last section, the authors introduce their position and the role of ontological networks in the design and implementation of DT in industry. Examples of further formalization of standards within the proposed approach based on the OSTIS Technology are given.

Keywords: Digital twin · Industry 4.0 · Ontological production model · Complex production automation · Ontology · Knowledge base · OSTIS Technology

1 Introduction

Currently, Industry 4.0 technologies are becoming increasingly significant in various branches of industry. The technologies behind the concepts of Industry 4.0 and Industrial Internet of Things (IIoT) offer new opportunities in relation to products and services. Fast algorithms, high computing power, and amounts of available data, advanced Big Data, and IIoT analytics – all this allows modeling and optimizing the physical process taking into account real-time control. The digital representation of a physical twin known as a digital twin (DT) is

V. Golenkov et al. (Eds.): OSTIS 2021, CCIS 1625, pp. 310–335, 2022.
https://doi.org/10.1007/978-3-031-15882-7_16

one of the essential aspects of the Fourth Industrial Revolution. It accompanies the asset throughout its life cycle, starting from conception and before as well as after utilization. For automated control systems, which are also an asset, it is also advisable to develop the digital twin in combination with the control object. It is expected that at the operational stage, the digital twin of such technological complexes will provide an exact prediction of their future behavior and will help effectively maintain the quality of production processes by both simple visualization and integration of cognitive capabilities into a real system. However, there is no single methodological approach to the development and implementation of DT at industrial enterprises. Despite the presence of a large number of existing international standards, project engineers and developers of automated production control systems offer a variety of DT solutions that differ in purposes, functionality, architecture, etc. In turn, representatives of specialized software, such as SCADA, SAV, MES/IOM, offer alternative solutions for the implementation of DT at their corresponding automation level.

When developing and applying DT, additional problems arise:

- the lack of a single unified industrial thesaurus;
- the diversity of large amounts of information to be processed;
- a single DT model, which in fact should describe "everything" (all aspects of the behavior of the system and its parts) from different points of view and is aimed at usage for different purposes.

As described in many sources, in particular, in [1], there is no single thesaurus that can unite various branches of the industrial sector. In particular, the relevant identified activities for the standardization of ontological semantics used in IIoT are eCl@ss (ISO 13584-42 and IEC CDD classes and properties), "Semanz4.0", "AutomationML" (IEC 62714), "WSDL" (Web Services Description Language by W3C), IEC SC3D with IEC 61360, IEC 62656, IEC CDD (the semantic and ontological repository based on IEC 61360 and IEC 62656). On the one hand, the problem in the cohesion of the digital twin model is contained in a need for a variety of heterogeneous, unrelated, and non-unified models. On the other hand, the interconnection of digital twins in a single system [20] requires their interaction, which expects the unification of such interaction at the level of concepts.

An effective way to overcome these problems is to use an ontology. In the context of DT, the ontology can be used:

- as a knowledge storage base that stores information throughout the entire life cycle of the device – the structured storage for the DT data;
- as a knowledge base for the subject domain modeling, which works on a conventional historical database and extracts the necessary knowledge – a wireframe for structuring heterogeneous DT models;

- as a base for the representation of meta-information about the digital twin for the possibility of its usage in the making of adapted interaction with other components of the system – WoT;
- as a means of information support for the DT, which works with open ontological databases on the network and is used to display auxiliary information – semantic WEB, OSTIS, etc.

Thus, the DT in industrial enterprises combines data and models, which are represented by the corresponding standards, with a knowledge base as a wireframe for the information exchange of the enterprise data. The latter is accompanied by the building up of a unified ontological production model, which is also the core of the complex information service of the enterprise. At the first stage of building up such a model, it is necessary to embed data on the lower production level, namely, on the production process and equipment. As the source of this data, P&ID-schemes of production can serve. Therefore, the formalization of the ISA 5.1 standard [25] is required to work with P&ID schemes, which are widely used in control systems jointly with the ISA 88 standard [26] and allow fully describing the lower production level. At the same time, it is also necessary to consider the approach of formalization of the subject domain based on the ISO 15926 standard [10,22] that describes the integration of life cycle data for processing enterprises into a single ontological storage. New users will be also added: an automation engineer and a master who implement new intelligent search functionality together with the developed model. For the current user – the production process operator – the implementation of a mechanism for obtaining intelligent information that covers both particular and general issues of the production process, equipment, components, and automated control systems becomes relevant.

In this article, attention is paid to the continuous development of the ontological model of the formulating enterprise on the example of the "Savushkin product" JSC, in particular, the construction of the DT for the lower production level, which describes the diverse connections of the technological and technical components of production. An Open semantic technology for the design of intelligent systems (OSTIS) is used and the results represented in the articles [41,42] are being developed.

2   Standards and Problems of Their Implementation

2.1   Ontologies in Manufacturing

International organizations for standardization, such as ISO, IEEE, OMG, W3C, and others, are engaged in the development and standardization of ontological systems. Some ontological structures have been developed, which, though have not been approved by international standards, have become standards de facto. They can be divided into several groups:

- ontological systems, models, languages, and their parts for general and industrial purposes;

– the ontological model of the hierarchical production structure in the processing industry [22];
– the technical dictionary [17, 27];
– a series of standards for the development of a top-level ontology, which is
currently in progress;
– formal semantic models of global production networks [21];
– a semantic approach for information exchange related to production and other
discrete processes [9];
– general and specialized top-level ontologies:
  • MOF (Meta Object Facility) is a meta-object environment for model engi-
    neering [18];
  • BFO (Basic Formal Ontology) is a basic formal ontology common for
    biomedicine [28];
  • ZEO (Zachman Enterprise Ontology) is the ontology of an enterprise for
    the description of its architecture [16];
  • DOLCE (Descriptive Ontology for Linguistic and Cognitive Engineering)
    is a descriptive general-purpose ontology for linguistic and cognitive engi-
    neering, quite popular in the field of ontological engineering [12];
  • GFO (General Formal Ontology) [13];
  • SUMO (Suggested Upper Marged Ontology) is the proposed unified top-
    level ontology, a source document for a workgroup of IEEE employees
    from the branches of engineering, philosophy, and computer science [38];
  • Semantic Web: it includes all standards and rules for semantic processing
    of documents on the Internet, such as the Resource Description Frame-
    work (RDF) [7] as well as its RDFS extension [8]; the Web Ontology
    Language (OWL) [11]; the SPARQL query language [15]; the Rule Inter-
    change Format [14], and a number of formats for saving RDF N-Triples,
    Turtle, RDF/XML, N-Quads, Notation 3 triples.

The basic (fundamental) ontology, or a top-level ontology, is a general ontology that is applied to various subject domains. It defines basic concepts, such as
objects, relations, events, processes, etc. The most famous fundamental ontologies are listed above. BFO and DOLCE are the most commonly used in the
development of engineering ontologies. These two ontologies are formal and provide a logical theory for representing common assumptions. When forming an
ontology of a subject domain based on one of the specified top-level ontologies,
it can be more easily integrated with other subject ontologies. The problem is
that there are quite a lot of top-level ontologies and giving preference to one of
them becomes a certain search problem that requires a lot of time and effort. In
addition, some of them do not have open access and are also badly compatible
with the language peculiarities of applied ontologies and the Semantic Web.
    The ISO 15926 ontology [35] is considered separately. This standard is not
only a top-level ontology but also a thesaurus of the processing industry, including the structure of retention and access to the ontological base. Standardization
is performed by using well-defined templates for technical and operational information, that include classes and relations of the invariant and temporal parts

of the ontology. The advantages of this ontological model are the typification and identification of data located on the Internet; information is stored in RDF-triplets, access to triplet storages occurs using the SPARQL query language, etc. When creating this model, the developers tried to cover all aspects of requests that may arise in manufacturing. As a result, the model has hundreds of nested classes and attributes at the lower production levels (description of technological equipment), most of which may not be used in practice. The temporal part increases the complexity of the model several times.

In addition, there are various applied usage options of ontological networks, for example, OSTIS that is developed according to ISA-88 [42], as well as highly specialized domains and cores [37].

In any case, the building of a unified ontological system of the enterprise should be based on some international standards in the field of Industry 4.0, which includes a hierarchy of manufacturing entities: ISA 5.1 – the lower-level entities, ISA 88 – manufacturing entities up to the level of the working center, ISA 95 – the manufacturing enterprise entities up to the upper level. Besides, the ontological model should provide tracking of asset entities in the context of the hierarchy and functions of manufacturing, the life cycle, etc.

2.2   Digital Twin: Specifications and Standards

According to the architecture proposed by Dr. Michael Grieves, the Digital Twin conceptual model (Fig. 1) consists of three parts:

1. a physical product in the real world;
2. a virtual product in the virtual world;
3. data and information connectivities that link virtual and physical products.

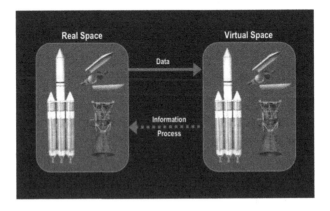

Fig. 1. The Digital Twin concept model by Dr. Michael Grieves (the source – [33])

In the White Paper published by the efforts of the Industrial Internet Consortium and Plattform Industrie 4.0 [29], the applicability of the digital twin conception in various branches of Industrial Internet of Things is described, including smart manufacturing, automotive, supply chains, and logistics, building automation, smart cities, and critical infrastructures. Today, the Digital Twin Consortium is engaged in the popularization of the usage of digital twins in various fields, the development of digital twin technologies, engineering facilities, and the requirements of new standards to maximize the benefits of digital twins. Unlike IIC, German Plattform Industrie 4.0 specializes in the implementation of the concept only in the manufacturing sector and with a focus on mechanical engineering.

The Digital Twin Consortium defines a digital twin as follows: "A digital twin is a virtual representation of real-world entities and processes, synchronized at a specified frequency and fidelity" [39]. Unlike the conceptual model by Dr. Michael Grieves, the definition of a digital twin focuses on real-world entities, because the things for which virtual reflection is implied can be non-material things, such as organizations, supply chains, work orders. The official documents of the Digital Twin Consortium have not yet been published. However, in accordance with the works of the organization [30], the digital twin is implemented by the digital twin system. It consists of a virtual representation, services, service interfaces, and various applications in compliance with the usage purposes of the twin. The virtual representation includes stored structured information that reflects the states and attributes of entities and processes, computational algorithms, and auxiliary data, which represent entities and processes from a dynamic point of view.

As part of the development of the Industrie 4.0 initiative, Reference architecture model industry 4.0 (RAMI 4.0) was developed to build smart manufacturing. The model assumes the representation of all assets of the enterprise, including personnel and software, in the form of equal I4.0 components compatible with each other due to the I4.0 compatible connection. The Industrie 4.0 components are globally and uniquely identified participants capable of communication, which consist of an administration shell and an asset (as in Fig. 2) with a digital connection in the I4.0 system. As a 14.0 component, a production system, a separate machine, an aggregate, or a module in a machine can serve. Assets should have a logical representation in the "information world", which is called the Asset Administration Shell (AAS). In fact, AAS is an implementation of the digital twin for industrial usage. It has been denoted and designed to enable interaction between companies throughout the value chains. AAS includes asset information collected throughout the life cycle in a structured form. AAS consists of properties, which in turn are grouped into submodels. Such properties are standardized data elements. To define such properties, it is recommended to use repositories, such as IEC CDD (Common Data Dictionary) or eCl@ss. A world unique identifier associates a property type with a definition, which is a set of clearly specified attributes.

There are various activities regarding standardization of digital twins. IEC 62832-1 – "Digital Factory" – is a well-established standard, which defines a digital factory framework with the representation of digital factory assets. A lot

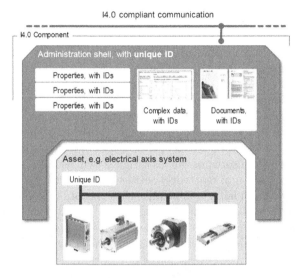

Fig. 2. Asset Administration Shell (the source – [5])

of standards are on the development stage, such as IEEE P2806.1 – "Standard for Connectivity Requirements of Digital Representation for Physical Objects in Factory Environments", IEEE P2806 – "System Architecture of Digital Representation for Physical Objects in Factory Environments", ISO/DIS 23247-1 – "Automation systems and integration – Digital Twin framework for manufacturing – Part 1: Overview and general principles".

Analyzing the above approaches, it is necessary to highlight the advantages and disadvantages regarding their further partial or full implementation in enterprise applications. The approach of the Industrie 4.0 platform focuses on the manufacturing that corresponds to the authors' area of interest. However, introduction into the RAMI 4.0 reference model suggests that this model is mostly focused on discrete production. In turn, the Digital twin consortium began its intensive activity to develop approaches for building digital twins, regardless of the domain of their usage. The amount of available information about improvements of both organizations differs significantly. DTC does not provide clear recommendations, but there is already a general structure, the elements of which were described above. In turn, Industry 4.0 is quite actively developing the RAMI 4.0 model, which has official recognized as IEC PAS 63088 [3]. In addition, the platform publishes many educational documents that provide a detailed description of the digital representation of the Asset Administration Shell real entity, namely the meta-model [4] and the description of the interaction interface [6]. Except for the documental description, there are publicly available software templates. However, according to the authors, the relevant publications of the platform (AAS description) contradict the fundamental principles of the RAMI 4.0 reference model. Also, in the context of AAS, there is no clear definition of how the digital representation of an asset will include predictive, simulation models, various analytical applications, machine learning mechanisms, and services. The digital twin system represented by DTC takes into account these key elements of digital twins, including the usage of ontologies. In any case, the introduction of digital twins in manufacturing should be based on existing standards and technologies that have stood the test of time.

2.3 ISA-88, ISA-95, and the Classification of Lower-Level Equipment

Since a digital twin is a virtual representation of a real entity, which aggregates information about an asset from different data sources, its formalization requires the usage of ontologies. At the same time, it should be noted that assets exist at different hierarchical levels of the manufacturing enterprise. In addition to being represented in the control system, it is also registered in the ERP system. Therefore, when developing a digital twin and building up its ontological model, all aspects of the direct explicit existence of a real entity should be taken into account. The ISA-95 standard (IEC 62264) is the foundation for the interaction of production subsystems and enterprise control systems, which implies the organization of all enterprise assets according to a Role-based equipment hierarchy model (Fig. 3). First of all, ISA-95 describes the integration mechanisms for hierarchical levels of the automated control system and business processes. At the same time, the standard denotes a functional model of the production level (the level of the enterprise and control system integration). The description of functions is accompanied by the definition of information flows and the information model itself, based on which the interaction between domains, subsystems, business processes, and the control system is made. That is, it describes the functionality and the interaction model for the resources of the entire enterprise (material, personnel, equipment) from the level of business process control to units – the level of automated technological process control. ISA-88 (IEC 61512) deals with the description of the lower levels of batch production equipment up to control modules.

According to ISA-88, the choice of the equipment role in ISA-88 depends on what function it will perform in the production process. Thus, the technological procedural elements should be known. The equipment is designed and at the same time used to perform technological operations. The knowledge base should be created to assist the technologist when generating a recipe (using PFC), that is, to provide the necessary choice of equipment, answering such questions:

- "What equipment can perform such a list of classes of procedural elements?";
- "What methods can be available for developing a product?";
- "Which method is the most optimal from the point of view of the selected criterion?"

However, the ISA-88 standard has some disadvantages, which are connected with the need for correct function identification for the procedural elements, which is aimed at predicting the development of new recipes. There are also a number of classical problems inherent in the building of hierarchies, in particular, dividing into very small procedural elements can lead to lengthy and

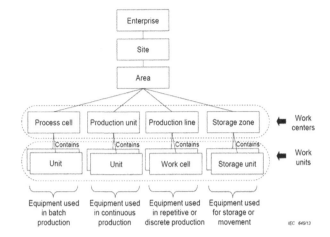

Fig. 3. A Role-based equipment hierarchy model

impractical recipes. Right up to the limiting case – the usage of a procedural element as a reference to basic functions, such as "unseat the valve", which does not correspond to the standard at all.

The presence of a database can simplify and speed up the search process, but the availability of a knowledge base about all production equipment, according to ISA-88 and ISA-95, would be the best option. The developer of the control system could get the necessary information by asking the system various questions:

- to find the equipment that is used in the charging/output/washing line of the tank;
- to find equipment at the crossing of the paths;
- to find the list of equipment for the specified set of conditions.

One of the labor-intensive problems is the implementation of a Master Recipe for a certain process cell by the General or Site Recipe.

In the article [31] about ISA-88, how to use the knowledge base on the ground of the OSTIS ontologies to train the operator with complex concepts, search for objects according to ISA-88, and their interrelations is described.

2.4   ISA-5.1 Representation Standard of Lower-Level Equipment

This standard describes the rules for drawing up block diagrams for the automation of production processes [25]. Such schemes allow graphically representing the production technology and equipment as well as measuring and control tools. ISA 5.1 also defines rules for the identification of equipment, measuring, and automation tools for design and maintenance. This allows classifying lower-level devices.

In the ISA 5.1 standard, it is specified that "the symbols and designations are used as conceptualizing aids, as design tools, as teaching devices, and as a concise and specific means of communication in all types and kinds of technical, engineering, procurement, construction, and maintenance documents, and not just piping and instrumentation diagrams (P&IDs)", therefore, in a system built on the concept of this standard, the ontological knowledge base can receive information that comes from P&ID, in particular, in the following form:

– lists of asset tools or indexes: specification, integration, and installation documents;
– lists of various equipment types, for example:
  • engine lists: size, power, voltage;
  • piping: line lists, size, function, and purpose;
  • technological equipment: information about the basic, intermediate, and additional technological equipment;
  • lists of Line symbols: an instrument to process and equipment connection and instrument-to-instrument connections.

All this information allows determining, if necessary, the asset position both on the real object and on the block diagram, which can be the basis for determining equipment at the design stage, ongoing system maintenance, and the formation of specifications for the procurement of necessary equipment.

An example of a block diagram of a coagulator heating assembly is shown in Fig. 4. This fragment allows overviewing, which devices are used and how they are interconnected.

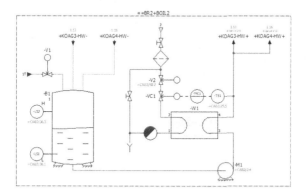

Fig. 4. A block diagram of a coagulator heating assembly according to ISA 5.1

2.5 Choice Justification of the Concept for Building a Production Model

The need for an ontology is specified in TR [1], however, it is not yet clear what its final form will be. The only thing mentioned in this document is two ways to use the introduced semantics: to provide an information model (related to a specific ontology) for querying or reasoning purposes and to provide a system dynamics model that supports checking inconsistencies during interoperation. Both possible interpretations shall be related to semantics web descriptions.

Data models and ontologies play various functional roles in the digital twin system. It is proposed to use sustainable data models for stored structured information. Service interfaces embody a logical data model that describes the structures and data types used by the API or protocol. Conceptual data models compatible with a common ontology can be used in a digital twin system that integrates information from diverse structured data storages, each of which has sustainable and logical data models. Various data modeling languages can be used, in particular, Digital Twins Definition Language or OWL.

RAMI 4.0 architecture defines a number of W3C standards that reflect the semantic representation of the data model on the network; they include OWL, RDF, RDFS, SPARQL, RIF/SRWL. RDF, OWL, and SPARQL are at the core of the Semantic Web. The first three technologies are used to represent metadata, the fourth is used to form queries to the ontological database, the fifth is the language for forming axioms and the format for exchanging rules. Such semantics has some advantages, such as reasoning over data and working with heterogeneous data sources, a single structure that allows data to be exchanged and reused between applications.

In fact, these recommendations are insufficient to build a complete distributed network for IIoT, therefore, since 2017, new recommendations from the W3C, that cover IoT, have appeared. They include OWL-Time [23], SSN ontology [19], and WoT [24]. OWL-Time describes the subclasses and properties of two generalizing classes of temporal position and temporal duration of resources on WEB pages. SSN ontology describes the ontology of sensors and actuators, built on a simple core ontology (self-contained core ontology) SOSA (Sensor, Observation, Sample, and Actuator) and designates several conceptual modules that cover the key concepts (sensor, actuation, and sampling ones): observation/actuation/sampling, deployment, system, system property, feature, condition, procedure, result. WoT recommends the general conception of the IoT existence on the network. In particular, the architecture, Thing Description, Interaction Model, Protocol Binding, WoT Interface, etc. are described. Thus, a set of templates for Web of Things is formed. However, no matter how the W3C standards develop today: they are still not enough for industrial scales. One confirmation of this is the appearance and development of the ISO 15926 standard, which is based on OWL.

Let us emphasize a number of disadvantages inherent in OWL-based systems:

1. the need to describe metadata, in either case, leads to duplication of information. Each document should be created in two copies: marked up one for reading by humans and one for a computer;
2. an important issue is the openness and validity of the metadata used – such systems are more fragile to threats from the outside;

3. the multiformat representation of knowledge fragments complicates their processing;
4. limited possibilities of tools for viewing and using the information provided by media resources.

The usage of the OSTIS Technology allows getting a solution without these disadvantages and with the following advantages:

1. the variety of types of knowledge stored in the system knowledge base;
2. the variety of types of questions that the system can answer;
3. the presence of a built-in intelligent help system for end-users, which provides a substantial improvement in the efficiency of the system operation;
4. the possibility of using the terminology in various natural languages;
5. availability of comprehensive facilities for knowledge visualization, including different styles of visualization of semantic space fragments and convenient means of navigation through this semantic space;
6. system integrability with other related systems, including ones built on the basis of the OSTIS Technology [40];
7. availability of means of self-diagnosis, self-analysis, and self-improvement [34].

The OSTIS Technology (an Open semantic technology for the component design of compatible computer systems controlled by knowledge) is based on a unified version of information encoding and representation grounded on semantic networks with a basic set-theoretic interpretation called an SC-code and with various formats of information representation based on it (SCg, SCs, SCn) [32]. The systems that are the target of formulating enterprises are developed on the OSTIS Technology platform.

3   Ontological Model of the ISA-5.1 Standard on OSTIS

3.1   General Principles of Building a Lower-Level Model

In the context of equipment ontology development each knowledge engineer faces a number of problems, one way or another related to the need to take into account various factors. The greater the number of equipment in the recipe scheme and the more connections between them, the more difficult it is to distinguish the semantic neighborhoods of the concepts corresponding to them. In addition, the standard may not regulate how the equipment objects should be connected, which creates additional problems at the level of describing the logical ontologies of the subject area. Therefore, this problem should be considered from the limitations and functional requirements of the ISA-88 standard and from the experience of best practices. Both can be put into the knowledge base [2].

The first it is needed to highlight clear restrictions, using which it is quite easy to determine if the equipment belongs to one of the hierarchy levels. According to ISA-88 standard, these levels are:

1. the level of the process cells;
2. the level of units;
3. the level of equipment modules;
4. the level of control modules.

According to the standard, "a process cell is a logical grouping of equipment that includes the equipment required for production of one or more batches". From the point of view of the production of a batch of products the concept of a process cell stands out. It is also necessary to include in the process cell even the equipment, that does not belong to the process cell, but is used to manufacture a batch of intermediate products. Within the boundaries of one process cell, there may be several related items of equipment capable of producing several batches of products in parallel, if this is considered possible. In addition, a process cell must contain at least one unit.

The allocation of units is a little less obvious. There are several clear criteria:

1. one unit contains only one batch;
2. each technological action occurs simultaneously with all the materials within one unit;
3. a technological operation begins and ends within the same unit.

Less obvious conditions for choosing and combining are the statements:

– the unit can include all the equipment and control modules involved in technological actions;
– the unit can work with part of the batch.

All equipment, except for the control module, can implement procedural control. That is, from the point of view of technology, it contains some procedural elements that perform a technological operation, separating itself from the method of its implementation. There are operational directives, for example, "heat to the required temperature", as opposed to the directives "open valve 1" or "if TE101 > 23, close the valve". The last control directive refers to equipment, not technology, and is called "basic control" in the standard. This is the main criterion that determines the principle of allocating the control module – this equipment does not contain procedural control. In addition, this part of the hierarchy enables real interaction with concrete equipment, while the other levels are more role groups. Therefore, the level of control modules cannot be omitted in the hierarchy.

The concept of procedural control is also not clear enough. It is difficult to formalize, and therefore, to define in the ontology. However, according to the standard, there are certain properties inherent in it, unlike basic control, such as visibility at the recipe level, a characteristic state machine, abstraction from equipment, etc.

As for the control module, there is one indirect but very useful property as a selection criterion – this type of equipment is shown in the P&ID-schemes

as instrumentation. According to the standard, the control module can include other control modules, creating combined control modules.

The most vague criteria concern the equipment module. First, they are not required. Secondly, this group of equipment consists of an equipment module or other control module, which may contain procedural control, but at the same time does not fit the criteria for either a unit, much less a process cell. The presence of the word "may" is confusing, since a non-procedurally controlled equipment module has the same meaning as a control module. If we accept this as a strict limitation, then it remains to introduce criteria that determine how the equipment module differs from the apparatus. Unit membership criteria can be used, and thus the most important selection criteria are:

- unit performs procedural control;
- unit doesn't work with the entire batch or part of the batch at the same time.

Thus, if a process action is to take place in a flow, such as heating/cooling in heat exchangers or in-line dosing, but within the boundaries of a process cell, then it should be assigned to the equipment module. If it is necessary to dispense a component into different units, then the dosing system is an equipment module, since it cannot belong to any unit.

All objects of the equipment hierarchy, with the exception of the lower level, are always a group of control modules that are combined to perform a specific role. The control system design engineer needs to understand how a group of equipment can collectively fulfill these roles. To do this, the knowledge base that helps in this must contain all the necessary knowledge about the lower level of the equipment. As mentioned above, this can be done by moving knowledge from P&ID schemes into it, which are always present in project documentation for batch production.

3.2   Content of the KB

The knowledge base, according to the ISA-5.1 standard [36] describes a complete, consistent and sufficient system of designations and symbols for tools, processes and functions, describing the lower level of production process control, including the specification of the conventions for the tools used.

As mentioned earlier, the ISA-5.1 standard solves the problem of unifying the designations and specifications of technological process tools for various types of prescription production. The notation system allows you to describe any process of prescription production and its components in any of its branches. Specific relationships between instances of different tool classes are described by signs represented as a knowledge base.

The OSTIS knowledge base of the recipe production system is based on a strictly formalized hierarchy of subject areas and their corresponding ontologies, which allows localizing problems and related tasks that need to be solved, as well as describing the relationship between various concepts. Within the framework of the considered knowledge base, the hierarchy of subject areas was formed in such a way that the concepts studied in a particular area correspond to entities that have a certain common function (goal). At the top level of the hierarchy, the following set of subject areas is allocated, corresponding to the ISA-5.1 standard (Fig. 5).

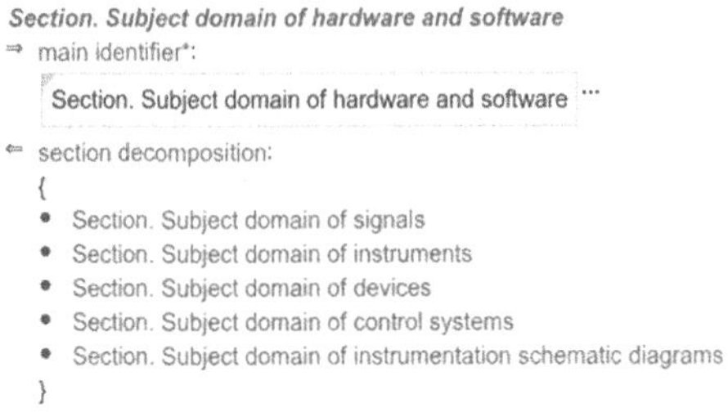

Section. Subject domain of hardware and software
⇒ main identifier*:

    Section. Subject domain of hardware and software ···

⇐ section decomposition:
    {
    • Section. Subject domain of signals
    • Section. Subject domain of instruments
    • Section. Subject domain of devices
    • Section. Subject domain of control systems
    • Section. Subject domain of instrumentation schematic diagrams
    }

Fig. 5. A hierarchy of subject domains of the ISA-5.1 standard

The subject area of hardware and software, which is a key sc-element of the corresponding section of the knowledge base, which, in turn, is decomposed into private subsections, describes general concepts and properties specific to instruments, devices, and other systems. These properties from the point of view of the subject area are non-maximal classes of objects of study or relations under study. The level of detail of the description of the concept depends on the tasks for which it is planned to use this information.

Each subject domain has a corresponding structural specification, which includes a list of concepts studied within this domain. In Fig. 6, the structural specification of the root subject domain – the subject domain of hardware and software – is shown.

3.3   Hierarchy of Subject Domains

Each hardware or software type is described at the level of a certain subject domain (Fig. 7).

The presented hierarchy is not complete, however, it was agreed and verified by a team of experts and developers. The knowledge base of the intelligent system for recipe production should be improved. To achieve this goal, it is necessary to fully describe the relationships between concepts, thereby eliminating incompleteness and information holes in the knowledge described by the standard. The structural specification of some of the given subject areas is considered below. They describe not only the roles of the concepts included in their composition, but also links with other subject areas.

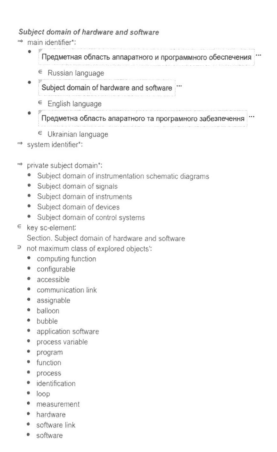

Fig. 6. The specification of the Subject domain of hardware and software

Subject domain of hardware and software
⇒ private subject domain*:
• Subject domain of instrumentation schematic diagrams
  ⇒ private subject domain*:
  • Subject domain of electrical circuits of instruments, loops, and application software functions
  • Subject domain of functional diagrams of instruments, loops, and application software functions
  • Subject domain of of instrument to instrument lines
  • Subject domain of instrument to process lines
  • Subject domain of signal processing function block symbols
• Subject domain of signals
• Subject domain of instruments
  ⇒ private subject domain*:
  • Subject domain of binary logic elements
  • Subject domain of instrumentation
• Subject domain of devices
• Subject domain of control systems

Fig. 7. A hierarchy of subject domains of the ISA-5.1 knowledge base

3.4   Description of a Particular Concept, Its Relations with Others

The subject domain allows obtaining only that knowledge that can and could be common to the concepts contained in it. Thus, the more information about the object there is, the more clear it is to the user. Let us consider the principles of describing a specific concept and its relations with others using the example of the following system of concepts: discrete tool (SD of instruments) $\longrightarrow$ device (SD of devices) $\longrightarrow$ hardware (SD of hardware and software) $\longrightarrow$ controller (SD of devices).

The specification of the concept "device" is shown in Fig. 8.

Fig. 8. The absolute "device"

A device is the maximum class of objects of research in the Subject domain of devices. It is worth considering that the knowledge base includes the internationalization of systems of concepts necessary for the end-user of this system. In this case, an employee of a manufacturing enterprise or an engineering company may be the end-user. It is possible to map back not only the concepts of the same subject domain but also the interrelations of the subject domains themselves.

Let us consider the concept "discrete instrument" from the Subject domain of instruments, which is also a subclass of the device class. It has the main identifier in three languages – Russian, English, and Ukrainian – and a single system one. The "instrument" class includes entities of the "discrete instrument" class. The definition of this concept is given in a hypertext format with links to the used concepts described in the knowledge base. Different understanding of this term is incorrect, and it is inadvisable to divide it into synonyms or homonyms (Fig. 9, 10 and 11).

Fig. 9. The absolute "discrete instrument"

An outstanding feature of the knowledge base, according to the ISA-5.1 standard, is the usage of logical formulas that allow describing logical conformities, which characterize the features of the entities being described. Within the knowledge base consistent with the ISA-5.1 standard, the most interesting from this point of view are the features of binary logical elements, which are central to

application software

⇒ main identifier*:

application software ⋯

∈ key sc-element:

> **Application software** is an *software* specific to a user application that is *configurable* and in general contains logic sequences, permissive and limit expressions, control algorithms, and other code required to control the appropriate input, output, calculations, and decisions; see also *software*.

∈ not maximum class of explored objects':
Subject domain of hardware and software

Fig. 10. The absolute "software"

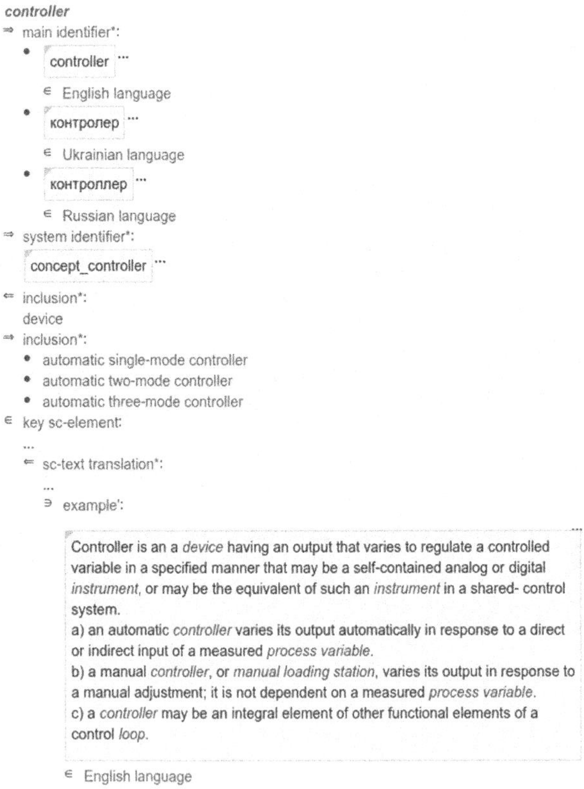

controller

⇒ main identifier*:

- controller ⋯

  ∈ English language

- контролер ⋯

  ∈ Ukrainian language

- контроллер ⋯

  ∈ Russian language

⇒ system identifier*:

concept_controller ⋯

⇐ inclusion*:
device

⇒ inclusion*:

- automatic single-mode controller
- automatic two-mode controller
- automatic three-mode controller

∈ key sc-element:

⋯

⇐ sc-text translation*:

⋯

∋ example':

> Controller is an *device* having an output that varies to regulate a controlled variable in a specified manner that may be a self-contained analog or digital *instrument*, or may be the equivalent of such an *instrument* in a shared- control system.
> a) an automatic *controller* varies its output automatically in response to a direct or indirect input of a measured *process variable*.
> b) a manual *controller*, or *manual loading station*, varies its output in response to a manual adjustment; it is not dependent on a measured *process variable*.
> c) a *controller* may be an integral element of other functional elements of a control *loop*.

∈ English language

Fig. 11. The absolute "controller"

the Subject domain of instruments and are the basis of hardware and software of formulating. To write logical statements about binary logical elements, the SCL – a sublanguage of the SC-code – was used. As an example, let us consider a qualified logical element OR, equal to "n" (Fig. 12).

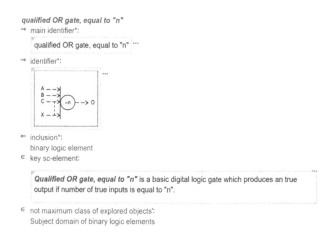

Fig. 12. The semantic neighborhood of the "qualified logical element OR, equal to n" concept

A device KB fragment can be a semantic neighborhood of a certain concept, which includes an identifier both in text format and in the form of an illustration adopted by the ISA-5.1 standard, a definition, a class membership, and a logical formula describing the principle of operation of this device.

A logical formula is a structure that contains sc-variables. An atomic formula is a logical formula that does not contain logical connectives. By default, the existential quantifier is superposed on sc-variables within the atomic logical formula. Thus, the formula below means that there is a _gate entity that is a qualified logical element OR, equal to "n", which has a set of inputs of power "n", and if at least one input has the logical value "true", then the output of the formula is also "true" (Fig. 13).

4   Examples of the System of Formulating Operation with the Display of Information in Natural Languages

In order for the information to be clear and understandable to the reader, it must be presented in a unified form. The system interface for recipe production allows you to display the structures of subject areas and ontologies in natural language. Such a translation procedure from the internal representation of knowledge to the external one is performed by the graphical interface component.

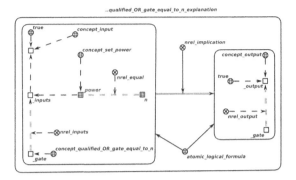

Fig. 13. The logical formula of the "qualified logical element OR, equal to n" concept

As examples of the usage of the component, answers to questions in any language can serve. In Figs. 14 and 15, a variant of the section decomposition for the SD of formulating enterprises in the SCn-editor and in natural language, respectively, is shown.

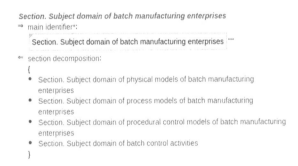

Fig. 14. The section decomposition for the SD of formulating enterprises in SCn

The system should also be able not only to localize and display the necessary knowledge, but also to initiate a dialogue and interact with the user. The dialogue between the system and users can be built on the basis of the question-answer mode. A natural language question can be any of the standard questions to the ostis system. The Figs. 16 and 17 provide an answer to the question about the set to which the indicated concept belongs and about the roles it performs in this set.

With the help of the translation component of knowledge base fragments into natural language, it is possible to represent the semantic neighborhoods of absolute and relative concepts in the knowledge base of the system. Knowledge about the concepts "apparatus" and "equipment phase" can have the forms of representation contained in the Figs. 18, 19, 20 and 21 respectively.

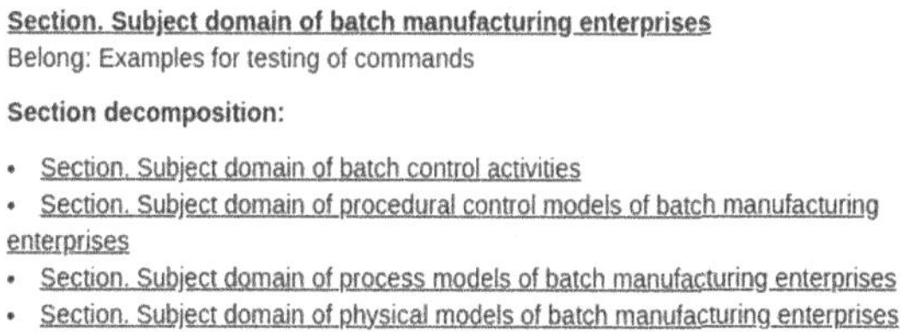

Section. Subject domain of batch manufacturing enterprises
Belong: Examples for testing of commands
Section decomposition:
Section. Subject domain of batch control activities
Section. Subject domain of procedural control models of batch manufacturing enterprises
Section. Subject domain of process models of batch manufacturing enterprises
Section. Subject domain of physical models of batch manufacturing enterprises

Fig. 15. The section decomposition for the SD of formulating enterprises in English

Элементом каких множеств является формовка творожной массы и какие роли она там выполняет
формовка творожной массы
∈ немаксимальный класс объектов исследования':
Предметная область семантики языка PFC

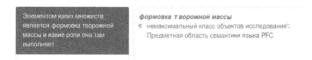

Fig. 16. The answer to the question "What sets is the molding of the curd mass an element of and what roles does it take on there?" in SCn

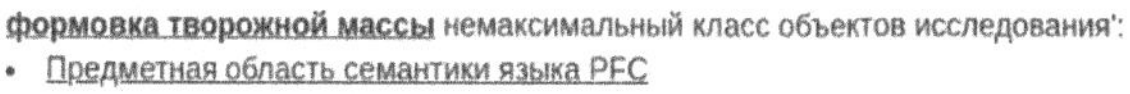

формовка творожной массы немаксимальный класс объектов исследования':
Предметная область семантики языка PFC

Fig. 17. The answer to the question "What sets is the molding of the curd mass an element of and what roles does it take on there?" in the Russian language

unit
⇒ main identifier*:
unit
⇐ inclusion*:
equipment_entity
∈ key sc-element:
технологічний вузол
unit
∈ not maximum class of explored objects':
Subject domain of physical models of batch manufacturing enterprises

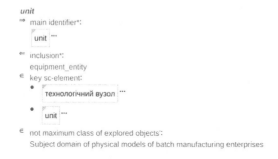

Fig. 18. The absolute "unit" in SCn

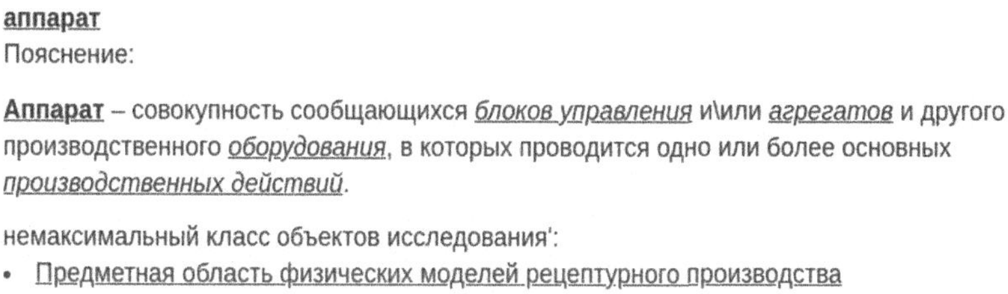

аппарат
Пояснение:
Аппарат – совокупность сообщающихся блоков управления и\или агрегатов и другого производственного оборудования, в которых проводится одно или более основных производственных действий.
немаксимальный класс объектов исследования':
Предметная область физических моделей рецептурного производства

Fig. 19. The absolute "unit" in the Russian language

equipment phase
⇒ main identifier*:

> equipment phase ⋯

⟺ inclusion*:
  atomic procedural element
∈ key sc-element:

> A *phase* that is part of *equipment control.* ⋯

∈ not maximum class of explored objects':
  Subject domain of procedural control models of batch manufacturing enterprises

Fig. 20. The absolute "equipment phase" in SCn

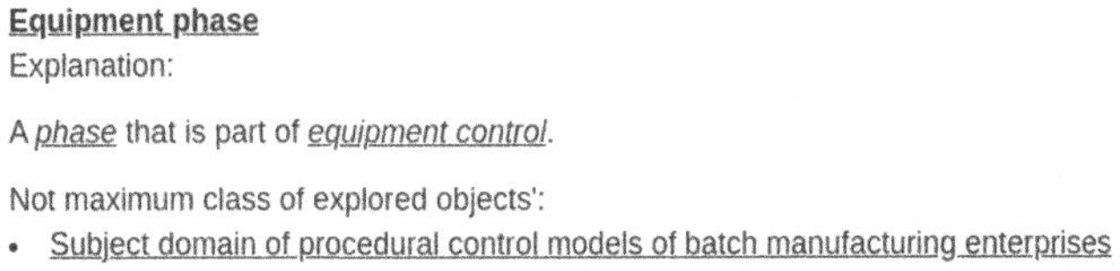

Equipment phase
Explanation:

A *phase* that is part of *equipment control*.

Not maximum class of explored objects':
  • Subject domain of procedural control models of batch manufacturing enterprises

Fig. 21. The absolute "equipment phase" in the English language

The main problem in the development of this component is the need to expand the vocabulary of key concepts used to build links between fragments of the neighborhoods of other concepts. The possibility of internationalization of concept systems gives rise to the problem of storing and presenting the means used to discover and build such relationships.

5   Conclusion

In the article, standards and documents for the development of DT from leading industry organizations and committees – ISO/IEC, W3C – are considered. Both in standards and in DT applied developments, semantic and ontological networks are proposed to combine and formalize heterogeneous parts of DT. However, there is no single systematic solution nowadays.

The principles of building up a system for automating the activities of a process engineer based on the ontological approach within the Industry 4.0 concept are highlighted. The developed system includes a number of international industrial standards that are used to build a subject domain, and therefore the system can easily be combined with other ontological subject domains of the enterprise (MOM, ERP, etc.). The complex of tools and methods for developing ontology bases on the ground of the OSTIS Technology is a powerful tool for designing systems of formulating enterprises. The technology used, with many of its principles and the resulting advantages over other technologies, allows developing and multiplying the potential of existing formulating systems. At present, the complex of information management systems is not just a knowledge base with a subsystem for processing user, including engineering, issues – it also has the right to be considered as a complete help system of a process engineer. The general purpose of the following problems of system design is to achieve the maximum level of integration of the accumulated knowledge. The need for knowledge bases for manufacturing is not restricted to the above. Among the most complex problems that can be solved using knowledge bases grounded on ontologies, there are:

– decision support in unforeseen situations as well as start-ups and ends;
– the determination of equipment failures and their causes;
– integration between systems with different data representation and functions of engineering problems.

Thus, such an ontological model of the enterprise is an integral part of the digital twin of the entire enterprise.

Acknowledgment. The authors thank the Departments of Intelligent Information Technologies of the Belarusian State University of Informatics and Radioelectronics (Minsk) and the Brest State Technical University (Brest) as well as the Department of Automation and Computer Technologies of Control Systems of the National University of Food Technologies (Kyiv) for the help and valuable comments.

References

1. ISO/IEC TR 30166:2020. Internet of Things (IoT) - Industrial IoT. https://www.iso.org/standard/53286.html
2. Knowledge Base for the ISA-88 Standard. https://github.com/savushkin-r-d/s88-ostis
3. Smart Manufacturing - Reference Architecture Model Industry 4.0 (RAMI 4.0). http://webstore.iec.ch/preview/info_iecpas630887Bed1.07Den.pdf
4. Smart Manufacturing - Reference Architecture Model Industry 4.0 (RAMI 4.0). https://www.plattform-i40.de/IP/Redaktion/EN/Downloads/Publikation/Details_of_the-_Asset_Administration_Shell_Part1_V3.html
5. SPECIFICATION Details of the Asset Administration Shell. Part 1 - The Exchange of Information between Partners in the Value Chain of Industrie 4.0. https://www.researchgate.net/publication/330142853
6. SPECIFICATION Details of the Asset Administration Shell. Part 2 - Interoperability at Runtime - Exchanging Information via Application Programming Interfaces (Version 1.0RC02). https://www.plattform-i40.de/IP/Redaktion/EN/Downloads/Publikation/Details_of_the-_Asset_Administration_Shell_Part2_V1.pdf?__blob=publicationFile-&v=6
7. World Wide Web Consortium (W3C). Resource description framework. Model and syntax specification (1999). https://www.w3.org/TR/1999/REC-rdf-syntax-19990222/
8. World Wide Web Consortium (W3C). Resource Description Framework (RDF) Schema Specification (1999). https://www.w3.org/TR/WD-rdf-schema/
9. ISO 18629 PSL: Industrial Automation Systems and Integration (ISO TC 184 SC4) - Process Specification Language (2004). https://www.iso.org/obp/ui/fr/#iso:std:iso:18629:-1:ed-1:en

10. GOST P/ISO 15926–1-2008 Integration of Life Cycle Data for Processing Enterprises, Including Oil and Gas Production Enterprises (2008). https://docs.cntd.ru/document/1200076803
11. World Wide Web Consortium (W3C). OWL 2 Web Ontology Language. Structural Specification and Functional-Style Syntax, 2nd edn (2012). https://www.w3.org/TR/2012/REC-owl2-syntax-20121211/
12. Descriptive Ontology for Linguistic and Cognitive Engineering (DOLCE) (2013). http://www.loa.istc.cnr.it/dolce/overview.html
13. General Formal Ontology (GFO) (2013). https://github.com/Onto-Med/GFO
14. World Wide Web Consortium (W3C): RIF Overview, 2nd edn (2013). https://www.w3.org/TR/rif-overview
15. World Wide Web Consortium (W3C). SPARQL 1.1 Overview (2013). https://www.w3.org/TR/2013/REC-sparql11-overview-20130321/
16. Zachman Enterprise Ontology (ZEO). (2013). https://www.zachman.com/resources/zblog/item/the-zachman-framework-requires-zero-documentation
17. GOST/ISO 22745-1-2016 - Open Technical Dictionaries and Their Application to the Main Data (2016). https://docs.cntd.ru/document/1200143361
18. Meta Object Facility (MOF) (2016). https://www.omg.org/spec/MOF/
19. World Wide Web Consortium (W3C): Semantic Sensor Network Ontology (2017). https://www.w3.org/TR/vocab-ssn/#Sampling-overview
20. Digital Twins for Industrial Applications, an Industrial Internet Consortium White Paper (2018). https://www.iiconsortium.org/pdf/IIC_Digital_Twins_Industrial_Apps_White_Paper_2020-02-18.pdf
21. ISO 20534: 2018 Industrial Automation Systems and Integration - Formal Semantic Models for the Configuration of Global Production Networks (2018). https://www.iso.org/standard/68274.html
22. ISO 15926 Industrial Automation Systems and Integration - Integration of Life-Cycle Data for Process Plants Including Oil and Gas Production Facilities (2019). https://www.iso.org/standard/68200.html
23. World Wide Web Consortium (W3C) (2020). Time Ontology in OWL. https://www.w3.org/TR/owl-time/
24. World Wide Web Consortium (W3C). Web of Things (WoT) Thing Description (2020). https://www.w3.org/TR/wot-thing-description/
25. ISA5.1 Standard (2021). https://www.isa.org/standards-and-publications/isa-standards/isa-standards-committees/isa5-1/
26. ISA88 Standard (2021). https://www.isa.org/isa88/
27. ISO/IEC 21838–1:2021 Industrial Automation Systems and Integration - Open Technical Dictionaries and Their Application to Master Data (2021). https://www.iso.org/standard/71954.html
28. Arp, R., Smith, B., Spear, A.D.: Building Ontologies with Basic Formal Ontology. MIT Press, Cambridge, August 2015. http://basic-formal-ontology.org/
29. Boss, B., et al.: Digital twin and Asset Administration Shell Concepts and Application in the Industrial Internet and Industrie 4.0, an Industrial Internet Consortium and Plattform Industrie 4.0 Joint. White Paper (2020)
30. DigitalTwinSystems. https://www.digitaltwinconsortium.org/glossary/index.htm#digital-twin-system
31. Golenkov, V.V., Gulyakina, N.A.: Semantic technology of component design of knowledge-driven systems. In: Golenkov, V. (ed.) Open Semantic Technologies for Intelligent Systems, pp. 42–50. Belarusian State University of Informatics and Radioelectronics Publ, Minsk (2015)

32. Golenkov, V.V., Gulyakina, N.A., Davydenko, I.T., Shunkevich, D.V.: Semantic model of knowledge base representation and processing. In: Data Analytics and Management in Data-Intensive Fields: A Collection of Scientific Papers of the XIX International Conference. DAMDID. Federal Research Center "Informatics and Management" of the Russian Academy of Sciences, Moscow (2017). https://libeldoc.bsuir.by/handle/123456789/29503

33. Grieves, M.: Digital twin: manufacturing excellence through virtual factory replication. White Paper (2015)

34. IMS Metasystem. http://ims.ostis.net

35. Jordan, A., Selway, M., Mayer, W., Grossmann, G., Stumptner, M.: An ontological core for conformance checking in the engineering life-cycle (2014). https://15926.org/topics/

36. Knowledge Base for the ISA-5.1 Standard. https://github.com/savushkin-r-d/isa-5.1-ostis

37. Lutskaya, N., Vlasenko, L., Zaiets, N., Shtepa, V.: Ontological aspects of developing robust control systems for technological objects. ICO 2020. In: Advances in Intelligent Systems and Computing, vol. 1324, pp. 358–371 (2020). https://doi.org/10.1007/978-3-030-68154-8_107

38. Niles, I., Pease, A.: Towards a standard upper ontology systems. In: Niles, I. (ed.) Proceedings of the International Conference on Formal Ontology in Information, pp. 2–9. Las-Vegas: Nevada (2001)

39. Reections Digital Twin Consortium. https://blog.digitaltwinconsortium.org/2020/12/digital-twin-consortium-denes-digital-twin.html

40. Shunkevich, D.V.: Models and means of knowledge processing machines component design on basis of semantic networks. In: Golenkov, V. (ed.) Open Semantic Technologies for Intelligent Systems, pp. 269–280. Belarusian State University of Informatics and Radioelectronics Publ., Minsk (2013). https://libeldoc.bsuir.by/handle/123456789/4366

41. Taberko, V.V., et al.: Design principles of integrated information services for batch manufacturing enterprise employees. In: Golenkov, V. (ed.) Open Semantic Technologies for Intelligent Systems. pp. 215–224. Belarusian State University of Informatics and Radioelectronics Publication (2019)

42. Taberko, V.V., Ivanyuk, D.S., Shunkevich, D.V., Pupena, A.N.: Principles for enhancing the development and use of standards within Industry 4.0. In: Golenkov, V. (ed.) Open Semantic Technologies for Intelligent Systems, pp. 167–174. Belarusian State University of Informatics and Radioelectronics Publication (2020)

The Approach to the Evaluation of Telecommunications Company Functioning Quality

Globa Larysa[(⊠)] [iD], Novogrudska Rina[(⊠)] [iD], and Moroz Anastasia[iD]

National Technical University of Ukraine, Igor Sikorsky Kyiv Polytechnic Institute,
Kyiv, Ukraine
lgloba@its.kpi.ua, rinan@ukr.net

Abstract. The paper presents the approach to the evaluation of telecommunications companies functioning quality. The use of such approach can help in increasing the efficiency of identifying factors and patterns of statistical data sets that affect the subscriber's decision to stop using the services of a mobile operator. Through the research machine learning methods as: associative rules, decision trees and bagging were considered. Input data from one of the largest mobile operators on Ukraine were analyzed. The method for determining the outflow of subscribers from a mobile operator using a set of machine learning methods was proposed. Patterns and factors were identified that most affect the subscriber's decision to refuse the services of a telecom operator.

Keywords: Telecom operator · Quality assessment · Customer churn · Data Mining · Modeling

1 Introduction

The billing model, in which the collection and processing of data was carried out by one specialized automated billing system that perfors only finensial calculations, does not satisfy the needs of the telecom operator. It is being replaced by models where a separate system is involved in collecting, processing and preparing data. The main reasons for the development of such a system are:

- The market demands from the operator a variety of offered tariff plans and service packages, quick commissioning of services, and therefore carrying out various analyzes of the accumulated data and according to various criteria.
- Telecom operators are forced to provide services on dissimilar equipment, which significantly complicates the collection of statistics through a variety of accounting data formats.
- Large telecom operators are expanding geographically to include regional companies. This leads to a sharp increase in heterogeneous equipment and the volume of accounting data.

V. Golenkov et al. (Eds.): OSTIS 2021, CCIS 1625, pp. 336–348, 2022.
https://doi.org/10.1007/978-3-031-15882-7_17

At the same time, there is a need for centralized accounting of the provided communication services in the conditions of operation of several different billing systems in the regions. In the course of their development, operators developed their own data preprocessing systems. The complexity of the operation of such systems lies in the need for their constant revision in connection with the emergence of new services, new equipment, and changes in the data formats coming from the equipment. In this case, the operator is forced to use the resources of a team of highly qualified programmers to constantly improve the system. A standard situation is when the data preprocessing is carried out by various systems at a telecom provider company.

With the modern development of telecommunications, systems that calculate the consumed services by users provided on the basis of one or another telecommunications equipment have received the same development. Such systems are usually called billing systems [1]. Their main purpose is to display the number of services consumed by the subscriber and write off funds in accordance with the cost per service unit. Based on this, it is possible to give a definition: billing system (BS) is a software complex that records the volume of services consumed by subscribers, calculates and debits funds, according to tariffs. In terms of relationships with content providers, the billing system must provide the following capabilities: firstly, it must guarantee the transmission of information to partners about the use of their services by specific subscribers, and secondly, bill the end consumer for using the service (or the content provider independently issues an invoice).

In the context of the rapid development of the communication network, replacement and addition of switching equipment, the provision of new types of services, it becomes expedient to switch to an industrial solution of data preprocessing problems. Products of this class have long been successfully used by large operators in countries with developed communication infrastructure. They are called Mediation systems. Mediation systems represent the level between the network infrastructure and OSS/BSS (Operation Support System/Business Support System) systems. The main purpose of Mediation systems is to transform data received from network elements into information that can be interpreted by the billing system and other business systems of the operator. Also, such systems are called previous billing systems.

In the context of sustainable development of telecommunications, as well as the presence of a sufficient number of provider companies in the telecom services market, important tasks are to assess the quality of telecom operators' functioning and develop a strategy to prevent subscriber churn. However, for this it is necessary to increase the level of intellectualization of OSS/BSS systems and to include in their structure tools for processing and analyzing large volumes of accumulated data.

2 State of Art and Background

2.1 Customer Relationship Management and Strategies to Prevent Customer Churn in Telecom Communications

Currently, the usual methods of increasing the loyalty of old customers and attracting new customers (mass advertising, traditional marketing, low prices) do not produce the desired positive result. That is why concepts that allow personalized sales of goods and services are becoming a priority all over the world.

As an example can be used Customer Relationship Management (CRM) [2]. CRM is not a technology or software product. This is a business strategy based on a customer-oriented [3] approach, that is, we can say that the main task of CRM is to increase and improve the efficiency of business processes, directly aimed at attracting new and retaining existing customers [4].

Technologically, a CRM system is a collection of software products linked into a single entire and integrated into the informational environment of a company. Any CRM system has the following main functions:

- Collection of information.
- Storage, processing and analysis of information for futher export in accordance with the specified criteria.
- Providing information to users.
- Customer relationship managment systems are divided into two classes by the way they are used.
- Operational use systems. They are applied for day-to-day management purposes.
- Analytical systems. Used by marketers to process large amounts of data (in order to gain new knowledge).

According to written above, the following conclusion can be drawn: CRM systems are most effective in those areas of business where it is possible to accumulate a large amount of useful information about each client. Here, the CRM strategy is used primarily to combat customer churn. In telecommunications, this term refers to the process of enticing customers from one telecom operator to another, or simply the outflow of customers from an operator [5]. Annual rates of customer churn reach 25–30%. Operators who have this indicator at the maximum do not receive a return on investment in new subscribers, since it takes about three years to return the funds spent on replacing each lost customer with a new one, that is, to acquire customers [6].

2.2 Overview of the Architecture of the OSS/BSS System and the Prospects for Their Development

ÎSS/BSS – Operation Support System/Business Support System – support systems for the operational and business activities of telecom operators, with the help of full or partial automation of these activities. Operational activities include processes that interact mainly with network equipment and the network, such as: accounting and planning of network resources, management and provision of services, management of quality characteristics of services. Business activities include customer-centric processes such as processing and invoicing, collecting payments, proposing new products, and much more [7].

Business support systems (BSS) also include CRM systems, water treatment, ERP systems.

The main elements of the OSS are the collectors of traffic and telephony statistics with a single rate. Transmission collectors for collecting, aggregating and storing raw data about consumed data services. The number of collectors may vary depending on the size of the network. For the entire OSS/BSS complex, the tariffifier is the only one. It maintains a central user base, stores aggregated information about the services used, on the basis of which funds are debited from subscribers' accounts [7].

The configuration of the OSS/BSS complex is always created based on the needs of a particular enterprise. Expansion of functionality is usually achieved by connecting additional modules.

2.3 Data Mining in Telecommunications

Today, the Data Mining solution [1] is widely used by telecom operators, network operators and Internet providers in order to improve the processing of unstructured large amounts of data for making better decisions in their business. Analytics enables telecommunications providers to significantly improve the cost-effectiveness of their service delivery.

Data Mining models are positioned on a dataset with known results and are used to predict results from other datasets. These are classification models (they describe the rules by which the description of an object can be attributed to one of the classes) and sequence models (they describe functions by which the change in continuous numerical parameters can be predicted). The scope of data mining technology is limited solely by the availability of a large amount of information. Therefore, executives and analysts can gain tangible competitive advantages using this technology.

In telecommunications, it is very important to identify categories of customers with similar stereotypes for using services, as a result, a pricing policy is being developed; analysis of failures; prediction of peak loads. Telecom systems generate an extremely large amount of data that needs to be processed and analyzed. Machine learning mainly uses a range or spectrum based on a method to optimize a large number of parameters.

Thus, Data minning methods are rapidly becoming a very important and widely implemented part of business processes in telecom operator systems [8].

Methods of data mining make it possible to effectively solve the problems of structural engineering design of innovative technical systems in telecommunications [9]. These methods make it possible to interpret the patterns that form the basic rules for including objects in equivalence classes. The use of Data Mining methods for telecommunications companies is necessary for:

- Reducing the computational complexity of big data processing methods for the operator to provide services to a subscriber with a given quality of service.
- Predicting the risks that may arise as a result of the operation of the telecommunications system.
- To be able to identify faults in the system and find out the cause of their occurrence.

Some of the existing algorithms can be adapted to compute large distributed information arrays. At the same time, serious difficulties can arise in the visual presentation of the results – due to the huge amount of information entering the input, the number of different reports at the output increases dramatically.

3   The Method of Telecom Operator Data Clustering

In data mining tasks, using cluster analysis, a complex construction of data for classification is created, patterns are identified, hypotheses are formed and tested, etc. In addition, cluster analysis is often used to identify data that "stands out" from others, since such data correspond to points located at a distance from any cluster. Cluster analysis is used to compress and summarize data. A method for clustering big data of a telecom operator is proposed, the use of which allows assessing the quality of functioning of telecommunication companies [10]. The method uses decision trees, association rules, and bagging to predict customer churn from a carrier. The method proposed in the study allows you to go through all the stages of preparation, processing and analysis of big data of a telecom operator. The method includes next stages:

- Subject domain analysis.
- Problem statement.
- Data preparation.
- Model development.
- Model checking.
- Model selection.
- Model preparation.
- Model updating.

The following systems are responsible for the first three stages: analysis of the subject area, statement of the problem, preparation of data: billing, OSS/BSS. The following steps are performed by the CRM system.

All of the above stages together give a high-quality result in solving the problem of customer churn in the telecommunications sector. This question is very important for doing business and determining the new course of the company.

The first thing to do is to analyze the telecommunications structure. Data that will be processed in the future are collected from network equipment. Further, in order to solve the problem of determining the cause of customer churn, it is necessary to identify which factors influence this, which data components are of the greatest importance.

After collecting the data, they need to be structured. To do this, the "raw" data must go through the following steps:

- Verification.
- Correction.
- Consolidation.
- Filtration.
- Separation.
- Routing.
- Representation.
- Distribution.

The next stage is modeling.

4   Modeling and Predicting the Churn of Telecom Operator Subscribers

The input data for the modeling were real customer data obtained from one of the leading telecom operators in Ukraine (Fig. 1). We will call such data "raw". There are spaces in the data table, which is invalid for analysis. Gaps can introduce additional prediction errors.

ABON_CODE	STATUS	COUNT_DAYS_OVER_1MB	COUNT_DAYS_OVER_5MB	DUAL_SIM_PROBABILITY	SIM_PRIORITY	OBLAST	CITY
1	0			High	SECOND	Donets'ka	Rodyns'ke
2	0			Very high	SECOND	Kharkivs'ka	Izium
3	0			Very high	SECOND	L'vivs'ka	Novoiavorivs'k
4	0			High	SECOND	Kharkivs'ka	Kharkiv
5	0	10	9	Very high	SECOND	Kharkivs'ka	Bohodukhiv
6	0	23	19	Very high	FIRST	Donets'ka	Makiivka
7	0	27	23	Low	FIRST	Kyivs'ka	Kyiv
8	0			Very high	SECOND	Kharkivs'ka	Kharkiv
9	0			Very high	FIRST	Kharkivs'ka	Bilyi Kolodiaz'
10	0			High	SECOND	Kharkivs'ka	Zavhorodnie
11	0			Very high	SECOND	Donets'ka	Artemivs'k
12	0			Very high	SECOND	L'vivs'ka	Kolodentsi
13	0			UNDEF	UNDEF	L'vivs'ka	Khodoriv
14	0			Low	FIRST	Odes'ka	Shyroka Balka
15	0			UNDEF	UNDEF	Kyivs'ka	Kyiv
16	0			Very low	FIRST	L'vivs'ka	Boryslav
17	0			Low	FIRST	Ternopil's'ka	Ternopil'
18	0			High	SECOND	Donets'ka	Makiivka
19	0			High	SECOND	Kyivs'ka	Kyiv
20	0			High	FIRST	Kharkivs'ka	Artil'ne
21	0	6	4	Very high	SECOND	Ternopil's'ka	Romanove Selo
22	0	2		Very high	SECOND	Zhytomyrs'ka	Berdychiv
23	0	4	3	Very low	FIRST	Zakarpats'ka	Chop
24	0			Very high	SECOND	L'vivs'ka	Hirne
25	0			Very high	SECOND	Rivnens'ka	Sarny
26	0	8	7	Low	FIRST	Rivnens'ka	Zdolbuniv
27	0			Very low	FIRST	L'vivs'ka	L'viv
28	0			Very high	SECOND	Mykolaivs'ka	Mykolaiv

Fig. 1. Initial modeling data.

For the correct execution of the process of analyzing the dataset, you need to fill in the gaps that are present in the input table. To do this, use the search function for gaps and fill them with zeros (Fig. 2). Thus, when simulating, we get a high probability of truthful results. As a result, we will receive "preliminary prepared data".

STATUS	COUNT_DAYS_OVER_1MB	...	INET_SLOPE	REFILL_SLOPE
0	0	0.0	...	0.000000	0.000000e+00
1	0	0.0	...	0.022223	-4.350000e-36
2	0	0.0	...	0.046196	3.710257e-02
3	0	0.0	...	-0.026511	3.838383e-02

Fig. 2. Pre-prepared data for modeling.

When modeling customer behavior in order to predict subscriber churn the random forest method was used, with the help of which the modeling is carried out. The random forest is one example of ensemble classifiers. The modeling was performed in the Python programming language. In the course of the study, a sample of subscribers inclined to outflow from the given probabilities was determined (Table 1).

Table 1. Subscribers who are prone to churn.

$N^{\underline{o}}$	prob_true
1977	0.9333
2696	0.9167
2708	0.9233
2924	0.9041

The work uses Data Mining methods: associative rules, decision trees and bagging in order to increase the efficiency of prediction by increasing the accuracy of the probabilities of subscriber churn.

Carrying out further modeling on the data and using the method of associative rules, we get the following results:

Accuracy: 0.7258

Table 2. Partition of the set in accordance with the method of association rules.

	Predicted False	Predicted True
Actual False	1811	747
Actual True	667	1754

When modeling the method of association rules showed the following results, which are reflected in Table 2. This table shows the amount of correctly and incorrectly estimated data. Errors of the first and second order are shown for the Data Mining method, namely, for the method of association rules. Using this data, you can build a graph of the ROC dependence, which is reflected in Fig. 3.

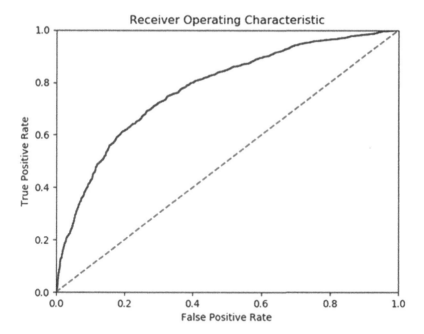

Fig. 3. Plot of ROC-curve for the method of association rules.

Then the simulation was carried out using the decision tree method and the following results were obtained:

Accuracy: 0.7805

Table 3. Partitioning of the set in accordance with the decision tree method.

	Predicted False	Predicted True
Actual False	2044	459
Actual True	650	1838

When modeling, the decision tree method showed the following results, which are reflected in Table 3. This table shows the amount of correctly and incorrectly estimated data. Errors of the first and second order are shown for the Data Mining method, namely, for the decision tree method. Using these data, we will build a graph of the ROC dependence, which is reflected in Fig. 4.

Then the simulation was carried out using the Bagging method and the following results were obtained:

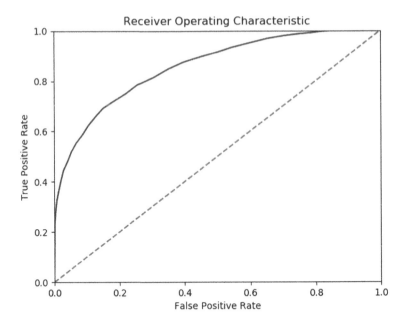

Fig. 4. Plot of the ROC-curve for the decision tree method.

Accuracy: 0.7884

Table 4. Partitioning of the set according to the bagging method.

	Predicted False	Predicted True
Actual False	2009	493
Actual True	664	1832

When modeling, the decision tree method showed the following results, which are reflected in Table 4. This table shows the amount of correctly and incorrectly estimated data. Errors of the first and second order are shown for the Data Mining method, namely, for the decision tree method. Using this data, we will build a graph of the ROC dependence, which is reflected in Fig. 5.

It was found that the bagging method allows you to get more accurate results, by 7% compared to the method of association rules and up to 1% better than the value of the metric of the decision tree method, the accuracy of the results obtained is 78.84%.

Also, in the process of modeling, the problem of identifying the factors that most affect the decision of the subscriber to switch to the services of another telecommunications company was solved. The modeling revealed the following

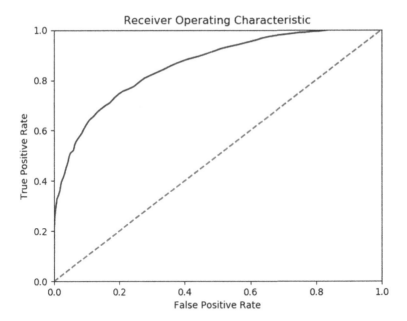

Fig. 5. ROC chart for Bagging method.

parameters that most affect the churn of customers, they are presented in Table 5. These parameters are:

- duration of using the services of the telecommunications company;
- the number of days during which the subscriber does not use the services;
- average value of all days during which the subscriber does not use services;
- average value of all active days outgoing calls to numbers of other mobile operators.

The simulation revealed the subscribers who are most susceptible to the transition to the services of another telecommunications company. Table 6 shows a sample of subscribers prone to churn from a mobile operator. The churn rate percentage is shown next to each subscriber. It can be concluded that, based on the consideration of these data, it is possible to influence individual users and provide each of them with those services in which the subscriber is most interested. This way you can prevent customer churn.

Based on the values of the probability of the outflow of telecommunication network subscribers, a classification was proposed, which is presented in Table 7.

According to the classification, all subscribers are divided into groups with a corresponding churn probability. Thanks to this information, telecom operators can prevent customer churn by introducing amendments to their business plan that take into account the groups of subscribers with the highest propensity to churn ("high" and "very high" indicators of the probability of subscriber churn)

Table 5. Impact of parameters on the customer churn process

№	importance	labels
3 2	0.075648	Duration of using the services of the telecommunications company
2 3	0.068619	The number of days during which the subscriber does not use the services
2 1	0.060132	Average value of all days during which the subscriber does not use services
2 2	0.055328	Average of all active days
1 9	0.045268	Outgoing calls to numbers of other mobile operators

Table 6. Subscribers who are prone to churn.

№	prob_true
13788	0.99256
13859	0.99121
17185	0.98286
11595	0.95789
10842	0.94865

and by offering the most favorable terms of cooperation for of these groups, in turn, will satisfy the needs of the subscriber.

Table 7. Classification of subscribers according to the propensity to churn.

The indicator of the probability of subscriber churn	Percent
Very low	Up to 20%
Low	Up to 50%
Average	Up to 70%
High	Up to 90%
Vety high	Above 90%

The results of modeling and predictions regarding the solution of the problem, as well as the analysis of these parameters for accuracy and reliability for different algorithms are presented in Table 8. Analysis of the results allows us to draw the following conclusions: among the selected methods, the Bagging method shows the best result, the results of which are up to 7% better than the metric value of the association rule method and is up to 1% better than the metric value of the decision tree method. It outperforms the association rule method in its completeness, accuracy, and truthfulness of forecasting, and outperforms the decision tree method in processing speed.

Table 8. The value of the metrics obtained for the considered methods.

Model	precision	recall	F1	F0.5	Accuracy
Association rules	0,710	0,733	0,718	0,711	0.7258
Decision trees	0,803	0,75	0,776	0,792	0.7805
Bagging	0,825	0,759	0,776	0,799	0.7884

Conclusion

A telecom operator collects large amounts of data in the course of its work; for full processing, this data must be structured. Large amounts of data are processed using systems: OSS/BSS, billing, CRM. Correct storage, structuring and analysis of this data in aggregate with high accuracy allows predicting the behavior of the subscriber and his use of the operator's services, as well as the possibility of the subscriber's transition to another operator.

Mathematical modeling for predicting customer churn was performed using the methods of association rules, decision trees and bagging. Such methods allowes to get more accurate results, by 7% compared to the method of association rules and up to 1% better than the value of the metric of the decision tree method, the accuracy of the results obtained is 78.84%. Also, as a result of the study, patterns and factors were identified that most affect the subscriber's decision to refuse the services of a telecom operator.

The use of data obtained in the course of research is especially effective at the stage of concluding an agreement with a client, which allows you to build relationships with a client in the most beneficial way for the company.

References

1. Nechiporuk, D.V.: Features of Data Mining Technology, Don State Technical University, Rostov-on-Don, Russian Federation
2. Skorbota, V.S.: How Ukrainians choose a mobile operator (2017). https://biz.nv.ua/experts/skorbota/kak-ukraintsy-vybirajut-mobilnogo-operatora-1930612.html
3. Dyakonov, P.V.: Handbook on the Use of the PC MATLAB System. Fiz-Matlit, Moscow (1993)
4. Palmov, S.V.: Comparison of the capabilities of various methods of Data Mining technology in the analysis of personal traffic. XII Russian Scientific Conference of Professors and Teaching Staff, Researchers and Graduate Students, Samara, PDATU, thesis, pp. 285–287 (2005)

5. Sasaki, Y.: The truth of the F-measure, 26 October 2007
6. Scholl, F.: Deep Learning in R. Peter Publishing House, St. Petersburg (2018)
7. Alexander, S., Larysa, G., Tetiana, K.: Applying business process modeling method when telecommunication services development. In: 2011 21st International Crimean Conference "Microwave & Telecommunication Technology", pp. 457–458. IEEE (2011)
8. Globa, L.S., Novogrudska, R.L., Koval, A.V.: Ontology model of telecom operator big data. In: Proceedings of IEEE International Black Sea Conference on Communication and Networking (BlackSeaCom), pp. 1–5 (2018). https://doi.org/10.1109/BlackSeaCom.2018.8433710
9. Breiman, L.: Random Forests, Machine Learning, $N^{\underline{o}}$, vol. 45, pp. 5–32, October 2001
10. Buhaienko, Y., Globa, L.S., Liashenko, A., Grebinechenko, M.: Analysis of clustering algorithms for use in the universal data processing system. In: Open Semantic Technologies for Intelligent Systems. Research Papers Collection, Issue 4, Belarusian State University of Informatics and Radioelectronics, Minsk, pp. 101–104 (2020)

Methodological and Technical Solutions for the Implementation of Clustering Algorithms in the GeoBazaDannych System

Valery Taranchuk$^{(\boxtimes)}$

Belarusian State University, Nezavisimosti avenue, 4, 220030 Minsk, Belarus
`Taranchuk@bsu.by`

Abstract. In this paper, from the perspective of creating and maintaining geological or geoecological models, methodological and technical issues, ways of developing the system GeoBazaDannych (GBD), expanding its functionality are considered. The new functionality provided by the inclusion of executable data mining modules of the Wolfram Mathematica computer algebra system into the GBD is noted. In particular, it illustrates tools for preparing benchmark geodata sets for validating, testing, and evaluating related neural network models. Examples on representative data sets illustrate options for choosing the best clustering algorithms.

Examples of representative datasets illustrate the options for choosing the best clustering algorithms. A series of calculations illustrate the effects of choosing the number of clusters, the clustering method, and metrics. Separately, options are considered when clustering takes into account not only the coordinates of observation points, but also the values in them.

Keywords: System GeoBazaDannych · Intelligent adaptation of digital fields · Clustering

1 Introduction

Digital geological, geoecological models are now a mandatory component of expertise in many areas, they occur in oil and gas production, in chemical industries, in the treatment of municipal and industrial liquid waste, in the construction industry, in biotechnology and many other industrie. Geological modeling includes the improvement of mathematical methods and algorithms; development of computer programs that provide a cycle of creating models; database design, their filling and maintenance. The data used in geological and geoecological models are a representative part of the geodata, which classify, summarize information about processes and phenomena on the earth's surface [1].

The features of solving the problems of developing and implementing computer-based geological and geoecological models with the means of their adaptation and self-adjustment, the main approaches to processing, analysis,

V. Golenkov et al. (Eds.): OSTIS 2021, CCIS 1625, pp. 349–360, 2022.
https://doi.org/10.1007/978-3-031-15882-7_18

interpretation of the data used and obtained are noted in [2–5]. It is emphasized that at this stage, data mining is among the priority areas of research and development, the corresponding classes of systems for its implementation are listed [6]. The mentioned publications [2–5] provide several basic solutions to the issues of preprocessing, intelligent analysis of geodata by means of the computer system GeoBazaDannych. The results and methodological recommendations of cluster analysis of geodata obtained with the environment of the system GeoBazaDannych are discussed below.

The solution to the problem of cluster analysis (segmentation) [7,8] is the partitions that satisfy the accepted criterion. The criterion is usually a functionally formalized set of rules for determining the levels of differences in partitions and groupings (the objective function). In data mining, segmentation can be used as an independent tool for making decisions about data distribution, for monitoring characteristics and subsequent analysis of data sets of certain clusters. Alternatively, cluster analysis can serve as a preprocessing stage for other algorithms. Segmentation is also used to detect atypical outlier objects (values that are "far" from any cluster), in other words, it is a novelty detection, such objects may be more interesting than those included in clusters. An important advantage of cluster analysis is that when it is performed, it is possible to divide objects not only by one parameter, but by a set of features. In addition, cluster analysis, unlike most mathematical and statistical methods, does not impose any restrictions on the type of source data under consideration.

It is well known that cluster analysis is widely used in many fields, in particular, in computer systems for pattern recognition, image analysis, information retrieval, data compression, computer graphics, bioinformatics, machine learning. The educational aspect should be noted separately. For example, in [9] it is emphasized that any activity in the field of artificial intelligence combines a high degree of research intensity, the complexity of engineering work, and involves highly qualified performers. The combination of fundamental scientific and engineering-practical training of specialists is a complex educational and pedagogical problem. When learning specialists in the field of artificial intelligence, it is necessary to simultaneously form their research and engineering-practical skills, an understanding of the high demands on the quality and reliability of the results and conclusions obtained. Representative examples are given below and cluster analysis tools implemented in the GeoBazaDannych system environment [10] are noted.

2   Brief Information About the Software System GeoBazaDannych

The interactive computer system GeoBazaDannych is the complex of intelligent computer subsystems, mathematical, algorithmic and software for filling, maintaining and visualizing databases, input data for simulation and mathematical models, tools for conducting computational experiments, algorithmic tools and software for creating continuously updated computer models.

By means of the system GeoBazaDannych, it is possible to generate and visualize digital descriptions of spatial distributions of data on sources of contamination, on the geological structure of the studied objects; graphically illustrate solutions to problems describing the dynamic processes of multiphase filtration, fluid migration, heat transfer, moisture, and mineral water-soluble compounds in rock strata; design and implement interactive scenarios for visualization and processing the results of computational experiments GeoBazaDannych subsystems allow you to calculate and perform expert assessments of local and integral characteristics of ecosystems in different approximations, calculate distributions of concentrations and mass balances of pollutants; create permanent models of oil production facilities; generate and display thematic maps on hard copies

The main components of the system GeoBazaDannych [4, 5, 10]:

- the data generator Gen_DATv;
- the generator and editor of thematic maps and digital fields Gen_MAPw;
- the software package Geo_mdl – mathematical, algorithmic and software tools for building geological models of soil layers, multi-layer reservoirs;
- software and algorithmic support for the formation and maintenance of permanent hydrodynamic models of multiphase filtration in porous, fractured media;
- modules for three-dimensional visualization of dynamic processes of distribution of water-soluble pollutants in active soil layers;
- modules for organizing and supporting the operation of geographic information systems in interactive or batch modes;
- software and algorithmic support for the formation and maintenance of permanent hydrodynamic models of multiphase filtration in porous, fractured media;
- the Generator of the geological model of a deposit (GGMD) – the integrated software complex of the composer of digital geological and geoecological models, which includes software components:
  - • tools and patterns for preparation of reference (calibration) model of digital field, which corresponds to the specified properties ("Digital field constructor");
  - • tools and several options of "distortion" of reference model;
  - • tools for data capture simulation, which are used in simulation practice ("Generator of profile observer");
  - • modules for calculation, visualization, comparison of digital fields approximation by several different methods ("Approximation component");
  - • tools and adaptation modules for digital model being formed ("Adaptation component");
  - • clustering tools.

To explain the novelty of the results presented in this paper, we note that [4, 5] provide examples of interactive formation of digital models of geological objects in computational experiments that meet the intuitive requirements of the expert Examples of approximation and reconstruction of the digital field, its interactive adaptation by means of the system GeoBazaDannych were discussed. The

examples of approximation and reconstruction of the digital field, its interactive adaptation by means of the system GeoBazaDannych and evaluation of the accuracy of results using the tools of the GGMD complex illustrate the unique capabilities of the developed methods and software. In [2,3] the results of the use of artificial neural networks in the analysis and interpretation of geospatial data are presented and discussed, the possibilities of obtaining and visualizing errors are described. This paper discusses variants and provides tools for implementing cluster analysis of geodata in the environment of the system GeoBazaDannych; recommendations are given for choosing the optimal parameters of classification algorithms when dividing the studied objects and features into groups that are homogeneous in the accepted sense.

3   Preparation of Source Data

The examples below are calculated with the data [5] for surface *zSurfF*. Explanations of why exactly such a surface is representative of the corresponding class of models are given in [5]. It is noted which disturbances of the base surface are added, and how the possibilities of their numerical description are analyzed by approximation based on the results of measurements on a scattered set of points. Figure 1 illustrates the used expression, it shows: the surface on the left and the volume bounded by it on the right.

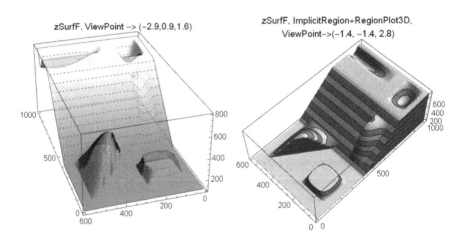

Fig. 1. Visualization of the *zSurfF* reference surface in the Plot3D and RegionPlot3D variants.

For clarity, Fig. 2 shows the isolines (contour lines) of the *zSurfF* levels. Also, signatures of the form (1), ..., (5) indicate the positions of perturbations of the base surface – they will be the objects of search during clustering.

Data for demonstration of methods and algorithms of intellectual analysis are obtained by simulation of measurements – the main is shown in Fig. 3.

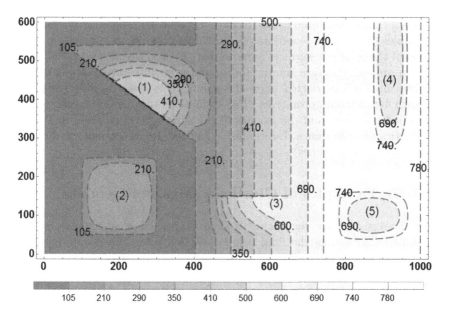

Fig. 2. Contour map of the reference surface *zSurfF*.

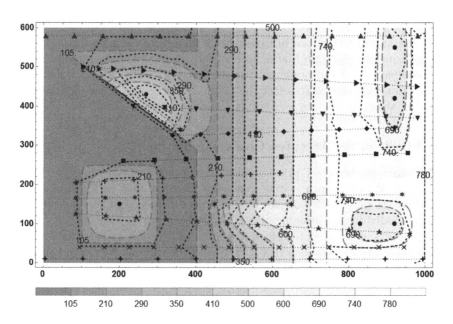

Fig. 3. A scheme of points with level measurements, a map of isolines of the reference and reconstructed surfaces. (Color figure online)

The data shown and used below in computational experiments, the calculated set of triples of numbers (coordinates and values) are points with the values of the level of the reference surface, representing (in fact) a scattered set of points. In this approach, they are interpreted as data on observation profiles, which are shown in Fig. 3 by dotted lines, the points themselves on different profiles are shown by different primitives. The isolines of the reference surface (thin long dashed red lines) and the isolines of the surface reconstructed in Wolfram Mathematica are also shown (Interpolation method, InterpolationOrder = 1, line format – black dashed lines).

4   Tools, Examples of Cluster Analysis of Geodata

Cluster analysis allows for many different types of clustering techniques/ algorithms to determine the final result [11]. Below are the results that illustrate the features of the most commonly used clustering algorithms.

4.1   Effects of the Number of Clusters

One of the most important problems of segmentation is determining the number of clusters. In a broader sense, this is the problem of initializing the algorithm: selection of optimal values of control parameters, evaluation functions used, metrics, stopping conditions, etc.

The series of illustrations in Fig. 4 shows the results calculated with default settings using the Wolfram Mathematica FindClusters function (details below).

A comparison of the presented variants gives grounds to assert that additional actions are needed to select the method, metric and other parameters of clustering algorithms.

4.2   Effects of the Accepted Clustering Method

In the examples below, a priori information is used, the number of clusters is set to 6. Why so much – it is taken into account that in the initial data, measurements were carried out for a surface that included 5 different distortions of it with individual positioning of perturbations.

The effects of the accepted clustering method (Possible settings for Method) are illustrated by the schemes in Fig. 5. In the illustrations (to remind the data source), the isolines of the reference surface are given in long dashed red lines. Clustering in the examples of this series was considered only for pairs of coordinates, i.e. the relative position of the points of the scattered set was taken into account, moreover, the FindClusters function with different criteria was used in the program module, the norm in the examples of the series Fig. 5 was calculated using the DistanceFunction EuclideanDistance metric.

Representative clustering options are shown, namely: KMeans [12], k-medoids [13], Spectral [14], Optimal.

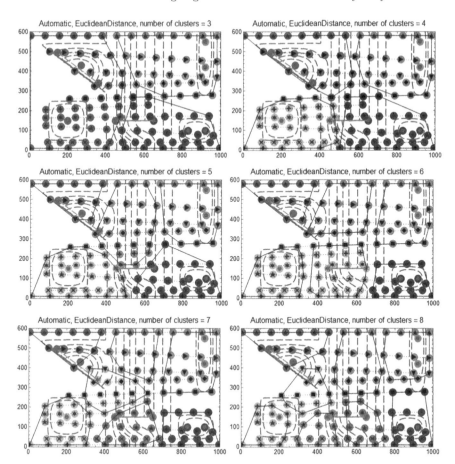

Fig. 4. Influence of the number of clusters.

Generally speaking, the corresponding software application included in the system GeoBazaDannych from the Wolfram Mathematica allows variants of the clustering method (Criterion function): Automatic, Agglomerate (find clustering hierarchically), Optimize (find clustering by local optimization), DBSCAN (density-based spatial clustering of applications with noise), GaussianMixture (variational Gaussian mixture algorithm), JarvisPatrick (Patrick clustering algorithm), KMeans (k-means clustering algorithm), KMedoids (partitioning around medoids), MeanShift (mean-shift clustering algorithm), NeighborhoodContraction (displace examples toward high-density region), SpanningTree (minimum spanning tree-based clustering algorithm), Spectral (spectral clustering algorithm). What segmentation methods are used in the calculations are recorded in the headers of the diagrams.

The results shown in Fig. 4 and Fig. 5 (Automatic, KMeans, KMmedoids, Spectral, Optimal) are markedly different. At the same time, given the digital

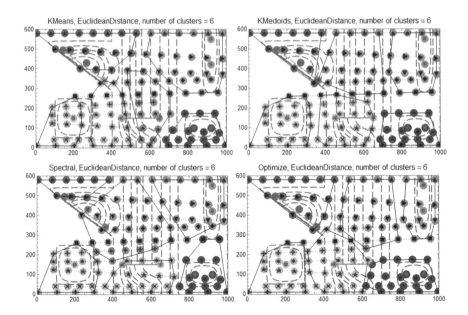

Fig. 5. Clustering methods. (Color figure online)

field of the original, it is difficult to name the preferred variant, we need to refine the algorithms.

The results shown were obtained in calculations when the number of clusters was set by the user of the program. By default, the FindClusters function tries various methods and selects the best clustering. However, there are possibilities [15] to specify additional options, in particular, you can determine: the average radius of the neighborhood of a point (NeighborhoodRadius), the average number of points in the neighborhood (NeighborsNumber), initial centroids/medoids (InitialCentroids). ClusterDissimilarityFunction specifies the intercluster dissimilarity. The methods KMeans and KMedoids determine how to cluster the data for a particular number of clusters k. The methods DBSCAN, JarvisPatrick, MeanShift, SpanningTree, NeighborhoodContraction, and GaussianMixture determine how to cluster the data without assuming any particular number of clusters. The methods Agglomerate and Spectral can be used in both cases.

The results of calculations using the MeanShift function and two representative options for setting NeighborhoodRadius values are shown in Fig. 6. It should be noted that in the case of NeighborhoodRadius = 10, the automatically selected number of clusters was 5, in the variant 20–8. And the same number of clusters for the data set in question is obtained by increasing NeighborhoodRadius to 100.

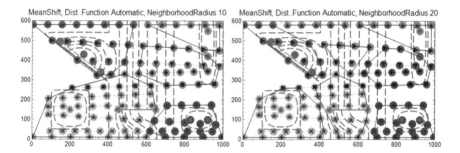

Fig. 6. Clustering method MeanShift, different NeighborhoodRadius.

4.3 The Impact of the Metric

In the examples discussed above, as well as in this series of results, the similarity or difference between the classified objects is established depending on the metric distance between them. The issues of measuring the proximity of objects have to be solved with any interpretation of clusters and various classification methods, moreover, there is an ambiguity in choosing the method of normalization and determining the distance between objects. The influence of the metric (DistanceFunction) is illustrated by the diagrams in Fig. 7.

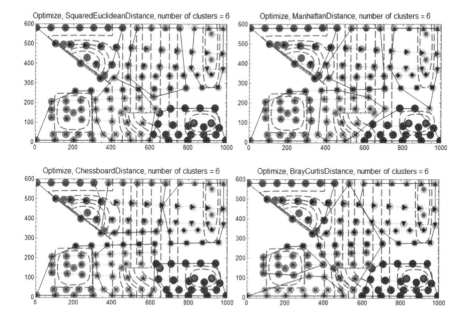

Fig. 7. Influence of DistanceFunction.

The results presented in this series are obtained by means of the corresponding software application included in the GeoBazaDannych from the Wolfram Mathematica, which allows different options for setting DistanceFunction (Possible settings for Method). In the Wolfram Mathematica system, different measures of distance or similarity are convenient for different types of analysis. The Wolfram Language provides built-in functions for many standard distance measures, as well as the capability to give a symbolic definition for an arbitrary measure. In particular, the following metric variant ware available for analyzing digital data [15]: EuclideanDistance, SquaredEuclideanDistance, NormalizedSquaredEuclideanDistance, ManhattanDistance, ChessboardDistance, BrayCurtisDistance, CanberraDistance, CosineDistance, CorrelationDistance, BinaryDistance, WarpingDistance, CanonicalWarpingDistance. The algorithmic features of the listed metrics can be clarified in the articles [16–18]. As in the examples above, clustering algorithms were considered only for pairs of coordinates, i.e. the relative position of the points of the scattered set was taken into account, the k-medoids method was used. What methods of DistanceFunction are used in calculations is recorded in the headers of the schemes. Representative variants are shown, namely SquaredEuclideanDistance, ManhattanDistance, ChessboardDistance, BrayCurtisDistance.

5   Influence of XYZ-Accounting for Values in Points

In the results considered and shown in Fig. 4, Fig. 5, Fig. 6 and Fig. 7, the similarity or difference between the classified objects is established depending on the metric distance between them. Figure 8 shows classification options using the Wolfram Mathematica ClusterClassify function. This function uses data to group into clusters and works for various types of data, including numerical, textual, and image, as well as dates and times and combinations of these. Options of ClusterClassify function [15]: DistanceFunction (how to compute distances between elements), ClusterDissimilarityFunction (how to compute dissimilarity between clusters), Weights (weights for different data elements), PerformanceGoal (whether to optimize for speed, memory, quality, training time, etc.), CriterionFunction (how to assess automatically selected methods), Method (manual override for automatic method selection).

In the results presented below, the ClusterClassify function is used to perform clustering not only taking into account the coordinates of the points of the scattered set, but also the values in them. In other words, in the results presented in this series, the algorithms take into account not pairs X_i, Y_i, but triples - X_i, Y_i, Z_i. The results are shown in Fig. 8. The illustrations on the left show the results of clustering by pairs (coordinates only), and on the right – by three values; at the same time, calculations are performed using the same methods and metrics.

It follows from the results that for the data set under consideration, taking into account the values at the points does not give an additional obviously positive effect in the implementation of clustering. But such results are useful and

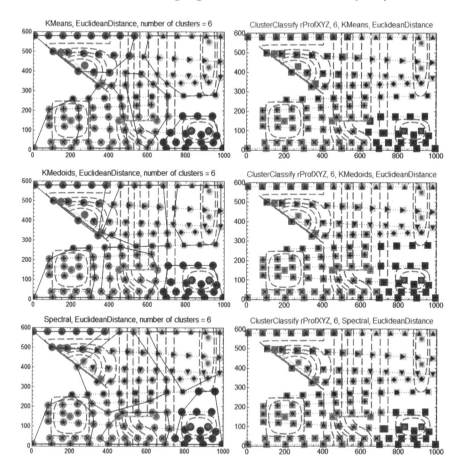

Fig. 8. Results of using the ClusterClassify function.

important, since it is clear from the comparison where additional source data is needed.

6   Conclusion

The article deals with the issues of instrumental filling and the use of the interactive computer system GeoBazaDannych. The results of clustering of a representative data set of a typical digital model of a spatial object are presented and discussed.

References

1. Savinyh, V.P., Tsvetkov, V.Y.: Geodannye kak sistemnyi informacionnyi resurs. Vestnik Rossiiskoi akademii nauk **84**(9), 826–829 (2014)

2. Taranchuk, V.B.: Examples of the use of artificial neural networks in the analysis of geodata. Open Semantic Technologies for Intelligent Systems. Research Papers Collection **3**, 225–230 (2019)

3. Taranchuk, V.: Tools and examples of intelligent processing, visualization and interpretation of GEODATA. In: Modelling and Methods of Structural Analysis. IOP Publishing (2020). IOP Conf. Ser. J. Phys. Conf. Ser. **1425**(012160), 1–9 (2020)

4. Taranchuk, V.B.: Examples of intelligent adaptation of digital fields by means of the system GeoBazaDannych. Open Semantic Technologies for Intelligent Systems. Research Papers Collection **4**, 243–248 (2020)

5. Taranchuk, V.B.: Interactive adaptation of digital fields in the system GeoBazaDannych. In: Golenkov, V., Krasnoproshin, V., Golovko, V., Azarov, E. (eds.) OSTIS 2020. CCIS, vol. 1282, pp. 222–233. Springer, Cham (2020). https://doi.org/10.1007/978-3-030-60447-9_14

6. Shaitura, S.V.: Intellektual'nyi analiz geodannyh. Perspektivy nauki i obrazovaniya **18**(6), 24–30 (2015)

7. Charles, D.T.: Concepts of clustering. In: Indexing, and Structures Data Architecture, pp. 241–253 (2011). https://doi.org/10.1016/B978-0-12-385126-0.00013-9

8. Everitt, B.S., Landau, S., Leese, M., Stahl, D.: Cluster Analysis, 5th edn. Wiley, Hoboken (2011)

9. Golenkov, V., Guliakina, N., Golovko, V., Krasnoproshin, V.: Methodological problems of the current state of works in the field of artificial intelligence. Open Semantic Technologies for Intelligent Systems. Research Papers Collection **5**, 17–32 (2021)

10. Taranchuk, V.B.: Komp'yuternye modeli podzemnoi gidrodinamiki. BGU, Minsk (2020)

11. Kriegel, H.P., Kröger, P., Sander, J., Zimek, A.: Density-based clustering. WIREs Data Min. Knowl. Discov. **1**(3), 231–240 (2011). https://doi.org/10.1002/widm.30

12. Bock, H.: Clustering methods: a history of k-means algorithms. In: Brito, P., Cucumel, G., Bertrand, P., Carvalho, F. (eds.) Selected Contributions in Data Analysis and Classification. STUDIES CLASS, pp. 161–172. Springer, Heidelberg (2007). https://doi.org/10.1007/978-3-540-73560-1_15

13. Park, H., Jun, C.: A simple and fast algorithm for K-medoids clustering. Expert Syst. Appl. **36**(2), 3336–3341 (2009)

14. von Luxburg, U., Belkin, M., Bousquet, O.: Consistency of spectral clustering. Ann. Stat. **36**(2), 555–586 (2008). https://doi.org/10.1214/009053607000000640

15. Distance and Similarity Measures. https://reference.wolfram.com/language/guide/DistanceAndSimilarityMeasures. Accessed 24 Oct 2021

16. Amigó, E., Gonzalo, J., Artiles, J., et al.: A comparison of extrinsic clustering evaluation metrics based on formal constraints. Inf. Retrieval **12**, 461–486 (2009). https://doi.org/10.1007/s10791-008-9066-8

17. Grabusts, P.: The choice of metrics for clustering algorithms. In: Environment Technology. Resources. Proceedings of the International Scientific and Practical Conference, pp. 70–76 (2011). https://doi.org/10.17770/etr2011vol2.973

18. Zhu, W., Ma, C., Xia, L., Li, X.: A fast and accurate algorithm for chessboard corner detection. In: 2nd International Congress on Image and Signal Processing, pp. 1–5 (2009). https://doi.org/10.1109/CISP.2009.5304332

An Approach to Ontology-Based Smart Search in E-commerce

Gleb Guskov⬤, Vladimir Zarayskiy, Aleksey Filippov$^{(\boxtimes)}$⬤, and Anton Romanov⬤

Ulyanovsk State Technical University, Ulyanovsk, Russia
guskovgleb@gmail.com, v-zar@list.ru, al.filippov@ulstu.ru,
romanov73@gmail.com

Abstract. The article presents the implementation of a intelligence search system for an CS-Cart platform online store. The system is based on the formation of a domain products ontology. The system assumes the processing and expansion of the user request. This article describes the structure of an OWL ontology. The article describes the algorithm for processing custom queries, as well as the results of experiments.

Keywords: Knowledge base · Ontology · Smart search · E-commerce

1 Introduction

The term "information retrieval" was first introduced into scientific circulation by the American mathematician Calvin Moers in 1951. Information retrieval is actions, methods and procedures that provide the selection of certain information from a data array.

The problems of modern information retrieval are reflected in the work processes of the online store. It's that users can not quickly and accurately find the desired item and leave the online store.

Currently, the platform for the CS-Cart online store by default search by matches in the name or description of the product with the entered user request.

In this research, process of implementing a intelligence search system will be considered. Intellectual search system is part of an online store based on CS-Cart platform, which allows you to expand the capabilities of the standard functionality of the search engine.

Any Internet resource must have a search panel, as it is an integral part of the graphical user interface. Most systems today are based on the Boolean search model.

Boolean variables get the value "true" or "false" depending on the occurrence or not occurrence of the query terms in the corresponding document.

V. Golenkov et al. (Eds.): OSTIS 2021, CCIS 1625, pp. 361–372, 2022.
https://doi.org/10.1007/978-3-031-15882-7_19

The search model is foundation for search technology in a particular system. The search model is a combination:

- the representations of documents form;
- an approach of forming representations of search queries;
- type of criterion of relevance of documents.

There are also systems that use external services to search through an array of data. Unfortunately, in this case, there is no way to control the behavior of the search engine, and the it's internal mechanisms are not available.

The growth of the World Wide Web has exposed the flaws classic search and indexing methods. Information retrieval can be based on a semantic structure. The Semantic Web allows connections to be created between terms, giving meaning to information and helping the machine integrate new hidden knowledge.Information retrieval can be based on a semantic structure, namely the relationship between information available on the network [1].This problem complicates the translation of user queries into an executable query for the information system, which leads to the loss of some of the relevant results when searching. Therefore, the identification of the semantics of search queries plays an important role in the development of search engines. This area of research is called semantic search. Semantic search aims to deliver contextually relevant results to the user by understanding the purpose and meaning of the query provided.

Most often, users know what they are looking for, but do not know how to formulate a search query. Users formulate a request based on the key characteristics or metadata of the sought object [2]. The online store provide to categorize products and set individual characteristics for each product. Presenting products, categories, characteristics and relationships between them as semantic network, and apply an inference engine to form the result of a search query, quality of the search engine will increase. The use of semantic search for an online store contains scientific interest.

On the basis of the ontological approach, there are platforms for creating information systems in which the advantages of semantic technologies are available [3–5].

Since with the help of ontology it is possible to formalize any subject area in the form of a set of statements and terms [6], that is, the possibility of using ontology for e-commerce. Ontological representation of knowledge will help customers can find the right products and make purchasing decisions. Ontologies can be applied in a search system to expand and adjust user queries.

The current article is an extended version of the following article [7].

2   Ontology Based Search System

The ontological approach to knowledge representation has many successfully solved problems in various industries. For example, the task of classifying documents in an electronic archive can also be solved using the ontological approach [8–12].

Ontologies are based on various description logics (DL). The base DL for all ontologies is $\mathcal{ALC}$. The OWL 2 standard is currently used for ontologies representing, and provides the following $\mathcal{ALC}$ extensions: $\mathcal{SROIQ}(\mathcal{D})$, $\mathcal{SHOIN}(\mathcal{D})$, and $\mathcal{SHIF}(\mathcal{D})$ [13].

Any ontology can be represented as a set of DL axioms:

$$O = \{TBox, ABox\},$$

where $TBox$ is a terminological box that contains concepts and relations between them; $ABox$ is a assertional box that contains axioms about relations between individuals and concepts.

Table 1 contains typical DL operators and axioms.

Table 1. Typical DL operators and axioms.

Description	DL
top (a special class with every individual as an instance)	$\top$
bottom (an empty class)	$\bot$
class inclusion axiom	$A \sqsubseteq B$
disjoint classes axiom	$A \sqcap B \sqsubseteq \bot$
equivalence classes axiom (or defining classes with necessary and sufficient conditions)	$A \equiv B$
intersection or conjunction of classes	$A \sqcap B$
union or disjunction of classes	$A \sqcup B$
universal restriction axiom	$\forall R.A$
existential restriction axiom	$\exists R.A$
concept assertion axiom (a is an instance of class A)	$a\colon A$
role assertion axiom	$(a, b) : R$

The top level classes of ontology are:

$$categories \sqsubseteq \top \quad features \sqsubseteq \top \quad products \sqsubseteq \top$$
$$categories \sqcap features \sqsubseteq \bot \quad products \sqcap features \sqsubseteq \bot$$

where $categories$ is a set of products categories;
$features$ is a set of products features;
$products$ is a set of products.

The $features$ class is disjoint with $categories$ and $products$ classes. The $categories$ and $products$ classes are not disjoint. An individual can belong to the classes $products$ and $categories$ at the same time. A set of categories form the structure of a store. One product can belong to several categories that are different in semantics.

The *products* class has the *hasFeature* object property. The *hasFeature* property allows defining a tie between some products and features:

$$products \sqsubseteq \exists hasFeature.features$$

An example of an ontology fragment is shown in Fig. 1.

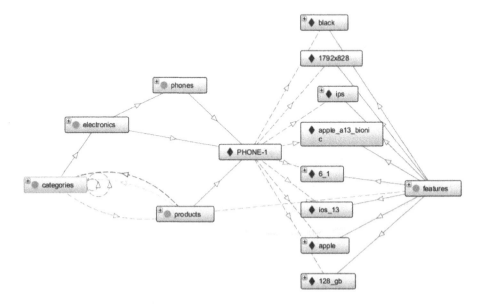

Fig. 1. The search results of the system

The intelligence search algorithm contains 3 stages:

- Query string preprocessing;
- Formation of logical conditions and definition of classes;
- Synchronization of the inference engine and getting a list of products.

2.1   Query String Preprocessing

The input query string is split into tokens and stop words are removed from the resulting array of terms. Bigrams are formed from the received tokens. Then, using an approximate string comparison, terms for autocomplete are compared with a bigrams list.

For example, a user enters the query "the blue medium t-shirt". The following array of tokens are obtained from the string: "the", "blue", "medium" and "t-shirt". The stop word "the" is removed from the array. The result is a new array containing the bigrams: "blue_medium" and "medium_t-shirt".

The algorithm for the approximate comparison of strings is based on the calculation of the Levenshtein distance. The function returns a number from 0 to 100 for compared strings. The number 100 means complete similarity. The strings are similar when rating values above 75. A partial comparison is executed on the first step. The partial comparison is based on matching of products data bigram with a bigram from a user query. The resulting set of matches is rechecked against the bigram using a word-by-word comparison on the second step. Thus, a list of concepts that exist in the ontology is distinguished.

2.2 Forming Logical Conditions and Determine Classes

At the second stage of the formation of logical conditions, it is checked to which class the element of the list of found concepts belongs:

$$products\_all\_categories \sqsubseteq products \quad products\_all\_features \sqsubseteq products$$
$$products\_any\_categories \sqsubseteq products \quad products\_any\_features \sqsubseteq products$$

where:

- $products\_all\_categories$ – products belonging to all categories from a set of conditions;
- $products\_all\_features$ - products that have all the characteristics from a set of conditions;
- $products\_any\_categories$ - products belonging to at least one category from a set of conditions;
- $products\_any\_features$ - products that have at least one characteristic from a set of conditions.

The top level conditions classes have subclasses that represent the intersections of the sets of found concepts:

$$products\_all\_features\_and\_all\_categories \sqsubseteq products$$
$$products\_all\_features\_and\_any\_categories \sqsubseteq products$$
$$products\_any\_features\_and\_all\_categories \sqsubseteq products$$
$$products\_any\_features\_and\_any\_categories \sqsubseteq products$$

where:

- $products\_all\_features\_and\_all\_categories$ are products that have all characteristics and belong to all categories from a set of conditions;
- $products\_all\_features\_and\_any\_categories$ are products that have all characteristics and belong to at least one category from a set of conditions;
- $products\_any\_features\_and\_all\_categories$ are products that have at least one characteristic and belong to all categories from a set of conditions;
- $products\_any\_features\_and\_any\_categories$ are products that have at least one characteristic and belong to at least one category from the set of conditions.

For each characteristic from the general set of conditions automatically generated a new axiom $(products_i, features_j)$: $hasFeature$.
Classes for describing conditions are described in the ontology in order of decreasing precision level (see above):

- from the high level – all conditions must be fulfilled;
- to the low level – a minimum one of the conditions must be fulfilled.

The sets of conditions are combined using the logical operators "AND" and "OR". The combination of "AND" and "OR" logical operators allows to customize the search: increase the recall or precision values. Logical operators determine the existence of properties and categories of some product to evaluate the relevance degree between search query and data about a product.

For example, the ontology contains the following axioms for t-shirt with the following features:

- t-shirt is a clothes and a t-shirt:

$$clothes \sqsubseteq categories \quad tshirt \sqsubseteq clothes$$
$$blue\_thirt: products \quad blue\_thirt: clothes \quad blue\_thirt: tshirt;$$

- t-shirt has colors: blue, black and white:

$$color \sqsubseteq features$$
$$blue: color \quad black: color \quad white: color$$
$$(blue\_thirt, blue): hasFeature$$
$$(blue\_thirt, black): hasFeature$$
$$(blue\_thirt, white): hasFeature;$$

- t-shirt has sizes: small, large, medium:

$$size \sqsubseteq features$$
$$small: size \quad large: size \quad medium: size$$
$$(blue\_thirt, small): hasFeature$$
$$(blue\_thirt, large): hasFeature$$
$$(blue\_thirt, medium): hasFeature.$$

The following conditions classes were generated after analyzing the bigram of search query 'the blue medium t-shirt':

- for $products\_all\_features\_and\_all\_categories$ is
  $hasFeature$ $blue$ and $hasFeature$ $medium$ and $tshirt$ and $clothes$;
- for $products\_all\_features\_and\_any\_categories$ is
  $hasFeature$ $blue$ and $hasFeature$ $medium$ and ($tshirt$ or $clothes$);
- for $products\_any\_features\_and\_all\_categories$ is
  ($hasFeature$ $blue$ or $hasFeature$ $medium$) and $tshirt$ and $clothes$;
- for $products\_any\_features\_and\_any\_categories$ is
  ($hasFeature$ $blue$ or $hasFeature$ $medium$) and ($tshirt$ or $clothes$).

2.3 Synchronizing the Inference Engine and Forming List of Products

The third stage starts the synchronization of the inference engine. Subclasses that allow you to identify the intersection of the sets of found concepts contain products that match the conditions. It is necessary to traverse all four classes in order from more precise to more complete list. More precise is a class that contains products that satisfy all the conditions, connected by the "AND" operator. And less accurate, but more complete, through the "OR" operator. The HermiT inference engine was used to synchronize the classes.

After inference engine synchronizing the following axiom was added to the ontology *blue_thirt: products_all_features_and_any_categories*.

The search results can be represented as:

$$search\_results \sqsubseteq products$$
$$products\_all\_features\_and\_all\_categories \sqsubseteq search\_results$$
$$products\_all\_features\_and\_any\_categories \sqsubseteq search\_results$$
$$products\_any\_features\_and\_all\_categories \sqsubseteq search\_results$$
$$products\_any\_features\_and\_any\_categories \sqsubseteq search\_results$$

2.4 Example of How the Proposed Approach Works

The request 'apple iphone 128 gb' was introduced into the system to test the proposed approach. The search results of the system are shown in Fig. 2.

The search results are formed as a result of the operation of the inference engine. The inference engine uses automatically generated rules. An example of the rules is shown in Fig. 3.

The result of the operation of the inference mechanism is shown in Fig. 4. The result is a list of ontology individuals (instances), which properties correspond to the generated rules.

3   Information System Developed During the Research

The architecture of the developed system is presented on the Fig. 5.

The process of searching for goods in the system consists of the following elements:

1. User request;
2. Two repositories of information (database and knowledge base);
3. Two developed program modules (search controller and search service);
4. An auxiliary module required for preprocessing a request.

As part of the research, a web service in python was developed using the REST API of the flask framework and a module for an online store on the CS-Cart platform version "4.11.2 Ultimate" in php.

The ontology is stored in an owl file on the web service server. Interaction with the ontology is carried out using the owlready2 [14] library for python. Autocomplete words are stored as a list in a json file.

Fig. 2. The search results of the system

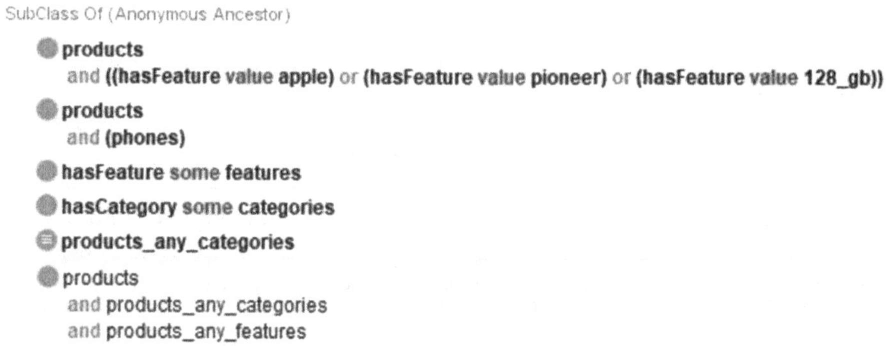

SubClass Of (Anonymous Ancestor)
products
and ((hasFeature value apple) or (hasFeature value pioneer) or (hasFeature value 128_gb))
products
and (phones)
hasFeature some features
hasCategory some categories
products_any_categories
products
and products_any_categories
and products_any_features

Fig. 3. Automatically generated rules

Instances
B00F3IUN24
L0239KVQ9F
PHONE-1
PHONE-12
PHONE-13
PHONE-14
PHONE-2
PHONE-4
PHONE-6
PHONE-7
Q0238LW6GY

Fig. 4. The result of the operation of the inference mechanism

StoreServer
<<component>>
asearch.php
API
SearchService
<<component>>
index.py
<<use>>
<<use>>
<<use>>
Database
Resoner
Knowledge base
Autocomplete words base

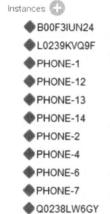

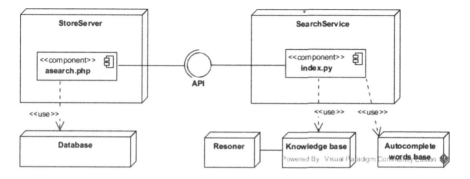

Fig. 5. The architecture of the developed system

4   Experimental Results

Experiments were run on demo store data, which contains 83 categories, 300 products, and 35 types of characteristics.

The time for filling the ontology with all concepts and relations between them ranged from 0.2 to 1 s, depending on the amount of data.

To check the synchronization time of the inference engine on the same user request, larger data sets were formed based on the existing ones. The library for interaction with ontology allows to automatically launch two inference machines: HermiT and Pellet. The results of the execution time of queries are presented in "Table 2".

Table 2. The running time of the algorithm with different reasoners.

Total goods	Founded goods	HermiT	Pellet
300	10	4,5 s	9 s
600	20	15,8 s	18,2 s
1000	30	26,5 s	46,3 s
2000	60	72,1 s	180 s
5000	150	529 s	1010 s

The results of the experiments, HermiT is faster at coping with inference almost twice as fast as Pellet. The larger the total number of products included in the ontology, the longer the search takes.

The results of executing queries by the intelligent search system(ISS) and the standard search algorithm(SSA) based on word coincidence are presented in "Table 3".

Table 3. Comparison of query results

Query	Goods count		Relevant goods count	
	ISS	SSA	ISS	SSA
blue medium t-shirt	1	0	1	0
apple iphone 128gb	10	0	2	0
windows 7 premium	9	0	8	0
monitor ips fullhd	29	0	7	0
huawei notebook	18	0	16	0
huawei	3	3	3	3
games	1	11	1	5

The results of the experiments, the standard search algorithm cannot find any product based on user queries consisting of several words. When searching for the word "huawei", the standard search system found all relevant products, since this word was present in the name of the products. When searching for the phrase "huawei notebook", the standard search system did not find the products, as it was in the previous query, since this phrase is missing in the name or description of the goods.

The intelligent search system was able to find the same products for the query "huawei" as the standard search algorithm, since in this case, among the characteristics of the products found, there was a brand characteristic with the value "huawei". When performing the query "huawei notebook" among the products that have the brand "huawei" and the type of notebook "notebook", there was no combination of such characteristics. However, there are products that have either the first or the second characteristic. Therefore, the system strives to offer the user products that may be of interest to him, and not leave him with an empty search result.

The average accuracy of the smart search system according to the results of the experiments from Table 2 was 70%.

5 Conclusion

As a result of the work, an intelligent search system was developed for an online store based on the CS-Cart platform using ontology.

The experiments carried out show that the developed system gives out products with characteristics and categories by which the user searches, in contrast to the standard search. The standard search algorithm does not find products for the query, for which smart search returns products. The running time of the algorithm with the HermiT inference engine is less than 10 s for a small number of products, which can be used for online stores with a specific subject area.

To increase the accuracy of the algorithm, you can add additional information about the product to the ontology and modernize the query preprocessing process. To reduce the query time, you need to add an inference engine written in python to the library.

Acknowledgment. This work is supported by the Russian Foundation for Basic Research (projects No. 19-47-730006, and 19-47-730003).

References

1. Saravanaguru, K., Shekhar, M.: Semantic web search based on ontology modeling using Protégé reasoner. School of Computing Science and Engineering, p. 10 (2013)
2. Sayed, A., Al Muqrishi, A.: IBRI-CASONTO: ontology-based semantic search engine. Egypt. Inform. J. **18**(3), 181–192 (2017)
3. Shunkevich, D.V., Taberko, V.V., Ivaniuk, D.S., Pupena, O.N.: Ontological approach for standards development within. Open Semantic Technologies for Intelligent Systems, pp. 31–42 (2013)

4. Yarushkina, N., Filippov, A.A., Moshkin, V.S., Guskov, G.: Development of a system based on a fuzzy knowledge base filled from various formats documents. In: Shahbazova, S.N., Kacprzyk, J., Balas, V.E., Kreinovich, V. (eds.) Recent Developments and the New Direction in Soft-Computing Foundations and Applications. SFSC, vol. 393, pp. 147–159. Springer, Cham (2021). https://doi.org/10.1007/978-3-030-47124-8_13

5. Yarushkina, N., Filippov, A., Moshkin, V.: Development of a technological platform for knowledge discovery. In: Misra, S., et al. (eds.) ICCSA 2019. LNCS, vol. 11619, pp. 533–544. Springer, Cham (2019). https://doi.org/10.1007/978-3-030-24289-3_39

6. Clarke, S.G.D.: The information retrieval thesaurus. KO Knowl. Organ. **46**(6), 439–459 (2019)

7. Guskov, G.U., Zarayskiy, V., Filippov, A.A., Romanov, A.A.: Development an ontology based intelligence search system for goods for an online store on the CS-Cart platform. In: The Proceeding of "Open Semantic Technologies for Intelligent Systems, vol. 5, pp. 277–280 (2021)

8. Elhadad, M.K., Badran, K.M., Salama, G.I.: A novel approach for ontology-based dimensionality reduction for web text document classification. Int. J. Softw. Innov. (IJSI) **5**(4), 44–58 (2017)

9. García-Díaz, J.A., Cánovas-García, M., Valencia-García, R.: Ontology-driven aspect-based sentiment analysis classification: an infodemiological case study regarding infectious diseases in Latin America. Future Gener. Comput. Syst. **112**, 641–657 (2020)

10. Qazi, A., Goudar, R.H.: An ontology-based term weighting technique for web document categorization. Proc. Comput. Sci. **133**, 75–81 (2018)

11. Elhadad, M.K., Badran, K.M., Salama, G.I.: A novel approach for ontology-based feature vector generation for web text document classification. Int. J. Softw. Innov. (IJSI) **6**(1), 1–10 (2018)

12. Saleh, A.I., Al Rahmawy, M.F., Abulwafa, A.E.: A semantic based Web page classification strategy using multi-layered domain ontology. World Wide Web **20**(5), 939–993 (2017)

13. Baader, F., Calvanese, D., McGuinness, D., Nardi, D., Patel-Schneider, P.F.: The Description Logic Handbook: Theory, Implementation, and Applications. Cambridge University Press, Cambridge (2003)

14. LAMY Jean-Baptiste Owlready2 Documentation Owlready2. https://owlready2.readthedocs.io//en//v0.31//. Accessed Dec 2021

Linking FrameNet to Russian Resources

Natalia Loukachevitch[1], Olga Nevzorova[2][(✉)], and Dana Zlochevskaya[3]

[1] Research Computing Center, Lomonosov Moscow State University, Moscow, Russia
[2] Kazan Federal University, Kremlevskaja str., 18, Kazan 420008, Russia
onevzoro@gmail.com
[3] Computational Mathematics Faculty, Lomonosov Moscow State University, Moscow, Russia

Abstract. In this paper we study three approaches for creating a Frame-Net-like resource for Russian, which can be very useful for semantic analysis of Russian texts. These approaches include two methods of linking the FrameNet frames with Russian words: via WordNet and via parallel corpus. Also we study a method for connecting FrameNet and Russian semantic resource FrameBank. We plan to use created bilingual resource fir developing a new Russian semantic resource.

Keywords: Semantic analysis · Frames · Language transfer · Parallel corpus · Neural networks

1 Introduction

Semantic analysis aimed at constructing semantic representations of natural sentences is important for developing natural language understanding systems. It remains one of the most difficult tasks in natural language processing. Such an analysis is based on special resources and corpora, such as FrameNet [1], Verb-Net [2] or PropBank [3], which are mostly created for English.

One of the most known semantic resources models is the Charles Fillmore's FrameNet lexicon of frames [1] based on his Frame semantics model. The idea of the Frame Semantics approach is as follows [4]: the senses of words can be represented using situations, their relations and roles. For example, the situation of "cooking" (see Fig. 1) in most cases can be described with the help of the following participants and relations between them as: "the subject who cooks" (the cook), "the object that is cooked" (food), "the source of heat for cooking" (heat source) and "cooking container" (utensils). In this case, it is possible to say that the cooking frame has been introduced, in which "cook", "food", "heat source" and "containers" are elements of the frame. Frame elements, which are "markers" of the frame, that is, they often signal the location of this frame in the text (for example, "fry", "cook", "stew", etc.) are called lexical units.

The work was funded by the Russian Science Foundation according to the research project no. 19-71-10056.

Frames can be of different complexity, can have different numbers of elements and lexical units. The main task in constructing semantic frames is to show how the elements of the frame are related to each other.

Fig. 1. Apply_heat frame from FrameNet.

FrameNet is a basis of numerous works on the first step of semantic analysis called semantic role labeling [5–8]. However, such data are absent for most languages, and development of FrameNet-like resources from scratch is a very laborous process, requiring a lot of resources and time [9,10]. Therefore various approaches for automatizing of framenet creation for other languages are discussed [11–13].

In this paper we describe three approaches for creating a FrameNet-like resource for Russian. These approaches include:

- the method of linking Russian words to FrameNet semantic frames via a chain of semantic resources: FrameNet – English WordNet – Russian Word-Net (RuWordNet) – Russian words and expressions;
- the method based on the transfer of semantic frames identified in English sentences using a parallel Russian-English corpus. We train a model on the FrameNet data, then apply it to the English part of a parallel Russian-English corpus, at last we match English frame elements with Russian words in parallel sentences. The resulting set of semantic frames in Russian is used to train and evaluate the models for identifying semantic frames in Russian;

– the method for connecting FrameNet and Russian semantic resource Frame-Bank.

From the results of this linking, a new Russian semantic resource is planned to be created.

2   Related Work

There is an interest of researchers in many countries to have a semantic resource similar to FrameNet for their own languages. However, to create a FrameNet-like resource from scratch is a very difficult, expensive, and time-consuming procedure [9,10]. Therefore automated methods for generating a framenet for a specific language are used. Such methods can be subdivided into two groups: cross-lingual transfer, and generating frames in unsupervised manner from a large text collection [11,14,15]. Cross-lingual transfer can be made via linking FrameNet with WordNet [16,17] or via parallel corpora [18]. Cross-lingual transfer of frames based on a parallel corpus requires a preliminary extraction of frames in English texts, which usually includes the following main steps [19,20]:

– recognition of lexical units, which can express frames, in a text. This stage can be reduced to the task of binary classification for each word of the text;
– recognition of semantic frames. For each lexical unit, it is necessary to determine what frames are expressed by this unit. This task can be considered as a problem of multiclass classification (with several labels) for each of the selected lexical units at the previous stage. The classes in this case are the semantic frames themselves, and several frames can correspond to one lexical unit. The main difficulties at this stage are the possible ambiguity of a lexical unit and/or its absence in the training set;
– recognition of the remaining elements of the frame such as roles. Most often, this problem is solved using named entity extraction methods with the condition that the set of roles strongly depends on the frame being processed. In the current work, this stage is not studied.

The solutions for these three tasks can be very different. In the work of the winners of the SemEval 2007 competition [20], to solve the problem of identifying lexical units, morphological and syntactic rules were used. To define semantic frames, classifiers were trained for each frame separately using support vector machine (SVM) method, the features for which were both morphological and syntactic characteristics of a lexical unit, and semantic information about it from WordNet [21].

The widely used SEMAFOR algorithm [22] has become an improvement of this algorithm. To recognize lexical units, an improved version of linguistic rules is used. To identify a frame, a probabilistic model is trained on a similar feature set. In [23], an approach based on recurrent neural networks is proposed for both tasks: recognizing lexical units and recognizing semantic frames. In recent years, works have also appeared that solve this problem using transformers, for example, BERT [24,25].

Another approach of creating FrameNet like resources is based on linking between English semantic resources: FrameNet [1], VerbNet [2], PropBank [3] and WordNet [26]. One of the latest integrating resources is the Predicate Matrix project. The developers of this project applied a variety of automatic methods to extend SemLink project coverage [27].

3   FrameNet Structure

FrameNet [1] consists of several components:

- the base of semantic frames, containing a description of each frame: its structure, roles and relations between frames;
- examples of sentences annotated with semantic, morphological and syntactic information. These sentences are examples of the use of semantic frames in natural language;
- lexical units linked to frames as well as links to examples of annotated sentences.

At the moment, the FrameNet database contains more than 13000 lexical units, of which 7000 are fully annotated with more than 1000 hierarchically related semantic frames. The number of sentences annotated with semantic information is about 200,000. The base exists in several versions and is in the public domain for research purposes. Basic concepts from the terminology of the FrameNet project are as follows:

- semantic frame is a semantic representation of an event, situation or relationship, consisting of several elements, each of which has its own semantic role in this frame;
- frame element is a type of participants (roles) in a given frame with certain types of semantic links;
- lexical unit – a word with a fixed meaning that expressed a given frame or a given frame element.

For example, in the sentence "Hoover Dam played a major role in preventing Las Vegas from drying up." The word "played" is a lexical unit that conveys the presence in the text of the semantic frame "PERFORMERS_AND_ROLES" with the frame elements "PERFORMER", "ROLE" and "PERFORMANCE" (who created, that created, what role the creator assumed in the creation). This example also shows that in one sentence there can be several frames with varying degrees of abstractness.

It is important to note that for the Russian language there is a FrameNet-oriented resource FrameBank [28]. This is a publicly available dataset that combines a lexicon of lexical constructions of the Russian language and a marked-up corpus of their implementations in the texts of the national corpus of the Russian language. The main part of FrameBank consists of 2200 frequent Russian verbs, for which the semantic constructions in which they are used are described, and examples of their implementations in the text are collected. Each construction is presented as a template, in which the morphological characteristics of the participants in their role and semantic restrictions are fixed.

Despite the fact that the semantic constructs of FrameBank are similar to frames from FrameNet, they are methodologically different. FrameNet frames are built around generic events with specific participants and relations between them. Frame-Bank constructs are built around the senses of specific words. It is supposed that the senses of each lexeme (mainly verbs) in FrameBank form a separate frame. Due to this methodological difference and the orientation of the FrameBank resource towards verbs as a center of constructions, the full use of this data set to solve the problem is impossible.

4   Linking Russian Words to FrameNet via WordNet

The Predicate Matrix Project provides links between several semantic resources including FraneNet frames and WordNet synsets. Russian WordNet-like resource RuWordNet has links from its units (synsets) to the WordNet's synset, therefore it is possible to link Russian words to the FrameNet frames.

4.1   RuWordNet and Its Links to WordNet

Russian wordnet RuWordNet currently contains 135 thousand Russian words and expressions [29]. It is created from the existing Russian re-source for natural language processing RuThes [30] in accordance with principles of wordnet development [20, 26], which includes:

- representation of the lexical system of a language in a form of a semantic net of units and relations between them;
- each units represents a set of synonyms, so called synset;
- each part of speech has their own semantic net; morphologically-related synsets in semantic nets of different part of speech are connected with special relations;
- main type of relations between synsets for nouns and verbs is hyponym-hypernym relation, connecting more general and more specific synsets.

RuThes is a bilingual resource, its concepts are connected with English and Russian lexical units, these data were used to provide initial linking of the Ru-WordNet synsets, because RuWordNet synsets origin from specific RuThes concepts. The following steps were used to connect RuWordNet and Princeton WordNet synsets [31].

First, automatic linking was implemented, the results of which were checked by linguists. The main problem in automatic linking is ambiguity of English words: for linking with WordNet synsets ambiguity should be resolved. Synsets were connected automatically via:

- non-ambiguous English words and phrases;
- several possibly ambiguous English words from a concept, which have maximum connections with a single WordNet synsets;
- automatic extension of links to other parts of speech: if for example noun synsets are matched, than derivational adjectives and verbs are also matched.

Second, five thousand core WordNet synsets were manually matched.

At the third stage, most frequent Russian words, with absent WordNet links were additionally manually linked with corresponding WordNet synsets.

Currently, about 23.5 thousand links connect RuWordNet and WordNet synsets. Small number of Russian synsets have more then one link to WordNet synsets. WordNet synsets are identified via so-called interlingual index (ili). In the Web-version links go to the rdf version of WordNet (http://wordnet-rdf. princeton.edu), where each synset has a separate page.

4.2   Results of Linking Russian Words to FrameNet via PredicateMatrix and Wordnets

The Predicate Matrix is a lexical multilingual resource resulting from the integration of multiple sources of predicate information including FrameNet, VerbNet, PropBank, WordNet and some other resources. The current version of the Predicate Matrix includes verbal predicates for English, Spanish, Basque and Catalan, as well as nominalizations for English and Spanish. Each row of this Predicate Matrix represents the mapping of a role over the different resources and includes all the aligned knowledge about its corresponding verb sense. Fragment of a line from the Predicate Matrix for a English verb abduct looks as follows:

id:eng id:v id:abduct.01 ... wn:abduct%2:35:02 ... fn:Kidnapping fn:abduct....

where wn:abduct%2:35:02 is indication of the WordNet sense, fn: fn:Kidnapping is a link to the FrameNet frame.

This gives possibility to attach Russian words to FrameNet via path RuWordNet synset - WordNet synset - Predicate Matrix - FrameNet frames. Table 1 contains examples of found connections.

One of the problems of this approach is unresolved ambiguity of WordNetFrameNet links in Predicate Matrix. For example, one synset of the word "boil" (immerse or be immersed in a boiling liquid, often for cooking purposes) is linked to three frames of FrameNet: fn:Absorb_heat, fn:Apply_heat, fn:Cause_harm. Also some links from RuWordNet lead to those RuWordNet synsets, which are not connected to FrameNet.

5   Linking Russian Words to FrameNet via Parallel Corpus

The method of linking Russian words to FrameNet via a parallel corpus is divided into several parts, each of which solves a specific subtask:

1. Training the model of recognizing lexical units and frames in English. At this stage, based on the FrameNet knowledge base, a model is created that can extract lexical units and semantic frames from any sentence in English. The quality of the models is evaluated on the test part of the FrameNet dataset and compared with the existing results.
2. Extracting lexical units and frames from the English part of the parallel corpus using a trained model.
3. Transferring the obtained semantic information into Russian using word matching through a pre-trained embedding model of the Russian language. At this stage, for each lexical unit from an English sentence, its analogue is searched for in a parallel Russian sentence. Transfer quality is evaluated on a test sample, annotated manually.
4. Extracting lexical units for each semantic frame. A set of annotated sentences in Russian is also formed for further recognition of semantic frames in Russian texts.

Table 1. Examples of found connections.

Frame identifier	Russian lexical units
fn:Make_agreement_on_action	vyrazit' soglasie, soglashat'sya, iz"yavit' soglasie, soglasit'sya
fn:Verdict	vynosit' opravdatel'nyj prigovor, opravdyvat' podsudimyj, opravdat' obvinyaemyj, snyat' obvinenie, opravdyvat' obvinyaemyj, opravdyvat' v sud, opravdyvat', opravdat' podsudimyj, sud opravdat', opravdat' v sud, opravdat', snimat' obvinenie, priznat' nevinovnyj, priznavat' nevinovnyj; priznavat' vinovnyj, prisudit', prisuzhdat', osudit', osudit' na, osudit' prestupnik, osuzhdat', osuzhdat' na, osuzhdat' prestupnik, vynesti obvinenie, prigovarivat', prigovarivat' k, prigovarivat' prestupnik, prigovorit', vynosit' obvinenie, vynosit' obvinitel'nyj prigovor, prigovorit' k, prigovorit' prestupnik, priznat' vinovnyj
fn:Cooking_creation	gotovit', stryapat', izgotovit' eda, gotovit'sya, sostryapat', gotovit' pishcha, gotovit' eda, sgotovit', prigotavlivat', prigotovlyat', nagotovit', prigotovit' pishcha, prigotovit' eda, prigotovit' blyudo, prigotovit', nagotavlivat', izgotovit' pishcha
fn:Apply_heat	svarit', povarit'sya, otvarit', varit', varit'sya, svarit'sya, dovarivat', otvarivat', dovarit', navarivat', navarit', povarit'

5.1   Training Models for Identification of Lexical Items and Frames in English

As in most studies, two sequential models are trained. The first model predicts potential lexical units that can express a semantic frame, and the second one, based on the predictions of the first model, determines which frames should be generated from the selected lexical units. Both models are trained and tested on the manually annotated FrameNet corpus of sentences.

For training and testing, the annotated corpus FrameNet version 1.5 was used. The entire corpus of annotated sentences contains 158399 example sentences with labeled lexical units and frames. They are presented in 77 documents, 55 texts of which were randomly selected for model training and 23 texts for testing. A modified CONLL09 format is used as a universal format for presenting annotations, in which the following set of tags is attached to each word of the sentence:

- ID – word number in the sentence;
- FORM – the form of a word in a sentence;
- LEMMA – word lemma;
- POS – part of speech for the given word;
- FEAT – list of morphological features;
- SENTID – sentence number;
- LU – lexical unit, if the word is it;
- FRAME – a semantic frame generated by a word if it is a lexical unit.

The task of predicting lexical units in a text is reduced to the task of binary classification for each word in a sentence. In some cases, a lexical unit may not be one word, but a phrase, but in this work, the most common variant with one word as a lexical unit is investigated. To solve this problem, a bidirectional recurrent neural network (BiLSTM) was used. Such models were actively used in previous studies for identification of lexical units and frames [23].

A sentence is sent to the input of the neural network, each word in which is represented by a vector representation of a word from a pretrained embedding model. In addition to this classical representation of words, new features responsible for semantic and morphological information were studied such as: part of speech and the initial form of a word. These features are represented as a one-hot vectors, which is fed to the input of fully connected layers of the neural network. During training, the outputs of these fully connected layers can be considered as vector representations of these features. These features can help the model to memorize morphological and semantic schemes for constructing frames from the FrameNet annotation.

All obtained feature vectors for a word are joined by concatenation into the final vector representation, which is fed to the input of the neural network. In the learning process, only vectors of tokens from the pretrained embedding model are fixed, the rest of the vector representations are formed during training. A sentence is sent to the input of the neural network, each word of which is represented as a vector according to the algorithm described above. The network consists of several BiLSTM layers, to the output of which a fully connected layer with the sigmoid activation function is applied for each word. As a result, at the output of the network, each word of the sentence is matched with the probability of a given word to be a lexical unit in a given sentence.

To optimize the parameters of the neural network, the logistic loss function was used. The adaptive stochastic gradient descent Adam [32] was chosen as an optimizer. To prevent overfitting of the neural network, the Dropout technique [33] was used, based on random switching off of neurons from the layers of the neural network for greater generalization of the trained models.

5.2 Semantic Frame Identification

The purpose of the semantic frame identification model is to recognize frames that correspond to lexical items in a sentence. Formally, this is a multi-class classification problem with multiple labels, since the same lexical unit can correspond to several semantic frames in a sentence. To solve this problem, a model was used that is similar to the model of the selection of lexical units, but with several changes. The main difference is adding information about whether a word is a lexical unit using one-hot coding. If the word is not a lexical unit in a given sentence, the lexical unit representation vector will consist entirely of zeros and will not affect the prediction. It is important to note that the predictions of the model are taken into account only for words that are lexical units in a given sentence. The remaining components of the vector representation of a word are similar to the model for extracting lexical units – a vector of tokens from a pretrained embedding model and one-hot coding that encodes a part of speech.

5.3 Implementation and Results

The following hyperparameters were chosen for training the models:

- the Glove model trained on the English-language Wikipedia[1] was chosen as an embedding model. The vector dimension is 100;
- the size of the vectors encoding the lemma, lexical unit and part of speech is 100, 100, and 20, respectively;
- number of BiLSTM layers is 3, output dimension is 100;
- the number of training epochs is 40;
- the Dropout coefficient is 0.01.

The results of lexical unit identification obtained on the test sample are presented in Table 2. For comparison, the SEMAFOR algorithm was applied, which determines the lexical units on the basis of linguistic rules. For this, an available author's implementation[2] was used, trained on the same data as the tested models. It can be seen from the results that adding information about the word lemma does not give a significant improvement, however, information about the part

---

[1] https://nlp.stanford.edu/projects/glove/.
[2] https://github.com/Noahs-ARK/semafor.

Table 2. Results for lexical units recognition in English.

Model for lexical units	P	R	F1
$SEMAFOR$	74.92	66.79	70.62
$BILSTM$	74.13	66.11	69.89
$BILSTM_{token}$	76.01	67.15	71.3
$BILSTM_{token,lemma}$	76.12	67.98	71.8
$BILSTM_{token,lemma,partofspeech}$	79.47	68.31	73.46

of speech allows obtaining quality that is superior to the classical SEMAFOR model. To evaluate the results of the semantic frame model, the SEMAFOR algorithm was also used, which identifies a frame based on the probabilistic model. In addition, for comparison, the model of the SemEval 2007 [18] was recreated. The obtained results are presented in Table 3.

Table 3. Results of model of semantic frame recognition for English.

Model	P	R	F1
SVM	79.54	73.43	76.36
$SEMAFOR$	86.29	84.67	85.47
$BILSTM$	83.78	79.39	81.52
$BILSTM_{lu}$	88.19	81.54	84.73
$BILSTM_{lu,token}$	88.83	88.12	85.34
$BILSTM_{lu,token,partofspeech}$	89.87	83.91	86.78

It can be seen that the trained model has a quality comparable to the performance of the SEMAFOR model. In this way, models for identification of lexical units and semantic frames in English were trained. At this stage, for any sentence in English, a set of frames and corresponding lexical units are identified. To transfer this information to the Russian part of the parallel corpus, it is necessary for each lexical unit from the English sentence to find its analogue in Russian. Since in this study only single-word lexical units are considered, the task is reduced to the comparison of words between sentences in a parallel corpus.

5.4 Translation of Annotations from English into Russian in a Parallel Corpus

For the study, we used the English-Russian parallel corpus[3], gathered by Yandex. It consists of 1 million pairs of sentences in Russian and English, aligned by lines. The sentences were selected at random from parallel text data collected in

---

[3] https://translate.yandex.ru/corpus.

2011–2013. Like most parallel corpora, this resource is sentence-aligned, not word-aligned, so word-level matching requires further refinement. A simple dictionary translation of an English word into Russian does not provide the desired effect due to the ambiguity of words and differences in structure of languages. Therefore, in addition to direct translation of words, a matching algorithm was implemented based on the similarity of words in an embedding model of the Russian language.

The FastText model in the Skipgram version trained on the Russian National Corpus[4] was chosen for word matching. Thus, the algorithm of matching between languages consists of the following steps:

1. Translation of a lexical unit in English, for which we are looking for an analogue in a parallel sentence in Russian. In this step, all possible translations into Russian are collected using the Google Translate API[5].
2. Further, between each obtained translation and each word of a parallel Russian sentence, the cosine similarity according to the embedding model is calculated.
3. A word in the Russian sentence is considered as an analogue of the original word in English if between the translation of an initial word and the Russian word, the cosine similarity is higher than 0.9.

To evaluate the quality of word matching, the transfer of lexical units in 100 parallel sentences was manually assessed. Both precision (in how many sentences the word was translated correctly) and recall (in how many sentences an analogue of the word in English was found in general) were considered. A simple search for a translation of a word in a parallel sentence was taken as the basic algorithm; the comparison results can be seen in Table 4. It can be seen that the use of the embedding model increases the recall of word matching with a slight decrease in precision.

Table 4. Results of matching words between sentences in a parallel corpus.

Word translation search method	P	R
Direct translation matching	91%	72%
Distributive word matching	90%	87%

Thus, applying this algorithm to each pair of sentences in a parallel corpus, it is possible to transfer the selected lexical units and the corresponding semantic frames from English into Russian.

5.5 Characteristics and Evaluation of the Resulting Corpus

The sentences in Russian obtained after the transfer with annotated lexical units and semantic frames form a dataset similar to a of the FrameNet knowledge base.

---

[4] https://rusvectores.org/ru/models/.
[5] https://cloud.google.com/translate/docs/.

In it, for each of the 755 frames, lexical units with frequency of use in the context of the frame are presented. This frequency can be interpreted as a certain "reliability" of the lexical unit belonging to the frame. A total of million lexical units were analysed out of 1 million sentences. They belong to 755 semantic frames from the FrameNet project. In total, 18150 lexical units have been identified, including 6894 unique words.

Table 5 shows an example of the obtained semantic frames and lexical units as-signed to it. Each column refers to a frame, the first line contains its name from the original FrameNet knowledge base, and the second contains lexical units assigned to it in Russian with the frequency of use.

Table 5. Examples of linking Russian lexical units to the FrameNet frames.

Fear	Labeling	Reason
strah : 1042	termin : 1045	prichina : 3287
boyat'sya : 552	ponyatie : 139	osnova : 755
boyazn' : 42	etiketka : 119	osnovanie : 533
opasat'sya : 40	yarlyk : 78	motivaciya : 247
uzhas : 28	terminologiya : 24	povod : 118
strashit'sya : 3	marka : 11	motiv : 110
strashno : 3	brend : 9	poetomu : 2
ispug : 1	klejmo : 2	imenno : 1

The resulting dataset can be used as a separate semantic resource for various natural language processing tasks. In addition, annotated Russian sentences are also valuable. They make it possible to conduct experiments on the selection of lexical units and semantic frames using supervised machine learning methods.

5.6 Training and Testing Model for Identification of Lexical Units and Frames in Russian

The resulting set of annotated sentences in Russian was used to train models for the selection of lexical units and semantic frames in Russian, similar to the already trained models in English. Out of 970 thousand sentences, 90% were used for training models, the rest were used for testing.

The architecture and method of constructing the vector representation of words are similar to the models for the English language, with the exception of the embedding model – instead of Glove, the FastText model of the Skipgram architecture was used, trained on the National corpus of the Russian language[6]. The vector dimension is 300. The results of the obtained models are presented in Tables 6 and Table 7.

---

[6] https://rusvectores.org/ru/models/.

Table 6. Results of the Russian lexical unit identification model.

Lexical Identification Model	P	R	F1
$BILSTM$	71.67	59.14	64.80
$BILSTM_{token}$	76.09	61.04	67.73
$BILSTM_{token,lemma}$	77.65	61.33	68.53
$BILSTM_{token,lemma,partofspeech}$	78.44	61.72	69.08

Table 7. Results of the model for identifying semantic frames for the Russian language.

Semantic Frame Identification Model	P	R	F1
SVM	80.28	72.43	76.15
$BILSTM$	84.10	76.99	80.38
$BILSTM_{lu}$	86.54	78.04	82.07
$BILSTM_{lu,token}$	87.01	78.20	82.40
$BILSTM_{lu,token,partofspeech}$	90.83	83.91	84.66

The obtained results for Russian are lower than the results of similar models in English. This can be explained by the fact that during the automatic transfer, there is a loss of data and the introduction of noise at each stage - both when using the models for extracting semantic information in English, and when directly transferring the resulting annotation. In addition, some frames and lexical units can be rarely represented in a parallel corpus, which leads to a low quality of their prediction.

Thus, the results show that the obtained dataset for the Russian language can be used to develop methods for extracting semantic frames and use it for other natural language processing tasks.

6 Linking FrameNet and Russian FrameBank

6.1 FrameBank Structure

FrameBank is a bank of annotated samples from the Russian National Corpus. The main task of FrameBank is to identify frame elements in texts, namely to identify participants in situations indicated by predicates (verbs, nouns, adjectives, etc.), and to mark the way they are expressed, regardless of whether the units denoting participants are related syntactically or not.

FrameBank presents information:

- about the lexical constructions and the system of frames in Russian;
- about the semantic-syntactic interface in a more general sense;
- about the ambiguity of predicate tokens and how the system of meanings is related to the constructive potential of tokens.

The bank of lexical structures includes:

- construction patterns of verbs and predicatives;
- morphosyntactic patterns of predicate nouns (include not only control, but also attributive and other syntactic relations);
- morphosyntactic patterns of adjectives, adverbs, introductory phrases, various adjuncts;
- small syntax constructions (phrasemes, idiomatic constructions).

The basic units of FrameBank are individual verb constructions, not generalized frames. The vocabulary of lexical constructions represents each construction as a template, which specifies:

a) morphosyntactic characteristics of structural elements;
b) the syntactic rank of the participant;
c) role of the participant;
d) lexical and semantic restrictions of structural elements;
e) participant status (mandatory or optional);
f) a letter marking the participant in a short pattern, for instance "Y is brought from Z to W".

For example, Pattern: <Snom V na.PR+ Sloc>, Pjatno vystupilo na platje (ru) 'A stain appeared on the dress'.

6.2   Methods for Linking FrameNet and FrameBank

The purpose of linking is to establish a semantic correspondence between the predicate of a construction from FB and the semantic frame from FN. The predicate of the FB construction is expressed most often by a verb. Thus, the construction from FB and the frame from FN will be express general semantic meaning.

The data linking of these resources is carried out according to the following algorithm:

1. Corpus of examples of the selected construction from FB is being extracted.
2. The predicate of the construction is translated into English and a set of lexical units (FUs) for FN is formed.
3. Then, for each lexical unit (FU), one need to find a frame from FN that contains this lexical unit. In this way, a set of frame-candidates is formed.
4. For each frame-candidate from FN, a corpus of examples is extracted including the translated lexical unit.
5. For each example from the constructed corpora from FB and FN, one is constructed vector embedding using the word2vec model, and then vectors embeddings of the each corpus.
6. The vectors embeddings of the construction from FB and the frame from FN are compared in pairs using the cosine metric, and the frame with the largest cosine value is selected as a result.

To implement this algorithm, a software module was developed and the experiments on linking the resources were carried out. Fragments of the results obtained are shown in Table 8.

To check the quality of the program, manual testing was carried out, in which the corresponding semantic frames were found on a set of 200 constructions from FB. The accuracy of establishing correct links by this algorithm is 88%, which is a fairly good result.

Table 8. Linking constructions and frames.

Construction from FB	Translated lexical unit	Frame from FN	The result of comparing the vectors embeddings (the frame with the maximum value on the cosine measure is highlighted)
ostat'sya 1.x	stay	Avoiding	0.3038
		Temporary_stay	**0.6899**
		Residence	0.1057
		State_continue	0.5133
pisat' 1.x	write	**Text_creation**	**0.7724**
		Contacting	0.5586
		Statement	0.6551
		Spelling_and_pronouncing	0.6979
		People_by_vocation	0.5444
vyrazit' 1.x	express	Encoding	0.7236
		Expressing_publicly	**0.8019**
		Sending	0.5979
		Facial_expression	0.6978
		Roadways	0.4696
vorovat' 1.x	theft	Self_motion	0.5870
		Theft	**0.7041**

7   Conclusion

The FrameNet lexicon created for the English language is on of well-known lexical resources intended for semantic analysis. To create such a resource for other languages is very time-consuming and extensive procedure. In this paper we study three approaches for creating a FrameNet-like resource for Russian. These approaches include:

- the method of linking Russian words to FrameNet semantic frames via a chain of semantic resources: FrameNet – English WordNet – Russian WordNet (RuWordNet) – Russian words and expressions;

- the method based on the transfer of semantic frames identified in English sentences using a parallel Russian-English corpus. We train a model on the FrameNet data, then apply it to the English part of a parallel Russian-English corpus, at last we match English frame elements with Russian words in parallel sentences. The resulting set of semantic frames in Russian is used to train and evaluate the models for identifying semantic frames in Russian;
- the method for connecting FrameNet and Russian semantic resource Frame-Bank.

From the results of this linking, a new Russian semantic resource is planned to be created.

References

1. Baker, C.F., Fillmore, C.J., Lowe, J.B.: The Berkeley FrameNet project. In: 36th Annual Meeting of the Association for Computational Linguistics and 17th International Conference on Computational Linguistics, vol. 1, pp. 86–90 (1998)
2. Kipper, K.: VerbNet: a broad-coverage, comprehensive verb lexicon. Dissertations available from ProQuest (2005). AAI3179808. https://repository.upenn.edu/dissertations/AAI3179808. Accessed 14 Nov 2021
3. Palmer, M., Gildea, D., Kingsbury, P.: The proposition bank: an annotated corpus of semantic roles. Comput. Linguist. 31(1), 71–106 (2005)
4. Fillmore, C.J., et al.: Frame semantics. In: Geeraerts, D., Dirven, R., Taylor, J. (eds.) Cognitive Linguistics: Basic Readings, vol. 34, pp. 373–400 (2006)
5. Palmer, M., Gildea, D., Xue, N.: Semantic role labeling. In: Synthesis Lectures on Human Language Technologies, vol. 3, no. 1, pp. 1–103 (2010)
6. Carreras, X., Marquez, L.: Introduction to the CoNLL-2005 shared task: semantic role labeling. In: Proceedings of the Ninth Conference on Computational Natural Language Learning (CoNLL-2005), pp. 152–164 (2005)
7. He, L., Lee, K., Lewis, M., Zettlemoyer, L.: Deep semantic role labeling: what works and what's next. In: Proceedings of the 55th Annual Meeting of the Association for Computational Linguistics, vol. 1: long papers, pp. 473–483 (2017)
8. Cai, J., He, S., Li, Z., Zhao, H.: A full end-to-end semantic role labeler, syntactic-agnostic over syntactic-aware? In: Proceedings of the 27th International Conference on Computational Linguistics, pp. 2753–2765 (2018)
9. Park, J., Nam, S., Kim, Y., Hahm, Y., Hwang, D., Choi, K.-S.: Frame-semantic web: a case study for Korean. In: ISWC-PD 2014: Proceedings of the 2014 International Conference on Posters & Demonstrations Track, vol. 1272, pp. 257–260 (2014)
10. Ohara, K.H., Fujii, S., Saito, H., Ishizaki, S., Ohori, T., Suzuki, R.: The Japanese FrameNet project: a preliminary report. In: Proceedings of the 6th Meeting of the Pacific Association for Computational Linguistics, Halifax, Nova Scotia, pp. 249–254 (2003)
11. Pennacchiotti, M., De Cao, D., Basili, R., Croce, D., Roth, M.: Automatic induction of FrameNet lexical units. In: EMNLP 2008: Proceedings of the 2008 Conference on Empirical Methods in Natural Language Processing, pp. 457–465 (2008)
12. Cheung, J.C.K., Poon, H., Vanderwende, L.: Probabilistic frame induction. arXiv:1302.4813 [cs.CL] (2013)

13. Tonelli, S., Pighin, D., Giuliano, C., Pianta, E.: Semi-automatic development of FrameNet for Italian. In: Proceedings of the FrameNet Workshop and Masterclass, Milano, Italy (2009)
14. Ustalov, D., Panchenko, A., Kutuzov, A., Biemann, C., Ponzetto, S.P.: Unsupervised semantic frame induction using triclustering. In: Proceedings of the 56th Annual Meeting of the Association for Computational Linguistics (Volume 2: Short Papers), pp. 55–62 (2018)
15. Modi, A., Titov, I., Klementiev, A.: Unsupervised induction of frame-semantic representations. In: Proceedings of the NAACL-HLT Workshop on the Induction of Linguistic Structure, pp. 1–7 (2012)
16. De Lacalle, M.L., Laparra, E., Rigau, G.: Predicate matrix: extending SemLink through WordNet mappings. In: Proceedings of the Ninth International Conference on Language Resources and Evaluation (LREC 2014), pp. 903–909 (2014)
17. De Lacalle, M.L., Laparra, E., Aldabe, I., Rigau, G.: Predicate Matrix: automatically extending the semantic interoperability between predicate resources. Lang. Resour. Eval. **50**(2), 263–289 (2016). https://doi.org/10.1007/s10579-016-9348-5
18. Yang, T.-H., Huang, H.-H., Baker, C.F., Ellsworth, M., Erk, K.: SemEval 2007 Task 19: frame semantic structure extraction. In: Proceedings of the Fourth International Workshop on Semantic Evaluations (SemEval-2007), pp. 99–104 (2007)
19. Johansson, R., Nugues, P.: LTH: semantic structure extraction using nonprojective dependency trees. In: Proceedings of the Fourth International Workshop on Semantic Evaluations (SemEval-2007), pp. 227–230 (2007)
20. Miller, G.A.: WordNet: a lexical database for English. Commun. ACM **38**(11), 39–41 (1995)
21. Das, D., Chen, D., Martins, A.F., Schneider, N., Smith, N.A.: Frame-semantic parsing. Comput. Linguist. **40**(1), 9–56 (2014)
22. Swayamdipta, S., Thomson, S., Dyer, C., Smith, N.A.: Frame-semantic parsing with softmax-margin segmental RNNs and a syntactic scaffold. arXiv:1706.09528 (2017)
23. Devlin, J., Chang, M.-W., Lee, K., Toutanova, K.: BERT: pre-training of deep bidirectional transformers for language understanding. In: Proceedings of the 2019 Conference of the North American Chapter of the Association for Computational Linguistics: Language Technologies, Volume 1 (Long and Short Papers), pp. 4171–4186 (2019)
24. Quan, W., Zhang, J., Hu, X.T.: End-to-end joint opinion role labeling with BERT. In: Proceedings of IEEE International Conference on Big Data (Big Data), pp. 2438–2446 (2019)
25. Lyashevskaya, O., Kashkin, E.: FrameBank: a database of Russian lexical constructions. In: Khachay, M.Y., Konstantinova, N., Panchenko, A., Ignatov, D.I., Labunets, V.G. (eds.) AIST 2015. CCIS, vol. 542, pp. 350–360. Springer, Cham (2015). https://doi.org/10.1007/978-3-319-26123-2_34
26. Fellbaum, C. (ed.): WordNet: An Electronic Lexical Database, p. 423. MIT Press, Cambridge (1998)
27. Palmer, M.: SemLink: linking PropBank, VerbNet and FrameNet. In: Proceedings of the Generative Lexicon Conference, pp. 9–15 (2009)
28. Kingma, D.P., Ba, J.: Adam: a method for stochastic optimization. arXiv:1412.6980 [cs.LG] (2017)
29. Loukachevitch, N.V., Lashevich, G., Gerasimova, A.A., Ivanov, V.V., Dobrov, B.V.: Creating Russian wordnet by conversion. In: Computational Linguistics and Intellectual Technologies: Papers From the Annual Conference "Dialogue", pp. 405–415 (2016)

30. Loukachevitch, N., Dobrov, B.V.: RuThes linguistic ontology vs. Russian wordnets. In: Proceedings of the Seventh Global Wordnet Conference, pp. 154–162 (2014)
31. Loukachevitch, N., Gerasimova, A.: Linking Russian Wordnet RuWordNet to WordNet. In: Proceedings of the 10th Global Wordnet Conference, pp. 64–71 (2019)
32. Srivastava, N., Hinton, G., Krizhevsky, A., Sutskever, I., Salakhutdinov, R.: Dropout: a simple way to prevent neural networks from overfitting. J. Mach. Learn. Res. **15**(1), 1929–1958 (2014)
33. Bojanowski, P., Grave, E., Joulin, A., Mikolov, T.: Enriching word vectors with subword information. arXiv:1607.04606 [cs.CL] (2016)

Author Index

Printed in the United States
by Baker & Taylor Publisher Services